THE EARLY KENTISH SEASIDE
(1736–1840)

KENTISH SOURCES

VIII. THE EARLY KENTISH SEASIDE
(1736–1840)

Selected Documents

With a commentary by

JOHN WHYMAN, BSc.(Econ), Ph.D.

ALAN SUTTON
FOR
KENT ARCHIVES OFFICE
1985

Other books in the Kentish Sources Series:

Kentish Sources I.   *Some Roads and Bridges*
Kentish Sources II.   *Kent and the Civil War*
Kentish Sources III.   *Aspects of Agriculture and Industry*
Kentish Sources IV.   *The Poor*
Kentish Sources V.   *Some Kentish Houses*
Kentish Sources VI.   *Crime and Punishment*
Kentish Sources VII.   *Kent and the Oxford Movement*

(Volumes I–IV only available from Kent Archives Office; volumes V–VI out of print)

© John Whyman 1985

Published by Alan Sutton Publishing Limited,
30 Brunswick Road, Gloucester GL1 1JJ,
in collaboration with
Kent Archives Office.

ISBN 0-86299-238-9

Produced by Alan Sutton Publishing Limited
Printed in Great Britain by
Redwood Burn Ltd., Trowbridge, Wiltshire

TABLE OF CONTENTS

For my mother.

EDITORIAL NOTE

This volume, together with one on the later Kentish Seaside, is published to coincide with a major exhibition of the same topic to be held at Maidstone and Whitstable museums, and Margate and Folkestone libraries, between June and September 1985.

Until recently very little work had been done on the history of the English seaside resorts, apart from a few books of mainly nostalgic reminiscence. Within the last few years economic and social historians have at last appreciated that the seaside resorts made a vitally important and unique contribution to contemporary society, and several significant studies have been published. These, together with various unpublished theses and articles in learned journals, have been referred to in the main text and supporting footnotes. The present volume aims to provide a substantial addition to the national literature on the English seaside resorts, as well as a useful contribution to the economic and social history of Kent.

The appearance of this volume would have been impossible without the active co-operation of the custodians of source material, expert advisers and competent photographers, and I am particularly grateful to Gillian Wyatt and Penelope Ward (respectively Reference and Local Studies Librarians at Margate Library), to photographers J.T.R. Styles of the University of Kent, Tony Bryan of Margate, Ken Bernthal of Rainham and Slater-Crosby of Gillingham, and to those responsible for typing much of the volume, Mollie Roots, Ray Pearson and Anne Manuel of the University of Kent. I should also like to thank Michael Carter of the Kent Archives Office who drew the illustrations of the bathing machines in Doc. 50 based on the original pencil sketches, and those who have permitted the reproduction of copyright material as indicated in the references to sources. The exhibition and its supporting publications have also been assisted by a generous grant from the English Tourist Board.

John Whyman

September 1984.

LIST OF ILLUSTRATIONS

COMMENTARY

'Margate has charms the pain'd to ease,
The sick to cure, and dull to please'.

> *The Margate and Ramsgate Guide in Letters to a Friend*, 1797, 5.

'All travel . . . has its advantages'.

'Travelling, as the means of improving health, is sometimes highly necessary as well as desirable; and, as a pleasing indulgence, [fills] up a portion of that time in which it is usual to relax from the fatigues of . . . business'.

> L. Fussell, *A Journey round the Coast of Kent, . . . being Original Notes made during a Summer Excursion*, 1818, 1–2.

'At mention of any of our Watering Places, . . . how naturally the desire to be released from the Metropolis, its business, and bustle, arises!'

> *Colburn's Kalendar of Amusements*, quoted on the title page of *The Visitor's Guide to the Watering Places, or A Summer Excursion . . . in Pursuit of Health and Recreation*, 1842.

(1)   *Preliminary Thoughts and Questions.*

Travelling in persuit of health or pleasure has been closely bound up with the history of seaside holidaymaking and resort development since the eighteenth century. Immediately there springs to mind the important question of what is the point of a holiday unless it is a period of higher living standards, offering new experiences and opportunities, away from the domestic duties and routines of everyday life?[1]

---

[1] This question is justified with reference to twentieth century holidaymaking and the travel trade, but must have been no less true of pre-1900 holidays: 'the point of a holiday is lost unless it is of a period of higher living standards', Elizabeth Brunner, *Holiday Making and the Holiday Trades*, O.U.P., 1945, 19; or, people travelling away from home 'tend to spend at a relatively far higher rate than when they remain at home and this characteristic has a vital effect on the industry', L. J. Lickorish and A. G. Kershaw, *The Travel Trade*, London, 1958, 5.

Taking a holiday has always cost money, and how this has been found is one of three essential conditioning factors behind the development of extensive holidaymaking, namely

a) the existence within society of a sufficient number of people who can afford to go on holidays, which naturally cannot be divorced from such considerations as incomes and living standards, plus the fact that certain expenses are still attached to running a home while residing elsewhere at the seaside. In other words, the pleasures inherent in travel and holidays for those who exercise prudence can only be contemplated out of a margin of disposable income once all other expenses are capable of being met;

b) there must be resorts or places to which holidaymakers can go, so that the history of seaside holidaymaking is inseparable from the emergence and expansion of seaside resorts;

and c) there must be adequate transport facilities to and from the resorts themselves (Docs. 1–17).[2]

The whole purpose of this *Kentish Sources* volume, apart from trying to demonstrate what it was like to travel to and be at the seaside in the past, was amply set out in 1763 by a Margate schoolmaster, John Lyons, on the very first page of the first original guidebook to the Isle of Thanet, *A Description of the Isle of Thanet, and particularly of the Town of Margate*.

'Margate, May 1, 1763.

It gives me great pleasure to hear . . . that you design to spend some part of the Summer at this place. You are welcome to any

---

[2] Recently published histories of the seaside strongly support the view that communications have determined the fortunes of most English seaside resorts; notably in their lavishly illustrated study, Janice Anderson and Edmund Swinglehurst, *The Victorian and Edwardian Seaside*, London, 1978, 18, while, according to James Walvin, *Beside the Seaside: A Social History of the Popular Seaside Holiday*, London, 1978, 156.

'seaside resorts are united by their common historical reliance on communications with the major cities. Indeed, their history can often be written in terms of the changing methods of transportation.'

information which it may be in my power to give you concerning it. I think your questions respect the Isle of *Thanet* in general, the Situation of *Margate*, its Accommodations, Provisions, Manner of Bathing, and Amusements, Places which attract the notice of Strangers in the neighbourhood, and along the coast.'

If Margate features more prominently in this volume than any other Kentish resort, it is because 'Margate has long been the most popular of all Kentish coastal resorts, drawing large numbers of holidaymakers from the great London metropolis, arriving by road, rail and sea, [and being] drawn by extensive golden beaches, endless hours of sunshine and the highly developed entertainment industry for which the town is noted.'[3] Margate has been to Kent what Brighton has been to Sussex, in terms of resort development.[4]

The questions to which John Lyons applied himself in 1763 (compare Doc. 24o) were narrowly circumscribed. It is hoped that this volume provides answers to several more general but interesting questions, which inevitably present themselves for discussion in any historical study of the growth of seaside resorts and the holidaymaking centred about them, even though it succeeds in only scanning what is a voluminous printed, documentary and visual archive, on an important aspect of both urban and social history. The underlying questions can be posed as follows.

What were the principal factors causing the rise of Kentish seaside resorts from about the middle of the eighteenth century onwards?

Did their expansion assume an intermittent or sustained character?

How were entertainment facilities developed? How much pleasure did they bring to their customers, and profit to their proprietors?

In what numbers and at what cost did holidaymakers travel to Kentish resorts by road, water or rail?

Who were the holidaymakers to these resorts? How far is it possible to identify broad categories of visitors or specific individuals?

What changes were there in the social composition of visitors over

---

[3] Philip MacDougall, 'Dead Fish and Lively Company: An aspect of Margate's past', *Bygone Kent*, Vol. 4, No. 9, September 1983, 547.

[4] The lead which Brighton established and maintained over other English seaside resorts has been given added stress by John K. Walton, *The English Seaside Resort: A Social History, 1750 – 1914*, Leicester, 1983, 12, 53 – 4; also on Brighton, E. W. Gilbert, *Brighton, Old Ocean's Bauble*, London, 1954, reprinted 1976.

the eighteenth and nineteenth centuries? Were some resorts more
retired and select than others?

Is there any information on how individual holidays were or could be
spent?

Can anything useful be said about the cost of holidays and how they
affected the economies of seaside towns?

(2) The Chronology, Scale and Pattern of Kentish Resort Development.

Almost forty years separate Mr. J.A.R. Pimlott's 'splendid pioneering
work',[5] The Englishman's Holiday: A Social History (1947), as the first
classic history of English holidaymaking, from Dr. J.K. Walton's The
English Seaside Resort: A Social History, 1750–1914 (1983), as the most
up-to-date comprehensive study of the economic and social history of
English seaside resorts, from their infancy in the mid-eighteenth
century to their maturity well before the First World War. The latter
work pulls together much of the research which has been undertaken in
this area since the pioneering work of Mr. Pimlott in the 1940s. Despite
some intervening general histories of holidays and resorts,[6] plus a
proliferation of local case studies, particularly in thesis form, not
forgetting too a rich quarry of primary sources on holidays and resort
development – in contemporary guidebooks; topographical works;
trade directories; national and local newspapers and journals; printed
and MS letters or diaries; estate and business records; maps, and
original prints, photographs and postcards – only a minority of
historians have paid much attention to the rise of seaside resorts. The
growth of the seaside holiday industry, which ought to be a significant
theme in English economic and social history, often receives no more
than a passing mention in textbooks of the nineteenth and twentieth
centuries. Here is a serious gap in British historiography. It is the
added purpose of this volume to plug that gap so far as Kent is
concerned.

It is well established that holidays are as old as human society, and
'are to be found in some form in all civilizations, ancient and modern',
with their character varying 'from age to age and from country to
country according to differences in religious, political and social

---

[5] Walton, op.cit., 2.

[6] Including, apart from those studies noted already, A Hern, The Seaside Holiday: The
History of the English Seaside Resort, London, 1967.

conditions'.[7] Important religious origins are attached to the word holiday or 'holyday' which, over the centuries, has been secularized in meaning to refer to periods of absence from work, for purposes of leisure, recreation and amusement. Holidays in a modern sense are ordinarily thought of as vacations away from home, over a day, a few days, weekend, a week or a period of weeks. The custom of a holiday period in the summer months certainly grew throughout the nineteenth century, with the seaside being indeed an item of 'mass consumption' in later Victorian Britain.[8] It was inevitably the case that as seaside holidays and resorts developed, so they exerted an extending influence over a growing proportion of the population, whether as holidaymakers, entrepreneurs or investors, or, in the words of Dr. Walton, 'the sheer scale of seaside resort growth and popularity . . . could hardly fail to have important and revealing causes and consequences.'[9]

Among the more powerful and long-term underlying causes of resort development in England and Wales were the alleged medical virtues attached to sea water and sea air (Docs. 23 and 24) and the development of transport (Docs. 1–17), but on a par with these key factors in the rise of seaside resorts was consumer demand. Dr. Walton's book has the great merit of giving careful and detailed attention both to the demand and supply side of a developing seaside holiday industry. Constantly and powerfully he argues that consumer demand was the principal force shaping the overall growth and character of resort development in this country.[10] The demand for seaside holidays expanded and changed as between the eighteenth and twentieth centuries, alongside the transformation of the British economy and a tremendous growth in national wealth and personal well-being.

> 'The seaside holiday habit percolated downwards through the increasingly complex social strata of the first industrial nation. . . .The changing structure of demand for seaside holidays was an essential influence not only on the growth-rate of resorts, but also on their social characteristics. The pattern and style of resort growth was in large part determined by the number of holi-

---

[7] 'Holidays and Resorts', *Chamber's Encyclopaedia*, London, 1959, 172.
[8] Walton, *op.cit.*, 225.
[9] *Ibid.*, 2.
[10] *Ibid.*, Chapter 2: 'The demand for seaside holidays', 5–44.

daymakers and by their social background and cultural expectations. To understand the evolution of the English seaside holiday town, we must first try to come to terms with the changes which took place in the visiting public over time.'[11]

As between 1750 and 1914 seaside resorts emerged at different times all over the country. Those of Lancashire, Yorkshire or the North East were less remote from far reaching industrial and commercial transformation and expansion, or from dramatic examples of urban explosion, within their hinterlands, than were those of Southern England, but whereas the North and the Midlands witnessed notable developments in industry, commerce and town growth, counties in the South East of England, notably Kent and Sussex, were to the forefront in the rise and expansion of seaside resorts. It would be difficult to quarrel with the overall assertion that 'Kent and Sussex between them can claim to have done more than most counties to develop the seaside holiday.'[12] The pattern of resort development up to the middle of the nineteenth century reveals a notable 'concentration of the seaside holiday industry into Kent and Sussex.'[13] The conclusion which emerges from Dr. Walton's table of 71 seaside resorts in England and Wales in 1851, ranked by population size, is that '18 Kent and Sussex resorts accounted for nearly 44 per cent of the total seaside resort population in 1851.'[14]

TABLE 1: 18 SEASIDE RESORTS IN SUSSEX AND KENT RANKED BY POPULATION SIZE, 1851.[15]

Brighton	65,569	Hove	4,104
Dover	22,244	Eastbourne	3,433
Hastings	17,621	Herne Bay	3,094
Gravesend	16,633	Broadstairs	2,975
Ramsgate	14,853	Bognor	2,694
Margate	10,099	Shoreham	2,590
Folkestone	7,549	Littlehampton	2,436
Deal	7,067	Rottingdean	1,084
Worthing	5,370	Seaford	997

[11] *Ibid.*, 5.
[12] L. Taylor, *London's Coast and Countryside*, London, 1950, 17.
[13] Walton, *op.cit.*, 53.
[14] *Ibid.*, 54.
[15] Extracted from *ibid.*, 53.

Although several of these populations were 'considerably inflated by non-resort elements', it is also interesting to note that of eleven English 'watering places' of importance on the coast, as enumerated by the 1851 census, only one, namely Scarborough, lay north of a line drawn linking the Thames and Severn estuaries, whereas two, Brighton and Worthing, were in Sussex and three, Margate, Ramsgate and Dover, were in Kent.

Despite Dr. Walton's assertion that Sussex may claim 'pre-eminence', while 'growth in Kent had been much less impressive than in Sussex, with Margate, in particular, well down [his] list',[16] seaside resorts, nevertheless, featured very prominently in the Kentish urban scene by 1851. Almost 30 per cent of Kent's urban inhabitants, at a time when the county was about half rural and half urban, resided in nine of the county's major resort towns in 1851, in contrast to only 1.8 per cent of the nation's urban residents living in the eleven English 'watering places' of importance on the coast, as enumerated in the Census of that year. Moreover, as the following table shows, seaside resorts were notable among the towns of Kent which doubled or tripled their populations during the first half of the nineteenth century.

TABLE 2: POPULATION GROWTH BETWEEN 1801 AND 1851 IN THE MAJOR KENTISH RESORTS.

RESORT	1801	1851
Gravesend and Milton (a)	4,539	16,633
Sheerness	5,561	11,082
Herne and Herne Bay	1,232	3,094
Margate	4,766	10,099
Broadstairs and St. Peter's	1,568	2,975
Ramsgate and St. Lawrence	4,178	14,853
Deal	5,420	7,067
Dover (b)	7,709	19,000+
Folkestone (c)	3,704	7,549
9 Resort Towns	38,677	92,352

Notes:
(a) The jurisdiction of the Corporation of Gravesend covered the two adjoining parishes of Gravesend and Milton.
(b) Dr. Walton provides an 1851 population figure of 22,244, but

[16] *Ibid.*, 54.

attempting to calculate the population of Dover is severely complicated by the fact that parish boundary changes in the town have been so intricate that comparable population statistics are difficult to assemble over the nineteenth century.

(c) Between 1841 and 1851 the population of Folkestone rose sharply from 4,413 to 7,549, following the completion and opening of the South Eastern Railway during 1843.

Population figures are not necessarily the best guide to a resort town's importance or patronage, for several reasons. Dr. Walton reminds his readers that 'not all seaside resorts grew in a rapid, clear-cut manner from negligible origins'; indeed, in most 'the holiday industry was grafted on to a pre-existing town or village economy'.[17] Thus there were 'non-resort elements' within their populations.[18] Moreover many developing seaside resorts, quite apart from catering for visitors, wealthy residents or the retired, continued to have mixed economies as they expanded, through being also fishing, shipping, manufacturing, marketing or dormitory centres. Although several of Kent's nine major resort towns had other functions, such as servicing shipping at Gravesend or Deal, working in a dockyard at Sheerness [Illus.23b], conducting an important London-bound corn trade from Margate, fishing from Ramsgate or Folkestone [Illus.21b], or handling cross-channel traffic at Dover or Folkestone, their combined population not only more than doubled between 1801 and 1851 but also accounted for almost 15 per cent of the county's total population at the latter date.

Whether or not Kent lagged behind Sussex in the provision of holidays the two counties soon shared one feature in common. Their resorts quickly became havens of retirement or residence for people of independent means, which is an interesting social phenomenon to reflect on. These two counties escaped much of the factories, mills, slums, grime and industrial pollution of Midland and Northern counties, and attracted instead some of the income and wealth of Lancashire, Durham, Yorkshire or the Black Country, which found their way into genteel living or were spent on excursions of pleasure in the leading coastal resorts of South East England. People were attracted to those towns both as holidaymakers and as permanent

---

[17] *Ibid.*, 47.
[18] *Ibid.*, 53.

residents. While money may have been easily made in the Midlands or the North, it was most agreeably spent in Kent and Sussex!

That too much can be made of railways is very pertinent to the emergence and rise of Kentish seaside resorts. The idea of associating their rise with the construction of railways is an untenable thesis so far as Kent is concerned. Kentish resorts by and large were not railway creations; as coastal watering places their origins were much earlier. Gravesend, Sheerness, Whitstable, Herne Bay, Margate, Broadstairs, Ramsgate, Deal, Dover, Folkestone, Sandgate and Hythe all assumed some significance as pre-railway seaside resorts. Although the South Eastern Railway contributed enormously to the growth of nineteenth-century Folkestone, as a leading seaside resort from 1843 onwards, there are several references to indicate that many facets of early holidaymaking already existed in Folkestone during the opening decades of the nineteenth century (Docs. 32i; 33r; 40j, k; 41 ss; or 42 ii, jj). Effectively while all Kentish resorts underwent some expansion following the arrival of railways, with the longer-term exception of Gravesend, there were only three notable railway creations in Kent dating from the 1860s onwards, namely Tankerton-on-Sea, Birchington-on-Sea and Westgate-on-Sea.

In the pre-railway period of Kentish resort development two main sub-periods of growth can be identified which tally closely with the transport facilities which were then available. In the coaching and hoy/sailing packet era up to 1815, Margate, Broadstairs and Ramsgate developed substantially as seaside resorts, along with Deal, Dover, Folkestone, Sandgate and Hythe. The Thanet resorts and Dover underwent further substantial growth during the steamboat era from 1815 to the 1840s alongside the steamboat creations of Gravesend, Sheerness and Herne Bay.

Another way of looking at the chronology of embryonic resort development in Kent, whereby the sub-periods of the previous paragraph are modified to some extent, is to date the onset of sea bathing (Docs. 27 and 32). By this method the following time-scale can be constructed which is not wildly out of line with what has been argued above.

1736 – Margate.
1754 – Broadstairs, Ramsgate, Deal.
1768 – Dover, Whitstable.
1776 – Herne Bay, Sandgate,

1792 – Folkestone, Hythe.
1796 – Gravesend.

Beginnings, however, can prove not only small but also quite prolonged, which was certainly true of Gravesend, Whitstable, Herne Bay (see after Doc. 32f) and Folkestone, with particular reference to its ability to accommodate visitors (Doc. 20 x, y). Against the fact that 'in many seaside resorts . . . the provision of accommodation for holidaymakers became the single most important economic activity in the course of the nineteenth century, [even though] its suppliers are difficult . . . to count',[19] so wretched was the state of Folkestone that a leading national newspaper during 1841 reported on how 'a gentleman recently visiting at this place was so much impressed by the dismal dirty appearance of the houses in some of the narrow streets, that he actually whitewashed the houses on one side of South-street, at his own expense, just by way of example to the inhabitants'[20] [Illus. 21b].

It must not be imagined that all the seaside resorts of Kent enjoyed a continuous or uninterrupted growth. Gravesend and Herne Bay were two resorts which took some time to develop before suffering respectively an irreversible decline and a temporary setback. There survives today very little visual evidence to indicate that Gravesend was once a popular watering place, but time was when the town flourished as a resort, following the introduction of steamboats on the Thames in 1815. A guidebook of 1845 observed how

'increase and improvement have been the features of its career . . . The limits of the place extended themselves slowly, until steam made Gravesend a suburb of London, when ancient rates of progression were lost sight of, and the small river-side town increased with startling rapidity, [and] with this great increase came additional embellishments, conveniences and improvements'[21] [also see Doc. 47 c, d and after v].

Ten years after the introduction of steamboats the following claims were made about Gravesend (also see Doc. 9c).

'Although this town has been long and universally known as the

---

[19] *Ibid.*, 81.
[20] *The Times*, 23 August 1841.
[21] *The Pictorial Guide to Gravesend and Its Rural Vicinity: A Holiday Handbook*, London, 1845, 13.

goal of every young Cockney's Sunday excursion, it is only [recently] that any invalid thought of resorting to water bathing. Excellent accommodations for bathing of every kind have been provided for the visitors . . . Almost every day they are undergoing some additional improvement. To the westward of the town, upon his own ground, and close to the water, Mr. Ditchburn has erected a noble building, in the lower part of which are warm baths, shower baths, a reading room for company, etc. Besides he has 5 or 6 large-tilted machines, which may be used at any time of tide [Illus. 18a]. For some years past the numbers of people who resort to this place, chiefly for the purpose of bathing, have been increasing every summer. . . .The people of London, who may be observed every Sunday flocking down by hundreds in steam packets, . . . have taken such a liking to Gravesend, that a company of rich capitalists have resolved to build an entire new town in its vicinity, as soon as they can bargain for a convenient track of ground for that purpose.'[22]

At first, and for a few decades, the prospects for Gravesend as a resort were favourable; indeed,

'on several occasions during its long history Gravesend has had greatness within its grasp . . . The flood-time came. Steamboat companies were formed . . . Piers were proposed [and] erected [Doc. 17 a–f]. Baths were erected [Docs. 29 z, aa: 32k]. Pleasure gardens were founded and developed – Rosherville Gardens, Victoria Gardens, [and] the Terrace Pier and Gardens [Docs. 39 j–m; 40 a–b] . . . At one time . . . the town had every appearance of rivalling some of the more famous watering places.'[23]

That hope, however, was not to be fulfilled for a multiplicity of reasons which became apparent during the 1850s. The seeds of its decay were inherent in its very popularity. To the fashion conscious middle and upper classes it had failed to develop a sufficiently respectable image (see Doc. 9 g). Neither could Gravesend compete with rival resorts further afield which also enjoyed improved transport facilities both by steamboats (Docs. 7, 11–16) and railways, hence the observation of

[22] *The Maidstone Journal and Kentish Advertiser*, 31 May 1825.
[23] A.J. Philip, *A History of Gravesend and Its Surroundings*, Hythe End, Wraysbury, Bucks., 1954, 174.

1860 that 'we have too many distant places, too many real sea-sides to notice, to keep you here.'[24] Gravesend's rapid rise was arrested and with the slump in its prosperity 'the Clifton Baths (Docs. 29 z, aa; 32 k) ceased to function: the Albion Baths (Doc. 29 aa) disappeared entirely, and Gravesend was without swimming facilities other than those offered by the river [Thames].'[25]

'What ought to be a rising locality – Herne Bay' stood in sharp contrast in 1860 to 'RAMSGATE, MARGATE AND BROADSTAIRS, a triad of London's chief seaside outlets.'[26] Herne Bay originated on the basis of local patronage, followed by London visitors, as was pointed out in the 1820s.

> 'HERNE has a spacious and commodious bay for shipping, frequented by the Newcastle and Sunderland colliers, as well as by hoys for the conveyance of goods to and from London. It is also a bathing place, to which great numbers of the inhabitants of Canterbury and its neighbourhood resort, and also many families from the metropolis and other parts of the kingdom, several good houses having been of late years erected, and commodious warm and cold baths prepared for the accommodation and recreation of the visitors.'[27]

Many attempts were made to plan and design new watering places during the later eighteenth and nineteenth centuries and the Herne Bay of the 1830s provides one example, alongside Bognor, St. Leonards and New Brighton.[28] Herne Bay was a planned seaside resort of the steamboat era, being also a case study of property owners taking it upon themselves to develop the necessary transport facilities to their resort, but also it was a speculation which was only partly successful, falling 'short of the expectations of speculative promoters of the 1830s.'[29]

High hopes characterized the period 1830–42 followed by stagnation and decay over the next twenty years when Herne Bay hardly grew at

---

[24] Spencer Thomson, *Health Resorts of Britain; and How to Profit by Them*, London, 1860, 65–6.

[25] Philip, *op.cit.*, 179–80.

[26] Thomson, *op.cit.*, 67.

[27] Thomas Cromwell, *Excursions through the Counties of Kent, Surrey and Sussex*, London, 1822, 80.

[28] Walton, *op.cit.*, 114.

[29] *Ibid.*, 114.

all, with the town actually exhibiting symptoms of physical decay. The high hopes centred around the increasing perfection of steamboats (Docs. 7, 8, 11), the creation of the Herne Bay Pier Company under an Act of Parliament of 1831 (Doc. 17 h), the opening during 1832 of Herne Bay Pier to service steamboats (Docs. 17 i–1), the erection of hotels, lodging and boarding houses, shops, sea water baths, assembly rooms, circulating libraries, bazaars, etc (Doc. 17 j, 1; 19 k–m; 20a; 22m; 29 x; 33e; 41 ww; 42 oo–rr; following 44 m, and 52), with all these improvements leading in turn to the formation in 1834 of the Herne Bay Steam Packet Company with its two famous vessels, the City of Canterbury and the Red Rover (Docs. 10c., 13, 14, 15 a–f).

Despite all this enterprise, coupled with favourable comments about the sea air and bathing at Herne Bay (Docs. 24o; 33d, e; 52), a valetudinarian wrote disparagingly in c. 1835 of this rising resort (also see following Doc. 34b).

'HERNE BAY and the Ague are now synonymous terms. I dread the recollection of my sufferings in this place . . . The neighbourhood is pretty enough, and its short distance from Canterbury by land, and from Margate by sea, induces a few stragglers to visit it occasionally in the summer. The town, if it may be so called, lays very low – hence its tendency to produce ague. The bathing is good, [but] still Herne Bay will never answer as a watering-place, till Ramsgate and Gravesend shall be no more. For children, it is very unhealthy.'[30]

1835 saw the publication by 'A Lady' of *A Picture of the New Town of Herne Bay* which between its pages revealed an overall development which was still incomplete.

'The length of Herne Bay, which now is properly denominated a town, is about a mile. The pier is at the western extremity where the buildings, and every thing adjacent, are on a scale to harmonize with its magnificence [see Illus. 22a] . . . The streets and squares, some completed, and others in progress, all fall within the scheme of perfect uniformity and sufficient breadth to give the notion of a liberal mind in the projectors . . .

In the plan laid down in the beginning, by able artificers, for the

[30] By a Valetudinarian, *Sea-Side Reminiscences: A Few 'Odd Thoughts' on Our Fashionable Watering Places*, London, c. 1835, 21.

formation of New Herne Bay, several squares were included; these have not yet been built, but are to be proceeded with, as soon as the trustees have completed the objects of more pressing necessity, such as forming different roads, [or] building the sewers intended for making the drainage of Herne Bay superior to any other watering-place . . .

There is to be also an elegant crescent on the ground lying between the Pier Hotel and the Dolphin Inn [see Docs. 191, m]. It will be named Telford Crescent, in honour of the great man, now no more [he having drawn up the plans for Herne Bay Pier, Doc. 17i] . . .

This is, perhaps, the proper place to state that persons feeling an interest, or a curiosity respecting the formation of the present, or the future extended town of Herne Bay, may be supplied with a lithographic plan of the whole, by applying to Mr. Clift, 1, Copthall Court; or to Clift, Pocock and Fisher, Solicitors, 3b Ely Place, Holborn . . . On this plan, every square, street, crescent, promenade, road, or remarkable object of any kind, is shewn with its name. It exhibits, not only the great number of buildings already completed, but what it is intended still to do . . . The plan designates numberless new intended erections, including crescents and promenades. . . . The western cliff is now sold, and forming into detached plots . . .

The aim of the projectors is to make the place unrivalled as a resort in the summer season.'[31]

Observations of the 1850s drew attention to 'long lines of streets, many of them still unfinished, stretching out in every direction',[32] and to a 'new town,. . .well planned on an extensive scale, of which portions only are yet built.'[33] The planned development of Herne Bay turned out in other words to be a speculative enterprise which was never completed, largely on account of the opening of railway communication from London to Brighton (1841), Folkestone (1843), Dover (1844) and Ramsgate and Margate (1846), which diminished the steamboat traffic from London to and through Herne Bay (see Docs. 13, 14, 15d, e).

[31] By a Lady, *A Picture of the New Town of Herne Bay*, London, 1835, 10, 12, 13, 14.

[32] E.L. Blanchard, *Adam's Descriptive Guide to the Watering Places of England, and Companion to the Coast*, London, 1851, 155.

[33] Mackenzie Walcott, *A Guide to the Coast of Kent*, London, 1859, 122.

Stagnation and decay set in, and there was much talk of depression. Precarious letting and 'several unfinished houses' formed part of the evidence to an 1850 Select Committee on a Herne Bay Improvement Bill.[34] In 1847, and again in 1857, Herne Bay people argued for railway communications as good as those from London to Thanet. The oral evidence of contemporaries shows how they viewed the situation.

'The place was very considerably resorted to by Londoners before the railway traffic took our passengers away and I think by giving it a railway communication, that in combination with the steamboats will cause it to be very much resorted to . . . for health and recreation. In 1842 we had between 50,000 and 60,000 passengers pass over the pier'[35] (also see Doc. 15d).

'[When we] enjoyed at Herne Bay the same advantages that other watering places did, . . . we had a larger share of visitors. Houses then let at a large rent, . . . furnished houses letting at 11 and 12 guineas a week, which are now glad to be let at 5 or 6 guineas or less than that . . . [Visitors] complain of the want of communication . . . The South Eastern run a cheap fast train down on Saturday night to Margate and Ramsgate and back early on Monday morning [the railway's answer to "The Hats boat" or "The Husbands' boat", Docs. 16a, e]. That train does not call at Sturry [then the nearest station on the South Eastern network for Herne Bay]. Fathers, etc. are able to run down and spend the Sunday with their family and be back on Monday morning. That does not apply to Herne Bay.'[36]

When asked if he was sanguine enough to suppose that Herne Bay could compete successfully with Brighton, he replied that 'if we get a railway to Herne Bay, a large number of persons who now go to Brighton would come to Herne Bay.'[37] Yet another witness, who

[34] Mr. James Wilson, a Herne Bay resident, in evidence 29 April 1850, to the *House of Commons Select Committee on the Herne Bay Improvement Bill* (Group 18), HLRO, Committee Office Evidence, 1850, volume 22.

[35] Mr. Samuel Frederick Miller, a London Solicitor and Clerk to the Herne Bay Pier Company, in evidence 27 April 1847, to the *House of Commons Select Committee on [the] Herne Bay and Canterbury Junction Railway*, HLRO, Committee Office Evidence, 1847, volume 6.

[36] Mr. William Evans, a medical practitioner for eighteen years in Herne Bay, in evidence 31 July 1857, to the *Select Committee of the House of Lords on the Herne Bay and Faversham Railway Bill*, HLRO, Lords Evidence, 1857, volume 3.

[37] *Ibid.*

claimed to have invested £50,000 in Herne Bay, reckoned that up to 1857 property had deteriorated in value by 'more than 75 per cent'.[38] A partial solution to Herne Bay's problems and some recovery from the doldrums followed the opening in 1861 of a through railway communication with London, via Faversham, Sittingbourne and the Medway Towns.

The changes in fortune which afflicted Gravesend and Herne Bay did not occur in the Thanet resorts where boom times were never lacking from their inception during the middle decades of the eighteenth century (Docs. 27; 32 b, c; 47). Continuous expansion and prosperity in Dover resulted from several growth points in its economy, being as it was up to 1840 the leading cross-Channel port and a major defensive centre, in addition to functioning as a seaside resort.[39] Although Dover and Deal were more populous than either Margate or Ramsgate in 1801[40] their resort function at that time was 'still of minimal importance'.[41]

Unlike the Thanet towns and Dover, Deal suffered from a post-Napoleonic depression.[42] It had become fashionable as a small resort in the later eighteenth century (Docs. 20 g, 32 a, 42 ff) when the town was more important as a naval station and port of call in the Downs for shipping *en route* to and leaving London (Illus. 7b). With respect to the latter functions the 'Golden Age' of Deal's history coincided with the French and Napoleonic Wars between 1793 and 1815.[43] 'Years of great adversity'[44] followed the Napoleonic Wars,

> 'which ended the long years of naval and military activity at Deal. With the close of the war a new era was ushered in. The years of prosperity were followed by a period of stagnation and decay. The boatmen, . . . impoverished by loss of occupation, were further harassed by severer measures against smuggling. Bankruptcies

[38] Mr. J. Burge, having extensive interests in Herne Bay, in evidence 31 July 1857 to *ibid.*

[39] J. Whyman, 'Rise and Decline: Dover and Deal in the Nineteenth Century', 2 Parts, *Archaeologia Cantiana*, LXXXIV, 1969 and LXXXV, 1970, particularly Part II: 'Growth Points in Nineteenth-Century Dover', 35–54.

[40] See this section Table 2 above.

[41] Walton, *op.cit.*, 49.

[42] Whyman (1969), *op.cit.*, Part I: 'Depression and Adjustment in Nineteenth-Century Deal', 123–37.

[43] *Ibid*, 126–8.

became common [see Doc. 29 r] among the tradesmen, and it was only by the energy and far-sighted policy of a little band of townsmen, who were convinced of Deal's possibilities as a watering-place, that the town was saved from complete ruin.'[45]

The hope that salvation lay in this direction was expressed by *The Maidstone Journal and Kentish Advertiser* on 21 June 1825.

'Many improvements are going on at Deal and Walmer, where lodgings have at this early period of the season become scarce . . . From the high price of land in its immediate vicinity (some has sold at £200 per acre) and the preparations that are making for building, we have no doubt it will ere long rank as high in the estimation of the public as its beautiful situation justly entitles it to.'

Some degree of buoyancy in Deal as a seaside resort had the effect of only partly masking the decay of the town's traditional maritime activities. The optimism of 1825 was not realized, as can be seen by the failure to complete the town's first pier (see before and following Doc. 17 o) and the chequered history of the Royal Adelaide Baths (Doc. 29 r). Deal exhibited up to the 1840s distinct signs of economic depression, which even the Duke of Wellington's associations with Walmer Castle, in his office as Lord Warden of the Cinque Ports (see Doc. 51), could not overcome. Deal shared with Herne Bay the fate of being a poor relation to the Thanet resorts, and it was even alleged in a letter to the Editor of *The Deal, Walmer and Sandwich Telegram*, on 6 April 1859, that it was, as a seaside resort, 'half a century behind most watering-places.'

Beyond Folkestone, Sandgate (Doc. 49) and Hythe developed as small resorts, which derived some social patronage from officers stationed at the Shorncliffe Camp and other barracks built on the hills above Sandgate and Hythe (see Illus. 12a, 17b), as part of the Napoleonic defences of the county.[46] These three resorts, 'being situated nearly contiguous to each other', shared 'a sort of relationship and community of interest between them', as was rightly pointed out in

---

[44] J. Laker, *History of Deal*, 2nd Ed., Deal, 1921, 375.
[45] *Ibid.*, 340.
[46] J. Whyman, 'The Kentish Portion of an Anonymous Tour of 1809', in Ed: A. Detsicas and N. Yates, *Studies in Modern Kentish History*, Maidstone, 1983, 180, 183; also *Pigot & Co.'s Commercial Directory, 1832–4*, 830, 863.

1816[47] (also see Docs. 2i, 24 i, 40 m, 41 pp and following 43 g).

It was Thanet, however, which boasted the largest concentration of seaside resorts in pre-railway Kent, which gave rise to the following observation in 1803.

'THE Isle of Thanet, small and circumscribed as its limits are, contains no fewer than three sea-bathing places, Margate, Ramsgate, and Broadstairs, which are here arranged in the rank of celebrity they respectively hold.'[48]

Margate built up a lead and superiority over all the other resorts of Kent and this fact is very well illustrated with reference to the provision of assembly rooms, circulating libraries and a permanent theatre, which operated during the summer months (Docs. 41, 42, 43; also Illus. 8, 13a, 14a), Of Ramsgate it was noted in 1803 that

'though it may be considered as the rival of Margate, and certainly is filled with very respectable and even more select company, it is never likely to supplant that favourite place . . . Three fourths of the people who [come to] Margate by the hoy . . . are induced to stop where the voyage ends . . . [Also] the place itself wants many of those attractions which draw the young and the gay to its neighbour.'[49]

In the case of Broadstairs (Illus. 2b, 7a, 11a),

'THE success of a neighbour generally excites envy or emulation. Margate on the one side, and Ramsgate on the other, having risen into high reputation as bathing places, *Broadstairs*, adopting the common principle, has attempted to rival them, or at least to withdraw a share of their trade. The consequence has been, that starting with a small capital, it has [not] been able to injure them in any essential degree, . . . beyond obtaining a moderate competence . . . Of late years it has become the resort of many respectable families during the summer [see Docs. 41 kk–mm], who preferring retirement to the gaiety and bustle of a public place, find in the society and accommodations here, all the *agrémens* which they wish, . . . [so] what was originally a small

---

[47] *The Hythe, Sandgate and Folkestone Guide*, Hythe, 1816, 1.
[48] *A Guide to all the Watering and Sea-Bathing Places*, London, 1803, 281.
[49] *Ibid.*, 281.

village is become a pretty considerable town, . . . almost a new creation, . . . [and yet] as the amusements here are few, reading seems properly to constitute one of the first and best of the number',[50] [compare Docs. 41 kk – mm; 42 v].

The contiguity and the sharing of common facilities as between Folkestone, Sandgate and Hythe applied also to the Thanet resorts 'between which places a constant intercourse is kept up', with Margate and Ramsgate both lying 'within an easy morning ride, or even a walk'[51] from Broadstairs (also see Docs. 41 kk, 43 r). In case it is thought that this commentary has devoted insufficient attention to Margate, in particular, as against assessing the changing fortunes of Gravesend, Herne Bay and Deal, there is much by way of background historical information on the Thanet resorts already available in print,[52] some of which is incorporated in the Documents which follow. The third section of this particular introduction, therefore, highlights briefly four factors contributing to Margate's uniqueness among early seaside resorts.

(3) *Four Factors in the Uniqueness of Margate as a Seaside Resort.*

Historically Margate can claim to be unique among English seaside resorts for four reasons at least, beginning with the fact of sea bathing there since at least the mid-1730s (Docs. 27 a, b), coupled with some important contributions from its inhabitants in offering advice on the medicinal value of sea water, sea bathing and sea air (Doc. 23 c), in perfecting and making more comfortable sea bathing by means of

---

[50] *Ibid.*, 122–3.

[51] *Ibid.*, 123–4.

[52] J. Whyman, *Aspects of Holidaymaking and Resort Development within the Isle of Thanet, with Particular Reference to Margate, circa 1736 to circa 1840*, 2 volumes, Arno Press, New York, 1981; J. Whyman, 'Visitors to Margate in the 1841 Census Returns', *Local Population Studies*, No. 8, Spring 1972; J. Whyman, 'A Hanoverian Watering Place: Margate before the Railway', in Ed: A. Everitt, *Perspectives in English Urban History*, London, 1973; J. Whyman, 'The Uniqueness of Margate as a Seaside Resort', *The East Kent Critic*, New Series, Nos. 165–70, January to June 1977; J. Whyman, 'A Three-Week Holiday in Ramsgate during July and August 1829', *Archaeologia Cantiana*, XCVI, 1980; J. Whyman, 'Water communications to Margate and Gravesend as coastal resorts before 1840', *Southern History*, volume 3, 1981, and J. Whyman, 'Water Communications and their effect on the growth and character of Margate, circa 1750 to circa 1840', in Ed: E.M. Sigsworth. *Ports and Resorts in the Regions*, Hull College of Higher Education, 1981.

bathing machines and sea water baths (Illus. 4a; Docs. 26; 27; 28; 29 a–c, k–n; 33 f,g), not forgetting too that Margate provided for coastal medical care and the convalescent needs of the poor in the Margate or 'General Sea Bathing Infirmary' from 1796 onwards (Doc. 46; Illus. 21a). Secondly, water communications (Docs. 4–11, 16) played a decisive rôle in Margate's pre-railway rise to maturity as a major English seaside resort. Thirdly, in spite of the patronage of the wealthy and the great (Doc.45), there were few pre-railway resorts which catered for social classes beneath the artistocracy, gentry and clergy. Margate soon emerged as an exception to the general rule that spas and watering places were almost exclusively resorts for the upper classes, and what became apparent in Margate well before 1815 applied equally to Gravesend after 1815[53] (Doc. 9 g). Neither was royal patronage an early and significant influence on the development of Kentish resorts, other than at Ramsgate and Broadstairs during the 1820s and 1830s,[54] in stark contrast to the seal of royal approval bestowed on Weymouth, with 'the conversion of George III's court to the joys of sea bathing', leading to 'regular royal visits between 1789 and 1805',[55] (Doc. 45 n), while even 'more spectacular and long-lasting was the influence of the Prince of Wales on Brighton . . . from 1783 onwards'[56] (Docs. 47a, dd), with Worthing and Southend also benefiting from royal visits in 1798 and 1801 respectively.

These last two factors exercised collectively such an impact on the growth and character of Margate as to justify a more extended treatment, but not before noting how fourthly Margate was in several respects the first seaside resort to become 'popular' in the widest interpretation of that word. Here were pioneered many popular seaside amusements, including a camera obscura (Doc. 36 b), riding around on donkeys or asses (Docs. after 34 b; 38 p, q; also Illus. 13b), having sporting contests on its sands (Docs. 35 j, k) and, not least of all, the indoor attractions associated with auctions, dice, loo, lotteries, raffling and the town's post-Napoleonic bazaars and boulevards (Docs. 42 j; 44 a–g, i–l).

The lower fares which came to prevail on hoys and steamboats

---

[53] The lowering of Gravesend's social tone contributing ultimately to its decline as a resort, as was noted in the previous section above.

[54] Evidence of royal patronage to these two resorts is touched on in this section below.

[55] Walton, *op.cit.*, 12.

[56] *Ibid.*, 12.

(Docs. 4 a, b, e, g; 5 a, c, l; 6 f; 9 e; 16 d), compared to those by coach (Docs. 1 h, 2 a), introduced a cross-section of society as visitors to Margate, which certainly did not escape the observant eye of other eighteenth-century travellers and holidaymakers (Docs. 5 b–f, i). Travelling down to Margate presented no great obstacles, because hoys and, later, steamboats operated regular, frequent and cheap services from and to London. The resort's eighteenth-century expansion and prosperity rested on communications by hoy or sailing packet, exploiting the almost exclusive advantage of a direct and low-cost water-communication link with London, using the Thames as a natural highway. The number of vessels on this route doubled between 1763 and 1792 (Docs. 4 a, c). The minimum single fare ranged from 2s. 6d. (Doc. 4 a) to 7s. (Doc. 4 e) falling back to 5s. before 1815[57], with differential fares being introduced from the 1790s commensurate with greater comfort (Doc. 4 e).

While it is not easy to calculate the total traffic which was handled by the Margate hoys, they do seem to have carried more passengers than the coaches. Individual coaches accommodated up to six passengers inside (Doc. 2 a), with others riding on the outside, but even allowing for the 'great complaints' which were levied during August 1802 at the Brighton coaches for being 'loaded with passengers, not less than eight or ten persons being frequently stowed on the outside'[58] each individual coach, compared to a sailing packet or a steamboat, carried relatively few passengers. Up to 70 passengers per vessel could be conveyed as early as 1763 (Doc. 4 a), rising to 'above a *hundred* passengers at a time' by 1797,[59] this latter fact being supported by newspaper reports. *The Times* of 16 September 1797 noted, for instance, that 'so great is the rage for watering places, that [a] Margate packet had, the week before last, 152 passengers on board', while according to *The Observer*, of 24 August 1800, 'seven hoys last week conveyed to Margate 1,342 persons'. In 1792 it was calculated that the 'vessels bring and carry during the Bathing Season to and from London 18,000 passengers',[60] as against 21,577 in 1814–15.[61]

---

[57] Whyman, 'Water communications', *op.cit.*, 115.
[58] *The Times*, 18 August 1802.
[59] *The Margate and Ramsgate Guide in Letters to a Friend*, London, 1797, 15.
[60] *The Kentish Companion for the Year of Our Lord, 1792*, Canterbury, 1792, 160.
[61] *Report from the Select Committee on Ramsgate and Margate Harbours; Together with the Proceedings of the Committee [and] Minutes of Evidence* [660], 1850, 169.

The Margate hoy was instrumental in lowering the social tone of Margate as a seaside resort, with the 1770s and 1780s referring to travel by 'the middle and inferior classes', or by 'the inferior cast' (Docs. 5 c, d). On 5 August 1799 *The Times* observed how 'Margate is already beginning to be crowded, as usual, with all sorts, and for all purposes', with 'some tradesmen [having] gone down . . . to get rid of their money.' During and following the 1790s the social range of Margate's holidaymakers remained as wide as ever. The disreputable at one extreme included pickpockets: 'several of the London Pickpockets have gone down to *get a ducking* at Margate.'[62] At the other extreme were holidaymakers of immense wealth and respectability (Doc. 45; Illus. 5 a-c). Margate's ordinary visitors were commonly referred to as citizens or Cocknies.[63] What was clearly a cross section of visitors from many trades and professions was one of the themes of William Robinson's poem *A Trip to Margate* in 1805.

"'Tis not in bathing that you come to know
Who visit Margate. To the pier you go [see Illus. 6a],
And there a strange and motley crew you see,
Compos'd of ev'ry trade, and each degree
Up to nobility, of which a few
Are sprinkled now and then among that crew.
The rest made up of male and female cits;
Loungers in Bond-street, looking for their wits;
Some macaroni-sops from God knows where,
And some coarse clowns bred up in vulgar air;
Solicitors and Lawyers, never wrong
In quest of business, where there is a throng
. . . Surgeons and Doctors too,
And Undertakers also not a few . . .
To these must still be added Barbers, Taylors,
Slopsellers, Butchers, Bakers, and Toy-dealers.
Old waddling dames, with hobbling gouty men,
And prudish virgins threescore years and ten.'[64]

Some visitors were none too pleased by what they encountered at Margate, including Mrs. and Miss Meyer and Miss Green who had

[62] *The Observer*, 10 September 1797.
[63] For instance by *The Times*, 6 September and 13 September 1804.
[64] William Robinson, *A Trip to Margate*, London, 1805, 16–17.

moved on 20 August 1804 to Broadstairs 'not liking Ramsgate or Margate, the latter Mrs. Meyer said is London, – Cheapside, Wapping!'[65] (compare Doc. 41 kk). Six years later the accolade of 'London-by-the Sea' was strongly hinted at when *The Morning Chronicle*, of 8 September 1810, observed how Margate was 'crowded with company, and indeed may be considered as London in miniature, being in many circumstances an epitome of that vast metropolis.' It seems both logical and fair to apply at an earlier date the above label to Margate before extending it to Brighton.

It was from London that the first steamboats were introduced to Margate in 1815 (Docs. 6 a–d). Although a mixed reception was bestowed on them at first (Doc. 6), from the outset they greatly augmented the traffic to Thanet and very much enhanced the popularity and prosperity of Margate in particular. Of much greater significance than the two canals which were constructed in Kent (the Royal Military Canal and the Thames and Medway Canal) were steamboat developments down the Thames to Gravesend and beyond to Herne Bay, Margate and Ramsgate. The introduction of steamboats to Kent was at least as far reaching socially as was the subsequent construction of railways. Compared with road, river and harbour improvements, and canal and railway developments, the effects of steamboats were predominantly social rather than economic, being confined almost wholly to passenger transport, involving a substantial and expanding excursion element (Doc. 9).

The success and comfort of steamboats (Docs. 7, 8, 11) were such that there was a fantastic expansion of passenger traffic both to Gravesend and to Margate. The annual traffic to and from Gravesend more than tripled in a decade, so that by the early 1830s the number of passengers landing and embarking at the Town Pier (Docs. 17 a–c) had reached almost 300,000 annually. Ten years later the Gravesend boats were handling in excess of a million passengers annually at the Town and Terrace Piers[66] (on the latter Docs. 17 d, e.).

As between London and Margate the total number of passengers carried between 1820–21 and 1829–30 exceeded half a million, followed by a further 854,462 passengers between 1830–31 and 1839–40. All told

---

[65] Ed: J. Greig, *The Farington Diary*, volume II, London, 1923, 277; Mrs. Meyer was married to Philip James Meyer, see following Doc. 41 kk.

[66] R.P. Cruden, *The History of the Town of Gravesend in the County of Kent*, London, 1843, 537; also Table 44 and Graph 3 in Whyman (1981), *op.cit.*, volume II, 550–1.

Margate's steamboat traffic more than quadrupled between 1817 and 1835 (also Doc. 47u). Over the thirty five years falling between 1812–13 and 1846–47 the number of passengers arriving at and departing from Margate by water communication totalled 2,219,364. High annual peaks of traffic were achieved in 1835–36 at 108,625 and in 1842–43 at 102,647.[67]

An 1836 parliamentary committee had submitted to it a table showing the 'Present Amount of Traffic by Water.'[68]

TABLE 3: PASSENGERS BY STEAM PACKETS BETWEEN LONDON AND VARIOUS PORTS.

Gravesend	670,452	From
Herne Bay (compare Doc. 15 d)	30,102	Returns of
Margate	107,188	Pier Dues
Ramsgate estimated at	50,000	
Sheerness, Southend, The Nore, Dublin, Falmouth, Northern and Foreign Ports	200,000	
	————	
Annual Amount of Traffic	1,057,742	

viz: 10% to Margate
    5% to Ramsgate   } 18% to the Kent coast,
    3% to Herne Bay
BUT over 60% to Gravesend.

During the steamboat era of resort development competition intensified between rival companies; larger, more powerful and more comfortable vessels were constructed (Docs. after 10 b, 11, 14 a), and journey times were considerably reduced (Doc. 7). New companies were promoted (Doc. 10), with twelve different companies operating steamboats below London Bridge between 1829 and 1846,[69] and with six different companies competing for the Margate passenger traffic in

[67] *The Select Committee on Ramsgate and Margate Harbours* (1850), *op.cit*, 169; also Tables 43 and 44 and Graph 2 in Whyman (1981), *op.cit.*, volume II, 542–3, 544, 550–2.

[68] *The House of Commons Committee on the London and Blackwall Commercial Railway Bill*, HLRO, Committee Office Evidence, 1836, volume 15.

[69] F. Burtt, *Steamers of the Thames and Medway*, London, 1949, 29–59.

1836 and 1841.[70] The companies plying down the Thames included the General Steam Navigation Company (Docs. 8, 10 a, 16 b), the Gravesend and Milton Steam Packet Company (Doc. 7 f), the Star Steam Packet Company (Doc. 9 j), the New Gravesend Company (Doc. 9 g), the Diamond Steam Packet Company (Doc. 7 g) and the Herne Bay Steam Packet Company (Docs. 10 c, 13, 14 a, 15 d).

The keen competition which developed between rival steamboat companies resulted in lower fares. Initially fares were relatively high at 3s. to 4s. in the best cabin and 2s. in the fore cabin on the London to Gravesend run in 1815–16, while the lowest Margate fare was 12s. compared with an 1815 hoy fare of 5s. Thereafter fares declined until averages of 7s. and 6s. were reached from 1835 onwards, with much lower levels operating whenever competition between the steamboat companies was intense.[71] Between London and Margate there were very low fares over 1835–36. On 27 June 1835 *The Dover Telegraph and Cinque Ports General Advertiser* observed how some steamboats were charging only 2s. per person from London to Margate, out of which the proprietors had to pay 15d. pier duty for each individual. Receiving only 9d. from each passenger for a ninety mile journey was the equivalent of only one penny for every ten miles. Effectively this was one tenth of the one penny per mile which found its way into the coffers of the parliamentary trains after 1844.[72] A 2s. fare was sixpence less than the hoy fare had been in 1763 and 1780 (Docs. 4 a, b).

The Thames steamboats were important for pioneering not only very low fares, which applied also on the Gravesend run (Doc. 9 j), but also for pioneering daily, Sunday and weekend excursions to Gravesend, Sheerness, Herne Bay and Thanet (Docs. 9, 16), and daily commuting between Gravesend and London. Reductions in journey time (Doc. 7 b) were such as to permit day excursions to Margate before the end of the 1820s (Docs. 9 d, e). As with day excursions so too it was not railways which promoted early forms of commuting to and from London. By the 1830s businessmen were taking their families down to Gravesend to stay, from where they commuted to and from London on the steamboats, it being argued in 1831 that they were 'of great

---

[70] Whyman, 'Water communications', *op.cit.*, 127.
[71] *Ibid.*, 127; also Graph 4 in Whyman (1981), *op.cit.*, volume II, 555.
[72] Under the Regulation of Railways Act, 1844, better known as the Cheap Trains Act, all railways had to run at least one train daily charging a minimum fare of 1d. per mile third class.

importance to . . . mercantile men, who require to be in London early in a morning to fulfil their duties; to them speed is necessary.'[73] During 1835 the Gravesend and Milton Steam Packet Company advertised its first vessel as leaving Gravesend at 6.30 a.m. on weekdays, so as to arrive in London around 8.30 a.m.[74], there being 'many . . . persons who live at Gravesend or take lodgings for the summer months'[75] (also see Doc. 7 f). Weekend excursions or commuting to and from Margate, allowing fathers and sons who lacked guaranteed holidays to join their families for weekends on the coast, were typified by the late Saturday arrival of 'The Hats boat' or 'The Husbands' boat' (Doc. 16).

The fruitful relationship between Margate and its steamboats was stressed thus in 1831.

'Of all the watering places in England, Margate has now become the most attractive, from the salubrity of its air, the variety of its amusements [Docs. 44 a, b], and the short space of time in which the voyage is performed, by means of the numerous elegant steam-vessels which daily sail from the port of London [see Illus. 12b]. Some notion may be formed of the increase of visitors to this place, since the introduction of these conveyances, when it is stated that [formerly] the number of visitors did not average one tenth of [today's] amount . . . Margate stands pre-eminent among those summer retreats to which the nobility, gentry and citizens of London, annually retire from the noise and bustle of that overgrown Metropolis of the World [London]'[76]

More specifically the original steward of the Thames and Eclipse steam vessels (Docs. 6 a, f; 7 b) maintained in 1828 that 'the inhabitants of Margate ought to eulogize the name of *Watt*, as the founder of their good fortune; and *Steam Vessels*, as the harbingers of their prosperity'.[77]

[73] Mr. R.P. Cruden [the author of the work in Footnote 66 above] in evidence 23 September 1831, to *The Select Committee on Steam Navigation* [335], 1831, 81, 83, QQ 1447, 1486.

[74] *The Gravesend and Milton Journal*, 25 April 1835.

[75] Mr. Charles White, Proprietor and Director of the Star Steam Packet Company, in evidence 14 April 1836, to *The House of Commons Committee on the London and Blackwall Commercial Railway Bill*, op.cit.

[76] G.W. Bonner, *The Picturesque Pocket Companion to Margate, Ramsgate, Broadstairs, and the Parts Adjacent*, 2nd Ed., London, 1831, 1–2, 44.

[77] R.B. Watts, *A Topographical Description of the Coast between London, Margate and Dover. . .With an Account of the First Application of Steam. . .in Propelling Vessels*, London, 1828, 10.

The trend whereby Margate attracted holidaymakers from all social classes became increasingly pronounced during the 1820s and 1830s (Doc. 45 following dd; also ee). Steamboats clearly played a part in this process, along with the fact that holidaymaking along English shores came within the reach of increasing numbers of middle class and trading folk, as one social consequence of expanding national wealth, itself a product of sustained economic growth. Margate attracted more ordinary holidaymakers and fewer visitors of distinction, as was all too clear to *The Morning Herald* of 11 July 1827.

'Margate having been so long under the bann of fashion, the names of distinguished visitants are seldom found amongst the arrivals. Such visits, however, like those of angels, "few and far between", when they do happen, form a remarkable event in [its] annals.'

Among the ordinary holidaymakers staying in Margate in the later 1820s were Mary Figgins and her sister Rose and brother Vincent[78] (see Docs. 20 l, 35 f, 37 j, 41 dd, 44 i). Associating the pre-1815 Margate hoy with vulgar company (Docs. 5 a, e) remained ingrained in the mind of an 1828 visitor to Ramsgate who recorded 'flocks' of 'Margate "hoy" people' going 'in abundance' to Pegwell Bay (Doc. 38o).

By 1841 Margate was a solidly middle-class resort so far as resident holidaymaking was concerned. That year produced an early summer census on 7 June. Over 1,200 visitors were specifically recorded by means of a tick, cross or a small 'v' or 'L' entered against their names, or they were bracketed in groups in lodgings (Doc. 20 q), boarding houses or hotels (Doc. 19 n) as visitors. It is fortunate that the 1841 census was the first to formulate details on the occupational structure of the country. 601 of Margate's visitors shared among them 98 different occupations.[79] The largest single category comprised 352 visitors of independent means, followed by 89 servants and governesses. 222 of the 352 were women, some of whom had left husbands behind in London, leaving, therefore, 130 male visitors of independent means, some of whom were elderly or retired. They as a group stood alongside 70 tradespeople, 32 merchants or manufacturers and 27 drawn from

[78] *MS Diary of Mary Figgins, 30 August – 21 September circa 1828*, Margate Public Library, Local Collection, YO60.41; also Whyman (1981), *op.cit.*, volume II, 669–74.

[79] Table 58 in Whyman (1981), *op.cit.*, volume II, 683–5.

the professions. Tradespeople, merchants, dealers, factors, the professions, engineers, mechanics, manufacturers and clerks, numbering 146, exceeded in total the 130 male visitors of independent means. Titled visitors numbered no more than three, and visitors drawn from the church or farming were also well down the list.[80]

It is scarcely surprising, therefore, that the fashion-conscious Mrs. Elizabeth Stone could write in the year (1845) before the South Eastern Railway linked Thanet to London (1846) that

> 'it requires marvellous courage now to confess any interest in places so utterly discarded by fashion as are Margate and Ramsgate. They are still crowded, but by decidedly unfashionable people.'[81]

This social decline in quality was more than compensated for by the quantity of visitors to Margate (Docs. 44 c, d), and the presence there of a bustling scene on Margate sands (Doc. 34 f).

The steamboats by providing day excursions at low fares permitted working-class travel, which was most evident at Gravesend (Docs. 9 c, g, j). Respectable passengers complained about too much drinking on board, and at having 'their morals shocked at the low orders of passengers.'[82] It was also felt that recklessly low fares tempted 'loose characters',[83] including pickpockets who continued to make their presence felt. Steamboats provided rich pickings for pickpockets. *The Maidstone Journal and Kentish Advertiser* of 16 September 1828 noted how on one Margate steamer they had committed robberies to the value of £300, while on another occasion it was alleged that company agents had failed to rectify 'the presence of three notorious thieves', thereby allowing '320 passengers to be subjected to robbery'.[84]

Where better to finish this section than on the highest possible note with the patronage of British and foreign royalty to Ramsgate and Broadstairs during the 1820s and 1830s? Other and earlier instances of royal patronage were largely isolated occurrences, such as in 1793 when the second son of George III, the Duke of York, stayed in Mitchener's New Inn, before embarking from Margate on an expedi-

---

[80] *Ibid.*, 685–7.
[81] Mrs. E. Stone, *Chronicles of Fashion*, volume II, London, 1845, 298.
[82] *The Gravesend and Milton Journal*, 30 August 1834.
[83] *Ibid.*, 13 September 1834.
[84] *The Times*, 28 August 1835.

tion to Flanders, followed a year later by a hurried visit, again to Margate, by his elder brother, the Prince of Wales, afterwards George IV, for the purpose of welcoming his prospective bride. Caroline of Brunswick, whereupon the Prince and his fiancée patronized Benson's Hotel, attached to which were the assembly rooms (Docs. 19 e or 41 f). Resulting from these brief visits the New Inn and Benson's Hotel were renamed respectively the Royal York Hotel and the Royal Hotel (following Docs. 18 j and 19 e). The only really notable royal visits to Thanet before the 1820s occurred in 1797 when the Duke and Duchess of York visited Broadstairs (Doc. 45 n) and in 1803 when East Cliff Lodge, as undoubtedly the most famous Thanet marine estate dating from the 1790s,[85] 'a distinguished marine residence, environed by about 24 acres of land planted on the verge of the cliff', between Broadstairs and within half a mile of Ramsgate, served as summer residence to the Princess of Wales, later Queen Caroline[86] (on this seat also see Docs. 45 bb, dd).

The Duchess of Kent, the widowed mother of Queen Victoria, was in Ramsgate in 1822[87] (Doc. 45 gg) and again in 1823.[88] It was announced from Ramsgate on 14 August 1822 that 'H.R.H. the Duchess of Kent and the Princesses Feodore and Alexandrina and suite, having embarked yesterday morning at the Custom-house Stairs, London, on board the *Hero* steam packet [compare Doc. 9 e], at 8 o'clock, arrived here about 5 in the afternoon.'[89] On 12 September 1822 the Duchess of Kent hosted 'a grand ball and supper' in Ramsgate,

'in honour of the birthday of his Highness Prince CHARLES of Leiningen, her Royal Highness's son, who has completed his 18th year. In the evening a grand display of fireworks was exhibited on the Cliff near Nelson's Crescent [Illus. 23a]. . . . The company was very numerous and select.'[90]

[85] Whyman (1981), *op.cit.*, volume II, 579, 649.

[86] Rev. D.A. Jessurun Cardozo and P. Goodman, *Think and Thank: The Montefiore Synagogue and College, Ramsgate, 1833–1933*, O.U.P., 1933, 10, 11.

[87] *The Morning Post*, 15, 16 and 22 August 1822.

[88] The Marquis of Lorne, *V.R.I. Her Life and Empire*, London, 1901, 59.

[89] *The Morning Post*, 16 August 1822. Six years later Queen Victoria's half-sister, Princess Feodore, the daughter of the Duchess of Kent by her first marriage with the Prince of Leiningen, married the Prince of Hohenlohe-Langenburg, The Marquis of Lorne, *op.cit.*, 35.

[90] *The Morning Post*, 17 September 1822.

Queen Victoria paid her first visit to Ramsgate as Princess Victoria in 1824, when she was five years old; five years later she and her mother spent part of the summer of 1829 at Pierremont House in Broadstairs[91] (Illus. 11a; Doc. 51a). In 1834 H.R.H. the Princess Sophia Matilda while on holiday in Broadstairs presented £5 towards funding the 8th Annual Pegwell Bay Regatta[92] (Doc. 37 p and Illus. 16b).

In 1835 the Duchess of Kent and Princess Victoria paid another visit to Ramsgate, when the royal party also included the King and Queen of the Belgians. On 2 October 1835 *The Times* reported that 'the visit of Her Royal Highness the Duchess of Kent and the Princess Victoria to this town continues to give gaiety and animation to it'. They stayed at Albion House (Illus. 11b) which, 'together with two other adjoining private houses, they have taken for two months', added to which 'the hotels are . . . crowded'.[93] The royal visitors were honoured by an address of welcome.

> 'Yesterday was the day appointed by their Royal Highnesses to receive the address of the inhabitants on the occasion of the Royal visit. At 11 o'clock the committee of the inhabitants, headed by R. Thompson Esq., the Deputy, Sir. W. Curtis [and] and M. Montefiore Esq., proceeded to Albion-house, to present the address, where they were received in the drawing room. At 1 o'clock the committee proceeded to the Albion Hotel [Docs. 19a, c] to present an address to the King and Queen of the Belgians . . . King Leopold proposes to leave Ramsgate at 8 this evening [but] the Queen is to remain . . . for the present'.[94]

Moses Montefiore (1784–1885), 'the outstanding Jewish figure of a great part of the nineteenth century',[95] and Ramsgate's most illustrious resident, made available the secluded grounds of his East Cliff Lodge to the royal party, with the presentation of a key 'enwrapped in the handsomest mazarine blue ribbon that the town of Ramsgate could supply',[96] having succeeded in purchasing this estate four years previously for £5,500.[97]

[91] The Marquis of Lorne, *op.cit.*, 28, 50.

[92] *The Kentish Observer*, 28 August 1834.

[93] *The Times*, 2 October 1835.

[94] *Ibid.*, 2 October 1835.

[95] P. Goodman, *Moses Montefiore*, Philadelphia, 1925, 11; also see Whyman (1981), *op.cit.*, volume II, 649–50.

[96] Goodman, *op.cit.*, 38–9.

[97] Cardozo and Goodman, *op.cit.*, 12.

Subsequently, Princess Victoria and her sister stayed for some time in Broadstairs, whereupon Moses Montefiore had a special gate cut into the wall for the royal visitors' convenience. This act of courtesy produced an appropriately worded royal note from the Duchess of Kent.

'Sir John Conroy presents his compliments, and in obedience to a command he has just received from the Duchess of Kent, hastens to acquaint Mr. Montefiore that Her Royal Highness is exceedingly gratified and obliged by his attention in making a new access to his charming grounds from Broadstairs for her convenience, but Her Royal Highness fears she has given a great deal of trouble.'[98]

During October 1836 the Duchess of Kent and Princess Victoria were once more in Ramsgate residing on the West Cliff, and Moses Montefiore, one year before he was knighted,[99] received and accepted an invitation to dine with them. His diary of 11 October recorded how

'a little before 7 [we] went in our chariot to West Cliff, where I had the honour of dining with their Royal Highnesses . . . The other guests were Sir John Conroy, The Dean of Chester, Mr. Justice Gaselee, the Rector of St. Lawrence, the Hon. Col. Stopford, and one other lady and gentleman. I took down the Colonel's wife and sat opposite to the Princess. There were thirteen at table, and it was impossible for it to have been more agreeable . . . The Duchess was most kind and condescending, and all the party were extremely amiable and chatty. The entertainment was truly Royal, and after dinner, when the gentlemen had joined the ladies in the drawing room, where tea and coffee were served, the Duchess again spoke to each of us. The Princess Sophia Matilda was also present. I returned home quite enraptured with the very kind and obliging manner in which I had been distinguished by her Royal Highness.'[100]

[98] Goodman, *op.cit*, 39.
[99] *Ibid.*, 46.
[100] *Ibid.*, 44.

DOCUMENTS

1. *Coaching services between the Kent coast and London up to the early 1790s.*

Long-distance coaching services from London to Canterbury or Dover were already well established by the middle of the eighteenth century.

(a) [*The Kentish Post, or Canterbury News Letter*, 30 March-3 April 1754]

POST COACHES . . . every Day from the Swan, at Westminster-Bridge to Canterbury, at 15s., and Dover at £1, in a Day; and from the Cross-Keys, in Dover, and the George, in Canterbury, every Day to the Swan, at Westminster-Bridge. . . Persons that come from, or go to the City End of the Town, may be taken up or set down at St. George's Church, in the Borough, upon such Notice at taking their Places.

(b) [*The Kentish Post, or Canterbury News Letter*, 2–6 March 1754] Commonly called the 4 Wheel Chaise Machines.

. . . From the 1st April next the price to each passenger to and from London and Canterbury to be £1. To and from London and Dover 25s.

Samuel Carnell as coaching manager of this particular firm sought to justify these higher fares because they included the following passenger provisions 'for their greater Ease and Benefit'.

1. It having been found troublesome both to Passenger and Manager, to weigh all Baggage above 14 lbs., each Passenger may carry 30 lbs., free, or one Company who shall take the Whole Post Coach 100lbs.
2. As Robberies are at this Time too frequent, (tho' no such Accident has ever happened to these Carriages, and as carrying an armed Man behind may be attended with fatal Consequences, making Villains more Desperate) each Person is insured 10 Guineas.
3. As Foreigners are apprehensive of being imposed on upon the Roads, Breakfast of Tea and Coffee, a regular Dinner with Small Beer, and Tea and Coffee in the Evenings, are provided and paid

for by the Manager; so that the above Prices are the Whole that each Passenger will be at throughout the Journey; except Wines, the Price of which are set up in the Rooms.

(c)   [*The Kentish Post, or Canterbury News Letter*, 11–14 September 1754]

Messrs Thomas Hartcup and Robert Legayt inform the public of their intention of running thrice a week between Canterbury and the Golden Cross, Charing Cross, London, a glass coach or Landau, hung on springs, to carry 4 people only, at a fare of 12s. per passenger. [N.B.] If 4 people take places for Margate or Ramsgate, they shall be carried thither from Canterbury as Stage Passengers.
A proper Guard shall attend the coaches up and down the road. Journey performed in one day.

(d)   [*The Kentish Post, or Canterbury News Letter*, 31 December 1755–3 January 1756]

A Stage Machine sets out from the Fountain Inn in Canterbury, every Morning (Sundays excepted), to the Crown Inn at Rochester, and the Star Inn, near the Monument, London, in one Day – and vice versa every Morning (Sundays excepted).

12s. a Passenger to London.
 6s. a Passenger to Rochester.

Each Passenger allowed 40 lbs. Weight of Baggage.
Perform'd by THO. LAMPARD.

(e)   [C. Seymour, *A New Topographical, Historical, and Commercial Survey of the Cities, Towns and Villages, of the County of Kent*, Canterbury, 1776, 322]

As there is a continual influx of natives and foreigners who travel on the road from Dover to London, coaches set out and return from the metropolis every day, Sunday excepted.

Initially because long-distance coaches from London focussed their services on Dover and Canterbury, visitors travelling to Folkestone/ Sandgate/Hythe, to Deal and to the Thanet resorts reached their destinations on local coaches, which operated to and from these coaching centres.

(f) [C. Seymour, *A New Topographical, Historical, and Commercial Survey of the Cities, Towns, and Villages, of the County of Kent*, Canterbury, 1776, 389]

FOLKESTONE – John Bailey goes to and from Canterbury with a Machine on Saturday during the summer; in winter he sets out on Friday and returns on Saturday. He goes weekly with the same Machine to Dover and Deal.

(g) [*The Dover and Deal Directory and Guide*, Dover, c. 1792, 43]

DEAL – A diligence sets off every morning at nine o'clock to Canterbury, where it waits till the arrival of the coaches from London, and returns the same evening. A waggon for luggage goes to Canterbury to meet the London waggon every Monday and Friday, and returns the next day. . . Two go every day to Dover.

(h) [*The Gentleman's Magazine*, XLI, 1771, 167]

MARGATE – The land conveyance is . . . extremely cheap and commodious. The stage coaches set out from London every day (Sundays excepted) at five in the morning and reach Canterbury at four in the afternoon, fare 12s. each passenger. The machines that carry only four within side do not set out till six in the morning, fare 15s. From Canterbury another machine (which runs all the summer) takes the passengers on to Margate the same day at 4s. each. The whole distance 72 miles [is] performed in 13 or 14 hours, and the whole fare [is] only 16s. to 19s.

Although Beale & Co. advertised on 8–11 June 1768, in *The Kentish Gazette*, a 'Flying Machine' from Margate to London in one day, from the Fountain Inn, guaranteeing that 'those who are pleased to favor this Machine may depend on the Business being performed with Care and Dispatch', most Thanet visitors changed coaches at Canterbury. Thus,

(i) [*The Kentish Weekly Post and Canterbury Journal*, 22–29 May 1769]

This is to give Notice, That The MARGATE MACHINE Sets out this Day from Margate to Canterbury, and will continue every Day during the Summer Season.

(j) [*The Kentish Gazette*, 18–21 May 1774]

WILLIAM BRETT'S MACHINE SETS out from MARGATE to the
FOUNTAIN INN, CANTERBURY, every Day during the Season
(Sundays excepted) and waits the Machines coming in from LON-
DON. – Places taken for London Coaches to LONDON in One Day, if
required.

(k) [*The Kentish Traveller's Companion*, Rochester, 1776, 139]

RAMSGATE – a machine and several carriers set out every day for
Canterbury, during the season, and return the same evening.
The seasonal nature of the Margate/Canterbury link is clearly
established in newspaper advertisements and other sources of the
1760s and 1770s.

(l) [*The Kentish Gazette*, 9–12 May 1781]

This is to give Notice That JOHN THORNTON's Coach sets out
from Margate to the Dolphin Inn, Canterbury, on Monday, Wednesday and Saturday mornings at 9 o'clock and sooner, if required, to meet
the Coaches . . . at Canterbury, and returns to Margate the same day,
at 3s. 6d. each Passenger.

2. *Coaching services between the Kent coast and London from the mid-1790s.*

Compared with earlier decades there was a notable improvement
in road travel facilities, in terms of speed, comfort, frequency and
choice of service from the 1790s onwards. By the mid-1790s direct
and regular coach services were operating between Margate and
London, by which time also the number and choice of services had
expanded appreciably, as the following details dating from 1796
demonstrate.

(a) [*The Universal British Directory of Trade, Commerce and Manufacture*,
1796; *A Short Description of the Isle of Thanet: being chiefly Intended as a
Directory for the Company Resorting to Margate, Ramsgate and Broadstairs*,
Margate, 1796, 95–6]

Fare
£. s. d.

I. *Mail Coaches and Diligences*

A Mail Coach starts from the York at 5 every evening
and returns at 8 every morning.   £1 1s.
Also a Coach to carry 'six insiders' at 4 every morning.   £1 1s.
Also one to carry 'four insiders' starting at 4.00 a.m.   £1 3s. 6d.
A Diligence for three inside at 4.00 a.m.   £1 3s. 6d.
Baloon Coach from Benson's Royal Hotel, Cecil Square
and Diligence from the same place.   ?
From Mummery's Coach Office, a Coach for six inside at
4.00 a.m.   £1 1s.
Also Coach to carry four.   £1 3s. 6d.
Also a Coach to carry six at 5.00 p.m.   £1 1s.
Also a Diligence at 4.00 a.m. every morning.   £1 3s. 6d.

These take up passengers from the Fountain, White Hart and Duke's
Head.

II. *List of Diligences, Coaches, etc. Running between Margate and London during the Season. From Mitchener's Hotel*

A Diligence every morning at 4 o'clock, carries three
inside, to the White Bear, Piccadilly.   £1 6s.
Also a Night Coach, every evening at 5 o'clock, carries
four inside, to the Cross Keys, Gracechurch Street.   £1 5s.

From the Fountain

A Post Coach, carries four passengers only, every morn-
ing at 4 o'clock, to the Spread Eagle, Gracechurch
Street; Cross Keys, ditto; White Horse, Fetter Lane;
and the Golden Cross, Charing Cross.   £1 5s.
A Coach, carries six inside, every morning at 4 o'clock, to
the above inns.   £1 2s.
A Night Coach, every evening at 5 o'clock, arrives in
London early in the morning, carries six inside.   £1 3s.
A Diligence every morning at 4 o'clock.   £1 6s.

Although by the 1790s coaching services had expanded considerably,
an overland journey to and from Margate was not necessarily

D E

TABE GLANDULARI,

S I V E

De Usu AQUÆ MARINÆ

I N

MORBIS GLANDULARUM

DISSERTATIO.

Auctore RICARDO RUSSELL, M. D.

Θάλασσα κλύζει πάντα τ' ἀνθρώπων κακά.
Mare abluit omnia hominum mala.
Euripides Iphigen. in Taur. V. 1193.

E THEATRO SHELDONIANO,
Proſtant venales apud JACOBUM FLETCHER, Oxon. & J.
& J. RIVINGTON, Lond. MDCCL.

Title page of Russell's treatise on sea water published in 1750.

Illus. 1

37

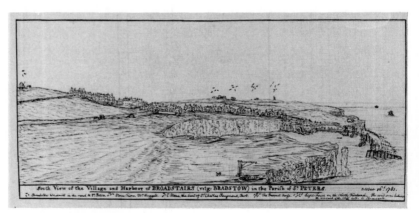

(a) The Old Margate Hoy, c. 1780.
(b) A view of Broadstairs, 1781.

Illus. 2

38

Two views of the bathing place at Ramsgate in (a) 1781 and (b) 1784.

Illus. 3

(a) A view of Margate, 1786.
(b) A public breakfast at Dandelion, c. 1790.

Illus. 4

Distinguished visitors to Thanet: (a) and (b) the Earl and Countess of Pembroke; (c) the Countess of Bessborough; (d) Joseph Farington, R.A.

(a) Landing at Margate, 1790.
(b) A view of Folkestone, 1790.

Illus. 6

something to be lightly undertaken. Overnight travelling, leaving at 5.00 p.m. was matched by early starts at 4.00 a.m. However, speeds and times certainly improved during the 1800s, as indicated by the following advertisement.

(b)   [*The Times*, 11 July 1815]

RAMSGATE – THE WELLINGTON, a new and elegant light COACH, every morning at 8 o'clock from the White Bear, Picadilly to the Albion Hotel, Ramsgate, when it arrives punctually at 7 o'clock evening. The Nobility and Gentry are respectfully informed, that the Proprieters have spared no expense to render this Coach, superior to any other on the road.

Coaches to Ramsgate also at 6 o'clock morning, and 6 and 7 o'clock evening, from the White Bear, Picadilly, and Cross Keys, Wood-street, Cheapside. MARGATE, ROYAL TELEGRAPH light 4 inside Coach every morning at 7 o'clock from the Cross Keys, Wood-street, two doors from Cheapside.

W.T. ROBERTS & CO.

Improvements to the Thanet coaching services were accompanied by higher fares.

(c)   [*Picture of Ramsgate, or A Guide to the Various Amusements, Public Libraries, Building Improvements, etc. of that celebrated Watering Place*, Ramsgate, 1833, 9]

Notwithstanding the safety, expedition, and cheapness with which the Steam Vessels travel, there are many persons, particularly ladies, who from timidity or choice prefer to travel by coach. For their accommodation several coaches run between London and Ramsgate, called Safety Coaches, built upon a principle which renders them secure from overturning, and conveniently fitted up with a roomy dickey, considerably below the roof of the coach. The price inside is £1 8s. and 15s. outside – nothing being charged for luggage. They start from London at eight o'clock every morning, . . . and arrive at Ramsgate about six o'clock in the evening. These coaches also stay some little time to take up passengers from the Elephant and Castle and the Bricklayer's Arms noted houses of call for stages on the Kent, Surrey, and Sussex roads.

Although coaches plying to Gravesend, Herne Bay or the Thanet resorts had to confront an intensifying competition from the Thames steamboats, the services on offer during the 1830s were much improved compared to earlier decades.

(d)   GRAVESEND [*Pigot & Co's Commercial Directory, 1832–4*, 819]

Call at the Prince of Orange.

To LONDON, the *Royal Mail*, every morning at three; the *Sons of Commerce*, every Monday morning at half-past six and every other morning (Sunday excepted) at seven; the *Wellington*, at ten; the *Commodore*, at a quarter before eleven; the *Faversham*, every alternate afternoon at half-past twelve; the *Telegraph*, at one; the *Eagle*, at two; the *Union*, every alternate afternoon at two; the *Express*, at three; the *Phoenix*, at four; the *Commodore*, every evening at a quarter before six; and the *Tally-ho!* at seven.

Call at the Nelson.

To LONDON, the *Nelson*, every morning at eight; the *Faversham*, every alternate afternoon at half-past twelve; and the *Union* coaches, at two and half-past four.

   The Following coaches, unless otherwise expressed, call at or go from the PRINCE OF ORANGE. To DEAL, MARGATE, RAMSGATE AND SANDWICH, branch coaches (from Canterbury), start for these places on the arrival of the Dover coaches from London.

To DOVER, the *Royal Mail* (from London), every night at eleven, goes thro' Chatham, Sittingbourne, Faversham and Canterbury; the *Union*, every morning at half-past ten, and afternoon at two; the *Eagle* and *Monarch*, every morning at eleven; the *Phoenix* and *Eagle*, every afternoon at one; and the *Express* at half-past one.

To MARGATE and RAMSGATE, the *Telegraph* (from London), every morning at half-past ten, goes thro' Chatham, Sittingbourne and Canterbury.

(e)   HERNE BAY [By a Lady, *A Picture of The New Town of Herne Bay*, 1835, 18]

Coaches and vans to and from Canterbury go and come several times in a day. A cross way is now forming from the west end of Herne Bay to the main road towards Canterbury, which will considerably abridge the distance. The fare is 1s. 6d.

Connecting with other places via Canterbury continued to be the case from Herne Bay during the 1840s.

(f) [S. Bagshaw, *History, Gazetteer and Director of the County of Kent*, II, Sheffield, 1847, 219]

Omnibuses are daily in attendance to convey passengers to Canterbury, Dover, Margate, Ramsgate, etc.

That part of the Kentish coast extending from Deal and Walmer round to Dover, Folkestone, Sandgate and Hythe relied much more heavily on coaching services to and from London, rather than water communication.

(g) DEAL AND WALMER [*Pigot & Co's Commercial Directory, 1832–4*, 800]

To LONDON, the *Auxiliary Royal Mail*, from Hook's coach office, 124 Beach st. and the Black Horse, every evening at half-past six.

To CANTERBURY, the *Defiance*, from Hook's office and the Black Horse, every morning at six, and the *Wonder*, every morning at nine.

To DOVER, postcoaches (from Margate), call at the Black Horse and Royal Oak, every morning at half-past ten and every evening at seven.

To MARGATE AND RAMSGATE, post coaches (from Dover), call at the Black Horse and Royal Oak, every day at twelve, and every afternoon at five, and during the summer months, every morning at six.

(h) DOVER [W. Batcheller, *A New History of Dover, to which is Added a New Dover Guide*, Dover, 1828, 354–6]

11 STAGE COACHES, etc. TO LONDON.

The Dover Royal Mail Coach leaves Wright's Ship Hotel daily (Sundays excepted) at eight in the evening, and returns at six in the morning.

Wright's Patent Safety Coaches from the Ship, Paris, Royal Oak, and Shakespeare Hotels, as follows:

The Courier, every morning at a quarter before eight, to the Golden Cross, Charing Cross, and to the George and Blue Boar, Holborn, in nine hours, without changing coach or coachman, and returns from the above places every morning, at a quarter before eleven.

The Sovereign, at ten in the morning, to the Golden Cross, Charing Cross. *The Regulator*, at six in the evening, to the Golden Cross,

Charing Cross, and to the Cross Keys, Wood-street.

The Union Safe Coaches, from the Union, Gun and Packet Boat Hotels, the Antwerp and Castle Inns, and from their Coach Office, 45, Snargate-street, every morning at eight and ten, and every evening at six, to the White Bear Inn, Piccadilly; Bell and Crown, Holborn; Blossom's Inn, Cheapside; and 11, Gracechurch-street; from whence they return every morning, at half past seven and eleven, and in the evening at a quarter before seven, in nine hours, without changing coaches or coachmen.

Chaplin's Safety Coaches from the Eagle Coach Office, Cross Wall; Chaplin's New London Hotel; and from the King's Head and Providence Inns, as follows:

The Mercury Fast Travelling Light Coach, every morning, at seven, to the Spread Eagle Office, 220, Piccadilly, and to the Spread Eagle, Gracechurch-street, and returns every morning, at eight o'clock.

The Eagle Patent Safety Coach, every morning at ten, in nine hours, to the above places, from whence it returns daily at ten, without changing coaches or coachmen.

The Swallow Superior Light Coach, every morning, at six, to the above places, from whence it returns every evening, at seven.

The Phoenix, every morning at half-past nine, from the York Hotel.

COACHES AND CARAVANS *To the Neighbouring Towns and Watering Places.*

The Union Coaches to Margate every day, and to Hastings every day during the summer, passing through Dover to Margate, at four in the afternoon, and to Hastings, at twelve, where it meets the Brighton coach, and forms a communication between Margate and Brighton.

The Brilliant Safety Coaches to Margate and Ramsgate, every morning at ten, and afternoon at four, from Chaplin's Eagle Coach Office, Cross Wall, and return daily at eight in the morning, and at four in the afternoon.

Ashtell's Coach from Hythe, every morning, and returns in the afternoon (Sundays excepted).

Bates's Coach to Margate, every morning at ten, and returns in the evening.

Williams and Johnson's Coaches from Margate, and return every afternoon, at four.

Austen's Van from Deal, every morning at eleven and returns at six in the evening.

(i) FOLKESTONE, SANDGATE, AND HYTHE [*Pigot & Co's Commercial Directory, 1832–4*, 815, 831, 863]

To LONDON, the *Times*, from the Rose Inn, every morning at eight; goes through Sandgate (the New Inn at half-past eight), Hythe (the Swan and White Hart Inns at half-past eight), Ashford, Charing, Lenham, Maidstone, etc.

To BRIGHTON and HASTINGS, the *Union* coach (from Dover), calls at the Rose Inn, every morning at ten, during the summer months; also via Sandgate and Hythe.

To DOVER, the *Union* coach (from Brighton) calls at Hythe (the Swan and White Hart Inns, every afternoon at one), Sandgate (the New Inn) and Folkestone (the Rose Inn), during the summer months.

3. *Recorded journeys to and from the coast by coach or chaise.*

(a) [Ed. P.C. Yorke, *The Diary of John Baker*, 1931, 417, 421–2]

In 1777 John Baker (also see Docs. 5g, 25e, 38b, 42c, 43j) travelled to and from Margate by chaise, accompanied by a Mrs. Woodington. Both the downward and homeward journeys were undertaken at a leisurely pace, with overnight stops in two of the major coaching towns on the London to Dover Road, Rochester and Canterbury.

September 9 – Set out for Margate, rose before 7 . . . Chaise came about 9 to the door . . . About 1 to the Bull at Dartford, where dined and stayed above an hour. At ½ past 6 to Crown at Rochester – drank tea and supt, to bed at 10.

September 10 – Breakfasted on tea and hot rolls, but relished them not . . . This is an excellent house, everything well ordered and the best one could wish. Came away about 10, and at 1 to Red Lion, Sittingbourne . . . dined – came away between 3 and 4 for Canterbury – At Booton's (Boughton) Hill, the horse would not go on, . . . 'tis a dreadful . . . hill. Mrs Woodington got out and walked a good way – kept us ¾ of an hour. To Red Lion, Canterbury, at 7, tea and supt in back room with 2 beds . . .

September 11 – This a bad house – alas! how short of last night . . . Came away a little after 10; at 2 miles through Sturry, a smart village – at 6 miles through Up-Street; stopt to water the horses at Half Way

House; got to Margate $\frac{1}{2}$ past 1. Mrs Woodington went out and got lodgings at Hall's, the bookseller, next door to Bathing House. Went thither and had dinner sent from hotel.

October 14 – At $\frac{1}{4}$ past 1 chaise came and in $\frac{1}{2}$ hour, after loading chaise, came away. Got to Canterbury (the King's Head) about 5. At $\frac{1}{2}$ past 8 had a roasted fowl and ate heartily a leg of it.

October 15 – Came away from Canterbury at 10 . . . To Red Lion at Sittingbourne about $\frac{1}{2}$ past 1; dined exceeding well on beef steak and cold roast beef . . . To Crown at Rochester, I supt on a little roast fowl at $\frac{1}{2}$ past 8.

October 16 – Came away $\frac{1}{4}$ after 9 . . . At Mrs Woodington's a little after 6. Gave the postillion a guinea, besides bearing his charges up and paying him a shilling per diem from the time we came to Margate this day 5 weeks.

Two days later he paid over to William Weston £28 10s. for three horses and a postillion to, from and at Margate, for 38 days, at 15s. per day.

(b)   [Ed. J. Greig, *The Farington Diary*, II, 1923, 1, 271, 278–9]

During 1802 and 1804 the famous topographical artist and diarist, Joseph Farington, R.A. (1747–1821) (Illus. 5d), travelled by coach, respectively to Dover, and to and from Thanet, with the first of these journeys being undertaken on the overnight mail coach.

August 28, 1802 – We left London on Friday evening . . . We made choice of the Mail Coach to Dover and had good reason to be satisfied with that mode of travelling, which is safe and expeditious. At 8 o'clock in the evening we drove from Lombard Street and were at Dover, 70 miles, at a quarter before Seven in the morning at the City of London Inn, where the people are very civil.

Two year later he set off with William Offley on a holiday to Broadstairs, breaking the downward journey overnight at Sittingbourne.

August 1, 1804 – At 9 o'clock left London in the Rochester Coach, . . . got there at $\frac{1}{2}$ past 3, and dined at the Bull . . . In the even'g we went in a Chaise to Sittingbourne, to the *Bell a good House*, but the *Rose* is most spoken of.

August 2 – Saw Lady Curtis [Wife of Sir William Curtis Bt., M.P. for the City of London, 1790–1818, and Lord Mayor of London in 1795] and her Family, who were at our Inn last night. They were going in a Barouche and 4 Horses to their House lately built at Ramsgate. – At 10 we set off for Canterbury and to Broadstairs, where we arrived at ½ past 2.

On the return journey a direct day coach from Margate was booked, which took fourteen hours to reach London, necessitating a previous overnight stay at Kidman's Hotel in Margate, where 'a bed may be had . . . at the rate of 2s. 6d. a night, but it is expected that those who lodge will . . . *eat there*.'

August 27, 1804 – Left Margate at 5 in the Coach, Miss Glover with me. We breakfasted at Canterbury, where 2 other passengers joined us. – We got to London at 7 in the evening. We remarked the *Hop Plantations* near the road [also see Docs. 19w, 20i, 38k, 41kk]

4. *The Old Margate Hoy.*

Hoys as a major means of conveying holidaymakers as well as commercial goods to and from Margate were already well established when Margate's first guidebook was published in 1763.

(a) [John Lyons, *A Description of the Isle of Thanet, and particularly of the Town of Margate*, 1763, 15]

They are sloops of eighty or an hundred tons burden. There are four of them, two of which sail in alternate weeks. Their station in the River is at *Wool-Key*, near the Custom-house. They usually leave *Margate* on *Friday* or *Saturday*, and *London* on *Wednesday* or *Thursday*. Passengers, of whom there are often sixty or seventy, pay only 2s. 6d. and the freight of baggage is inconsiderable. They sometimes make the passage in eight hours, and at others in two or three days, just as winds and tides happen to be for, or against, them. The best wind down is W.N.W., the best up E.S.E. The Hoy, like the Grave, confounds all distinctions: High and Low, Rich and Poor, Sick and Sound, are here indiscriminately blended together, . . . a motley crew, of all ages, tempers, and dispositions . . . Upon the whole, the passage is cheap, and in fine weather extremely pleasant and agreeable . . . The Masters are very careful, decent men, and allow of no impropriety of behaviour, which they can possibly prevent. They transact incredible business.

49

Within two decades they had been joined by yachts.

(b)   [*The Margate Guide*, 1780, 10, 18–19]

Having a quick and easy Communication with the Metropolis by Water, the Shops are well furnished, . . .in all Branches. The Hoys go to and return from London every Week. They are very good Sloops from 80 to 100 Tons . . . Passengers pay only Two Shillings and Sixpence for themselves, and the Freight of Baggage does not exceed Sixpence the Hundred Weight. – Besides the Hoys there are Vessels fitted up as Yachts, which pass regularly between London and Margate, for the Purpose of conveying Passengers. The Passage is frequently made in ten or twelve Hours.

By 1792 sailing yachts were plying between London and both Margate and Ramsgate.

(c)   [*The Kentish Companion for the Year of Our Lord*, Canterbury, 1792, 160, 161]

8 from Margate
   Prince of Wales, John Finch
   Endeavour, V. Kennard
   Robert and Jane, R. Kidd
   Neptune, J. Rowe, Jun.
   Dispatch, R. Laming
   Francis, E. Goatham
   Rose in June, John Rowe, Sen.
   Diligence, Jethro Sandwell.

2 from Ramsgate
   The Friends, Roger Strivens
   The Speedwell, George Ansell
   These sail every week with passengers from Ramsgate to London during the summer season and occasionally in the winter.

An emphasis on greater comfort and service was stressed in guidebooks and advertisements from the later 1790s onwards.

(d)   [By an Inhabitant, *The Margate Guide, A Descriptive Poem, with Elucidatory Notes*, Margate, 1797, 75]

During the season, eight Packets sail to and from *London* alternately . . .

They bring a great part of the company . . . These vessels are fitted up with a degree of elegance and convenience, that at once shows the emulative spirit of their owners, who are men of respectability, and to whose persevering exertions *Margate* must be thought not a little indebted for its present prosperity.

(e)   [*The New Margate, Ramsgate, and Broadstairs Guide*, 5th Ed., Margate, 1809, 53–4]

THE PASSAGE PACKETS are fitted up with different cabins and beds in the most commodious manner . . . Some of them have a state-room or after-cabin, which may be engaged by a select party for five or six guineas; but the passenger is conveyed in all of them at the moderate expence of 7s. and 9s. and his baggage proportionably cheap. It is perhaps owing to this, and the very superior accommodation which they afford, as well as to the civility and attention of the masters and seamen who navigate them, that Margate stands so highly distinguished in the list of watering-places.

(f)   [*The Times*, 3 July 1811]

For MARGATE – on Friday . . . at about 12.30 the PRINCESS OF WALES YACHT will leave Ralph's Quay, near Billingsgate. Capts. GORE and HUBBARD at the Gun Tavern, this evening, and all tomorrow, will feel additionally obliged by those who apply, enquiring for one of them personally . . . Carriages and persons passing down St. Dunstan's hill not only avoid Thames-street, and the unpleasantries of Billingsgate, but will face a clean paved passage to the vessel; and Ladies and Gentlemen can step on board without having other vessels to pass over, or any other annoyance.

(g)   [*The Times*, 16 and 22 July 1812]

RAMSGATE, BROADSTAIRS, and places adjacent, from Botolph-wharf, Lower Thames-street, fast sailing PACKETS

Wednesdays – SWIFT, Matthew Harman
Fridays – LORD HAWKESBURY, Richard Morris
Sundays – RESOLUTION, James Kelsey.

Best Cabin 7s., Fore Cabin 5s., Children in arms ½ price.

(h)   [*The Times*, 7 July 1814]

THE PRINCESS OF WALES YACHT – Capt. GORE or Mr PALMER, the Master, attends on board. Attendance will be given also at the Monument Coffee-house, Fish-street-hill and at the Newcastle Coffee-house, near Billingsgate. Takes in for Ramsgate, Sandwich, Deal and the adjacent villages. From Custom House Quay on Fridays, return on Tuesday morning.

(i)   [*The Times*, 12 July 1815]

RAMSGATE – The OWNERS of the RAMSGATE PACKETS beg most respectfully to acquaint the Nobility, Gentry and the Public, that from the increasing number of visitors to this delightful Watering-place, they have been induced to establish THREE additional fast sailing PACKETS. The superior style of accommodation in which they are fitted up; the continuance of the old prices, of 7s. the best, and 5s. the fore cabin; and the baggage, etc. being free of wharfage at Ramsgate, evidently render the passage by these packets preferable to that by the packets of a contiguous watering place; they will sail from Botolph Wharf, near London Bridge, this week, in the following order:

Royal Charlotte, J. Kelsey.	Thurs. 13th at 7 [compare Illus. 9].
Lord Hawkesbury, R. Morris.	Friday 14th at 8.
Duke Wellington, K.B. Martin.	Sat. 15th at 9.
Resolution, B. Belsey.	Sunday 16th at 10.
Marshall Blucher, W. Adams	Tuesday 18th at 11.
The Swift, Capt. M. Harman.	Wed. 19th at 12.

Three of the packets have private state cabins, which may be hired separately. The Captains to be spoken with at Botolph Wharf, where orders and baggage are taken in;
also at Mr. Rammel's, 92, King Street, Ramsgate.

> There are three points of interest about this advertisement; the rivalry which existed between Ramsgate and Margate as competing resorts, the mention of K.B. Martin who became subsequently a famous steamboat captain, employed by the General Steam Navigation Company (see Docs. 8, 12) and the naming of vessels after two heroes of the Battle of Waterloo, the Duke of Wellington and Marshall Von Blücher.

5. *Comments and observations on the merits or otherwise of travelling to and from Margate by hoy.*

'The Old Margate Hoy', as immortalized by Charles Lamb (see Illus. 2a), was subject to much critical comment as well as being a popular target for caricature and literary and poetic licence. On her first visit ever to the seaside Catherine Hutton (1756–1846) travelled to and from Margate by water.

(a) [Ed: Mrs. C. Hutton Beale, *Reminiscences of a Gentlewoman of the Last Century: Letters of Catherine Hutton*, Birmingham, 1891, 24–5]

London, May 19, 1780.

How little, my dear father, when we wrote last did we expect such a glorious excursion to Margate! It was Mrs. André's plan, and as sudden as it was agreeable. For four hours after we got upon the sea I was miserably ill and in strong hysterics . . . I passed three nights at Margate . . . Mrs. André was so disgusted with the hoy that she returned to town in the diligence . . . Mr. Drury, my brother, and I went back as we came, except that we came in nine hours and forty minutes, and went back in thirty-six hours.

Catherine's father was the contemporary historian of Birmingham, William Hutton. When John Lyons wrote his *Description of the Isle of Thanet, and particularly of the Town of Margate*, which was published in 1763, he warned of the hoy passage, 'I would not recommend it too strongly to Ladies of great delicacy' (p.15). It became distinctly unfashionable to be seen travelling to Margate in a hoy.

(b) [*The Times*, 10 September 1803]

We understand that at Margate the distinctive title of Fashionables is given without reserve to all the visitors of that agreeable watering-place, who do not arrive there by the Hoy.

This forthright assertion was backed up by other comments dating from the 1770s.

(c) [*A Tour Through the Island of Great Britain*, 8th Ed., 1778, 139]

The middle and inferior classes may have recourse to the benefits of this place by the cheapness of a sea voyage, as hoys and yachts are continually passing between this place and *London* for the conveyance of goods and passengers at a very cheap rate.

(d)　[*The New Margate and Ramsgate Guide in Letters to a Friend*, 1789, 12]

The chief of the company which come by the hoys are . . . of the inferior cast; very few persons in genteel life come by water, without they are recommended by their physicians so to do, to experience the sea-sickness, which is thought to be very beneficial in some complaints.

(e)　[George Saville Carey, *The Balnea; or, An Impartial Description of all the Popular Watering Places in England*, 1799, 34–5]

Should you be disposed to go by water to Margate, you will often be under the necessity of arming yourself with a great deal of patience, and a good store of victuals; you must shut your eyes from seeing indecent scenes, your ears from indecent conversation, and your nose from indelicate smells.

George Keate was one who decided to try the hoy during the 1770s.

(f)　[George Keate, *Sketches from Nature, Taken, and Coloured, in A Journey to Margate*, 5th Ed., 1802, 245–8, 251]

I HAVE been these three days balancing in my mind, whether I should return to town by land, or by water. The great road, however rich in beautiful prospects, hath no novelty to me, who have so frequently travelled it; – and the course of the THAMES, being perfectly new, made me rather incline to trust the sea . . . But then there is no conveyance on this element, but the HOYS! – And what does that signify? – there are always merry folks aboard . . . I have seen them so many times go off in such high spirits, that I shall not dislike to make one among them. – A crowd affords variety, and is never unpleasant to me, if I have the liberty of sitting still in it . . . Half MARGATE thronged the Pier-Head, and the deck of the HOY seemed already covered with passengers. – The morning was delicious . . .

No sooner had we begun to push off, when *a good voyage* was echoed from a hundred voices at once; while, *Do not forget that parcel – My love to Harry – Tell BETTY I shall soon be in town . . . Have you got your basket of cold meat? – Take care your bonnet does not blow off – Be sure give PEGGY that letter*, and a thousand such other mementos were resounded from various quarters.

I began now . . . to survey the cargo we ourselves had on board. – It consisted of a few gentlemen, who, like myself, enjoyed a passage by sea; – some decent shop-keepers, and their wives, who had been washing off the summer dust of LONDON, – and the remainder chiefly composed of the servants of families, that had left MARGATE, who were all extremely communicative, and appeared to have spent their time in that happy idleness, which such an excursion from home usually gives them.

The rolling of the ship gave a new turn to matters. Some put on a very serious countenance, – some turned pale, – others complained of a swimming in their head, – others, that everything moved *under* them, – and it was not long after, before it became very apparent, that everything moved *within* them, so I sat very quietly, and gathered up the flaps of my coat, for I hate to carry away the property of anyone . . . In about eleven hours from the time we left MARGATE were safely landed at WOOL QUAY.

> Two facts mentioned in the above account are confirmed by actual experiences as recorded in diaries or letters; firstly, wealthy families who avoided the hoy nevertheless found it useful for transporting their domestic servants, and secondly, the risk of sea sickness.

(g) [Ed. P.C. Yorke, *The Diary of John Baker*, 1931, 417–8] (compare Doc. 3a).

September 12, 1777.

The Hoy came in about 12 and in it the maid (Sally Matthews) Mrs. Woodington hired in London.

(h) [KAO, *Cobb MSS.*, U1453 C2]

> Addressed during 1800 to 'My Dearest Love',

I have particular pleasure in informing my getting safe here last night *past 8 o'clock*, and have had refreshing rest in my old bed Mark Lane.

Our passage was too fine to be expeditious, but . . . my female friends, . . . mild and fine as it was, were very sick indeed.

> Such was the reputation of the hoy that it inevitably attracted the attention of the caricaturist.

(i) [*The Morning Post and Fashionable World*, 17 August 1795]

Several caricaturists are now at Margate . . . The exhibitions of the *City Ladies* ascending from the Hoys . . . present daily the most *whimsical* exhibitions.

> One very famous caricaturist who visited Margate during 1807 was James Gillray. Residing some 150 yards from the beach gave him ample opportunity to observe the arrival and departure of the hoys [Illus. 6a].

(j) [D. Hill, *Mr Gillray The Caricaturist*, 1965, 136–7, 143]

Packet just arrived. People just landed from ye packet. Fatigued and faded – some Sick and Invalid wrapd up in Great Coats with their Bags and Baskets of Provisions. High wind. Ladies Petticoats blowing over their heads . . . Returning the cheapest way all sick. Mama Sucking ye Brandy Bottle. Captain Rowe at helm – Miss Puking up her inside – some eating, some smoking, some playing at Cards – some singing, some drunk.

> Both the arrival and departure of a hoy attracted great crowds which, as a social phenomenon, became well known as 'hoy fair'.

(k) [*The New Margate, Ramsgate and Broadstairs Guide*, 6th Ed., Margate, 1816, 56–7]

The Pier . . . is uncommonly crowded at the coming in or going out of the packets, which is generally termed *hoy fair* . . . On it are frequently to be seen upwards of a thousand persons of *all* distinctions, indiscriminately blended together . . . It can therefore be no wonder, if the humours of such a motley group, welcoming their new comers, should not now and then occasion such diverting scenes as to baffle all possibilities of description.

> Much quoted in this and other guidebooks of the time were the following lines attributed to John Wolcot (pseudonym Peter Pindar) describing the welcoming scene at Margate on the arrival of a hoy.

Soon as thou gett'st within the Pier,
  All Margate will be out I trow,
And people rush from far and near,
  As if thou had'st wild beasts to show.

Despite all the sarcasm meted out to 'The Old Margate Hoy' and its clientele, it was always compared to travelling by road both cheaper and more popular.

(1)   [*A Guide to all the Watering and Sea-Bathing Places*, 1803, 251, 254, 256]

MARGATE, conveniently situated in respect to the metropolis, . . . is always enlivened by a more numerous Company than any other sea-bathing place. The Hoys, which sail every tide from Billingsgate, are cheap, and sometimes agreeable and rapid conveyances, but as the distance by land is only 73 miles, the roads good, and the vehicles numerous and certain, . . . ladies especially prefer the passage by land . . . PASSAGE TO MARGATE.

There are plenty of conveyances, both by sea and land. Post-chaises and stage-coaches present nothing particular, being the same in most parts of the kingdom, except that on this road the drivers of such vehicles, as well as their masters, are said to be characteristically impertinent and imposing . . . A passage in the Margate hoy, which like the grave levels all distinctions, is frequently so replete with whim, incident and character, that it may be considered as a dramatic entertainment on the stage of the ocean. The fare being only five shillings for the common cabin, and half-a-guinea for the best, is a strong inducement for numbers to prefer this mode of travelling, though it cannot be recommended to persons of nice delicacy.

Here the high and low, the rich and the poor, the sick and the sound, the gentleman and the blackguard, are all jumbled together; and though there is much for the humourist to laugh at, there is more to offend the decent and well-bred . . .

Not less than 20,000 persons annually sail to and from this port. Hence with great truth live-stock may be regarded as the principal and most lucrative branch of commerce in which the people of *Margate* are engaged.

In consequence of this profitable trade, *Margate* has risen from insignificance to wealth and consequence.

6.   *The mixed reception accorded to steamboats in their early days.*

(a)   [*The Times*, 8 July 1815]

During 1814 Sir Marc Brunel had introduced to Margate harbour the first steam yacht, the Thames, powered only by one 16 h.p. engine. It was sensationally described as a 'rapid, capacious, and splendid vessel.'

She has the peculiar advantage of proceeding either by sails or steam, separated or united, by which means the public have the pleasing certainty of never being detained on the water after dark, much less one or two nights, which has frequently occurred with the old packets.

(b) [*The Gentleman's Magazine*, LXXXV, 1815, 272]

A *Margate* hoy of large dimensions, propelled by steam, goes constantly to and from London to Margate. From its novelty, and the certainty of its arrival within a given time (about twelve hours), it is much thronged with passengers.

(c) [Sir Rowland Hill and George Birkbeck Hill, *The Life of Sir Rowland Hill and the History of Penny Postage*, I, 1880, 134–6]

One enthusiastic admirer of steamboats from their inception was (Sir) Rowland Hill (1795–1879), who was staying in Margate during the summer of 1815.

Margate, July 3rd, 1815.

We went to see the steamboat come in from London. It is worked by means of two wheels, resembling water-wheels, one of which is placed on each side of the vessel, and about a-half sunk in the water. It comes from London and returns three times in each week. It generally performs the voyage in about twelve hours. In the best cabin there is a handsome library, draught-boards, etc. It is surprising to see how most people are prejudiced against this packet. Some say that it cannot sail against the wind if it is high; but when it entered the harbour the wind and tide were both against it, and the former rather rough, yet I saw it stem both. There was a great crowd, and much enthusiasm, though carpers predicted failure, and sneered at 'smoke-jacks'.

This extract is significant for being one of the first eye-witness accounts of steamboats at Margate. In essence it provides an almost perfect description of one.

(d) [*The New Margate, Ramsgate, and Broadstairs Guide*, 6th Ed., Margate, 1816, 59–60]

The number of passage vessels was last season augmented by three steam yachts, which from the general regularity of their arrivals, induced many to prefer them to the original packets, but as others cannot divest themselves of the idea that their motion . . . must be more liable to accidents, this invention, however ingenious, will probably never entirely supersede the old packets, though it may promote that kind of competition and attention to accommodation which will more effectually promote public convenience.

(e) [E.W. Brayley, *Delineations, Historical and Topographical, of the Isle of Thanet and the Cinque Ports*, I, 1817, 66–7]

The old fashioned Margate hoys or sailing packets soon yielded in fact to the technical superiority of the steamboats which improved with each passing season.

In consequence of the introduction of *Steam Packets* in the summer of 1815, and the general preference given to them by the visitants, several of the regular sailing Packets have been obliged to look out for other service.

Surviving sailing packets reverted to trading vessels, operating to and from London, or between British and Flemish ports.

(f) [Ed. Lady Dorchester, *Recollections of a Long Life by Lord Broughton*, II, 1909, 133–4]

As the technical performance and safety of steamboats improved so they were more favourably received. Lord Broughton travelled to and from Margate within days on two different steam vessels (Illus. 12b).

July 28th, 1820.

Went in the London Engineer steam yacht to Margate – 270 people on ·board – a magnificant spectacle altogether. A few years ago I recollect laughing at the notion of applying steam to these purposes.

July 31st.

Set out at eight in the *Eclipse* steam yacht. Beautiful sight leaving the shore – boats, spectators, and bands of music on board the yachts playing. We arrived by this extraordinary mode of making progress at Tower Stairs, quarter to four in the afternoon, passing by all sailing boats as if they were at anchor. I admired the *Eclipse's* engines much more than the other – more compact. The vessel made the passage in six hours and a half – 88 miles by water; passage money, 15s.; music, 1s.; sailors, 1s. Eighty passengers pay the expenses. All above – profit.

No doubt he was more than pleased with himself for the following reason.

Met on board Chabot of Malta. He told me I was not altered since 1810. Congratulated me on my eminence.

(g)   [Ed. E.H. Coleridge, *Letters of Samuel Taylor Coleridge*, II, 1895, 743]

Samuel Taylor Coleridge too was no less impressed by steamboats some five years later.

8, Plains of Waterloo, Ramsgate, October 10, 1825.

How impossible it would have been fifteen or even ten years ago for me to have travelled and voyaged . . . 120 miles with fire and water blending their souls for my propulsion.

7.   *Contemporary references showing how journey times were steadily reduced on steamboat voyages.*

(a)   [*The Thanet Itinerary or Steam Yacht Companion*, 1819, 25]

The benefits arising from the noble invention of *Steam Vessels* are nowhere more sensibly felt than in the Isle of *Thanet* . . . The *Sailing Hoys* have been known to be 72 hours in going from *London* to *Margate*. . . A *Steam Vessel* might actually make *nine* voyages, while the *Sailing Packets* are making *one*! Such is the great improvement that has lately been introduced into the mode of conveyance between *London* and *Margate*.

(b)   [*The Maidstone Journal and Kentish Advertiser*, 31 May 1825]

The expedition and certainty of the steam navigation is such that Captain Rule, of the Eclipse, Margate steam packet, on leaving London, . . . told many of his passengers within two minutes of the time he should arrive at his destination; and on Saturday his vessel left Margate at 8 o'clock in the morning and arrived at her moorings, near the Tower, before half past two in the afternoon, being a distance of 92 miles in 6½ hours, or 14 m.p.h. Sojourners to this asylum of health and pleasure may well call this *flying* by steam!

(c) [G.A. Cooke, *A Topographical and Statistical Description of the County of Kent*, 1830, i]

A JOURNEY to Margate, which thirty years ago might have occupied a whole week only in going and returning, may now be performed in a sunny afternoon; and before the week is elapsed, the whole of Margate may have been explored, and the traveller safe back to his own London residence.

(d) [*The Kentish Gazette*, 1 April 1831]

We are informed the Royal Adelaide performed the voyage from Margate to London, a distance of nearly 80 miles, in 5 hours and 17 minutes on Tuesday last, being the quickest passage ever made.

(e) [*The Dover Telegraph and Cinque Ports General Advertiser*, 23 and 30 May 1835]

The Herne Bay steam vessels start for London at 2.30 p.m. These Packets perform the Voyage in less than FIVE Hours.

(f) [*The Gravesend and Milton Journal*, 25 April 1835]

The Diamond, belonging to the Gravesend and Milton Steam Packet Co., left the Pier, at Gravesend, on Wednesday morning with her passengers at 6.30, and arrived at London Bridge at 8.17, thus performing the passage in 1 hour and 47 minutes, a distance of 32 miles.

(g) [*The Gravesend and Milton Journal*, 16 May 1835]

Gravesend is filling fast, and the various steamers have little cause for complaint . . . On Monday the Diamond came to the Pier in 1 hour and 45 minutes. This is by far the greatest feat ever performed by any Steamer on the River.

(h) [*The Times*, 27 June 1846]

The Prince of Wales frequently performs the voyage between Blackwall and Margate in less than 4 hours.

8. *The superiority of steamboats over sailing vessels in terms of safety and capacity.*

[Captain K.B. Martin, *Oral Traditions of the Cinque Ports and Their Localities*, 1832, 27–31]

Captain Kennett Beacham Martin commanded the City of London Steam Packet as an employee of the General Steam Navigation Company, which had been established and incorporated by an Act of Parliament in 1824. Having experience both of sailing packets and steam vessels, he was well qualified in assessing with approval the state of steam navigation as he saw it in 1832.

Properly to appreciate the value of steam-propelling power, we must draw some few comparisons with days gone by . . . When we consider the strong prejudices it had to combat – the extraordinary difficulties its infant progress encountered, . . . we [have] reason to admire the persevering industry of those individuals who (having expended their wealth and talent upon its improvement) have brought it to its present useful and efficient state . . .

The passage from London to the Isle of Thanet, by fast sailing packets, had existed for many years, and, as far as good pilotage and nautical skill could command success, was brought to a very great perfection. The vessels were handsomely modelled, fleet under canvas, and possessed excellent accommodations for one hundred passengers, . . . but the elements are fickle, and the voyage begun in pleasureable anticipations too often terminated in delay and disappointment: on these occasions the passengers' provisions became exhausted, and ill humour seated itself beside the empty hamper . . . I commanded one of those vessels six years . . .

In 1820, the first steam-vessel was prepared for Ramsgate. I was offered and accepted the command of her. This vessel, called the Eagle, had two engines of Bolton and Watt's best construction, and were equal to forty horse power. She is now his Majesty of Denmark's steam yacht. I had every reason, in all kinds of weather, to be satisfied of her complete efficiency. Since that period, in the continual command of steam packets, I have in no one instance been obliged to anchor upon the passage, or put back to port, in consequence of any fault, accident, or defect in the steam machinery.

During a period of six years, in sailing packets, my return of passengers conveyed amounted to 3,107 persons. With these I witnessed many unpleasant casualties, from the breaking of spars, and coming in contact with other vessels, and in more than one instance attended with loss of life. In twelve years, up to the present date, in the command of different steam vessels, I have had under my care 128,047 passengers, not one of whom received the slightest personal injury. If a sailing packet, to and from London and Ramsgate, conveyed 800 passengers in a month, it was thought an extraordinary affair; yet, during the last four weeks, our returns in the City of London steam-packet, give 5356 persons.

How beneficial is this to the health of this great and populous city! – Thousands embark daily on board steam vessels, to inhale fresh vigour from the ocean breeze. Let us then be grateful for these advantages, procured through the medium of civilization and science . . .

K.B. MARTIN
City of London Steam Packet, July, 1832.

9. *A sample of steamboat excursions.*

(a) [*The Times*, 2 July 1824]

On Sunday, July 4, 1824. The London Engineer Margate Steam Yacht, to Southend, Sheerness or the Nore returning Same Day. 5s.

(b) [*The Times*, 1 July 1825]

Gravesend Steam Packets – Sons of Commerce, Swiftsure and Favourite – Leave at 8.00. Return at 4.00. Chief Cabin, 3s. Fore Cabin, 2s. On Sunday, 3s.

(c) [*The Maidstone Journal and Kentish Advertiser*, 31 May 1825]

[Gravesend] has been long and universally known as the goal of every young Cockney's Sunday excursion . . . The people of London, who may be observed every Sunday flocking down by hundreds in steam packets . . . have taken such a liking to Gravesend, that a company of rich capitalists have resolved to build an entire new town in its vicinity.

(d) [*The Maidstone Journal and Kentish Advertiser*, 26 August 1828]

Tuesday the Columbine, Captain Grant, on an excursion from London to Margate and back in the day, exhibited her unprecedented freight of 660 merry souls, off Jarvis's Landing-place, and after taking a fresh supply of provisions and exchanging a few 'how do you do's', with the

gay inhabitants of this corner of England, she majestically moved off
with her numerous guests to complete her destined task.

(e) [*The Times*, 24 June 1829]

To Margate and back the same Day. Third annual, extra-ordinary and
interesting marine excursion. The HERO Steam Packet, Captain
Large, to Margate and back, 13–14 hours. This Packet has engines of
100 h.p. by Messrs. Watt & Co. Tomorrow June 25th. A military band
on board. Leaves Tower Stairs 7.30 am. Tickets 10s. each. Refreshments.

(f) [*The Times*, 16 July 1831]

Sunday Excursions to Herne Bay and back in one day during July and
August, Albion, Captain Read.

(g) [Mr. L. Gilson, in evidence, 25 July 1832, before *The Select
Committee on the Observance of the Sabbath Day*, P.P. 1832/697, pp.
205–7]

As Secretary to the New Gravesend Company he explained how up
to three vessels would arrive on a Sunday morning having each
250–300 passengers on board.

We have generally on the Sunday that class of people that cannot go
during the week – artisans and mechanics, and persons in business . . .
I do not find anything like indecorum on board . . . At Gravesend . . .
you generally find them spreading their little cloths, and taking their
refreshment on the grass . . . I have never seen anything like a tumult
or anything like disorder.

(h) [*The Times*, 5 July 1832]

Steam to Ramsgate and Back in one day – The Harlequin – going and
returning 6s, but not landing.

(i) [*The Gravesend and Milton Journal*, 2 May 1835]

Unrivalled Excursion, by the splendid New Steam Packet RED
ROVER, Captain Large, from Gravesend Pier daily at 10 o'clock to
Herne Bay, returning same day at 6 o'clock. Fare there and back 4s.
each; landing and embarking gratis. Commencing Saturday, 2nd May,
1835.

(j) [*the Times*, 1 July 1845]

'Fresh Air and Cheap Excursions for the Million'. STAR PACKETS, 9 and 10 every morning from Nicholson's East India and China Wharf, Lower Thames Street, to the New Royal Terrace Pier, Gravesend, and back in the afternoon, 9d. only down and up.
Star Office, Gravesend.
June 30, 1845.

(k) [*The South Eastern Gazette*, 17 May 1853]

On Whit-Sunday morning the Medway Company's steamboat 'City of Rochester' left Chatham on an excursion to Ramsgate and back. In consequence of the extraordinary state of the weather for this season, the number of excursionists was not so great as on former occasions, only about 50 from Chatham availing themselves of the opportunity of visiting that delightful watering place. At Sheerness a large number was added to the party, the whole of whom returned from Ramsgate on Monday.

10. *Three examples of steam packet company promotion, in 1824, 1829 and 1834.*

No fewer that eleven steam packet companies, apart from the General Steam Navigation Company, operated steam vessels below London Bridge between 1829 and 1846.

(a) [*The Times*, 1 July 1824]

GENERAL STEAM NAVIGATION CO. This Company has been formed by persons well experienced in steam navigation . . .
Capital £2,000,000 in 20,000 Shares of £100 each, upon which a deposit of £21 10s. per share will only be required in the first instance.
Application for shares until 31st July, 1824.

(b) [KAO, *Cobb MSS.*, U1453 Z47/18]

MARGATE AND LONDON NEW STEAM PACKET COMPANY.
At a Meeting of the Provisional Committee held at the Wellington Baths, 31 October 1829. Resolved,

'That the following Estimate of the Expences and probable Receipts of Two Steam Vessels be laid before the Public:- Showing that a Reduction of Fares will give to the Shareholder a fair and reasonable renumeration for Capital Invested.'

Capital £22,000. £

Receipts from Passengers to and from London for 20 Weeks, during the Season, average 120 per day, each way, at 6s. per Passenger, clear of Pier dues, Fares 7s. and 9s.   8,640

Expenditure

Establishment on Board	1,000
Offices and Agents in Margate	180
Printing and Advertising	100
Coals, Oil and Tallow	2,200
Damages and Incidentals	700
Annual Outfits	1,000
Dividend 10% on Capital	2,200
	7,380

Surplus Sinking Fund   1,260

'In this Statement it is presumed by the Reduction of Fares that the following Season 70,000 Visitants may arrive by Steam, of which nearly $\frac{1}{2}$ are supposed to be conveyed by the Margate Co., producing to the concern, upwards of £9.000'.

The above does not include the Benefits arising from Towing, Excursions, and Cocketing the Vessels for Conveyance of Goods and Luggage for the Inhabitants of Thanet. The Committee sit daily at Phillpott's Wellington Bathing Rooms, from 6 to 8 o'clock in the Evening, until Thursday, 5 November next, for the purpose of receiving Subscriptions and Communications, and on Friday the 6th, at 6 o'clock, the General Meeting of Proprietors.

In connection with the capital figure proposed above, Mr George Dodd, giving evidence before *The Select Committee Appointed to Consider of the Means of Preventing the Mischief of Explosion from Happening on Board Steamboats* [422] (1817), pointed out that steam vessels apart from costing initially anything between £5,000 and £10,000, their 'furniture and decorations alone form an expensive item; they are also very expensive to maintain . . . by reason of the great cost of coal', 37. One of the early steamboats, the Regent which on 2 July 1817 succumbed to fire off Whitstable had cost '£11,000 to construct', according to *The Maidstone Journal and Kentish Advertiser*, 8 July 1817. New steamboats were costing £20,000 by the mid-1820s, W. Bain, 'Remarks on the Progress of Steam Navigation', *Blackwood's Edinburgh Magazine*, XVIII (November 1825), 544. A Margate Steam Club was formed to help finance the Margate and London New Steam Packet Company [also KAO, Cobb MSS, U1453 Z 52/20]

From a firm conviction that the Company now establishing would materially increase the prosperity of the Town of Margate and the Isle of Thanet generally, a few Friends have resolved themselves into a Club for the purpose of aiding the exertions of the GOOD CAUSE, and respectfully invite those favourable to their Views to lend a helping hand.

The Deposit required is 1s. per Week, and as soon as the Funds amount to £10 a share is taken in the above Company, in the name of that Person whom the majority of the Club may appoint.

Each Depositor to receive interest in proportion to the Capital invested.

Depositors are requested to leave their Names with MR. T. ROBIN-SON of the New Inn, who will give every information.

New Inn, Margate, Dec. 14, 1829.

(c)   [*The Kentish Observer*, 17 July 1834]

A new steam Company is forming by the principal inhabitants of the Bay and neighbourhood, which is to be under the management of Directors, appointed for this place, and to be called THE HERNE BAY STEAM NAVIGATION COMPANY. This spirited move, with some others in agitation, cannot fail to make this delightful place one of the most attractive.

This company was established and became famous on account of two of its vessels, the City of Canterbury and the Red Rover, trading as The London and Herne Bay Steam Packet Company or The Herne Bay Steam Packet Company.

11. *Extracts relating to the comfort and cuisine of the steamboats plying from London to the Kent resorts.*

(a) [*The Times*, 8 July 1815]

Right from the inception of steamboat communication comes this description of the comfort and facilities to be found on board the Thames steam yacht.

Her cabins are spacious and are fitted up with all that elegance could suggest and all that personal comfort requires, presenting a choice library, backgammon boards, draught tables, and other means of amusement. For the express purpose of combining delicacy with comfort a female servant tends upon the ladies.

(b) [G.W. Bonner, *The Picturesque Pocket Companion to Margate, Ramsgate, Broadstairs, and the Parts Adjacent*, 2nd Ed., 1831, 6–7]

Those persons who have not been accustomed to steam-vessels, will, doubtless, be astonished at the accommodations which they will find on board; the cabins being fitted up in the most elegant manner, and with every possible attention to comfort. The company are also provided with draughts, chess-boards, etc., and an excellent band of music; and, when the weather permits, they often join in the dance, for which the clear and spacious decks of these vessels are peculiarly adapted. It would be an act of injustice towards the stewards, were we not to notice their great activity and civility, and the excellence of the refreshments provided. The dinner, which consists of joints, boiled and roasted, of the very best quality; all vegetables that are in season; and pastry, wines, dessert, etc., is served up in a style both pleasing and surprising, when the limited size of the kitchen is considered. The hour for this repast is commonly half-past one o'clock, and when it is over, the visitor generally finds himself off Reculvers, and not more than nine miles from Margate. In speaking of these accommodations, we must not omit to notice that there is always a female attendant on board to wait upon the ladies; and that there is also a very neat cabin fitted up for their particular reception.

(c) [*The New Ramsgate, Margate, and Broadstairs Guide*, Ramsgate, c.1842, 6]

[The cabins are] fitted up with absolute splendour – paintings and noble glasses adorn the sides and the floors are covered with the most expensive carpeting.

(d)   [*The Morning Herald*, 11 July 1827]

[In] the sojourn of a few days which the Duke of Devonshire made [to Margate] the week before last, . . . he came down and returned to town by the steamboats . . . He dined at the table-d'hôte, caused his own fruit to be produced at the dessert, and permitted his servants to wait upon the company at table.

(e)   [*Ms. Journal of a Visit to Herne Bay in 1835*, KAO, U2491]

We had not long left Gravesend when the bell sounded for dinner. Neither of us was tormented with the pains of hunger but we descended to the regions below to see what was going on. A parcel of men were seated round one of the tables and only one lady in spectacles . . . The hour and the viands brought temptation ergo, we took our seats . . . and dined infinitely well on a savoury roast chicken and charming potatoes, . . . [While] the mankind were at wine and walnuts, . . . we modestly retired to the women's apartment.

12.   *Travelling down to Ramsgate and back to London in July and August 1829.*
      [*MS Journal of an Excursion to Ramsgate in July and August 1829*, Tyler Collection (Ramsgate Scrapbook), Cathedral Library and Archives, Canterbury]

Monday, July 20.
   Started at 9.12 from off the Tower Stairs, London, in the Magnet Steam Boat and after a pleasant journey arrived at Margate at ½ past 4 precisely, thence in a coach to Ramsgate which we reached at precisely ½ past 5 . . .

	£ – s – d		
Paid Coach from 3 New Millman St. to Tower Stairs		3	6
Paid Waterman at the Stand for putting in the Luggage			6
Paid Porterage of Luggage from Coach to the Wherry		1	0
Paid Waterman to the Steam Boat the Magnet		1	6
Paid for *Times* Newspaper			9
Paid fares for Mrs. B. and myself 24s, Servant 10s, infant nothing	1	14	0

Paid Sailors' Box 1s, 1 bottle of Port 1s, Woman 6d		2	6
Paid Porterage of Luggage to Ramsgate Coach			6
Paid Coach fare to Ramsgate		3	0
Paid Porterage of Luggage from the Crown Hotel to our Lodgings		2	0
Total Expense of the Journey	2	9	3

Monday, August 10.

Rose at 5 and prepared for our return home by the City of London Steam Boat, commanded by Mr. Martin, whom we joined at 5 minutes before 8. Started at 8 and after a journey which was exceedingly wet till 12 o'clock, we arrived without accident at the Tower at $\frac{1}{4}$ past 5 whence, taking a Coach, we reached home at $\frac{1}{2}$ past 6, thankful for the kind protection of providence during our whole excursion.

Expenses of Journey Home:	£	s	d
Porter for Carrying Luggage to Steam Vessel		1	0
Passage in the Steam Vessel 2 at 12s and 1 at 10s	1	14	0
Gave the Ship's Crew		1	6
Bottle of Porter		1	0
Wherry to the Custom House		1	0
Porter for carrying Luggage to the Coach No. 476		1	6
Boy for getting a Coach			1
Jack at Waterside			2
Coach hired by mistake		1	0
Coach really hired		4	6
	2	5	9

The total cost of travelling to Ramsgate and back in this case amounted to £4 15s, or 22% of a total three-week holiday expenditure of £21 10s 0¾d. The infant was conveyed both ways on the steam vessel free of charge and the servant 10s. either way 'attending the family'. *The Times* during the 1820s quoted lower fares for 'servants attending families', one such advertisement on 28 June 1826, inserted by the General Steam Navigation Company, on behalf of the Royal Sovereign, stating a 10s. single fare for servants. The return journey was made on the City of London steamboat, commanded by Captain K. B. Martin (see Doc. 8) directly from Ramsgate, but on the downward journey the party disembarked at Margate. Until well into the nineteenth century passengers bound by water from London to Broadstairs or Ramsgate chose to disembark at Margate, thereby avoiding what was seen to be a hazardous voyage around the North Foreland. Also on the downward journey a wherry was the means at the London end of reaching a steamboat prior to the subsequent establishment of passenger wharves, which may well have been under construction in the summer of 1829, for by 1831 in order 'to facilitate the embarking and landing of passengers, two commodious wharfs have recently been formed: one close to *London Bridge*, and the other at *St. Katherine's Docks*, near the Tower,' so that 'the public are now enabled to go on board and land with perfect safety, without the aid of boats' [G. W. Bonner, *The Picturesque Pocket Companion to Margate, Ramsgate, Broadstairs and the Parts Adjacent*, 2nd Ed., 1831, 3–4]. On one or both journeys money was spent on purchasing reading material, on refreshment, on tips and on porterage. Both Margate and Ramsgate possessed officially appointed porters for conveying passengers' luggage to and from the steam vessels, while at the London end passengers were advised to have their luggage 'safely deposited in its proper place', as 'the Proprietors of the Steam Vessels are not answerable for the loss of any of the luggage, as they make no charge for its conveyance; so it behoves the Passenger to look after his own property', which at Ramsgate involved seeing 'your luggage safely in possession of one of the appointed ticket porters' [*Picture of Ramsgate, or A Guide to the Various Amusements, Public Libraries, Building Improvements, etc. of that celebrated Watering Place*, Ramsgate, 1833, 4, 8].

13. *Setting off on a steamboat 'Voyage to Herne Bay', 23 October 1835.* [*Ms. Journal of a Visit to Herne Bay in 1835*, KAO, U2491]

The following extract sets the scene very well on the commencement of a journey by water from London to Herne Bay in the City of Canterbury steamboat, which was frequently mentioned in guide books and newspaper reports at that time.

The morning grew from fair to fine. We arrived at St. Kath[erine]

Docks, where Lucy, I, and Arthur, abandoning ... the Carriage, embarked on board the often and justly praised City of Canterbury, whose decks were yet wet with dew of morning, and peopled only by a few stray cits. Soon, however, more passengers descended – a fellow with a rose escorting a lady with a very agreeable pair of hazel eyes seated her and himself in midships; a sick lady of a goodly countenance was laid on the continuation of the bench, attended by her ... papa; an officer in varnished boots appeared pacing the decks, which he continued to do without relaxation of muscle or feature for 4 hours by the clock, sending his wife, son and servants to the fore part of the vessel to keep their distance as behoved them. I had no time to take note of the other [passengers] before the signal was given, the chimney smoked, we moved slowly from the pier of the docks and simmered carefully away into the intricacies of the Pool [of London], which was more than usually crowded. A voice of command from the paddle box drew our attention to the Captain, in whom we at once recognized the original of the frontispiece and the celebrated Cap. Large of the dedication of the H. Bay Guide ... The extreme caution and activity he displayed in his office showed him at once to be a good Cap.[n] and a conscientious man. Down we went then thro' the Pool to the tune of 'Ease *her*', 'Stop *her*' and with all our care ... running foul of a coasting vessel whose bowspirit got entangled in our rigging.

By the mid-1830s there was mounting public concern as to overcrowding and safety in the Pool of London. Indeed, an 1836 parliamentary committee [*The House of Commons Committee on the London and Blackwall Commercial Railway Bill*, HLRO, Committee Office Evidence, 1836, volume 15] heard some interesting evidence concerning the steamboat traffic then passing up and down the Thames. Mr Taylor, a Thames pilot, alleged that 130 steam vessels passed through the Pool of London on a summer's day, and 'in consequence of the *speed* with which they go up and down they cause a very great swell and that swell endangers both coal craft, shipping and the tiers of small boats, ... I do not consider any boats are safe when those large steam boats go up and down at the rate at which they now go.' Captain Large himself had been involved in a collision with a long wherry off Globe Stairs, Rotherhithe, while proceeding up the river on the Herne Bay steamboat, the Red Rover, on Friday, 10 July 1835, whereby the wherry with five gentlemen on board was run down and two were drowned [*The Times*, 13 July 1835, and *The Dover Telegraph and Cinque Ports General Advertiser*, 18 July 1835]. On being called as a witness on 26 March 1836 before the above Commons Committee, Captain John Large revealed how he had been in charge of the City of Canterbury Steam Packet for two seasons, during which time 'the increase of passengers to Herne Bay has been very great'. He admitted to some difficulty in navigating the Pool of London, but he was governed by the wishes of his passengers who complained of any delays which they experienced. The accident of 10 July 1835 formed part of the evidence of Mr Charles Hay, Master of the Watermen's Company, on 25 July 1836, before the *Select Committee Appointed to Inquire into the State of the Port of London* [*P.P. 1836/557, p.246*].

14. Down to Herne Bay on the Red Rover steamboat, 29 August 1844.

  (a) [*MS. Journal compiled by S. Daniele in 1844*, KAO, U2666 F1, 1–8]

We started from Cloudesley Street in a fly, and proceeded to the Blackwall Railway Station, in order to take our place in the Red Rover packet for Herne Bay, . . . all in excellent spirits and full of anticipation . . . We waited nearly an hour and a half under a most scorching sun, before the beautiful vessel arrived, in which we were to sail . . . After embarking the vessel pursued its way without interruption down the noble Thames. The numerous vessels lying at anchor from all parts of the world; the meadows sloping to the sides of the river; the gentlemen's seats seen at a distance, with the smoothness of the water, and the beauty of the weather, made it as delightful a sail as could possibly be desired. Nothing particular occurred on board. The company was not very numerous, and amused themselves with promenading the deck, and reading. The Red Rover is a most splendid vessel, both as regards its size, fittings and accommodations. When we reached the mouth of the Thames we noticed the guardship, which marks its junction with the Ocean. We also passed the Isle of Sheppey which is rather an odd looking object. Owing to the calmness of the weather we did not feel the least inconvenience from sea sickness. We reached Herne Bay about half past 4 o'clock, and through the kind enquiries of some friends who had been staying there, were speedily installed into some very pleasant lodgings close to the sea. After arranging our dress, etc., we sat down, and made a very hearty tea, after which we took a stroll to explore the town . . .

The Pier is three quarters of a mile long, composed of piles of wood, and has rails laid down for facilitating the conveyance of luggage and passengers, to and from the steamers. The carriages are propelled by a sail, which is hoisted behind.

Three years later it was noted.

(b)   [S. Bagshaw, *History, Gazetteer and Directory of the County of Kent*, II, Sheffield, 1847, 218–9]

A sailing carriage runs upon iron grooves in the centre of the pier, for the purpose of conveying passengers and their luggage.

15.   *Steamboat to Herne Bay and coach to Dover, etc., or steamboat to Dover and Deal, from 1835 onwards.*

(a)   [By a Lady, *A Picture of The New Town of Herne Bay*, 1835, 18–19]

The conveyance from London to Herne Bay is much the cheapest and most agreeable journey to Dover or Deal, as the whole expense from the metropolis to Dover by this route is 10s. 6d.; being 5s. 6d. to land at Herne Bay, 1s. 6d. by coach to Canterbury, and 3s. 6d. by coach or van from Canterbury to Dover; while the expense, outside the coach, from London to Dover is 16s. and inside 30s.

An even lower fare of 8s. from Dover to London, by way of Herne Bay, was advertised in a Kentish newspaper for the same year.

(b)   [*The Dover Telegraph and Cinque Ports General Advertiser*, 23 and 30 May 1835]

'The Cheapest and most expeditious Route between Dover and London' for 8s. THE RED ROVER COACH from the York Hotel, and Dover Castle, Dover, every morning at 10.30 for Herne Bay to meet the Steam Packets which start for London at 2.30.

'These Packets perform the Voyage in less than FIVE Hours; Passengers are therefore only Eight hours on the Road between London and Dover'.

The Red Rover Coach leaves Herne Bay for Dover immediately on the arrival of the Packets.

'Passengers leaving London at 8.30 in the Morning arrive at Dover by 5 in the Afternoon'.

Coach Fare, Dover to Herne Bay:
  Outside 3s. Inside 6s.
Steam Fare, Herne Bay to London
  Fare Cabin 5s. Saloon 6s.

Six years later it was observed of Herne Bay and of the route to Dover how in

(c) [*The Dover Telegraph and Cinque Ports General Advertiser*, 4 September 1841]

This interesting watering place continues to attract a numerous and highly-respectable company. Those fast and well appointed steamers, the Red Rover and City of Canterbury, are daily crowded with passengers, many of whom land at the Bay and proceed by coach to Dover and other parts of the coast. This mode of transit, from avoiding the passage round the Forelands, has become the most frequented route from London to Dover.

There was a steady growth in the number of passengers conveyed to and from Herne Bay by steamboats between 1838 and 1842, prior to any threat from the South Eastern Railway reaching Folkestone in 1843.

(d) [George William Rohrs, Secretary to the Herne Bay Steam Packet Company, in evidence, 27 April 1847, to the *House of Commons Select Committee on the Herne Bay and Canterbury Junction Railway*, HLRO, Committee Office Evidence, 1847, volume 6]

Year	Herne Bay Steam Packet Company	By Other Boats	Total
1838	31,289		31,289
1839	37,829		37,829
1840	41,305		41,305
1841	40,033	6,441	46,474
1842	40,957	11,248	52,205

Up to 1840 no other steamboats ran regularly to Herne Bay other than the vessels of the Herne Bay Steam Packet Company and while no distinct account of the number of passengers travelling to and from Canterbury, Dover, etc., was kept, the number was estimated to be nearly half the total figures quoted above. No wonder that the same witness in 1850 could recollect this through traffic, as a temporary phenomenon.

(e) [*The Select Committee on Ramsgate and Margate Harbours*, P.P. 1850/660, p.151]

There used to be a very considerable traffic not only between Canterbury and Herne Bay, but likewise between Dover and Deal and Herne Bay. I recollect the time, twelve or thirteen years ago, that ten or a dozen coaches used to come into Herne Bay from these various places . . . All that is gone by, and there is only one single coach now.

(f) [*The Visitor's Guide to the Watering Places*, 1842, 198]

As the bay is but twenty-four miles from Dover, and seventeen from Ramsgate and Broadstairs, the most agreeable, nearest, and quickest route to any of these places will be, to go to Herne Bay by one of the steamers, and afterwards proceed direct by one of the coaches, which will be awaiting their arrival. The expense of this mode of travelling will be at least one-third less.

> The progressive opening of the South Eastern Railway to Ashford (1842), Folkestone (1843), Dover (1844) and Thanet (1846) reduced the number of passengers travelling to destinations beyond Herne Bay. Although from other resorts coaches continued to ply to and from London they found it increasingly hard to compete with the reliability, speed, comfort and cheapness of the steamboats during the 1830s. A bustling Dover was reported thus at the end of May 1835.

(g) [*The Dover Telegraph and Cinque Ports General Advertiser, 30 May 1835*]

Within the last fortnight many of our Marine Residences have been let, and several respectable families have arrived for the season . . . Sixty steam vessels enter or leave the harbour weekly, on their passage to France, Belgium, London or the Isle of Thanet; and twenty stage coaches or public conveyances, and two superior steam vessels – the Hero and the Dover Castle – carry on a daily intercourse with the Metropolis, and all the towns on the coast, from Margate to Brighton. [Also] a communication has been opened with Herne Bay, and from thence by steam to London. These, with the never ending transit of posting carriages, and the arrival and departure of the packets, offer an interminable variety.

The detrimental effects which the immense success of steamboats had on the coaching services from London did not pass unnoticed.

(h) [Mr Benjamin W. Horne, in evidence, 31 May 1837, to *The Select Committee of Internal Communication Taxation*, P.P. 1837/456, p.3, Q.39]

What competition do you meet with on the Kent Road? Steam-packets, at 1s. and 1s. 6d. to Gravesend, 5s. to Dover, 1s. 6d. to Ramsgate and 4s. to Boulogne.

(i) [John Poole, 'Margate', *The Amaranth*, 1839, 69]

I have not heard of one person, in his or her right senses, who has lately made an over-land trip to Margate, . . . apart from the driver and guard of the royal mail.

Dover and Deal, as well as Gravesend, Herne Bay, Margate and Ramsgate, continued to be supplied with visitors arriving on various steamboats from London during the 1840s.

(j) [*The Dover Telegraph and Cinque Ports General Advertiser*, 23 July 1842]

The influx of visitors to this fashionable marine resort is now very great: nearly all the houses on the Waterloo Crescent, Marine Parade, etc. are engaged. The steamers from London, Ramsgate and the Continent are thronged with passengers . . . The ECLIPSE in consequence of the fineness of the weather has, during the week, landed upwards of 300 passengers at Dover, from London.

(k) [*The Dover Telegraph and Cinque Ports General Advertiser*, 13 August 1842]

The long continued fine weather has caused a great influx of visitors at Dover during the week. The London Steamers, 'Royal Adelaide' and 'Isle of Thanet' have averaged nearly 100 passengers each voyage, while the coaches from Herne Bay and Ramsgate have been daily filled . . . But few residences in the town now display that ominous announcement 'to let'.

One week later the same newspaper reported, on 20 August 1842: The steamers from London to this port are daily thronged with

77

passengers. Upwards of 400 persons left London Bridge by them on Tuesday last.

(1) [*The Maidstone Journal, Kentish Advertiser and South Eastern Intelligencer*, 10 July 1849]

The communication with steamboats between Deal and Dover and the metropolis has been again opened by the Herne Bay Steam Packet Company.

16. *Weekend Visitations by 'The Hats boat' or 'The Husbands' boat'.*

(a) ['The Isle of Thanet', *The Land We Live In*, I, c. 1850, 147, 152, 154]

In the absence of paid or guaranteed holidays fathers and sons, who were employed in London in commerce, banking and so on, became weekend commuters to Herne Bay or Thanet, travelling on the steamboats to join their families for weekends on the coast.

The number of disembarkations from the steamers at Margate alone exceeded 100,000 in the summer of 1846. On the Saturdays during that season it was common to see 800 to 1000 landed there from the different steamers. But these must not all be taken as new arrivals; the male part of the visitors generally go up and down to London for their business, leaving their families on the coast . . .

The liveliest scene at this lively watering place is on the Saturday night. There is a late steam-boat, called in the language of the place, 'The Hats boat', or 'The Husbands' boat'. The good men wind up their week's business on the Saturday afternoon, and then embark to rejoin their wives and children. All circumstances favourable, the husbands' boat ought to arrive at nine, or half-past nine, in the evening, and the wives expect its arrival at that time, as if it could go, on every occasion, as regularly as the clock in the Margate clock-house. But tides and winds will at times be contrary, and impede even the progress of steam; off Herne Bay there are certain sand banks, and at particular states of the tides there is not water enough over these banks to float the vessel, so she either runs upon them and sticks fast, or she is backed into deep water, and kept paddling about. Any such delay throws Margate into a fearful state of excitement. Swoonings and convulsions take place at the Pier-head, . . . and anxious eyes, and hands with white pocket handkerchiefs in them, are directed towards Reculver and the Bay, and voices

are heard murmuring 'when will they come, where can they be!
Boatman, is there any danger?'. . . But comfort, good wives! The sea is
as smooth as a looking-glass; and, let it be Captain Large, or let it be
Captain Read, there is a right skilful mariner on board – a man
bronzed, through thirty years of this steam-boat service, . . . a man that
knows every sand-bank, reef, shallow, or point whatsoever, between
Margate Pier and London Bridge, as well as you know the corners of
your parlours or bedrooms . . . Through the shades of night, the
steamer comes boldly round, . . . broadside to the head of the Jetty, or
along the Pier. Then follows a babel of tongues. 'Ah, Tom! There you
are, all safe'. . . 'There's my Joe'. 'Stuck on the bank for a quarter of an
hour, that was all'. . . 'Captain Large is a trump'. . . 'Buss, ladies and
gentlemen'. 'Remsgett'. 'Broadsteers'. . . 'Step in here, ladies and
gentlemen, mine's a good un'. 'Lodgings – Lodgings'. 'Plenty of room
in the York Hotel, sir!' 'Wright's York Hotel'. . . 'Let the luggage pass'.
'Polly, what have you got for supper?' 'Shrimps – Shrimps'. . . 'Only a
guinea and a half a week, and close to the sea, and a fine view over the
Jetty'. 'A quiet lodging, and no children – say thirty shillings, ma'am'.
'A piano-forte and two telescopes, and a turn-up bed in the parlour for
a visitor'. 'I'm the best barber in Margate, take my card, sir'. 'Good
night, Captain'. . . Then the porters clear off with their luggage; the
Busses and Flies with their passengers, the happily restored husbands
with their wives; and in a few minutes nothing is heard from the end of
the Marine Parade to the furthest extremity of the Fort, but the
munching of shrimps and the cheerful explosions of bottled porter.

The antecedents of such weekend travelling facilities can be traced
back to the later 1820s.

(b) [*The Times*, 12 July 1827]

General Steam Navigation Company Margate Packets. To meet the
numerous and respectable applications which have been made to the
Directors . . . they have determined that one of their fast vessels shall
leave the Custom House every Saturday at 1 o'clock, . . returning
Sunday at 9.

(c) [*The Times*, 17 July 1827]

Margate Regular Steam Packets.
Eclipse, Venus, Magnet, Dart, Albion or Hero all furnished with

powerful engines by Bolton, Watt & Co. frequently perform the passage in 6 hours. Coaches are in readiness for Ramsgate, Broadstairs, Deal, Dover and Canterbury. The Margate Grand Regatta will take place on Monday, August 13th, and a splendid Marine Fête on Thursday 16th.

NOTE. The Public are earnestly requested to patronise the late Steam Packets at 12 from London, established at enormous extra expense, for the convenience of professional and commercial gentlemen, as well as of families and invalids . . . who, by this second conveyance, avoid the rivalry as to the speed of vessels starting together, and the annoying interruptions at the waterside complained of by early passengers.

As an encouragement to family and periodic travel the above company and steamboats advertised their services and fares as follows.

(d)   [*The Times*, 9 July 1827]

From the Tower twice a day at 9 and 12. Family Passage Tickets, in parcels containing 6 or 12, price 4 gns. per dozen. Personal Season Tickets 3 gns. each, offering great advantage to the purchaser as these vessels now make 26 passages a week.

NOTE. The packet Hero fitted with powerful Boulton & Watt Engines on the 4th inst. did the journey to Margate and back in less than 14 hours, with 300 passengers.

When railways appeared on the scene they competed with the steamboats in offering special Saturday to Monday tickets to the seaside.

(e)   [*The City Press*, 12 and 19 May 1860]

'Saturday to Monday at the Seaside'.
Cheap trains by the South Eastern Railway every Saturday afternoon from London Bridge to Margate at 2.30 p.m. and 5.30 p.m., returning on Sunday evening or Monday morning. Fare there and back 8s. 6d., 3rd Class; 12s. 6d., 2nd Class; and 17s. 6d., 1st Class.

17.   *The steamboat piers or jetties of Gravesend, Sheerness, Herne Bay, Margate and Deal.*

In any Victorian seaside resort of consequence its pier was

invariably one of the great attractions of the town. Notable seaside resorts were considered incomplete without their piers. Prior to their construction, however, as promenade extensions into the sea, marine parades and drives were about as close as the visitor could get to the ocean, short of bathing in the sea, or going out in a boat. All the early piers of Kent were built, sometimes of wood, as landing places for steamers, and no resort had more piers than Gravesend did in the steamboat pre-railway era of resort development.

(a) [Anon., *The Pictorial Guide to Gravesend and Its Rural Vicinity: A Holiday Handbook*, 1845, 8]

GRAVESEND boasts three landing places: the middle most – The Town Pier – being the senior, and the most frequented of the three.

This was the first to be constructed for £8,700, with the handling of passenger traffic being transferred from the Town Quay on Monday, 27 January 1834.

(b) [R.P. Cruden, *The History of the Town of Gravesend in the County of Kent*, 1843, 505–6]

It extends into the river 127 feet from the stone front of the Town Quay, and is 40 feet wide, being built upon cast-iron arches of 40 feet span, and a rise of 6 feet . . . At the extremity of the platform is a transverse head, commonly called a T head, 76 feet in length, and 30 feet wide, under which there are flights of steps, that communicate with a floating vessel rising and falling with the tide, [which] is always on a level with the packets alongside, for convenient access . . . The 26 cast-iron columns, supporting the whole Pier, are each 18 feet high, and 2 feet 9 inches diameter. The platform of the Pier is enclosed by an open parapet, and is used as a promenade . . . The wings or ends of the T head are roofed over, forming two pavilions for shelter in unfavourable weather. The roofs are each supported by cast-iron ornamental columns, with Greek entablatures, and panelled turrets, in one of which is a clock, and in the other a bell, which is rung to give notice for packets to depart . . . The entrance to the Pier is by an easy flight of steps, enclosed by handsome cast-iron gates.

(c) [*The Visitor's Guide to the Watering Places*, 1842, 10–11]

[The] TOWN PIER . . . constitutes not only a noble place of embarkation and debarkation, but a fashionable and much frequented promenade. Seats are placed at certain distances, for the accommodation of the company, and the view from it is very extensive, commanding a fine sweep of the river and adjoining coast, east and west, with a beautiful prospect of several villages . . . The *Diamond* Steam Packet Company's vessels arrive and depart from its head. The *Commercial* steam packets also call here on their way to and from . . . Sheerness, to London . . . In the centre is a high column, on the top of which is a lantern, which when lighted emits a strong red glare.

The second Gravesend pier to be built was the Terrace Pier.

(d) [*The Visitor's Guide to the Watering Places*, 1842, 11]

[The] TERRACE PIER is composed of wood, and is upwards of 200 feet long, by 9 broad. The erection of this structure, and laying out of the adjoining grounds, as a public promenade and garden [see Docs. 39 l,m] has not only caused this part of the town to be much frequented, but may likewise be esteemed one of the great improvements of Gravesend . . . Seats are placed on the pier, for the accommodation of the company, and omnibuses and vans wait the arrival of the *Star* and *Eagle* Steam Packet Company's boats . . . It is projected to erect a new pier, composed of stone, upon a noble plan, about forty yards eastward of the present structure.

> What had been a wooden pier was replaced by one built of more durable materials, namely the Royal Terrace Pier, erected in 1845, at a cost of £9,200.

(e) [*The Post Office Directory of the Six Home Counties*, 1851, 325].

The extreme length is 250 feet, width 30 feet; it rests on 22 cast iron columns, the underside of the pier being 8 feet above the level of high water at spring tides. It is covered with a wrought iron roof, supported on pilasters, forming panels at the side, between which sliding shutters are introduced. During the summer months a concert band is in attendance throughout the day; in the evening the pier is converted into a magnificient ballroom.

> Gravesend's third pier by 1840 was the Rosherville Pier, described as follows in 1842 and 1851.

(f) [*The Visitor's Guide to the Watering Places*, 1842, 13; *The Post Office Directory of the Six Home Counties*, 1851, 325]

ROSHERVILLE PIER is moveable, and ingeniously contrived to form a safe and pleasant landing-place at all times of the tide. ROSHERVILLE PIER . . . is a neat, commodious and substantial erection, within 150 yards of the entrance to Rosherville Gardens; steam-boats to and from the metropolis call here every hour in the day during summer.

A pier at Sheerness was erected in 1835 resulting from 'A BILL For maintaining the Pier at *Sheerness* in the Parish of *Minster* in the Isle of *Sheppy* in the County of *Kent* and for paving lighting watching cleansing and improving certains Streets, Lanes and public Passages and Places within the said Parish, 1828' [KAO, U713 018]

(g) [*Pigot & Co's Royal, National and Commercial Directory*, 1840, 361]

In 1835 a very handsome pier or jetty, extending nearly 500 yards over the bed of the Medway, and beyond low water, was erected, so that steam packets can land and embark passengers at all times: this is a great public accommodation, and has materially increased the celebrity of Sheerness as a watering place [Illus. 23b].

Herne Bay's first pier of 3,613 feet in length was built in 1831–2, and demolished in 1870, resulting also from an Act of Parliament, which received the Royal Assent on 30 March 1831.

(h) [An ACT FOR Making and maintaining a Pier or Jetty, and other Works, at *Herne Bay*, in the Parish of *Herne*, in the County of *Kent*, 1831, KAO, U713 017]

[The Preamble].
It would greatly conduce to the Convenience and Advantage of the Inhabitants of Herne, and Herne Bay . . . and all other Persons resorting there to . . . if a Pier or Jetty were made and maintained, which should extend into the Sea on the North Side of the Town of . . . Herne Bay, . . . and if convenient Quays, and other Works adjoining to, or connected with, such Pier or Jetty, and convenient Avenues and Approaches thereto were also erected, made, and maintained.

This Act created the Herne Bay Pier Company and allowed it to raise a capital of £50,000 in 1000 shares, of £50, with limited liability, the Company being also authorized

to make a Parade along the Shore of the said Bay, and Causeways, Avenues, and Approaches to the said Pier or Jetty, . . . and also to erect such proper and convenient Baths, Bathing-places, and Accommodations for Bathing-machines, . . . as the Directors shall from time to time deem necessary or expedient.

The initial deposit per £50 share was fixed at £2. It was no wonder that 'A Lady' wrote of an emerging 'New Town' in 1835.

(i)   [By a Lady, *A Picture of the New Town of Herne Bay*, 1835, 3–5, 6–7]

Early in the year 1830, two capitalists, intimate friends, drove to Herne Bay for a ride . . . They were soon struck with the unwrought condition, and the death-like inactivity of everything around them, . . . [also] with the capabilities presenting themselves at every step . . .
Here might a town, full and complete, be raised, where now lay stretched before them a nearly desolate expanse of shore! . . .
The mode of arriving at Herne Bay, previously to the year 1830, was either by coach, or by dropping from the steamers . . . into boats, which put out from the shore to receive the company . . .
A project of magnitude was now formed [Illus. 20b]. It was nothing less than erecting a pier, to enable passengers and goods to be landed at all times of the tide. After a complete investigation of the difficulties to be surmounted for carrying the plan into effect, the report from the engineers was found highly favourable, and a committee of the principal landholders and others was appointed, when they drew up a plan for forming a company, to be incorporated by Act of Parliament, and raising a sufficient sum for its execution. The list of shareholders was soon found sufficient to commence this important undertaking . . .
The first pile was drove on the 4th of July, 1831, in the presence of an immense concourse of spectators from all parts of the adjacent country, particularly from Margate and Canterbury . . . The plans were drawn up by the late Mr. Telford, whose abilities, as a skilful engineer, are so well known.
The Pier extends 3,000 feet into the sea, being in the shape of a T . . . [It] is 24 feet wide, and forms an agreeable promenade . . . A voluntary subscription has been opened, not exceeding 5s. from each person, for

the erection of a royal statue at the pier-head, in honour of his present Majesty [William IV] . . . The Pier is constructed of immense timber piles, shod with iron, having five in a row, the breadth of the platform, each row being 20 feet distant; they are secured in their position by equally strong cross and diagonal timbers, tied together by heavy iron bolts and screw nuts. The piles are sunk 14 feet below the water mark.

Some of the effects of all this enterprise was spelt out in 1832–4.

(j)   [*Pigot & Co's Commercial Directory, 1832–4*, 829]

The [previous] want of a landing-place has prevented its acquiring greater notoriety, and has been the only drawback to its becoming one of the most fashionable places of resort of the day . . . The company are making a parade of at least 30 feet wide, which will extend for a mile or more along the front of the town next the sea, for the accommodation of pedestrians and others, on payment of a small toll. Since the company has been formed, considerable improvements have already been made in the town; and several buildings, including a Hotel, have been erected. It is also intended to build a new church, for which a piece of ground has been given by Sir Henry Oxenden.

(k)   [*The Visitor's Guide to the Watering Places*, 1842, 197]

The Pier . . . extends . . . nearly $\frac{3}{4}$ of a mile over the sands and sea, where it terminates in the form of a T . . . Unrivalled in length, [it] affords a most delightful promenade, in addition to which a parade has been made on the shore adjoining it, above a mile in length, and nearly 60 feet wide.

(l)   [S. Bagshaw, *History, Gazetteer and Directory of the County of Kent*, II, Sheffield, 1847, 218–9]

THE ROYAL PIER . . . stretches imposingly into the bosom of the waters . . . On the western side of the pier is a long line of handsome shops, having a frontage to the beach, and one story in height; so designed in order to prevent their obstructing the view of the ocean from ST. GEORGE'S-TERRACE, a noble range of building flanked on one end by an assembly room of magnificent dimensions, together with reading and billiard rooms. THE PARADE extends about a mile on the coast, . . . forming a fine promenade on which is the CLOCK TOWER, standing conspicuously fronting the ocean, . . . [as] a considerable architectural ornament. It was completed in 1837 at the sole expense of Mrs. Ann Thwaites, at a cost of £4,000 [Illus. 24].

The first Kentish resort to acquire a pier or jetty was Margate in the shape of 'Jarvis's Landing-Place' in 1824, which was the same year as the incorporation of the General Steam Navigation Company.

(m) [G.W. Bonner, *The Picturesque Pocket Companion to Margate, Ramsgate, Broadstairs, and the Parts Adjacent*, 2nd Ed., 1831, 50–1]

Passengers are [thereby] enabled to reach the shore, when the water is too low for vessels to enter the harbour. This useful work was completed in 1824, at the cost of £8,000, . . . borne by the company of pier proprietors, from whom it must therefore be regarded as a munificent gift to the public. It is constructed of English oak, measures 1,120 feet in length, and at low and half tide is deservedly considered one of the most inviting marine walks which fancy can imagine, or experience realize . . . The handsome and richly ornamented cast-iron archway which adorns the entrance of the landing-place, was placed in that situation [in 1828] by the Pier and Harbour Company, as a tribute of respect to their Chairman, Dr. JARVIS.

(n) [*Picture of Ramsgate, or A Guide to the Various Amusements, Public Libraries, Building Improvements, etc., of that celebrated Watering Place*, Ramsgate, 1833, 62]

THE JETTY; or JARVIS'S LANDING PLACE.
This substantial wooden projection was erected at the suggestion of the late Dr. Jarvis, a public-spirited gentleman of the town, to whom it is indebted for many valuable improvements.

The 1830s produced proposals for constructing a wooden pier at Deal, the want of a harbour having always militated against the commercial progress of the town.
[John Laker, *History of Deal*, 2nd Ed., Deal, 1921, 378]
In 1838 a company was formed to build a wooden pier or jetty as a substitute for a harbour, an Act of Parliament sanctioning the formation of a Deal Pier Company, with an authorized capital of £21,000. The famous harbour engineer Sir John Rennie was commissioned to design a pier, 445 feet in length. This proposal was only partially completed.

(o) [S. Bagshaw, *History, Gazetteer and Directory of the County of Kent*, II, Sheffield, 1847, 355]

THE PIER – From the influx of visitors, and to facilitate communication with the shipping in the Downs, the inhabitants formed a Joint Stock Company, and in 1838 obtained an Act authorizing the construction of a wooden pier or jetty, and to make other improvements to enable passengers to land at all times without getting into small boats. Accordingly, a pier was built of wood to the extent of 250 feet, which it is intended to carry out to double its length as soon as the funds will admit.

£12,000 had been spent on getting so far, following which a further sum was then raised by an issue of £5 shares, but after that nothing more was done to complete the structure. Indeed 'year by year parts of it succumbed to the violence of the winter gales' until, in 1857, a sudden south-easterly gale brought the whole structure down.
[Laker, *op.cit.*, 378–9]

18.   *Seaside accommodation: the early years in Thanet.*

Guidebooks of the later eighteenth and early nineteenth centuries frequently commented on the physical transformation of traditional fishing and maritime communities which inevitably followed in the wake of a developing craze for seaside holidays.

(a) [Zechariah Cozens, *A Tour through the Isle of Thanet, and some other Parts of East Kent*, 1793, 2–4, 48, 49].

MARGATE is now, through the smiles of a generous public, become a populous thriving town. There are upwards of 700 families resident in the town, exclusive of the great number of visitants who annually spend some of their summer months in this place.
[The High Street was once] a long dirty lane, consisting chiefly of malt-houses, herring hangs, and the poor little cottages of fishermen; but now, such of those as were anyways calculated for it, have improved and converted into decent dwelling houses; and others have given place to more spacious buildings, purposely intended for the accommodation of the visitants: and another small village called the Dane . . . [is] now, by the multiplicity of the new buildings between them, connected into one town.

Also in Churchfield, on the Fort and in several other parts of Margate

are large squares, commodious crescents, and handsome streets, forming an assemblage of spacious buildings, every way adapted for the pleasure and convenience of the nobility, gentry, citizens, and tradesmen who visit the town.

While across in Broadstairs, and Ramsgate, respectively,

BROADSTAIRS, . . . now by the resort of visitants, . . . contains a number of good houses, . . . on the edge of the cliff; here is also a good hotel . . . The village promises fair to become a considerable thriving place.

RAMSGATE, . . . since the *rage* for sea bathing hath taken place, has had its share of visitants: and consequently is, every year, much improving in its buildings, and other accommodations. Here are many good lodging houses, several excellent hotels, inns, etc.; . . . in short, everything to make a summer residence comfortable.

(b) [*The Thanet Itinerary or Steam Yacht Companion*, 1819, 20]

When the *rage* for sea bathing became general, the vast metropolis poured forth her smokey thousands, who hastened to the sea coasts of *Thanet* . . . The effect was astonishing; – squares were laid out – streets built – places of public amusement erected – markets established.

The overall point was put more generally during the 1850s in the following observation on 'The Decay of Old Mercantile Coast Towns, and their Revival as Watering Places'.

(c) [George Roberts, *The Social History of the People of the Southern Counties of England in Past Centuries*, 1856, 540, 547]

They died out as mercantile coast towns; and when near to a point of extinction, they rose, phoenix-like, under a metamorphosed appearance, and enabled a large and new class in society to gratify their wishes and a novel taste . . . The middle of the eighteenth century is the epoch when this remarkable change, that has to be described, became perceptible.

It soon became clear to developing seaside towns that there was a pressing need for accommodation from visitors, many of whom were accustomed to the comforts and spaciousness of a country estate and a London home. The provision of residential accommodation, whether in the form of lodging houses, as opposed to inns, hotels or boarding houses, soon became urgent.

(d) [John Lyons, *A Description of the Isle of Thanet, and particularly of the Town of Margate*, 1763, 11, 12]

The Lodgings, tho' small, are neat and tolerably commodious, considering that they are now applied to the reception of Strangers, for which purpose they were never originally intended. Some good houses have been built within a few years, and others are building: The old ones daily receive all the improvements they are capable of . . .

The principal House of Entertainment is the New Inn, kept by *Mitchener*: the accommodations of it, with respect to neatness and good entertainment, can hardly fail to recommend it. Here is likewise a Coffee-house, as well as other Inns and Publick-houses; in one of which is a fine new Billiard-table.

There were real limits to the extent to which existing houses or premises could be adapted to the needs and demands of wealthy families, only a minority of whom could afford or chose to erect their own marine villas or estates. Giving a face lift to older properties was only a partial solution to the problem of housing increasing numbers of visitors. From the outset investment in new buildings was called for, involving land purchases, and the raising or mobilization of capital, materials and labour for construction. In short, it soon became a well-established feature of seaside towns of significance that they had to possess residential accommodation well in excess of the needs of their permanent populations. Waves of visitors resulted in building booms, settlement extensions and active property markets. Houses and lodgings had simply to be available in greater numbers. Much of the building enterprise which took place lacks actual documentation because it was either piecemeal or small scale. Margate witnessed, however, a continuous building boom which was sustained over seventy years, the initial effects of which were already apparent by 1770.

(e) [*The Margate Guide . . . In a Letter to a Friend*, 1770, 12–13, 15]

The New-square [Cecil Square], which is a large one, consists of some very handsome Houses, which have been lately erected by Persons of Fortune for their own Use, with several others, intended for the Reception of the Nobility and Gentry. Some of these are fit for present Use, and more are building for the same Purpose. A line of very neat Shops forms another Part of the Square, for the Convenience of such Strangers as may be desirous of inhabiting this new and elegant Part of the Town. The Fronts, both of the Houses and Shops, are paved in the same Manner as those in the principal Parts of London and Westminster; and the Scene, both of Business and Pleasure, seems to be transferring itself hither very fast.

The Assembly Room, which has been lately built [1769, also] stands in the New-square, and is thought to be one of the largest Buildings of the Kind in England . . . [Attached] is a Flight of Bed-chambers neatly furnished, for the Accommodation of such Persons as are not provided with other Lodgings at their first coming . . .

[Elsewhere] there are several good Lodging-houses . . . Many have been built of late Years, expressly with an Intention of their being hired for Lodgings.

> Mitchener referred to earlier in 1763 continued to flourish at the New Inn, 'on the Water-side . . . [which] is still much frequented both as a good Inn and Tavern, and has two fine Billiard-tables, and a Subscription Coffee-room' (p.14). John Mitchener was one of Margate's most enterprising eighteenth-century hoteliers. His son, John Mitchener junior, began playing an increasing rôle in the business from 1772 onwards. The Mitcheners had a long and honourable reign in the Margate hotel and bathing businesses which ended in 1807 at the death of John Mitchener junior. What started as an inn with an assembly room prior to 1770 became a thriving and expanding hotel, as can be seen from a succession of newspaper advertisements.

(f) [*The Kentish Post, or Canterbury News Letter*, 17 June 1761]

John Mitchener from Rochester has taken the New Inn and Assembly Room at Margate.

(g) [*Ibid.*, 5 May 1762]

John Mitchener has greatly improved the New Inn.

> Assembly room functions at the New Inn were abandoned once

the permanent new Assembly Rooms were opened in Cecil Square. However, by May 1775 the New Inn was being advertised as a hotel.

(h) [*The Kentish Gazette*, 17–20 May 1775]

Mitchener at the New Inn Tavern and Hotel, on the Parade, Margate, acquaints the public that he has made a number of additional lodging rooms.

The seasons of 1778 and 1779 were prefaced by announcements of further expansion and improvements.

(i) [*The Kentish Gazette*, 6–10 June 1778]

Mitchener at the New Inn Tavern and Hotel informs visitors that he has increased the Size of his house and [has] taken the wine vaults of the late Mr. William Smith.

(j) [*Ibid.*, 22–26 May 1779]

Mitchener of the New Inn has enlarged his house with a number of additional Lodging Rooms. He has erected a compact Livery Stable opposite his house for near 60 horses.

It was during his son's proprietorship that a final change of name to the Royal York Hotel occurred. In 1793 the New Inn was patronised by Frederick, Duke of York, the second son of George III, prior to his embarking from Margate on an expedition to Flanders. This patronage prompted John Mitchener II to rename his house the Royal York. Originating also as an inn on the Parade was the White Hart. These two hotels competed vigorously with each other and commanded an extensive patronage throughout the eighteenth and nineteenth centuries as two of Margate's leading seafront hotels. Ramsgate too was quick off the mark with the opening of a waterside inn during August 1751.

(k) [*The Kentish Post, or Canterbury News Letter*, 28–31 August 1751]

I take this Method of informing those worthy Gentlemen and Ladies of my Acquaintance, and others, that I have lately opened a Tavern (the Sign of the DOLPHIN) near the Water Side in Ramsgate, comman-

ding a near and fair Prospect of the Downs, and of the new Harbour of
Ramsgate; with very good Stabling and other Accommodations: Where
all who will be so good as to favour me with their Company, shall meet
with the best Usage, and a hearty Welcome from
Their most humble Servant,
ROBERT HINDS,
Musician.

Among the many developments which contributed to Margate's
early uniqueness and popularity as a seaside resort were the
existence by 1770 of boarding houses and possibly the first
mention in any English resort of the word 'hotel' in 1774.

(1) [*The Margate Guide . . . In a Letter to a Friend*, 1770, 15]

There are, likewise, Boarding houses kept in a very decent, reputable
Manner, for the Convenience of small Families, or single Persons, who
rather wish to have a Table provided for them at a certain and easy
Expence, than to be at the Trouble of keeping one of their own.

(m) [*The Daily Advertiser*, 2 June 1774]

MARGATE.
To the Nobility and Gentry. Mr. SMITH of the Devil Tavern,
Temple-bar, takes the Liberty to acquaint them, that he has taken the
New Assembly Rooms Tavern and Hotel for the ensuing Season, which
are now open for the Reception of Company, who may depend on
meeting with good Accommodation . . . They may be supplied with the
best of Wines, Arrack, Rum, Brandy, etc., in any Quantity, and equal
in Quality to any that are now selling in London.

And so by the mid-1770's the scenario of what was long to be
familiar seaside accommodation – the inn, the tavern, the hotel,
the boarding house and the lodging house – had become well
established in Margate, being destined for a wider overall expansion.

19. *Selecting a seaside hotel before the middle of the nineteenth century.*

The recommended hotels of Ramsgate and one very good reason
for choosing to stay in a hotel were clearly spelt out to visitors in a
famous guidebook of 1833.

(a) [*Picture of Ramsgate, or A Guide to the Various Amusements, Public Libraries, Building Improvements, etc. of that celebrated Watering Place*, Ramsgate, 1833, 15–16]

Persons intending to make a short stay cannot do better than take up their residence at one of the numerous Inns with which the place abounds. The following list will enable them to make a choice conformable to their taste and means [Illus. 15b].

The ALBION HOTEL, a large, commodious, and magnificent house, possessing every accommodation, both splendid and convenient; and conducted with spirit and liberality by its present occupier, Mrs. Jane Bear.

The KING'S HEAD, Zachariah Hiscocks, facing the harbour, possesses every comfort and convenience which either large or small parties may require.

The ROYAL OAK, Ann Cramp, and the CASTLE, Mary Ann Webster, are likewise comfortable and convenient houses, and possess the same advantages as the last mentioned hotel.

Those Hotels may be considered first-rate houses in the town.

The BULL AND GEORGE, kept by Hudson and Son, is considered a reasonable and yet commodious house, chiefly occupied by commercial men.

The SPREAD EAGLE, at the top of High Street, is kept by Mr. R. Cramp, and generally commands a respectable company.

The FOY BOAT, on Zion Hill, and several other Inns in which comfortable accommodation may be found at a somewhat less price than the larger hotels.

Recommendations were made also for Broadstairs and Margate [Illus. 15a]

(b) [*Ibid.*, 49, 61]

Broadstairs

The ALBION HOTEL, conducted by Mr. Peyton, yields to none in the Isle of Thanet for accommodation, either in wines, spirits, viands or even luxuries; [while] those who may take up their temporary abode at

The ROSE INN are certain to depart well satisfied with the attention and accommodation they have received.

Margate

The Visitor on arrival will find the Royal Hotel, York Hotel, and White Hart, houses possessing every accommodation, both splendid and convenient: and at the Duke's Head, King's Head, London Hotel, Crown and Anchor, Queen's Arms, and Ship, comfortable accommodation, at somewhat less price than the larger hotels.

The Albion Hotel and the Rose Inn in Broadstairs were equally commended in 1831, along with most of the other hotels and inns listed above for Ramsgate and Margate, adding respectively the London Hotel and the Fountain Inn. The comments attached to individual establishments varied slightly in 1831 but were no less flattering.

(c) [G.W. Bonner, *The Picturesque Pocket Companion to Margate, Ramsgate, Broadstairs and the Parts Adjacent*, 2nd Ed., 1831, 73–5, 160–1, 189]

Ramsgate

THE ALBION HOTEL is situate near the pier, and commands an extensive view of the Downs, and coast of France. The proprietor is polite and attentive and, therefore, receives marked and well deserved encouragement from the nobility and gentry who frequent this town. At this house are the assembly and card rooms.

There are several other good hotels and taverns, of which, as all are equally excellent, we shall only mention,

THE KING'S HEAD,
THE ROYAL OAK, at which is held an excellent Catch Club, . . .
THE CASTLE AND LONDON HOTELS, and
THE BULL AND GEORGE,
whose respective proprietors seem, by indefatigable exertion and polite attention to vie with each other for a share of public patronage and support.

Margate

HOWE'S ROYAL HOTEL, in Cecil Square, is a splendid and well arranged establishment, possessing billiard tables, a card room and a magnificent ballroom. The landlord of the tap belonging to the Hotel is in possession of a dog, who is found useful in fetching home the pewter-pots whenever he sees them standing at the doors of his master's customers. Weekly concerts are established here, and on Sundays there is a selection of sacred music.

THE LONDON HOTEL is pleasantly situated in Hawley Square, and is conducted by Mrs. Boncey, who is remembered and esteemed by some of the oldest visitors of Margate, whose patronage she continues to ensure, by indefatigable attention to their wants, and by an ardent desire to promote their comfort. This house, being removed from the noise and bustle of the town, is excellently calculated for a family abode.

THE YORK HOTEL is situate on the Marine Parade: the accommodations here are of a very superior and satisfactory kind, and the proprietor, Mr. James Wright, is well known to, and highly respected by, the many families and individuals, of the first respectablity and distinction, by whom this hotel is frequented; and his polite attention, and persevering endeavors to ensure their comfort, during their stay at his house, is sufficiently evidenced by the large share of patronage with which he is honoured [Illus. 19]

A short distance on, stands

CREED'S WHITE HART TAVERN, which next calls for our notice: this is a very good hotel, and well conducted . . .

THE DUKE'S HEAD, near the Pier, kept by Mr. James Adams, is equally entitled to our notice; its accommodations are good, and in summer this house is well frequented. There are several other good inns, but our space will only permit us to notice

THE FOUNTAIN, which is a comfortable house, . . . kept by Mr. Read.

As early as 1765 Margate boasted twelve inns or taverns, some of which evolved into famous hotels and all of which continued to trade during the 1790s.

(d)   [*A Short Description of the Isle of Thanet; Being Chiefly Intended as a Directory for the Company Resorting to Margate, Ramsgate and Broadstairs*, Margate, 1796, 16]

Besides the Royal Hotel there is another on the Parade of equal excellence, and several good Inns and Taverns, where families may be well accommodated until they have provided themselves with lodgings agreeable to their wishes.

(e) [By an Inhabitant, *The Margate Guide, A Descriptive Poem, with Elucidatory Notes*, Margate, 1797, 85]

Benson's [Royal] Hotel is a capital house, . . . and has every requisite to render it comfortable either to families or individuals; it may be the more desirable residence to some, on account of its being contiguous to the Assembly Rooms. The York Hotel, kept by *Mitchener*[also see Doc. 18], is most pleasantly situated on the Parade; it commands a fine view of the Harbour, and of the ocean: the house is commodious, and every way calculated to please the numerous visitants it receives. The Prospect Tavern is occupied by *Jenkins*, and is much frequented; it stands, attached to a large bowling green, on a delightful eminence, near the sea. *Rayner's* Shakespeare's Tavern is opposite the Theatre, in Hawley Square; during the Season, it is a resort for many genteel people, being in a very polite part of the town. The Fountain Inn, kept by *Stevenson*, is in King Street, near the Market and the Pier; it is a good house, affording excellent accommodation. In the same street, stands the George Inn, occupied by *Humble*; adjoining to it, are *Bloxham's* Livery Stables, which render it peculiarly convenient for those who have horses or carriages with them. The King's Head, near to the Bathing Houses and the sea, is both pleasant and convenient for strangers, and is well managed by Mrs. *Crickett*.

The other Inns are kept by Mrs. *Mitchener*, Mrs. *Adams*, and Mr. *Dunkin*: they are comfortable houses, whose occupiers do their utmost to oblige: and, though on a smaller scale, will perhaps be found as agreeable as those before mentioned.

As the eighteenth century drew to a close and on into the nineteenth century a vigorous rivalry developed between the White Hart, the New Inn/Royal York, and the Assembly Rooms Tavern/Royal Hotel (again see Doc. 18) as the leading Margate innkeeping/hotel businesses. The latter began its career in Cecil Square, in 1769, having been built in conjunction with the resort's new and permanent assembly rooms (see Doc. 41). In 1794, George, Prince of Wales, and afterwards George IV, paid a hurried visit to Margate, for the purpose of meeting his prospective bride, Caroline of Brunswick, daughter of Charles, Duke of Brunswick. The Prince and his fiancé patronized Benson's Hotel, in commemoration of which its name was changed to the Royal Hotel. It became a fashionable hotel in which to stay.

(f)   [E.W. Brayley, *The Beauties of England and Wales; or Delineations Topographical, Historical and Descriptive*, Vol. VIII: *Kent*, 1808, 960]

Adjoining to this building [the Assembly Rooms] is the Royal Hotel, which is very handsomely fitted up for the reception of the first company.

The letting of these extensive premises was widely advertised in the national press during July, August and September 1810.

(g)   [*The Times*, 2 July 1810; *The Morning Chronicle*, 18, 22, 28 and 30 August and 1 September 1810]

ROYAL HOTEL, MARGATE – To be LET, for a Term of Years, . . . now in the occupation of Mr. BENJAMIN KIDMAN, comprising large and elegant assembly rooms, coffee room, billiard room, and every requisite convenience for carrying on an extensive tavern business. The premises may be viewed by leave of the tenant, and further particulars may be known by application at the office of Messrs. Williams and Walker, Dartford; or of Mr. Floxney, Chancery-lane, London.

By 1816 this hotel had undergone yet further improvements and additions.

(h)   [*The New Margate, Ramsgate and Broadstairs Guide*, 6th Ed., Margate, 1816, 65]

The present occupier, Mr. Howe, conducts the business of this hotel in a manner that fully entitles him to the patronage of the public, and has lately built several new chambers with suitable conveniences, which, independent of improvement to the building in its external appearance, affords a larger scope for the accommodation of his numerous and respectable visitors. . . . For neatness, comfort or luxury, the Royal Hotel will not suffer in comparison with any house in the kingdom.

Meanwhile on the Marine Parade,

(i)   [*Ibid.*, 68]

Wright (the successor of the late Mr. Mitchener) has also a tavern of great excellence, most delightfully situated. . . . It commands a fine view of the harbour, and the ocean; the front is simply elegant; the house is in every respect well adapted to please the numerous visitants it receives. Mr. Wright became the possessor of these extensive premises in 1808. . . . If indefatigable attentions, with the greatest civility, deserve public recommendation and support, we are fully persuaded Mr. Wright will be entitled to a liberal share.

> Fifteen years later the Howe and Wright families continued to prosper in their respective hotels, as was noted in (c) above, which vindicates the hopes expressed in 1816; likewise Mr. Peyton in his highly recommended Albion Hotel in Broadstairs in 1833, as noted in (b) above, which in 1816, *ibid.*, 109, was introduced as one of 'two good houses of accommodation', being 'a new built house conveniently fitted up', with Mr. Peyton having moved to there from the Rose Inn, located lower down in the same street. The Ramsgate hotelier of 1833, Mrs. Jane Bear, prefaced the opening of the 1835 season by extending her Albion Hotel.

(j) [*The Dover Telegraph and Cinque Ports General Advertiser*, 24 January 1835]

The mania for building in this highly favoured town appears to supercede at this [winter] season of the year every other object of business. Besides terraces, crescents, Camden-place, and others of minor importance, the extensive range of buildings now adding to the Albion Hotel, give promise of great improvements for the better accommodation and comfort of visitors in that well-known establishment which, it is presumed, by the early part of spring, may vie with any of similar rank in the county. Too much credit cannot be bestowed on the worthy hostess (Mrs. Bear) for her liberality and courtesy to those who favour her with their patronage.

> The few stray visitors to Herne Bay in its early days had to rely on inns rather than hotels, but not so by 1818 and even less so by 1835.

(k) [L. Fussell, *A Journey round the Coast of Kent*, 1818, 72]

Only a few years have elapsed since the erection of one of those temporary stations for the military [1798], by which it was thought necessary to secure the coast, became a sort of signal to inform the visitors of Margate and Ramsgate that the spot was habitable. They soon afterwards flocked hither in such numbers, that a considerable increase in buildings and improvements speedily ensued. An hotel was erected, which, if not elegant, was capable of affording lodging to those who could not obtain a closet or cupboard in the little habitations contiguous.

(1) [By a Lady, *A Picture of the New Town of Herne Bay*, 1835, 14–16]

There are already three hotels established at Herne Bay [the Pier Hotel, the Kent Hotel and the Dolphin Inn]. . . . These, at a small distance from each other, are nearly the first objects which meet the eye on landing from the steamers [ditto at Margate the Royal York and White Hart Hotels]. We believe that an active rivalship, in the best sense of the word, stimulates their respective occupiers, for in each of these receptacles visitors find accommodations equal to the best houses in town, or those of the most fashionable resort in any part of England. Excellent wines, first-rate cookery, elegant apartments, and the charges fair.

In addition to the above prominent establishments, there are others on a smaller scale, no less deserving the patronage of travellers. We heartily wish them all the fullest success.

Seven years further on it was noted.

(m) [*The Visitor's Guide to the Watering Places*, 1842, 199]

The accommodations for visitors [to Herne Bay] are rapidly increasing; three new hotels have been built. The principal is the NEW PIER HOTEL, facing the sea; the Kent Hotel, situated a little to the left of the Pier; the Dolphin, built behind the original inn of the same name; and the Ship, about half a mile from the pier, formerly the only house of accommodation in the bay, now of course only a third-rate house.

Information concerning hotel occupancy and tariffs is sparse for the period before 1840. The summer census of 1841 throws some light on who was staying and working in the White Hart Hotel on the Parade at Margate over the census night of 7 June.

(n)   [P.R.O., H.O. 107/468/2]

The same family were running this hotel as ten years previously (see (c) above).

Names	Age & Sex M	F	Profession, Trade, Employment, Independent Means	Where Born, Y for Kent or No	
George Creed	55		Hotel Keeper	Y	
Mary do.		55		Y	
John Colley	21		Clerk	Y	
Charles do.	12			Y	
Mary Mastraw		30	Female Servant	Y	
Sarah Pain		35	Female Servant	Y	
Mary Doughty		14	Female Servant	Y	
Joseph Walker	20		Male Servant	Y	
William Johnson	25		Male Servant	Y	
Robert Elliott	80		Independent)	No	
Mary do.		60	Independent)	No	
Edmund Chalmer	45		Independent)	No	
Charles Fowler	58		Independent)	No	
Thomas Lambert	30		Engineer) . . .	No.	Visitors
Eliza do.		25	)	No	
Mary Depuse		50	Independent)	No	
Edward Collins	25		Solicitor)	No	
Eugenie do.		19	)	Y	

Also during 1841 the Royal Pier Hotel at Herne Bay advertised its tariff as follows.

(o)   [*The Dover Telegraph and Cinque Ports General Advertiser*, 11 September 1841]

[There are] some splendid suites of apartments.
Beds 2s. and 2s. 6d. per Night.
Sitting Rooms from 2s. per Day.
Breakfast 2s.; with Ham and Eggs, 2s. 6d.
Teas 1s. 6d.
Children Half Price.
N.B.   Gentlemen are begged not to be influenced by their Drivers.

This warning may be compared with that which emanated from John Benson and what was to be renamed the Royal Hotel in Margate when, through *The Kentish Gazette*, 31 May 1785, he advised 'the Company not to be persuaded by the disgusting Solicitations of some of the Inns, contrary to his Interest'. The above payment of up to 2s. 6d. for a bed for a night may be compared to what Joseph Farington expected to pay for a Margate hotel bed for the night on 26 August 1804 (see Doc. 3b). Again it was the Pier Hotel at Herne Bay which attracted favourable press comment earlier still in 1841, as if to underline the general comment about fair charges in 1835.

(p) [*The Dover Telegraph and Cinque Ports General Advertiser*, 7 August 1841]

The spirited proprietor of the Pier Hotel provides a dinner in his usual magnificent style at 2s. 6d. each!! Surely after this we shall hear no more about extravagant charges at watering places.

> This figure may be contrasted with some idea of the cost of hotel food at John Mitchener's New Inn, Margate (subsequently the Royal York Hotel, see Doc. 18) as stated in Margate's first guidebook of 1763.

(q) [J. Lyons, *A Description of the Isle of Thanet and particularly of the Town of Margate*, 1763, 69–70]

At the NEW-INN, *Margate, a house I have long used, the prices of provisions, etc. are as follows*:

Each person	s.	d.
Bread, cheese, or butter	0	1
Welsh rabbit	0	2
Beef steaks, veal cutlets, mutton or pork chops	0	9
Veal or beef collops	1	0
Tripe boiled or fryed	0	9
Ditto in fricasée	1	0
Eggs and bacon	0	9
Cold meat	0	8
Servant breakfast, dinner, or supper	0	6
Breakfast, tea, coffee, etc.	0	8
Pigeon roasted or boiled	0	8
Ditto boiled with bacon and greens	1	0

Each person	s.	d.
Ditto stewed	1	0
Chicken or fowl roasted or boiled	2	0
Ditto broiled with mushroom sauce	2	6
Ditto white or brown fricasée	2	6
Ditto roasted with egg sauce	2	6
Ditto boiled with bacon and greens	3	0
Duck roasted	2	0
Ditto with onion sauce	2	6
Capon roasted or boiled	3	0
Turkey roasted with sauces, etc.	5	0
Ditto boiled with oyster or lemon sauce	5	0
Goose roasted with sauces, etc.	5	0
Wild duck and dressing	2	6
Teal and dressing	1	6
Woodcock and dressing	2	6
Eels and dressing, by the pound	1	6
Trout and dressing by the pound	2	0
Cray fish, by the hundred	6	0
Ditto buttered	8	0

Other fish, as it shall be in season, at a reasonable price.

	s.	d.
Rabbit roasted or fryed	1	6
Ditto smothered with onions	2	0
Neck of mutton and broth	3	6
Ditto roasted	2	6
Ditto in chops	2	6
Shoulder of mutton and dressing	3	6
Leg of mutton and dressing	4	0

All other joints of beef, veal, pork, etc. at six pence by the pound dressed.

Made dishes, soups, puddings, tarts, fruits, asparagus, pease, beans, potatoes, greens, cucumbers, pickles, etc. as they come in season at reasonable prices.

Wines, etc. as usual.

Charles Dickens from 1837 onwards developed a high regard not only for Broadstairs but also for the Albion Hotel and its landlord, James Ballard (? 1806–74), who, as 'an excellent hotel-keeper' managed that hotel for 38 years.

THE EARLY KENTISH SEASIDE

(r) [Ed: M. House and G. Storey, *The Letters of Charles Dickens*, Volume I: 1820–1839, O.U.P., 1965, 303]
At the end of August 1837 he wrote to inform his friend and biographer John Forster (1812–76),

I have discovered that the landlord of the Albion has delicious hollands [Hollands gin].

In the years which intervened between the 1760s and the 1840s there were periods of inflation as well as complaints about the fleecing of holidaymakers. The hope that this might be avoided in Margate was expressed as early as 1776.

(s) [C. Seymour, *A New Topographical, Historical, and Commercial Survey of the Cities, Towns, and Villages of the County of Kent*, Canterbury, 1776, 559]

As all bathing-places are fashionable, like all those of public diversion, it is to be hoped that the inhabitants of Margate will understand too well their own interest, to give disgust to the company, by that spirit of extortion and rapaciousness, too often stimulated by the concourse of the profuse and the opulent.

A 1797 guidebook pointed out by way of a footnote how

(t) [*The Margate and Ramsgate Guide in Letters to a Friend*, 1797, 29]

when Margate overflows with company, as it generally does at the height of the season (when I am well informed *ten shillings* and *sixpence* is often given for a single bed for only *one* night) then *Ramsgate* and *Broadstairs* fill with the overplus, though some persons give the preference to these places, for quietness and retirement...

Here I cannot but make one remark, which, as I wish well to Margate, I hope the inhabitants will take in good part and attend to; and that is, *Beware of imposing, or making exorbitant demands on the company during the season, either respecting lodgings or provisions, lest you oblige them to go to other watering-places less expensive and more moderate in their charges.*

Extortion out of season was not unknown as experienced by William Ward (1727–1821), a Quaker, from Benenden in the Weald of Kent on 20 March 1803.

103

(u) [Ed: C.F. Hardy, *Benenden Letters: London, Country and Abroad 1753–1821*, 1901, 291]

I was used most infamously at Margate – 4s. 6d. for a dinner not worth 6d.; wine at 4s. a bottle; 2s. a night for my bed; charges for more than I had – on proof I caused them to abate 4s. from my bill.

> Obviously not all travellers were pleased with the accommodation and sustenance which were provided for them; least of all the Hon. John Byng on his 'Tour into Kent' in 1790, one principal theme of which is a castigation of all the inns which he stayed at.

(v) [Ed: C. Bruyn Andrews, *The Torrington Diaries*, 1970, Volume IV, 159–61, 162, 163]

Monday, September 20.
. . . Dinner being order'd at the Swan Inn [Hythe] . . . Our dinner consisted of Herrings split; and the Roes lost:- odd cookery this! With Beef Steaks, which is allways a tough Business. – Port Wine not drinkable: One starves in a tour, but . . . with the air, and exercise, consists the salubrity.

Rump Steaks	1s. 8d.
Herrings	8d.
Potatoes and Butter	6d.
Cheese and Bread	4d.
Port	2s. 4d.
	5s. 6d.

After Dinner, quitting Hithe, . . . Much bluster'd, and buffeted by wind, over the exposed Hills, We came, (leaving Shakespeares Cliff at a small distance to our Right) within Sight of Dover Castle; and soon into the Towne of Dover, To The York Hotel; where, amidst Noise, and Racket, we procured a mean dirty Parlour for ourselves, and a kind of ship-hold for our Horses. Bad specimen this, To the French, of English comforts! – Bread, and Wine, not to be endured, . . . and old tough Partridges! A Room fill'd with Wind; and ship Stinks!! . . .

Tuesday, September 21.
. . . Our dinner was ill served, and nasty as possible, with not-drinkable wine! . . . After a long, cold, and tedious walk, we had to endure a tedious evening, from the want of a good apartements . . .

Wednesday, September 22.
... Never did I Enter a more dirty, noisy, or more imposing Inn, than this York House; for we were charged most exorbitantly, for wine not drinkable, for musty Fowls, and stinking Partridges; never did I leave an Inn with greater Pleasure.

At the other extremity to bad food were luxuries of the kind which Joseph Farington observed at John Mitchener's Royal York Hotel during an afternoon visit to Margate on 14 August 1804.

(w)   [Ed: J. Greig, *The Farington Diary*, 1923, Volume II, 275]

He had two turtles in water, and had Turtle ready dressed to be sent anywhere: the price 18 shillings a quart.

What then of the hotels in that part of Kent visited by the Hon. John Byng between Hythe and Dover? By virtue of being the country's leading cross-channel port, as well as a rising seaside resort, Dover was naturally plentifully endowed with hotels, taverns or inns by the 1790s.

(x)   [*The Dover and Deal Directory and Guide*, Dover, c.1792, 22]

The principal inns in Dover are, the Royal Hotel, kept by Charles Marice: York House, by Rutley and Willimot; the Ship, by John Harvey; the City of London, by Sophia Belcher; and the King's Head, by William Crow. The above inns are amply provided with post-carriages of every description.

These same principal inns were said to offer

(y)   [*A Guide to all the Watering and Sea-Bathing Places*, 1806, 214]

good accommodations, . . . and excellent post-chaises.

Several of the fourteen inns listed for Dover in 1828 emphasized their proximity to the harbour, clearly with an eye to seeking the patronage of continental travellers.

(z)   [W. Batcheller, *A New History of Dover, to which is added a New Dover Guide*, Dover, 1828, 351–2]

Wright's Hotel and Ship Inn, Strond-street, and on the Quay, fronting the harbour, C. Wright.

York Hotel, fronting the sea, at the lower end of the Rope Walk, Freeman Payn.

Union Hotel, Snargate-street, Pent-side, John Jell.

New London Hotel, Council-house street, near the harbour, W. Chaplin.

City of Antwerp Hotel, Market-place, W. Huntley.

Shakespeare Hotel, Bench-street, Charles Elvey.

Royal Oak Inn, Canon-street, William Mowll.

King's Head Inn, Clarence-place, fronting the harbour, A. Podevin.

Packet Boat Inn, Strond-street, J. Hoad.

Gun Hotel, Strond-street and on the Quay, fronting the harbour, G. Hipgrave.

Castle Hotel, fronting the harbour, near the north pier head, T. Divers.

Cinque Ports' Arms Inn, Clarence-place, R. Eastes.

Flying Horse Inn, King's-street, Mrs. Chittenden.

Guildhall Tavern, Bench-street, Thomas Houghton.

> Most of these hotels and inns were again listed for 1832–4, along with Charles Crothall's Paris Hotel in Snargate Street

(aa)   [*Pigot & Co's Commercial Directory, 1832–4*, 804, 807]

The Hotels and Inns are numerous, and their management such as to impart convenience and comfort to the foreigner and general stranger.

Folkestone possessed 'one principal inn' in 1791.

(bb)   [*Universal British Directory of Trade, Commerce and Manufacture*, III, 1791, 117]

The Folkestone Arms, kept by George Janeway, where the traveller meets with good accommodation.

> This was also the case according to *A Guide to all the Watering and Sea-Bathing Places*, 1806, 229. Two commercial inns are listed for 1832–4.

(cc)   [*Pigot & Co's Commercial Directory, 1832–4*, 814–5]

There are two good Inns here; the 'Rose' is the one generally resorted to by the commercial traveller.

Folkestone Arms (and excise office), Daniel Cork, Bail st.

Rose, Thomas Payne, Broad st.

The visitor to Sandgate in the 1830's could choose between three inns.

(dd) [*Ibid.*, 863]

Here are [three] respectable Inns, [of which] the 'New Inn' [listed also for 1806] may be considered the principal.

New Inn (posting, commercial and livery stables), Richard Marsh.
Castle, Irvine Barton Beattie.
Ship (posting and commercial), Sarah Podevin.

> Sarah Podevin may well have been related to A. Podevin at the King's Head Inn in Dover, as noted in (z) above. The Hon. John Byng knocked the Swan Inn at Hythe in 1790, but not so two guidebooks of 1806 and 1816.

(ee) [*A Guide to all the Watering and Sea-Bathing Places*, 1806, 230]

Here are two good inns, the White Hart and the Swan.

(ff) [*The Hythe, Sandgate and Folkestone Guide*, Hythe, 1816, 7, 25]

HYTHE contains some good and spacious inns . . . Whist clubs for the gentlemen are held weekly at the Swan and White Hart inns during the winter; and there are occasional balls, particularly in the bathing season, and other amusements usual at watering places, and by the sea side.

The position in 1832–4 was as follows.

(gg) [*Pigot & Co.'s Commercial Directory, 1832–4*, 831]

There [is] an excellent Inn (the 'Swan'), [which] will be found to render perfect accommodation to the visitor or commercial traveller; it is likewise a posting house, and the excise office – and where, also, corn is sold by sample, by those attending the weekly market (which is likewise for hops); the day for holding the market is Thursday. [Three Inns].

King's Head, Henry Stokes.
Swan (posting and commercial, and excise office, and corn market), George Pilcher.
White Hart (posting and commercial), John Hills.

Hotels and inns catered for commercial travellers as well as tourists and holidaymakers and, no doubt, in Deal and Gravesend their patrons included coastal and river pilots. The most prominent hotel in Deal in 1840 was the Royal Hotel fronting on to the sea.

(hh)   [*Pigot & Co.'s Royal, National and Commercial Directory*, 1840, 271]

A very superior establishment, the proprietors of [which] are Messrs. Bleaden & Co. of the London Tavern, Bishopsgate-street, London, whose name is a sufficient guarantee for affording accommodation to the most fastidious visitor; while the marine view enjoyed from the premises is beautiful and extensive.

> There were seven inns and hotels in Gravesend in 1832–4, not to mention 62 taverns and public houses.

(ii)   [*Pigot & Co's Commercial Directory, 1832–4*, 818]

Falcon Tavern (and baths), Thomas Pallister, East st.
Lord Nelson, Robert Birch, New rd.
New Inn (and excise office), John Heard, King st.
Pier Hotel, Charles Moore, High st.
Prince of Orange, William James Newman, New road.
Rum Puncheon, Jas. Curtis, West st.
White Hart Tavern, George Gardner, High street.

> Each new season was prefaced by announcements designed to attract additional custom.

(jj)   [*The Gravesend and Milton Journal*, 18 April 1835; 25 April 1835]

ROSE TAVERN AND HOTEL, High Street, Gravesend [a public house in 1832–4].
WILLIAM KNIGHT, from Blackfriars Road, London, takes leave to inform the Inhabitants and Visitors, . . . that he has rebuilt the above Tavern, and commenced the Season.
PUNCHEON TAVERN.
J. CURTIS has re-opened his spacious room for the season. The Harmonic Meetings will take place every Friday evening until further notice.

Hotel accommodation was both plentiful and expanding in Gravesend early in the 1840s.

(kk) [*The Visitor's Guide to the Watering Places*, 1842, 1–2, 18]

Several handsome streets are now forming, in which are many fine hotels, and other public buildings, which, when completed, will add greatly to the beauty of the place . . .
HOTELS. – These places of public entertainment are numerous. Those most eligibly situate for temporary visitors are on the brink of the river, and they command from their windows extensive views. Among these are the Rum Puncheon and the Pope's Head. The latter deserves honourable mention – it being close to the Pier, and commanding a fine view of the passing scene. The proprietor has an ordinary daily, which is numerously and respectably attended. Visitors may secure beds here, at almost any hour, without the fear of being disappointed. The principal hotels in the town are the Pier Hotel, the White Hart, the Fountain, the Prince of Orange, the Nelson, and the New Inn (the last three are in the London road). The New Inn demands especial notice for its fine bowling green, extensive pleasure grounds, and neat gardens.

Some of Gravesend's leading hotels were singled out for particular mention in specific paragraphs.

(ll) [*Ibid.*, 4, 7–8, 19]

CLIFTON HOTEL (The) is situated close to the [Clifton] baths [see Doc. 29 aa], which form a handsome erection at the western entrance of the town. Its appearance from the river is very striking. The front is towards the water: a handsome and solid stone embankment, forty feet wide, having been constructed before it, forms an excellent promenade for company. The views from hence, both up and down the river, are exceedingly attractive. The same may be said of the opposite shore, on the Essex coast. . . . The building is of stone, and is an oblong square. The stabling and other offices attached to it form a handsome semi-crescent. In the construction of this part of the establishment, much judgement and good taste has been evinced, by making it a terrace, instead of allowing it to take the usual appearance of a mews. . . . What would otherwise be an unpleasing sight, is here converted into an object of attraction. The whole of the interior is admirably adapted to personal convenience and comfort. By means of various staircases, part of the hotel may be cut from the rest, so that a portion of it may be used as a separate family residence, with all the necessary accommodation for domestics; an object to be desired by those who wish the advantages of an hotel without its publicity.

LORD NELSON INN (The) is situated at the corner of New Road, and Windmill-street, opposite the High-street. Here most of the coaches call and exchange horses, alternately with the opposite Inn, 'The Prince of Orange'. Considerable posting business is done from this house; the accommodations are good and reasonable, and the situation very convenient for commercial travellers, being in the centre of the town.

WINDMILL INN. – From the rear there is a fine view. The house is much frequented by the admirers of archery, . . . bows, arrows, etc., being supplied in abundance, and at a moderate charge. Refreshments ditto.

THE OLD PRINCE OF ORANGE is a house of public entertainment at the foot of Windmill Hill, . . . celebrated far and near for its general amusements, excellent malt liquors, etc. The grounds are laid out for archery, trap-bat, etc. While some are amusing themselves at these games, others practise pigeon-shooting, and generally, after a long trial, manage to wing one bird out of fifty!

20. *The seaside lodging house.*

The largest slice of seaside property development concerned the provision of lodgings, but the business of the lodging house took time to evolve. In the early years of sea bathing once the local inns were occupied, there were only the fishermen's or small traders' cottages to fall back on. The tally of residential accommodation will probably never be known, since all sorts of people, besides hotels, inns, boarding establishments and lodging house keepers, offered accommodation to summer visitors. This was certainly the case in Herne Bay during the 1830s.

(a) [By a Lady, *A Picture of the New Town of Herne Bay*, 1835, 11]

The streets of Herne Bay are numerous, and contain shops furnished with every kind of provisions . . . Drapers, tailors, milliners, dressmakers, hatters, shoemakers, hairdressers, etc. Most of these let the upper parts of their houses, the neatness and cleanliness of which are truly remarkable.

With the passage of time it became much more common to rent houses or rooms, than to stay in hotels or boarding houses. Inn or hotel occupancy for the most part became temporary while alternative lodgings were sought. The majority of visitors chose to reside with a lodging house keeper, or occupied spare rooms or floors of a tradesman's house or business premises. A large and wealthy family would rent a single property, without a resident owner or keeper on the premises. Many families did not require the catering and other services of hotels. Their domestic servants were brought down to look after the domestic arrangements of lodgings and, no doubt, the change of air and scenery benefited their health and well being. Demands for complete lodging houses or for several floors could only be satisfied by a tremendous physical expansion. As the lodging house became, and remained, the most predominant and popular form of residential seaside accommodation, so fewer holidaymakers, as a proportion of the total number of visitors staying in Thanet and elsewhere, chose subsequently to reside in inns, taverns, hotels or boarding houses. Thus, well before 1815, the lodging house became the dominant architectural feature of a developing seaside urban landscape. The need to accommodate large and wealthy families plus servants explains the height and appearance of many Georgian residential properties in Margate, Ramsgate, Dover and elsewhere. They followed the pattern of Bloomsbury, having kitchens and work-places in the basement, ground and first floors for everyday living and entertaining, one or two floors of bedrooms, with the very top floor containing servants' rooms. Advertised for letting during May 1806 was a substantial Margate property which could accommodate either a large family with servants, or two families, each having access to a kitchen, a parlour, a drawing room and three bedrooms.

(b) [*The Times*, 24 May 1806]

MARGATE. – The WHOLE, or PART of a HOUSE to be LET, elegantly furnished, situated in the pleasantest part of High-street, with a double entrance, and commanding an extensive and beautiful view of the sea. It contains 2 kitchens, 2 parlours and 2 drawing rooms; 3 bedrooms on the second floor, and 3 on the attic. Apply to Mr Beck, Sadler, Oxford-street, near Portman-street.

Accommodation was secured in a variety of ways. Lodgings were secured in advance either by post or through the agency of bathing-room proprietors (see Docs. 29e, g; 32a, c), circulating libraries, London taverns, or City and West End tradesmen, as noted above. Having successfully moved his library into Margate's fashionable Cecil Square, Samuel Silver announced through *The Kentish Gazette*, 26 – 29 May 1773, that he had opened 'at his Circulating Library . . . a Register Office for Lodgings', which he continued to advertise in *ibid.*, 25–28 May 1774. Not all visitors, however, sought or found accommodation in advance. Some preferred to undertake initial inspections, so that they might be satisfied as to location, size, facilities and rent. Such was the advice profferred with very good reason in 1797.

(c)   [*The Margate and Ramsgate Guide in Letters to a Friend*, 1797, 5–6, 8, 24]

I take the first opportunity to inform [you] of my safe arrival at the Fountain Tavern, in King-street [Margate], about half after *eight*, yesterday morning. The reason for travelling in the *night*-coach*, . . . [is] because I have the whole day before me to look for lodgings in, and avoid, by this method, the necessity of lying at an inn, which I never am very fond of, and seldom do if I can possibly help it.

*Travelling by night in the summer, at the full of the moon, is doubtless pleasant, but better for *gentlemen* than ladies.

After breakfast I went to see an apartment in Fort-square, recommended to me by an intimate friend, and got settled in it by tea-time; from whence I have a prospect of the Parade in the front, and the sea, from my back chamber . . . Having little or no sleep in the coach, and the fatigue naturally attending travelling, . . . made me . . . wish to get to bed as soon as possible; this I accomplished about ten o'clock, after eating a light supper, and drinking your health in a glass of good red port, from *Pope's* wine-vaults in the High-street, from whom I always order my wine, as he is a civil honest man, and sells as good, and as reasonable as any other person in the place.+

+*Mitchener* and *Benson*, at their different hotels, and Mr *Hall*, the Postmaster, in Church-field, each of them keep wine-vaults, and sell very good commodities, but little by the *single* bottle, in which way many persons are obliged to have it; as they have no cellars or conveniences in some of the lodgings, for a larger quantity at a time than *three* or *four* bottles . . .

A view of the sea is what most persons wish for here; but those lodgings which have such a view are always let first, and are the dearest; one guinea per week for a parlour, chamber, and the use of a kitchen near the sea, is counted reasonable; many of the inhabitants make it a constant rule to raise the price of their lodgings in the height of the season, during *July* and *August*; and, if the town is nearly full at that time, some persons will not let their lodgings for less than a month certain; so that a family or single person coming here in the season, are obliged to pay for a *month's* lodging, though they may stay but a *week* or *two* . . .

Here, as well as at most public watering-places, the inhabitants in general have learnt the art of charging exorbitantly for *lodgings*, *provisions*, etc. They know the season lasts but a few months, and therefore they make the company pay handsomely for their accommodations, which in many houses about the town are but indifferent; this may at first sight appear good policy, but if they continue so doing, I am apprehensive, in a few years, they will do more hurt to the town than they are at present aware of; and other bathing towns, not far distant, may reap the benefit of it.

The resorts nearby included, of course, Broadstairs and Ramsgate. *The Observer* reported on houses being taken in various places during August 1797.

(d)   [13 August 1797]

The Duke of Clarence has taken a house for the bathing season at Dover, where he arrived on the 8th.

(e)   [13 August 1797]

Mrs Fitzherbert [privately married to the Prince of Wales, later George IV] has taken a house in Albion Place, Ramsgate, where at present she resides.

(f)   [27 August 1797]

The Lord Chancellor has taken the house at Kingsgate, formerly Lord Holland's [see Docs. 38b, c, d, f). The Lord Chancellor, who sailed from London in the Trinity yacht, arrived on Monday at Kingsgate.

Of Deal it was noted in 1776.

(g)   [Chales Seymour, *A New Topographical, Historical and Commercial Survey of the Cities, Towns, and Villages, of the County of Kent*, Canterbury, 1776, 282]

An Apartment towards the Sea has been of late years modernized. It is intended for the accommodation of the Rt. Hon. Francis Marquis of Carmathen . . . during the bathing season.

> Disgruntled visitors complained of the shortage, quality and price of lodgings. One Northamptonshire country gentleman on a visit to Margate in 1796 took the first lodgings which he happened to find vacant and then rued that decision.

(h)   [Henry Homelove, 'On Watering Places', *The Annual Register*, 1796, 479–80, 481, 482–3]

The chief gratification proposed [from our visit] was an entire freedom from care . . . We should find everything requisite in our lodgings . . . It was not until after we had taken them, that we discovered how far ready furnished lodgings were from affording every article in the catalogue of necessaries. We did not indeed give them a very scrupulous examination, for the place was so full . . . We eagerly engaged the first lodgings we found vacant, and have ever since been disputing about the terms, which from the hurry were not sufficiently ascertained . . . We are continually lamenting that we were obliged to buy things of which we have such plenty at home . . .

The spirit of greediness and rapacity is nowhere so conspicuous as in the lodging-houses . . . In this manner, sir, has the season past away. I spend a great deal of money . . . I am cooped up in less room than my own dog kennel, while my spacious halls are injured by standing empty . . . As to the great ostensible object of our excursion, health, I am afraid we cannot boast of much improvement. We have had a wet and cold summer; and these houses, which are either old tenements vamped up, or new ones slightly run up for the accommodation of bathers during the season, have more contrivances for letting in the cooling breezes than for keeping them out, . . . apartments which, during the winter, have only been inhabited by the rats, and where the poverty of the landlord prevents him from laying out more in repairs than will serve to give them a showy and attractive appearance . . .

I am told by the good company here, that I have stayed too long in the same air, and that now I ought to take a trip to the Continent, and spend the winter at Nice, which would complete the business. I am entirely of their opinion, that it would complete the business.

> Joseph Farington, R.A. (1747–1821) found lodgings to his satisfaction when he visited Broadstairs in 1804 (Illus. 5d).

(i)   [Ed: J. Grieg, *The Farington Dairy*, II, 1923, 271]

August 2–

. . . We arrived at ½ past 2, and found John Offley [wine merchant] and his wife and Miss Glover [her sister] agreeably lodged at Barfield's Library for four guineas a week. – We dined with them and lodged near them [probably in the Albion Hotel facing the sea].

August 3–

Passed the day with our friends, and in walking and reading. We took lodgings a little removed from the Sea side, two minutes walk from Barfield's Library – at Mrs Redmans, a small neat House, for which Wm. Offley and I agreed to pay two guineas a week for three weeks, – and she undertook to make our beds, etc. Linen we agreed to Hire.

> The practice of taking houses or rooms which grew out of the eighteenth century was sustained during the nineteenth century, as the most common form of seaside accommodation.

(j)   [*The Maidstone Journal and Kentish Advertiser*, 16 September 1817]

Albion House, formerly the residence of James Simmons Esq. and lately of Lord Edward Bentinck, in Albion Place, Ramsgate [Illus. 11b, 15b], is engaged for a month, for the reception of the family of the Archbishop of Canterbury.

(k)   [Ed: E.H. Coleridge, *Letters of Samuel Taylor Coleridge*, II, 1895, 721–2]

Mrs Gillman has been determined by your letter, and the heavenly weather, and moral certainty of the continuance of *bathing* weather at least, to accept her sister's offer of coming into Ramsgate and to take a house, for a fortnight certain, at a guinea a week, in the buildings next to Wellington Crescent and having a certain modicum and segment of sea peep.

Two personal diaires of the 1820s provide insights into the taking, quality and domestic arrangements of lodgings in Margate, circa 1828, and in Ramsgate, in 1829.

(1) [*MS Diary of Mary Figgins, 30 August – 21 September circa 1828*, Margate Public Library, Local Collection, Y060. 41]

August 30.
. . . We [Rose and I] had a very pleasant voyage and we landed at the pier at ¼ past 4 where Vincent was waiting to receive us. We then proceeded to our lodgings in Union Crescent at the back of Hawley Square [Illus. 15a], had our tea, unpacked and went to bed at ten.

August 31.
Got up at 8. After breakfast we went to market and laid in a store . . . In the evening after supper we had a game at whist with a dummy and retired to bed at 11.

September 2.
. . . In the morning I went with Vincent first to market . . .

September 3.
Up at 8. We all went to market . . .

September 5.
We were down by ½ past 7 as Vincent was going to town by the 9 o'clock packet . . . Vincent before he went agreed to take the lodgings for a month. They are in a large house at the back of the town. We are very well waited upon and we are very comfortable with the exception of one thing, namely, the person at whose house we are lodging is a music master and whenever he is in he is what Vincent calls tormenting his violin. Mr Wilson [our fellow lodger, an old school fellow of Vincent's] likewise plays so that between the two we have scraping nearly all day. In the afternoon it rained . . . We had Mrs Wilson's baby in for about an hour . . .

Further visits to Margate's market, dating from 1777, occurred on 8, 10, 13, 15, 16, 17 and 20 September. The existence of markets and shops was vital to the provisioning of lodging houses and of Margate it was noted in 1831 by G.W. Bonner's *Picturesque Pocket*

Companion to Margate, Ramsgate, Broadstairs, and the Parts Adjacent (page 64) that 'in 1777 Francis Cobb and John Baker obtained a grant or patent, empowering the inhabitants to hold a market on Wednesdays and Saturdays, but it is now generally open daily, for the sale of fish, vegetables and fruit'. Moreover, 'in 1820 the old market was pulled down, and the present very convenient one, with the new hall, . . . erected at an expense of £4,000, . . . and perhaps there are very few markets in the kingdom better supplied with both the necessaries and luxuries of life'. Ramsgate too had a market which features prominently in the next extract.

(m) [*MS Journal of an Excursion to Ramsgate in July and August 1829*, Tyler Collection (Ramsgate Scrapbrook), Cathedral Library and Archives, Canterbury]

Monday, July 20.
. . . Found our old lodgings engaged [referring to a previous visit in 1826], therefore took a sitting room and 2 bedrooms at Mr Cullen's in Hertford Place which place was erected in 1813 . . . After having given my friend Hunt of Burgess's Library a call and taken some refreshment we retired to rest greatly fatigued by the day's exertion [the downward journey in the Magnet steamboat described in Doc. 12].

Tuesday, July 21.
. . . After Breakfast [Mine was the Yolks of 2 Eggs mixed in a Pint of milk and Tea] walked with Charlotte to Market . . . Dinner at 2 o'clock consisted of roasted Lamb, Peas and Currant and Raspberry Pie . . .

The variety and prices of the provisions which were obtained that day were recorded as follows.

Paid:	£	s.	d.
½ lb. Butter fresh			7½
1 lb. Candles – ½ common ½ Rush Lights			7½
½ lb. Mould Candles			4½
1 lb. Figs			9
Anniseed Cordial for the Child			3
2 lb. Loaf of Bread			5¾
½ Pint of Milk			1½
1 Pint do.			3
5 English Eggs			6

Paid:	£	s.	d.
¾ lb. of Lard for Pie and Pudding Crust @ 10d lb.			7½
4 lbs. Flour			10¾
1 Pint of Porter (Mrs. Benham) [Charlotte]			3
Baking Pie			1
2 lb. Loaf of Bread			5¾
½ Peck of Peas (Prussian Blues)			4
1 lb. Black Currants			2½
½ Gallon of Potatoes			3
1 Leaf of Raspberries			2½
2 lb. red Currants			4
Cake of Brown Bread			2
1 lb. Brown Sugar			7
Salt and Pepper			3
Gooseberries ripe			1
3¾ lbs. Ribs of Lamb @ 9d. per lb.		2	10

11s. 6¾d.

Wednesday, July 22.

. . . After [breakfast] went with Mrs B— to market . . . At ½ past 12 to 1 called on my friend Hunt and bought red ink, pencil and rubber. At 2 returned to dinner which was Soles fried and Cold Lamb and potatoes and currant and raspberry Pie.

> On this second day of their holiday 1s. was paid for '1 pair of Soles', with the overall cost of dinner being reduced by using the cold left-overs of the day before, which suggests a careful attention to the details of household management.

Friday, July 24.

. . . Walked to market with Charlotte about one hour . . . For dinner shoulder of Lamb, potatoes and blackcurrant pie [the Shoulder of Lamb 4 lbs. 14 oz. at 9d. per lb. costing 3s. 8d.]

Saturday, July 25.

After breakfast went to Market with Charlotte and walked for about an hour. This being Market day we had an opportunity of observing its extent. It has 3 divisions – Meat – Vegetables – Fish – and these were well stocked with every common thing in season . . . Dinner at 2 . . . consisted of Lamb Pie and blackcurrent pie [Baking 2 Pies, 2d]

The Benhams during their stay in Ramsgate took advantage both of the soft fruit season and of the custom of having pies baked locally for a penny apiece. Apart from one other visit to the market on 1 August, unrecorded visits by their servant and nursery maid, Betsy Thornton, occurred no doubt on other days. The quality of some of the goods purchased were also commented upon, such as 10d. spent on a pound of white sugar which was 'very indifferent', on 23 July, as against 4½d. for a '2 lbs. Brown Loaf from the Calais Cottage – very good', on 3 August, or 6d. for a half peck 'of very fine peas', on 8 August. The total cost of accommodation in a lodging house comprised two major items, rent and food and drink. Rent for the sitting room and two bedrooms, respectively for Mr and Mrs Benham and for their infant child and Betsy Thornton, was paid at weekly intervals as follows.

	£	s.	d.
Monday, July 27.			
One Week's Lodging	1	11	6
Monday, August 3.			
Week's Lodging	1	11	6
Sunday, August 9.			
For the Week's Lodging	1	11	6
A Broken Tumbler Glass		1	2
Attendance during the 3 Weeks Miss C., 7s. 2d., Girl, 1s. 6d.		8	8
	£5	4s.	4d.

By the time Mr Benham had returned to London on Monday, 10 August 1829, his three-week holiday to Ramsgate had cost £21.10s. 0¾d., of which 24%, or £5. 4s. 4d., had been spent on basic lodging, plus attendance during their stay and making good the cost of a broken tumbler glass. Miss C. mentioned above was possibly Miss Cullen, the daughter of Mr. Cullen, who owned or occupied the house in Hertford Place where the Benhams stayed.

Food and drink, as the second major item of accommodation expenditure, had absorbed £4 16s. 0¾d, or just over 22% of the total holiday outlay, broken down as follows:

	£	s.	d.
Meat	1	6	5½
Bread and Flour		12	11¾
Butter and Eggs		9	3
Fruit		8	10½
Milk		8	1½
Fish		7	5
Beer and Porter		6	3
Vegetables		3	11½
1 Bottle of Sherry Wine		2	6
Salt, Sugar, Coffee, Lard, etc.		10	3
	£4	16s.	0¾d

The Benhams enjoyed obviously a varied diet during their holiday, involving a high animal protein content, with meat forming the largest single item of expenditure, accounting for 27% of the total food bill, while total expenditure on bread and flour did not greatly exceed that on butter and eggs, or fruit, or milk. The total cost of accommodation in Ramsgate for this family, embracing rent, food and drink, candle lighting at 2s. 4½d. and having clothes washed at 8s. 2d. amounted to £10 10s. 11¼d., or just over 48% of the total outlay. Assuming two adults in a boarding house at two guineas a week for three weeks would have cost twelve guineas, without even allowing for the infant or the domestic servant in this case. Thus, a family could save on expenditure by taking furnished lodgings and providing their own food, compared to the cost of hotel or boarding-house accommodation. Mr Benham through having recorded the smallest items of daily expenditure right down to the cleaning of shoes between 20 July and 10 August 1829, has left behind him a unique document on how a pre-Victorian holiday was spent and how much it cost. Readers interested in this holiday in its entirety are referred to John Whyman, 'A Three-Week Holiday in Ramsgate during July and August 1829', *Archaeologia Cantiana*, XCVI, 1980, 185–225.

By the 1830s the habit of spending holidays away from home in seaside lodging houses commanded widespread support, as the next two extracts show.

(n) ['Amusements at Margate', *Chambers's Edinburgh Journal*, 1833, 155]

The place [enjoys] the visits of nearly 100,000 persons in the course of a season. Families, respectable in every sense of the term, . . . have houses or lodgings in the squares, or best parts of the town . . . They [include] the affluent merchants and tradesmen of the metropolis . . . Another description of persons rent houses or lodgings, less expensive, and regulate their establishments on principles of economy and respectability . . . These are select in their intimacies, enjoying all the amusements of the place unostentatiously.

(o) [*Picture of Ramsgate, or a Guide to the Various Amusements, Public Libraries, Building Improvements, etc., of that celebrated Watering Place*, Ramsgate, 1833, 16–17]

Persons having families usually prefer furnished lodgings, of these there are great variety, but the best way to procure them is by means of some friend residing at Ramsgate, who has leisure and opportunity to select the best situation and the most convenient houses, which are not always to be got in the season at short notice; if this cannot be done, it will be advisable to go to an Inn for a day or two, which will enable the Visitor to gratify his taste, both as to situation and comfort, by a personal inspection. The lodgings on Wellington and Royal Crescent, the former on the Eastern and the latter on the Western Cliff [Illus. 15b], are the most expensive; whole houses let at from eight to five guineas a week, and upwards, according to the number of beds and other conveniences found; lodgings, consisting of a sitting room and two or three bedrooms, from two to three and four guineas per week. In parts of the town having no sea view they are proportionately cheaper; but no rooms, possessing any respectable appearance or comfort, can be had in any part of the town at less than two guineas per week.

A personal experience which confirmed the previous account dates from 1844.

(p) [*MS Journal compiled by S. Daniele in 1844*, KAO, U2666 F1]

About noon we reached Ramsgate and as soon as possible turned out in quest of Lodgings. This was found no easy matter, the town being very full and those commanding a sea view exceedingly expensive. After walking about for five hours we at last found some that suited us exactly, commanding an entire view of the Harbour. We were quite exhausted as it was a very sultry day. So after arranging ourselves in our new abode staid quietly at home the rest of the evening.

Since 1801 there have been three summer censuses, 30 May 1831, 7 June 1841 and 20 June 1921. The 1921 census is closed to public inspection, and the 1831 census is lacking in useful occupational data. Although not asked specifically to do so, the Margate enumerators of 1841 identified visitors staying in the resort by entering against their names a bracket, tick, cross or small 'v' or 'L'. The Enumerators' Schedules for Margate confirm an important feature of Victorian holidaymaking, namely that few holidaymakers chose to stay in hotels or boarding houses. Most visitors rented complete lodging houses, resided with lodging-house keepers, or occupied spare rooms of floors of tradesmen's houses or business premises. Extracted from the Census Enumerators' Schedules are some examples of lodgings occupancy in Margate over the census night of 7 June 1841 (also see Illus. 15a).

(q) [P.R.O., H.O. 107/468/2, 107/468/3]

Location Within Margate	Houses	Names	Age & Sex		Profession, Trade, Employment, Independent Means	Where Born. Y for Kent or No
			M	F		
High	1	James Gostling	30		Draper	No
Street		Sarah do.		30		Y
		Louise do.		1		Y
		Mary Moyan		30	Female Servant	Y
		Hannah do.		15	Female Servant	Y
		Richard Kingsford	20		Shopman	Y
		(Lewis Ling	50		Independent)	No
		(Lewes do.	25		Independent)	No
	Lodgers	(Walter do.	20		Independent) . . .	No. *Visitors*
		(Eliza do.		20	)	No
		(Harriet do.		15	)	No

Location Within Margate	Houses	Names	Age & Sex M	F	Profession, Trade, Employment, Independent Means	Where Born. Y for Kent or No
Parade	1	Ann Trike		60	Lodging House Keeper	Y
		Ann do.		20		No
		Mary Sacket		19	Female Servant	Y
		William Cummins	50		)	No
		Sarah do.		45	) Visitors	No
		Mary McGora		25	)	No
Vicarage	1	Mary Stewart		55	Lets Lodgings	No
Terrace		Hannah do.		25		No
	L	James Wood	20		Independent	No
Vicarage	1	Simon Sullivan	40		Stone Sawyer	Y
Place		Harriet do.		40		No
		Sarah do.		15	Clerk	Y
	L	Henry Mitten	25		Clerk	No
	L	Marie do.		20		No
	L	Henry do.	3			No
	L	Benjamin Adams	35		Clerk	No
	L	Ann do.		35		Y
Broad	1	Ann Busden		40	Staymaker	Y
Street		Ann do.		20	Staymaker	Y
		Sarah Burtinshaw		10		Y
		V Ann Worley		55	Independent	No
		V Ann do.		25		No
		V Daniel do.	20		Independent	No
Bridge	1	Thomas Scott	41		Grocer	Y
Street		Elizabeth do.		33		Y
		Stephen do.	12			Y
		Eliza do.		10		Y
		William do.	7			Y
		Elizabeth do.		4		Y
		Thomas do.	6			Y
		Joanna do.		2		Y
		Elizabeth Cook		20	Female Servant	Y
		V J.R. Rucktro	34		Independent	No
		V Sarah Mitin		74	Independent	No
		V Thomas Rucktro	6			No
		V Sarah Colman		20	Independent	No
		V B. Brooks	50		Independent	No
		V L. Brooks		50	Independent	No

Location Within Margate	Houses	Names	Age & Sex M	F	Profession, Trade, Employment, Independent Means	Where Born. Y for Kent or No
		V L. Brooks		18	Independent	No
do.	1	Richard Deveson	46		Coachmaster	Y
		Theresa do		45		No
		Mary Norris		19	Female Servant	Y
		V William Johnson	29		Lawyer	No
		V Mary do.		24		Y
		V Percy Dunshill	28		Independent	No
		V Mary do.		20		No
		V William Watson	69		Independent	Scotland
		V E. do.		68		Y
		V John Smith	50		Innkeeper	Y
		V Mary do.		22		Y
Buenos Ayres	1	V Sarah Read		35	Independent	No
		V Sarah do.		15		No
		V Helen do.		10		No
		V Margaret do.		10		No
		V William do.	5			No
		V Francis do.	4			No
		V Thomas do.	2			No
		V Sophia Hayes		35	Female Servant	No

Lodgings accommodation was scattered all over Margate by the 1840s; likewise in Gravesend.

(r) [*The Visitor's Guide to the Watering Places*, 1842, 17–18]

The inhabitants have, with a view to profit in letting apartments, etc., lately caused to be erected a number of pretty dwelling-houses. These are not confined to any particular spot, but may be found scattered in every direction of the town; so that the visitor may choose his own situation without loss of time, and study his convenience with regard to expense. Apartments may be hired at a very reasonable rate, either for a shorter or a longer time. Houses, also, may be engaged at a moderate rent.

Dover suffered from a deficiency of good lodgings during the 1800s.

(s) [*A Guide to all the Watering and Sea-Bathing Places*, 1806, 214]

It must be confessed that there are few elegant lodgings, or even handsome houses, in *Dover*.

> Following the conclusion of the Napoleonic Wars this situation changed somewhat.

(t) [*Horn's Description of Dover*, Dover, 1817, 23]

It is in contemplation to build a line of handsome houses upon the upper rope walk commencing at the parade, which would add greatly to the accommodation of families visiting this romantic and most delightfully situated sea port.

(u) [W. Batcheller, *A New History of Dover to which is added a New Dover Guide*, Dover, 1828, 348]

At the time of the last census, in 1821, the population of Dover, including the divisions of Charlton and Hougham, amounted to 11,468. Since that period, many elegant lodging houses and private dwellings have been erected, and the number of residents, has very much increased.

(v) [*Pigot and Co's Royal, National and Commercial Directory*, 1840, 281]

Within the last ten or twelve years the town has been very much improved, and enlarged, by the addition of upwards of one hundred handsome dwelling-houses, chiefly fronting the sea, all of which are excellently fitted up and tastefully furnished for visitors.

> Within twenty five years Dover had witnessed building expansion in the following areas of the town: Marine Parade, Liverpool Terrace, under the East Cliff, Guilford and Clarence Lawns, the Esplanade, and Waterloo and Camden Crescents, and during the 1840s further extensive building projects attracted the attention of the national press.

(w) [*The Times*, 26 March 1844]

We understand that the Earl of Guilford, the noble proprietor of the Frith Farm, near [Dover] Castle, is about to apply to Parliament for a private act to enable him to let a portion of the valley on lease for building purposes; and that plans for the erection of splendid terraces, said to be equal in design and magnitude to any in the kingdom, have been prepared, as also for detached villas; altogether nearly 1,500 residences are contemplated to be formed on this delightful spot . . . It will prove a good speculation.

> Folkestone lagged most of all in the provision of residential accommodation prior to the opening of the South Eastern Railway in 1843.

(x) [*A Guide to all the Watering and Sea-Bathing Places*, 1810, 242–3]

On the heights at the entrance of the town from Sandgate, the ground is laid out for a handsome row of houses; and as the company of late years has been more numerous, there is little doubt the accommodations will increase, and that Folkestone will become a distinguished watering-place.

(y) [*Pigot and Co's Royal, National and Commercial Directory*, 1840, 293]

As yet there is a lack of lodging-houses as compared with the demand, but great facility is afforded for the erection of new ones. A large extent of land, most eligibly situate, has been laid out by the Earl of Radnor for building purposes; and there are few places, it is presumed, that would better repay a well-directed building speculation.

> Compared to Folkestone the provision of lodging houses was much more pronounced in Sandgate.

(z) [*A Guide to all the Watering and Sea-Bathing Places*, 1806, 229]

THIS is a pretty little village, exactly half way between *Folkestone* and Hythe, and which has suddenly started into notice . . . Lodgings may be obtained here on reasonable terms: and of late there have been erected some very good houses.

(aa) [*A Guide to all the Watering and Sea-Bathing Places*, 1815, 423]

Nearly one hundred houses are appropriated as lodging-houses in the season.

(bb) [*The Hythe, Sandgate and Folkestone Guide*, Hythe, 1816, 28]

The houses though in general small, are commodious, and remarkably clean, light and cheerful. The greater number of them have been erected within the compass of a few years, for the reception of visitors who resort hither for the purpose of sea-bathing.

Hythe was subject to conflicting assessments concerning the rented accommodation which it could offer to visitors.

(cc) [*A Guide to all the Watering and Sea-Bathing Places*, 1806, 230 and 1819, 32]

The lodgings here are not the most commodious.

The lodgings are not numerous.

(dd) [*The Hythe, Sandgate and Folkestone Guide*, Hythe, 1816, 8]

There are many pleasant houses upon ledges of the cliff, above the town, which command delightful and extensive views both of the sea and the neighbouring country, as also numerous convenient habitations appropriated to the use of strangers during the bathing season, and others usually occupied by the families of officers of rank in the army stationed here, who greatly contribute to enliven and improve the society constantly to be met with at Hythe.

21. *The occupancy and income of one Margate lodging house, 1778–1796.* [KAO, *Cobb MSS.*, U1453 A2]

In the previous document there are references suggesting that the cost of lodgings rose during the height of the season and that accommodation could be taken over short or long intervals of time. These two points are very well illustrated in this particular document which exists in the Cobb MSS and details William Stone's lodgings lettings during each of the years falling between 1778 and 1796. William Stone retired from business in January 1777 possessed of the following assets:

	£	s.
Dwelling house	714	14
Loan to Cobb	500	
Cash	1,187	
	£2,401	14s

Included among his papers are 'An Acct. of the Purchis of my New

Dwelling and Additions made to the same in the Year 1777', and
'Lodgings Let to Sundry Persons', 1778–1796. William Stone saw
that a retirement income could result from letting lodgings during
the summer months. In 1777 he purchased a house for £200 and
paid £19 to 'J^{no} Fagg by Bill for Conveyance'. The purchase of the
property and its conversion into a lodging house absorbed
£645.9s.11d. The largest bills were £193.7s.6d. paid to Orpin, a
carpenter; £87.0s.7d. to Bayley, a bricklayer; £27.9s.7d. to Stone,
a plumber; £16.2s. to Wilds, another bricklayer; £20 to Friend for
bricks; and £16.10s. for making a vault. The work of conversion,
which put money into various hands, involved expenditure on
bricks, timber, paper, £3.15s. on Newcastle stone, and cartage;
and among the tradesmen called in were bricklayers, carpenters,
plumbers, a stonemason, and blacksmiths. At least fifteen different
names were involved in the work.

The house became ready for letting during 1778, and produced during that season £37.16s. for 18 weeks rent between 13
June and 18 October, from a Mr. William Franks at 42s. per
week. Thereafter the lodgings entries read as follows:

Year	Occupant	Period	No. of Weeks	Rent per W.
1779	Wm. Barber	7 June–5 July	4	42s.
	Wm. Martindale	9 July–16 August	7	52s.
	Mrs. Patterson	16 August–30 Sept.	4	63s.
			10 days	6s. per day
	John Southerby	3–29 October	4	31s.6d.
1780	Wm. Franks	5–24 May	3	31s.6d.
	Leonard Ellington	1–21 July	3	42s.
	Ann Wilton	22 July–10 Nov.	16	52s.6d.
1781	Richard Halford	17 June–21 July	5	39s.9d.
	Contis, De, Salis	23 July–7 Oct.	11	52s.6d.
	Robert Dormer	8 Oct–5 Nov.	4	31s.6d.
1782	Charles Hoskins			
	Masters	18 April–30 May	6	21s.
			2	31s.6d.
	Jno. Gutteridg	22 June–31 August	6	42s.
			4	52s.6d.
	Geo. Brewster	31 Aug–6 Oct.	5	63s.
	Charleton Palmer	6–28 October	3	31s.6d.
	Geo. Dempster	1–22 November	3	31s.6d.
1783	Rev. Leath Hoskins Masters	13 Feb–4 June	14	21s.
			2	31s.6d.
	Wm. Legayt	15 June–27 July	2	42s.
			4	52s.6d.

Year	Occupant	Period	No. of Weeks	Rent per Week
	Mrs. Montrap	28 July–18 August	3	63s.
	Charles Carter	18 August–14 Sept.	4	63s.
			1	52s.6d.
	Mr. Silvester	22 Sept–20 Oct.	4	52s.6d.
	Rev. Mr. Barrett	24 Oct–20 Nov.	4	26s.3d.
1784	Rev.Leath Hoskins Masters	13 April–3 June	7	21s.
	Wm. Pitt Esq.	5 June–30 Oct.	3	42s.
			4	52s.6d.
			11	63s.
			3	42s.
1785	R.C. Bricay (?)	31 May–12 July	6	42s.
	Mrs. Seliar Scott	?	?	11 gns.
	Robt. Baxter Esq	2 Aug–17 Oct.	11	63s.
	Miss Lewis	19 Oct–15 Nov.	4	21s.
1786	Jer. Watson Esq	2 June–26 Aug.	12	52s.6d.
	Peter Cazelet Esq	26 Aug–31 Oct.	4	$3\frac{1}{2}$ gns.
			4	3 gns.
			1	$1\frac{1}{2}$ gns.
1787	Taylor Esq	23 May–5 June	2+2 days	2 gns.
	Mr. Leyget	16 June–28 July	2	2 gns.
			4	$2\frac{1}{2}$ gns.
	Mrs. Woodamson	30 July–27 Aug.	4	3 gns.
	Henry Gardner Esq	27 Aug–8 Oct.	6	$3\frac{1}{2}$ gns.
	Smith Esq.	7–17 October	$1\frac{1}{2}$	2 gns.
1788	Mrs. Sharp	13 March–? June	12	£11.11s.6d.
			2	31s.6d.
	Mr. Thompson	29 June–3 August	4	$2\frac{1}{2}$ gns.
			1	3 gns.
	Mrs. Halghers	4 Aug–6 Oct.	3	3 gns.
			6	$3\frac{1}{2}$ gns.
	Rev.L.H. Masters	6 Oct–3 Nov.	3	31s.6d.
			1	21s.
1789	Mrs. Sharp	2 April–25 July by Agreement	16	£22.1s.
	Mr. Wright	25 July–8 Sept.	4	3 gns.
			2	$3\frac{1}{2}$ gns.
	Mr. Cutler	8 Sept–6 Oct. as per Agreement	4	£15.15s.
	Mr. Dormer	6 Oct–3 Nov.	4	2 gns.
1790	Mr. Fish	17 March–30 Nov. by Agreement		£63
1791	Mrs. Young	1 June–5 Oct.	4	2 gns.
			4	$2\frac{1}{2}$ gns.
			10	$3\frac{1}{2}$ gns.
	Rev. L. Hoskins Masters	7–28 October	3	31s.6d.
1792	Wm. Anderson	1 May–30 July	4	1 gn.
			4	2 gns.

Year	Occupant	Period	No. of Weeks	Rent per Week
			4	2½ gns.
	Thos. Dyke	4 Aug–15 Sept.	6	3½ gns.
	Sir Charles Morton Bowe	16 Sept–14 Oct.	4	3½ gns.
			3 days	18s.
	Rev. John Phillips	19 Oct–29 Nov.	6	1 gn.
1793	Peter Campbell	18 June–19 Aug.	6	2 gns.
			3	3 gns.
	Thos. Dyke	21 Aug–21 Oct.	6	3½ gns.
	Benjamin Horans Esq. Foots Cray Place	10 Oct–7 Nov.	4	1½ gns.
1794	Joseph Foskell Esq.	17–30 May	2	2 gns.
	Wm. Abott Esq	2–30 June	4	2 gns.
	Thos. Dyke Esq	7 July–6 Oct.	3	2½ gns.
			10	3½ gns.
	Geo. Collyer	6 Oct–3 Nov.	4	1½ gns.
1795	Thos. Dyke Esq	1 July–29 Sept.	4	2½ gns.
			9	3½ gns.
	Mr. Simpson	29 Sept–27 Oct.	2	3½ gns.
			2	1½ gns.
	Mr Fish	30 Oct–14 Nov.	2	1½ gns.
1796	Mr. Richardson	27 April–20 July	6	1½ gns.
			3	2 gns.
			3	2½ gns.
	Thos. Dyke Esq	22 July–7 Oct.	1	2½ gns.
			10	3½ gns.
	Mr Simpson	10 Oct–	4	1½ gns.

This record of lettings by one Margate lodging house keeper over the years 1778 to 1796 reveals two points of interest. The rates for letting varied according to the season, except for those periods negotiated by agreement, possibly by post beforehand, thereby confirming the point noted earlier that lodgings cost more at the height of the season. The names of some lodgers appeared over several years, suggesting regular holidays and a preference for staying in one particular resort.

Name of Visitor	Year and Duration of Stay	
William Franks	1778 (18 weeks),	1780 (3 weeks).
Rev. Leath Hoskins Masters	1783 (16 weeks),	1784 (7 weeks),
	1788 (4 weeks),	1791 (3 weeks).
Mrs Sharp	1788 (12 weeks),	1789 (16 weeks).
Mr. Dormer	1781 (4 weeks),	1789 (4 weeks).
Thomas Dyke	1792 (6 weeks),	1793 (6 weeks),

Name of Visitor	Year and Duration of Stay	
	1794 (13 weeks),	*1795* (13 weeks),
	1796 (11 weeks).	
Mr. Simpson	*1795* (4 weeks),	*1796* (4 weeks).
Mr. Fish	*1790* (the entire season), *1795* (2 weeks).	

Mr. Fish in occupying these lodgings by agreement for the entire season of 1790 paid £63 to William Stone. William Pitt paid £57.15s. for a twenty-one week stay in 1784, and Mrs. Young £55.13s. for eighteen weeks during 1791.

For William Stone the letting of his lodging house provided a regular income for nineteen years.

Year	No. of Weeks Let		Amount Realised		
	Weeks	Days	£	s.	d.
1778	18		37	16	0
1779	20	3	48	13	6
1780	22		53	0	6
1781	20		44	7	0
1782	29		57	15	0
1783	38		72	19	6
1784	28		65	2	0
1785	21 +		63	0	0
1786	21		60	7	6
1787	Almost 20		56	14	0
1788	32		65	13	0
1789	30½		67	14	6
1790	Season by agreement		63	0	0
1791	21		60	7	6
1792	28½		67	1	0
1793	19		50	8	0
1794	23		63	10	6
1795	19		57	4	6
1796	27		69	6	0

From this one source of income William Stone derived £1,124, which was not far short of being double the purchase and original outlay on the house at £645.9s.11d. In no year after 1781 did the amount realized fall below £50 annually. Letting lodgings produced a steady retirement income in excess of £1 per week over nineteen years, added to which there was £40 interest per annum on the £500 loaned to the Cobbs, besides the proceeds from other bonds, stock and loans. William Stone spent a comfortable retirement employing two female servants, Ann Crane and Ann Matthews, paying them annually 4gns. each between 1780 and 1798.

22. *The seaside boarding house.*

Although fewer in number and less well patronized than inns, hotels or lodging houses, an earlier document (181) has drawn attention both to the existence of boarding houses and their *raison d'etre* in Margate as early as 1770. An enterprising boarding house proprietor caught the eye of Charles Seymour in 1776.

(a) [C. Seymour, *A New Topographical Historical, and Commercial Survey of the Cities, Towns, and Villages, of the County of Kent*, Canterbury, 1776, 558]

Crow, who keeps a Coffee-House and Bathing Machines, has a convenient neat house, where small families, or single persons, may find a genteel table and decent lodgings, upon easy terms; he is a good natured, civil and obliging man, and takes a delight in making his house agreeable to his guests; he has lately fitted up a Music-Room.

Two years previously the facility of board and lodging was advertised in two national newspapers.

(b) [*The Gazetteer and New Daily Advertiser*, 2 June 1774 and *The Daily Advertiser*, 3 June 1774]

Lodgings and Board, at Margate, in Kent.
A Small Family having taken a large handsome house at Margate, would be glad to accommodate about 4 ladies or gentlemen with lodgings and board if agreeable, on reasonable terms . . . Please to enquire at the Half-moon Tavern, Holborn.

Why single visitors or small families might prefer a boarding house to any other kind of seaside accommodation was made quite clear on at least two occasions during the mid–1790s.

(c) [*A Short Description of the Isle of Thanet; Being Chiefly Intended as a Directory for the Company Resorting to Margate, Ramsgate and Broadstairs*, Margate, 1796, 25–6]

[There are] several good boarding houses, furnished in a modern taste, whose tables are covered in a style of plenty and elegance; at any of which such ladies and gentlemen as may wish to decline the fatigue of an establishment at private lodgings, will find themselves very comfortably and agreeably accommodated.

(d)   [*The Margate and Ramsgate Guide in Letters to a Friend*, 1797, 35–6]

There are several boarding-houses about the town [Margate], for the accommodation of small families or single persons, who having not brought down their own servants (as many do), nor intending to stay here above two or three weeks (it may be), do not think it worth while to lodge and board themselves: The terms for lodging and board at these houses are from £1.11s.6d. to £2.2s. per week:* And there are frequently in the height of the season, near thirty sit down together at each boarding-house.

> *The principal boarding-houses are *Lautier's* and *Rogers's* in Cecil-square; *Mrs Brazier's* opposite to it in the Church-Field; *Humble's*, in the High-street, opposite Surflen's Coffee-room; and *Mrs Eden's*, opposite the post office.

> By 1811, according to *Holden's Annual London and Country Directory*, Margate possessed at least eight boarding houses. Information about them is fairly readily available from newspaper advertisements and guidebooks.

(e)   [*The Times*, 1 July 1807, 13 August 1807]

MARGATE – Mrs. DAVIS begs to inform her Friends and the Public [that] her BOARDING HOUSE, No. 21 Hawley-square, is now open for the reception of Ladies and Gentlemen; its delightful situation, joined with her exertions and attention to the comfort and accommodation of those who honour her with their patronage, will, she trusts, meet with that approbation she is solicitous to obtain. Particulars may be known on enquiry, at No. 23, Red Cross-street, Cripplegate.

> Three years later James Cotterill (or Cotterell) announced that he had taken over Mrs. Brasher's boarding house in Cecil Square, Margate.

(f)   [*The Morning Chronicle*, 13 August 1810]

No expense has been spared in repairing the House, and furnishing it in a style that he flatters himself will be found superior to any in the above line of business. The bed rooms are lofty and airy, with a sea view, which, together with the beds, require only to be inspected to be approved.

This boarding house became famous under the management of the Cotterell family.

(g) [*The New Margate, Ramsgate and Broadstairs Guide*, 6th Ed., Margate, 1816, 69]

Boarding Houses,
Of which there are several well furnished, with good accommodations, and the society in general pleasant and select. Of this description are Surflen's and Cotterell's both situated in Cecil Square; Webb's in Hawley Square; and Mrs. Fleming's in the High-street.

> In 1819, according to *The Thanet Itinerary or Steam Yacht Companion* (page 45), the Cotterells owned or ran one of 'several very respectable private *Boarding Houses*'. Mrs. Mary Pilkington (1766–1839), the authoress of over sixty children's books, confronted during her two months' residence at Margate in the summer of 1812 a female shrimpseller, among whose customers was the Cotterell boarding house.

(h) [Mrs. Pilkington, *Margate!!! or Sketches Amply Descriptive of that Celebrated Place of Resort*, 1813, 108, 113–4, 118–9]

Mrs. P. proposed taking a walk upon the Fort . . . a healthy and inviting promenade. . . . A poor woman approached them with a basket of shrimps, covered with a clean napkin.

> 'Please to buy a few shrimps, ma'am', she said,
> 'for I have not more than a pint and a half left. . . . Every day of my life I walks as far as Pegwell's Bay, and gathers shrimps, greater part of which Mrs. Cotterell, at the great boarding-house, always buys of me. Mrs. Cotterell, God bless her, often gives me a bit of meat.' . . .

'Does Mrs. Cotterell give victual to all those ladies and gentlemen, mamma, who dine there every day?', enquired Fitzmaurice, not comprehending the nature of a boarding-house.

> 'No, my love, for each of those ladies and gentlemen she receives three guineas a week, for which they are furnished with an excellent table, and a separate bed-room; but when a gentleman and his wife are together, under the consideration of their occupying only one sleeping apartment, the terms for board and lodging are reduced to five.'

Information on how many guests a particular property could accommodate occurs infrequently, but one good example relates to a Margate boarding house which was for sale in 1829.

(i) [*The Times*, 2 July 1829]

Commanding, both in situation and the respectability of its connexion, a first-rate business in this much frequented place, established seven years. There are 17 bed chambers, several double bedded . . . The drawing rooms and dining rooms are well planned and spacious; from 40 to 48 persons have been comfortably accommodated at one time during last season. A small premium is expected for the goodwill and 18 years lease at a low rent. Furniture and fixtures to be taken at a valuation and possession without delay. For terms apply at Mr. George Robin's offices Covent-garden.

The domestic and social arrangements of a pre-Victorian boarding house were no different from those of the present century.

(j) ['Amusements at Margate', *Chambers's Edinburgh Journal*, 1833, 155–6]

Ladies ever form a considerable part of boarding-house society . . . In the boarding-house, the meals are announced by jingling a large bell in the passage or hall. At these meetings parties are made [for] a ride to Ferrry Grove [Grove Ferry] – a trip to Pegwell Bay – a sail to the Reculvers – a stroll on the Parade – a walk on the Pier, or on the Jetty. . . .
The charges for board and lodging, where both are good, are about two guineas per week – wine, spirits, or ale, exclusive.

By this time all three Thanet resorts could offer their visitors a choice of boarding houses.

(k) [*Picture of Ramsgate, or A Guide to the Various Amusements, Public Libraries, Building Improvements, etc., of that celebrated Watering Place*, Ramsgate 1833, 17, 50, 61]

RAMSGATE.
Many persons from a principle of economy, or for the pleasure of associating with others, prefer the establishment of a Boarding House, in which comfort and good living are combined, without the care and

inconvenience of housekeeping. There are many houses of this description, varying their prices according to the quality of the table kept, from £2 2s. to £3 3s. a week each person.

Mr. Sackett's, on Rose Hill, is one of the best, and has for many years been established with reputation.

BROADSTAIRS.

Those who from economy or from the pleasures of society prefer the establishment of a Boarding House, are invited to enjoy comfort and good living at Miss Edgar's, No. 1, Chandos Place, the residence of the late Lord Henniker, or Mrs. Blackburne's Flint House, in Harbour Street, both fronting the sea; either of which houses bear high character for respectability and attention. Terms per week in the height of the season are about £2 2s. more or less as the season advances or declines.

MARGATE.

[There are] Boarding Houses, numerous and respectable, from £1 10s. to £2 12s. 6d. per week.

> Mr. Sackett of Ramsgate was highly recommended along with Mrs. Sandford in 1842.

(1) [*The Visitor's Guide to the Watering Places*, 1842, 178]

There are two excellent boarding-houses in Ramsgate, one occupying the extensive rooms over Messrs. Sackett and Fuller's Library on Sion Hill, under the direction of the proprietor, Mr. Sackett, furnished in modern taste, and whose table is covered in a style of elegance, and so plentifully supplied, as to afford the utmost satisfaction to the numerous visitors who frequent this old establishment; the other is kept by Mrs. Sandford, No. 15, Wellington-crescent, and also possesses every accommodation for those who prefer a boarding-house to the retirement and fatigue of an establishment of their own.

> Herne Bay's boarding house terms were lower than those of Thanet, at least in one instance, judging from the following advertisement which was placed in 1845.

(m) [*The Times*, 9 July 1845]

At this delightful and improved watering place ladies or gentlemen may be comfortably accommodated with BOARD and LODGING for 25s. per week. Address to Mr. Tupper, Herne Bay.

(a) A view of Broadstairs, 1796.
(b) A view of Deal, c. 1800.

Illus. 7

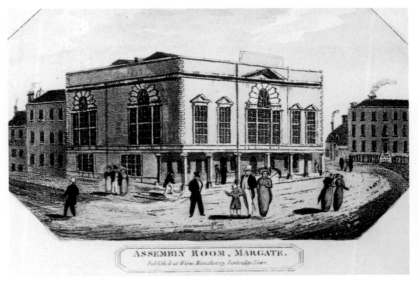

ASSEMBLY ROOM, MARGATE.

The exterior and interior of the Margate assembly rooms in c. 1800.

Illus. 8

138

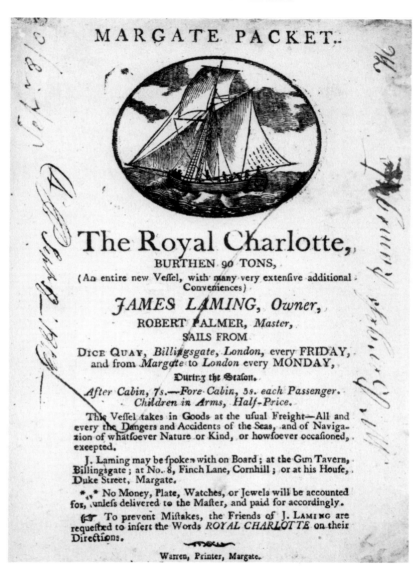

MARGATE PACKET.

The Royal Charlotte,

BURTHEN 90 TONS,

(An entire new Vessel, with many very extensive additional Conveniences)

JAMES LAMING, Owner,

ROBERT PALMER, *Master,*

SAILS FROM

DICE QUAY, *Billingsgate, London,* every FRIDAY, and from *Margate* to *London* every MONDAY,

During the Season.

After Cabin, 7s.—Fore Cabin, 5s. each Passenger.
Children in Arms, Half-Price.

This Vessel takes in Goods at the usual Freight—All and every the Dangers and Accidents of the Seas, and of Navigation of whatsoever Nature or Kind, or howsoever occasioned, excepted.

J. Laming may be spoken with on Board; at the Gun Tavern, Billingsgate; at No. 8, Finch Lane, Cornhill; or at his House, Duke Street, Margate.

*** No Money, Plate, Watches, or Jewels will be accounted for, unless delivered to the Master, and paid for accordingly.

☞ To prevent Mistakes, the Friends of J. LAMING are requested to insert the Words *ROYAL CHARLOTTE* on their Directions.

Warren, Printer, Margate.

Margate packet advertisement, 1803.

Illus. 9

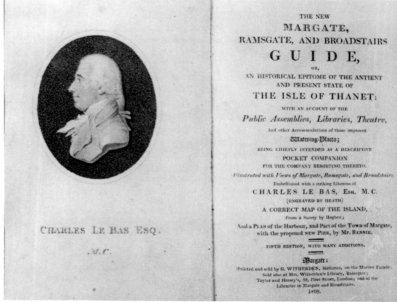

(a) The great storm at Margate, 1808.
(b) Title page of Thanet guidebook, 1809.

Illus. 10

(a) A view of Broadstairs, 1809.
(b) Ramsgate town and harbour, 1809.

Illus. 11

(a) A view of Sandgate, 1815.
(b) Steam packets at Margate pier, 1820.

Illus. 12

23. *Insights into the advice offered by eighteenth-century medical treatises on sea water and sea bathing.*

In 1750 the merits of applying sea water as a form of medical treatment, either internally through drinking it or externally by means of bathing in it, were given great publicity by the pen of Dr. Richard Russell, F.R.S. (1687–1759). The medical work, which made him famous at the age of sixty three, was first published in Oxford in Latin (see Illus. 1). The first English translation appeared in 1752.

(a) [R. Russell, M.D., *A Dissertation on the Use of Sea-Water in the Diseases of the Glands, particularly The Scurvy, Jaundice, King's Evil, Leprosy and the Glandular Consumption,* 1752, 67, 73, 112–3, 118]

In one famous passage he described how children who were sent to him for treatment, pale and delicate, over-clothed and with long hair, were returned to their parents much improved in their health after a course of sea bathing.

I have often had Boys brought to me weak, pale, with long thick Hair hanging down their Necks, and covered up with the greatest Care, lest the tender Creatures should be killed with the Cold, the whole Texture of the Body being relaxed with the Heat of their Cloathing . . . I have sent them back to their Parents, with their Hair cut off, their Necks bare, with a florid youthful Countenance, having first strengthened their Limbs by bathing in the Sea.

Dr. Russell introduced his readers to 39 cases illustrating the medical value of sea water as he saw it. Case 2 concerned

A Servant of the most noble Duke of ——— . . . I sent him to *Brighthelmstone* [Brighton], . . . *drinking a Pint of Sea-Water in the Morning.*

Case 32 was the most sensational, indicating once again the importance which he attached to the drinking of sea water.

As this Patient took *Sea-Water,* several Months, I . . . insert this Case, that it might be a confutation of those Persons, if there are any such, who condemn the long Use of *Sea-Water,* as being too strong a Medicine.
In the mean Time, I do not offer to those who cultivate the Art of Physic, a trifling worthless Remedy, but one that is of great Worth and Efficacy, and doubtless very safe, if it is directed by the Judgement of a

skilful Person . . . The woman in the present case took 25 gallons of *Sea-Water*, not at stated Intervals, but in one continued Course of Purging, at a Pint every Morning (which makes in all 200 Pints) and while she was drinking it, she had . . . a keener Appetite, and the strumous Swellings were dispersed . . . If this vast Quantity of *Sea-Water* drank, (which was followed by the cure of the strumous Swellings, and a better State of Health than before) does not procure and demonstrate its harmless Virtues; I fear there will never be any Argument strong enough to remove the unjust Prejudices of some People.

Case 34 combined both forms of treatment.

A Man 44 Years old was troubled with hard scrophulous Tumors upon both Knees, and the very same scorbutic Disorder upon his right Wrist. . . At last he came to me, and by my Advice went to Brighthelmstone, where, for four Months without any Intermission he drank a Pint of *Sea-Water* every Morning. When the Tumors began to decline he went into the Sea as a Cold Bath, and went away restor'd to his Health.

> Dr. Russell's *Dissertation* commanded such an extensive readership as to enjoy a 6th Edition in 1769, but he was not the only physician who explored the medicinal properties of sea water. The independent researches of a Dr. Speed were also published prior to 1760. He was less enthusiastic about the drinking of sea water and took issue with Dr. Russell as follows.

(b) [Dr. Speed, *A Commentary on Sea Water*, included in the 1760 4th Edition of Dr. Russell's *Dissertation*, 153, 173–4]

I have known that Sea-Water would not purge at all, and then it created a very great Uneasiness in the Stomach . . . Others, who have drunk it unadvisedly, have been . . . thrown into an almost incurable Looseness, . . . which has sometimes proved fatal . . .

There may be some Things in which I seem to clash with Dr. RUSSEL'S Account of Sea Water, and some may think I have done it with Design. But this is so far from being true, that I had written the greatest Part of this Commentary before I had even heard of Dr. *Russel's* Book or Name. But I could not help taking Notice while I was reading this Book, that though the Author says a great deal concerning the internal Use of Sea Water, yet in all his Cases which he wrote himself, or received from his Friends, which he thought proper to publish, there are only four who experienced the internal Use of Sea

Water alone . . . In the rest it is joined to the external Use, to which the principal Effects seem to me to be owing, or also with other Medicines, which have been noted for their Efficacy against particular Diseases; and in most, both these Assistances were used . . .

He . . . affirms that Patients may indulge themselves in the plentiful drinking of Sea Water, from the Example of a Woman who drank a large Quantity, *viz*: 25 Gallons, without any Harm, perhaps forgetting we cannot infer Universals from particular Cases.

I must needs own I have not been so fortunate as to make the same Observation, nor have I been so happy as never to have perceived any Inconvenience from the free Internal Use of Sea Water.

Doctors Russell and Speed prepared the way for an extensive literature on the medicinal value of sea water which continued into the nineteenth century. Originating from the pen of a 'Physician to, and A Director of, The General Sea Bathing Infirmary at Margate', which, at Westbrook, opened its doors, during 1796, as the country's first specialist hospital for tuberculosis, was the following advice, published in 1795.

(c) [John Anderson, M.D., F.A.S., C.M.S., etc., *A Preliminary Introduction to the Act of Sea Bathing; Wherein is Shewn its Nature, Power and Importance; With Some Necessary Hints for the Attention of Visiters, at the Watering Places, Previous to, and During a Course of Bathing*, Margate, 1795, 3–4, 8, 9, 12, 15–16, 21]

In compliance with the request of some highly distinguished gentlemen of the faculty, I have undertaken to write on the nature, power, influence, and effect of Sea-Water and Sea-bathing, cold and hot. The subject matter, thus assigned me . . . stands in much need of further investigation . . . What I deliver [is] the result of long practical experience, . . . supported by respectable living evidence of gentlemen of the faculty on the coast, and long-standing sagacious sea-bathing guides, male and female, at MARGATE . . .

Sea-bathing comprehends in it the powers and qualities of fluidity, gravity, pressure, attraction, repulsion, stimulation, friction, attrition and velocity; cold, heat, humidity, dryness, effluvia, etc . . .

Neither the advantages of Sea-bathing, at *Margate*, nor the salubrious property of the air of *Thanet*, have hitherto commanded medical attention equal to what their importance deserve . . . Sea bathing has certainly worked its own way . . . None have suffered at MARGATE except the indiscreet and unthinking, or who have been so unfortunate as to be badly advised and injudiciously directed . . . I have observed some to have come, and, under judicious direction, receive much benefit . . .

Nine years ago I happened to come to MARGATE in quest of strength, after a long and severe fever; and receiving a very sensible benefit the first season by sea-bathing, and the salubrious air of *Thanet*, I was thereon led to make enquiry into their special effects on other visitors . . . Since that time, I have had frequent opportunity of observing more minutely their effects on others under various states, circumstances, and conditions of body: in simple and complicated, acute and chronic, casual and inherent complaints; and every year's experience gives manifold proofs of their very great utility to health: they restore and preserve. There are but few distempers incident to human nature in which either the cold, the warm, or vapour sea-water bath, and the air of a salubrious spot on the margin of the main, such as *Thanet*, are not equal to meet and prove more or less beneficial in. . . . These baths are certainly most excellent auxiliaries to medicine, diet, exercise, and amusement, . . . which accounts for the great flux and re-flux of company, from the king to the beggar, to and from the sea-watering places, during the temperate seasons . . .

The bountiful ocean answers the peremptory demands of thousands and tens of thousands of proper claimants every year.

24. *The value attached to sea air, with topographical and climatic considerations.*

Physicians quite naturally explored and exploited the medical properties of sea air during the eighteenth century. Dr. Ingenhousz carried out experiments at Gravesend, at three miles from the mouth of the Thames, in the middle of the English Channel and between the Kent coast and Ostend and published his conclusions in 1780.

(a) [*Philosophical Transactions*, 1780, 354]

It appears from these experiments, that the air at sea and close to it is in general purer and fitter for animal life than the air on the land, . . . so that we may now with more confidence send our patients, labouring under consumptive disorders, to the sea, or at least to places situated close to the sea, which have no marshes in their neighbourhood.

The scourge of marshy areas was ague or malarial fever. The above experiments and conclusions were noted along with others in

(b) ['Sea Air', *The Encyclopaedia Britannica*, XVII, 3rd Ed., Edinburgh, 1797, 193]

Sea air has been found salubrious and remarkably beneficial in some distempers . . . Dr. DAMMAN, an eminent physician and professor royal of midwifery at Ghent, told Dr. INGENHOUSZ, that when he was formerly a practitioner at Ostend, during seven years, he found the people there remarkably healthy; that nothing was rarer there than to see a patient labouring under a consumption or asthma, a malignant putrid, or spotted fever.

With a dry easily-draining chalky soil and cliffs, rather than marshes, dominating the Thanet coastline from Birchington to Pegwell Bay, it was not long before the Isle of Thanet became highly renowned for its salubrious sea air, which was frequently measured in terms of the longevity of its inhabitants.

(c) [*The Gentleman's Magazine*, XLI, 1771, 167]

The salubrity of the air of the Isle of Thanet, and the longevity of its inhabitants, speak likewise not a little in favour of Margate. There are now living in that town many healthy people from 80–90 years of age . . . In short, this island . . . enjoys all the beauties of fine prospects and clear healthy air.

(d) [*The Margate Guide*, 1780, 5–6]

The Soil is dry, and the Air remarkably pure . . . The Inhabitants are remarkably healthy; and the Salubrity of the Air tends to make them long lived and prolific. Several Instances of Longevity may be adduced. I will mention a few only. Out of seventy three Persons, who were buried at St. Peter's (the Parish adjoining to Margate), in the Year 1762 ten of them were of the Age of seventy eight Years and upwards and in the Year 1760 five old Persons were interred whose Ages as they died in successive Order, amounted to four hundred Years. Several Persons of very advanced Years are now living in and near Margate; and in last April (1780) an old Lady was buried there, in her hundredth Year.

Inevitably it was not long before other resorts began to stress or have recommended for them the merits of their own sea air, with or without reference to their own geographical setting.

(e) [*The Kentish Gazette*, 27–30 April 1790]

SANDGATE is allowed to be an exceeding pleasant Place, and its Air very salubrious, as a Proof of which it is much frequented by a very large and respectable Company during the Summer.

(f) [*The Dover and Deal Directory and Guide*, Dover, c. 1792, 1]

The delightful situation of Dover, the purity of the sea, and the advantages of a fine beach for bathing, has caused this place to be much frequented in the bathing season; and it now promises to become one of the most fashionable watering places in the kingdom . . . The salubrity of the air, the strength and purity of the water, the ease and safety of the mode of bathing, make the situation equally desirable to those who visit the coast for amusement, or the valetudinarian who is in search after health.

(g) [*Horn's Description of Dover*, Dover, 1817, 23]

The air is . . . remarkably salubrious, the surrounding lands being dry; as the basis is constituted almost entirely of chalk.

> The Hon. John Byng, later the fifth Viscount Torrington (1742–1813) was mindful of the benefit of sea air when, on Monday, 20 September 1790, he rode from Ashford down to Hythe.

(h) [Ed: C. Bruyn Andrews, *The Torrington Diaries*, IV, 1970, 159–60]

We joined The Road; and in 3 more miles, after smelling the salubrious Sea-Breeze, Descended by a fine dip into The Town of Hythe . . . Walk'd up the Hill To the Church; whence is a fine Sea View [Illus. 17b] . . . This is a good Station for Sea-Bathing, and Retirement . . . With the air, and exercise, consists the salubrity.

(i) [*The Hythe, Sandgate and Folkestone Guide*, Hythe, 1816, 1–3, 24, 27–9]

HYTHE, SANDGATE, and FOLKESTONE, being situated nearly contiguous to each other, and the daily intercourse of their inhabitants having long established a sort of relationship and community of interest between them (also compare Doc. 40m), it will not be deemed improper to connect together the most leading features . . . of the respective places . . . This Guide is therefore very respectfully presented to the notice of those who visit the Kentish Coast, either for health or amusement . . .

HYTHE is situated near the sea shore . . . On approaching the town . . . from Ashford, as the road descends, the principal buildings appear to rest at the foot of a precipice, or are seen clinging to its side and stretching out towards the margin of the sea. [Illus. 17b]. On the right, the extensive level of Romney Marsh and its variegated patches of verdure and sterility, interspersed with here and there small tufts of trees and brush wood, and the high hills of Sussex bounding the horizon in that direction, are finely contrasted by the charming expanse of sea in front, . . . with the neighbouring heights on the left sheltering the town of Hythe from the keenness of the north and north-east wind . . .

The shelter which these high hills afford . . . and the mildness of the sea breezes on this shore, . . . invite an earlier attendance of bathers in the spring, as well as encourage them to protract their stay in the neighbourhood longer in the autumn than is usual elsewhere, [being] advantageous to . . . invalids and persons of weak health.

The society of Hythe is respectable and genteel . . .

The neat and picturesque Village of SANDGATE [Illus. 12a] . . . consists principally of one street of a handsome breadth which runs nearly due east and west, at the foot of a range of lofty eminences and on the very brink of the sea, of which it commands a boundless and delightful view . . . Indeed, there are few situations between Dover and the Lands-end better adapted for the residence of invalids who are desirious of enjoying the combined advantages of the water, the saline breezes, and exercises either on foot, on horseback, or in a carriage, free from the annoyance of a crowd, and the fatigue and bustle incident to larger and more populous towns . . . The charming expanse of ocean on the south, the softness and salubrity of the air, the remarkable purity of the water, and the accommodations which it affords for bathing, are strong recommendations of this spot to those who travel in search of health.

Dover too claimed to offer a panoramic shelter from cold and boisterous winds.

(j)   [W. Batcheller, *A New History of Dover to which is added a New Dover Guide*, Dover, 1828, 348–9]

The town, by its south-eastern aspect, affords all the advantages of a seaport, without the inconvenience of that extreme cold, to which many others are subject. Had its original founders anticipated, that it would one day become a favorite resort of the invalid, they could not have selected, within a compass of many miles, a better shelter from the northern blast, than the lofty castle hill. The heights to the west, and Shakespeare's cliff, at a distance, to the south-west, afford a cover from the wind in those directions. And, in order to secure a free current to the wholesome breeze, a most beautiful and shaded valley opens to the north-west.

A vast expanse of sea spreads before the town, enlivening the prospect from the balconies and windows; and those who have been charmed with the fixed beauties of rural scenery, look with no less delight on the moving panorama of boats and vessels gliding along before them. [Illus. 20a].

The variety of the scenery is truly delightful. Mountain and valley, land and water, rural and marine beauties, conspire to shift the scene at every instant . . .

But the sea bathing is . . . one of the greatest attractions. The town is but a few hours' ride from London, and a fewer hours' sail from Margate and Ramsgate.

Much the same points were made about Gravesend in 1842.

(k)   [*The Visitor's Guide to the Watering Places*, 1842, 1–2]

The salubrity of the air, the beauty of the surrounding scenery, the short distance from the metropolis, and the facility of communication therewith [steamboats], have combined to bestow great prosperity upon Gravesend. The consequent increase of buildings has been immense . . .

Gravesend is situated on a gentle acclivity from the south bank of the Thames . . . From many of the dwellings are fine prospects of the river (which is here half a mile across), its shipping, and the wide sweep over the coast of Essex, . . . altogether forming a magnificent and varied panoramic view. This town will vie with most of the watering-places in point of beauty, health, and pleasure . . . [It] abounds in springs of the finest water, which cannot be too highly appreciated . . . The air is dry, pure, bracing, and extremely healthy. Numerous instances have occurred of invalids being restored to health, upon a short residence here.

No less an emphasis was bestowed on the virtues of Herne Bay, Deal and Margate during the 1840s.

(l)   [*The Visitor's Guide to the Watering Places*, 1842, 198]

The salubrity of the air of Herne Bay has been long noted,. . . from its gentle elevation, clear of those stagnant pools and marshes, and low woodlands, which prevent a free circulation of the air on many other parts of the coast.

(m)   [S. Bagshaw,*History, Gazetteer, and Directory of the County of Kent*, II, Sheffield, 1847, 352–3]

DEAL is . . . situated between the north and south Foreland . . . The air is considered very healthy, on which account numbers resort to it in summer, as well for pleasure as for the benefit of sea bathing, for whose accommodation suitable improvements have been made.

(n)   [Edward Cresy, *Report to the General Board of Health on a Preliminary Inquiry into the Sewerage, Drainage, and Supply of Water, and the Sanitary Condition of . . . Margate*, H.M.S.O., 1850, 3]

Margate contains about 12,000 inhabitants, and from its contiguity to the North Foreland, and other great local advantages, it has long been esteemed one of the most salubrious places within an equal distance of London . . . Upwards of 60,000 visitors are annually induced to frequent this parish for the benefit of sea air.

Quite apart from the impossibility of isolating sea air from sea bathing (see Doc. 25o), the real benefits of a seaside holiday have always come from a complete change of environment, to which sea air makes a contribution – coupled with good food, exercise, relaxation, and to some extent sea bathing. It seems fitting that a lady writing in 1835 about Herne Bay should have the final word.

(o)   [By a Lady, *A Picture of the New Town of Herne Bay*, 1835, 8]

The first question that arises when choice is to be made of a watering-place, is the salubrity of the air; the next in importance are, the facilities and concomitants for bathing; for taking exercise; for the means of gratifying various tastes, whether in pursuit of amusement or reflection; for ready supplies of articles for the table; for clean, commodious, well arranged lodging-houses; and for short, agreeable modes of conveyance . . .

The [Herne Bay] air has been pronounced, by medical men who have resided there, to be the desired medium between the mildness of Hastings and the bleakness of Margate, and having resemblance to that of some favoured spots in Devonshire.

25. *Wallowing in sea water and sea air: contemporary experiences and evaluations.*

Letters and diaries tell of visits to the seaside for medical reasons while guide books sought to assess the medicinal virtues of exposure to sea water and sea air. Bishop Pococke observed what was happening in Margate in September 1754.

(a) [Ed: J.J. Cartwright, *The Travels through England of Dr. Richard Pococke, during 1750, 1751, and Later Years, Camden Society*, II, 1889, 86]

Sandwich, Sept. 11, 1754. On the 10th I left Canterbury, crossed into the Isle of Thanet, and . . . came to Margate . . . This is a fishing town, and is of late much resorted to by company to drink the sea water, as well as to bathe.

(b) [*1757 MS.*, Margate Public Library]

Of late years since the physicians of London have in several cases prescribed drinking and bathing in salt water, the town of Margate has become much frequented in that account as the shore is flat and sandy.

(c) [John Lyons, *A Description of the Isle of Thanet, and particularly of the Town of Margate*, 1763, 14]

I do not think myself a proper judge of the efficacy of Sea-bathing, having never had occasion to consider it but as an amusement. I will, however, venture to say, that in all cases where Bathing can be of service, this must be at least equal to any other; and in all disorders of the skin, or where the complaints are external, infinitely superior. Its salutary effects are daily experienced in the Rheumatism, and in scorbutick and scrophulous habits; nor is it found that Patients are more liable to a relapse who have been cured by this method, than by other medicines. Nevertheless, it must sometimes happen, from the injudicious use of it, that the sick will go away disappointed of the relief they expected to have received.

Not everyone in the early days felt inclined to adopt the fashionable habits of drinking sea water and bathing in it. For the poet Thomas Gray these were in 1764 the practices of 'common people' but he did warm to the sea air.

(d)   [Quoted by C.H. Woodruff, 'The Making of Margate', *The Home Counties Magazine*, IV, 1902, 171]

My health is much improved by the sea, not that I drank it, or bathed in it, as the common people do.

Sea bathing in the hope of restoring health was very much on the cards for John Baker (1712–1779), a barrister of the Middle Temple and sometime Solicitor General of the Leeward Islands, when between 9 September and 16 October 1777, he spent five weeks on a trip to Margate with Mrs. Woodington. he was then 66 and the entries in his diary indicate that he was a hypochondriac.

(e)   [Ed: P.C. Yorke, *The Diary of John Baker*, 1931, 417–21]

11 September – afterwards Mr. Slater, apothecary, about my bathing.
13 September – Up soon after 6; by help of Mitchener and Charles hobbled to bath at the very next door. Mitchener, vast stout man, dipt me . . . back and to bed near 2 hours. Mrs. Woodington gone to market.
14 September – Bathed as yesterday. Mitchener says he is 55 – a stout, tall man that dips me.
16 September – Continued ill and suffering.
19 September – I am now very bad indeed everywhere.
28 September – My father died wanting about 22 days of compleating his 66th year. I want more than 4 months of compleating my 66th year which I think it utterly impossible I should ever do, for I grow daily weaker. The sea-bath, sea-air, or any air, has no effect to make me better, but all are flat and useless and I have neither pleasure nor amendment from them.
2 October – My body all disordered . . . I am now in a dreadful condition indeed – all pain and wretchedness . . . Come at 4 Mr. Slater; seemed to think all will go away with dissipation and exercise.

4 October – Mr. Slater came – much talk with him and Mrs. W. about my case; he thinks right to bathe again.

7 October – I believe the air disagrees with me – it is too damp so near the sea.

8 October – Went into the sea the 9th time – seem well after it.

11 October – Mr. Slater still insists on my bathing, tho' it weakens me so.

Three days later they set off for London but not before paying 4 guineas to Mr. George Slater for his medical advice.

In the previous year to John Baker's visit, James Essex (1722–84), an architect, travelled down to Margate.

(f) [Ed: W.S. Lewis and A. Dayle Wallace, *Horace Walpole's Correspondence with the Rev. William Cole*, II, 1937, 26]

According to a letter written on 19 September 1776 by the Rev. William Cole,

I sent Mr. Essex the contents of your letter the day after I received it, and saw him a day or two after. He was just then returned with his wife from Margate, where they had both been for the use of bathing.

(g) [Ed: J. Fergusson, *Letters of George Dempster to Sir Adam Fergusson, 1756–1813*, 1934, III, 196–7]

During September 1782 George Dempster took his wife and sister down to Margate.

to bathe for both their healths.

A few years later in July 1789

Mrs. J.H.D. writes me from Margate that her little boy has uniformly mended for his last fortnight.

(h) [By an Inhabitant, *The Margate Guide, A Descriptive Poem, with Elucidatory Notes*, Margate, 1797, 7, 61–3]

Thousands can testify, ... for we annually see many who come to Margate, even on crutches, after bathing a few weeks, not only throw aside their auxiliary legs, but are restored to such health and florid countenances that scarcely their most intimate friends can recognize them. Sea bathing can no where be enjoyed with a greater possibility of success than here; and its beneficial effects, in all glandular and cutaneous disorders, are so well established, that they need no eulogium ... If anything were wanting to prove the efficacy of sea-bathing, which seems now to be fully established, our numerous visitors would be sufficient testimony; few of them leave Margate without having realized their most sanguine expectations. Those who wish to make themselves acquainted with the good and bad effects of salt water, may consult a *Practical Essay* on that subject, lately published by Dr. Anderson, a resident Physician [see Doc. 23c], who for many years has made sea-bathing the peculiar object of his study, and has thereby been enabled so to appropriate these waters to the various ills of human nature, as to give great success to his practice.

The benefit of the warm salt-water bath has been experienced in the removal of many obstinate complaints, which had baffled the power of medicine; and in most cases, where the cold-bath disagrees or fails, the tepid has the desired effect. It is frequently recommended preparatory to a course of the former; as it tends to relax the fibres, open the pores, and give greater energy to the powers of the natural bath.

> Drinking sea water as well as a belief in the efficacy of sea bathing continued to attract their adherents during the nineteenth century, as Charles Lamb could point out in a letter to John Rickman, written on 16 September 1801.

(i) [Ed: E.V. Lucas, *The Letters of Charles Lamb to which are added those of his Sister Mary Lamb*, I, 1935, 272]

Your Letter has found me at Margate, where I am come with Mary to drink sea water and pick up shells.

(j) [Ed: E.H. Coleridge, *Letters of Samuel Taylor Coleridge*, II, 1895, 700]

Ramsgate, August 20, 1819.
Whether from the mere intensity of the heat, and the restless, almost sleepless, nights, ... or whether simply the change of air and the sea bath, ... I have been miserably unwell for the last three days ... Finding myself convalescent this morning, I bathed, and now am better, ... having had a glorious tumble in the waves, though the water is still not cold enough for my liking.

(k)　[*MS Journal of an Excursion to Ramsgate in July and August 1829*, Tyler Collection (Ramsgate Scrapbook), Cathedral Library and Archives, Canterbury]

Tuesday, July 21.
Charlotte, myself and the Servant each took half a pint of Warm salt Water – Breakfast at 9.

> In the meantime published works continued to advocate the merits of sea water treatment.

(l)　[W.C. Oulton, *Picture of Margate and Its Vicinity*, 2nd Ed., 1821, 54]

In cases of langour and debility, hysterical affections, epilepsy, St. Vitus's dance, convulsions in children, . . . bathing, at proper times, has been found remarkably efficacious.

> A medical pamphlet of 1828 recommended cold and warm sea water baths as being effective in the treatment of a number of diseases.

(m)　[William Harwood, *On the Curative Influence of the Southern Coast of England*, 1828]

Acute and chronic rheumatism, gout, consumption, asthma, indigestion, diseases of the liver, scrofula, rickets, measles and whooping cough.

> In 1841 Dr. A.B. Granville, F.R.S. recommended applying sea water both externally and internally in his famous study of *The Spas of England and Principal Sea Bathing Places*. In 1860 the recommended dose of sea water was half a pint, proving perhaps more palatable if mixed with port wine, milk or beef tea, according to Dr. Spencer Thomson on pages 29–30 of his *Health Resorts of Britain; and How to Profit by Them*. Some of the advice on offer in Victorian times was more cautiously expressed.

(n)　[*The Visitor's Guide to the Watering Places, or A Summer Excursion Round the Coast of England, in Pursuit of Health and Recreation; with An Introductory Chapter on the Use and Abuse of Warm and Cold Water Bathing*, 1842, xvi–xviii]

If a person in the full enjoyment of health be immersed in the cold bath, and continue in it but a short time, the sensation experienced on emerging from the water is highly pleasurable . . . When the body is dried, a glow of warmth pervades the whole system, and the physical powers become refreshed and invigorated . . . When a person, from timidity, stands for a time upon the brink, or enters the bath by degrees, instead of plunging in at once, the sensation of cold is more striking, . . . succeeded by shivering, excessive langour, head-ache, nausea, and often distressing symptoms . . . Where the system has been debilitated by great and continued exertion, or by disease, cold bathing is not only improper, but in the highest degree injurious . . . The cold bath should never be taken when the body is heated by exercise or other exertion . . . It is customary with many persons, who find their bodies excited to a gentle perspiration, to wait for some time in a state of nudity before they plunge into the water. This is an error which is frequently productive of the most serious consequences . . .

As to the proper time of cold bathing, it is not of much consequence to a healthy person; but, were a question to arise, perhaps one might say two or three hours after breakfast . . . It is wrong to drink a large dose of salt water; the only benefit is to produce a discharge of bile . . .

When an individual rises from his bed refreshed and active the bath may be taken early in the morning, before breakfast.

In using exercise, previous to the bath, with the view of rendering the circulation more vigorous, care must be taken not to induce fatigue, or much perspiration. A slight moisture on the skin should be wiped off before bathing.

Our first object should be to ascertain if bathing agrees with us . . . When it does not, perseverance is worse than folly. The test is very simple. We should, on coming out, feel a good deal refreshed . . . If we shiver much, if the teeth chatter, or if the fingers are white or numbed, it does not suit us, and ought to be discontinued.

The impregnation of salt, in reference to mere bathing, is not worth a consideration.

> In the final analysis, and whatever the cure proposed, it was quite impossible to isolate the effects of sea bathing from those of sea air, as was fully appreciated in 1910.

(o) [Ed: Dr. Montague Murray, *Quain's Dictionary of Medicine*, 3rd Ed., 1910, 1469, 1470–1]

The physiological and therapeutical effects of sea-bathing cannot be separated from those of sea-air; for it is impossible to take sea-baths without being under the influence of sea-air . . . A stay at the seaside alone, without sea-bathing, produces on many constitutions all the effects which are usually ascribed to sea-bathing.

Should cold sea bathing be contemplated, however, delicate persons ought not to bathe with a perfectly empty stomach; but also never after a full meal . . . Weakly persons ought not to remain in the water over five minutes . . . Immersion for one or two minutes is in many cases all that is useful or permissable; while stronger individuals may remain from five to ten minutes.

26. *An immense publicity boost for Margate in 1771 concerning bathing in the sea.*

A safe and convenient location for 'dips into the sea' was of immense importance to people who, having perhaps never set eyes on the sea before, were scared of the water. To eighteenth-century contemporaries the open sea had a childlike novelty about it, as something visualized from conversation, paintings, prints or the pages of books. Many people were naturally terrified of the sea. In the actual promotion of sea bathing Margate had several distinct advantages, two of which attracted much publicity from contemporary writers:

(a) The fact of Margate Bay being what is termed a 'weather shore', and

(b) the perfection within Margate of the bathing machine (see Docs. 27, 28).

Sea bathing, whether for medical reasons or for pleasure, was promoted from certain natural facilities which the resort possessed, coupled with entrepreneurship in perfecting the bathing machine and providing early on sea-water baths, which enabled sea bathing to be undertaken by visitors and invalids of all ages (see Docs. 27, 28, 29). In 1771 an important and reassuring article gave to Margate an immense publicity boost in its early days as a seaside resort
[By Philomaris, 'Some Peculiar Advantages which Margate pre-eminently Enjoys, for the Benefit of Bathing in the Sea', *The Gentleman's Magazine*, XLI, April 1771, 166–8]

The town and harbour of Margate are situated on the east side of a fine clean sandy bay, . . . directly open to the northern ocean . . . It may be truly asserted, that no particles of fresh water from any river can mix or incorporate with the ocean near Margate. The Thames and Medway are at 30 miles distance, and are both salt for 30 miles from their mouths. Besides the waters of these rivers do not run on the ebb tide half way down to Margate road, before the flood tide turns them back again.

Another advantage peculiar to Margate is, its being a weather shore, during the greatest part of the summer; or, in other words, the southern winds, which generally prevail in that season, blow on from the land; by which means the sea is rendered perfectly smooth, and the water so clear, that, in a considerable depth, a pin may frequently be seen at the bottom; whereas most of the places on the sea coast, in the English Channel, from the North Foreland to the Land's End, are on a LEE SHORE during the greatest part of the summer, and are incommoded very much by the southerly winds before-mentioned; for these grateful gales, which produce the warm fine weather, and render Margate a smooth plasant shore, never fail to occasion at the same time a continual swell and surf of the sea, on the south coast of England, which not only makes the water there foul and thick, but annoys, frightens, and SPATTERS the Bathers exceedingly.

The Bay wherein the Company bathe at Margate is about half a mile in breadth, and has not its equal in this kingdom, or perhaps any other, for the purpose of bathing. The surface is a fine clean sand, perfectly free from rocks, stones, sea-weed, and all manner of soil and sullage; and lies on so gentle and regular a descent, that the sea at low water, ebbs away about half a mile from the shore. The west side of this bay is defended by a long ridge of rocks, which projects a very considerable distance into the sea, and dries at low water upwards of half a mile from the Cliff. The east side of the bay is covered and defended by another rock, called, The First Rock; so that, Margate Bay being thus happily fenced off by these two walls of nature, the swell and surf of the sea, when the wind blows obliquely upon the shore, is broken and repelled; insomuch, that tho' the weather in this case, be very bad and windy, excepting with a hard gale from the N.N.W. to the N.E. points of the compass, which seldom happen in the summer, the company go into the water in the open ocean with security and ease; and when the sea, by mere chance, is too rough and boisterous in the bay, the bathing machines find a safe retreat in the harbour; so that the going into the salt water at Margate can never be defeated through the means of bad weather, excepting by violent storms and tempests, which harrow up the ocean in every corner.

Another mighty convenience attending this bay ought not to escape notice; namely, that there is in a manner no . . . current in it; for the two rocks before-mentioned so break it off, that the sea, with propriety, may be said to sleep between them.

For the foregoing, and several other reasons which might be added, Margate has the superiority over every place in England, for the conveniency and propriety of bathing in the salt water. [Also] the bathing machines THERE have their merits too; and are universally allowed to be the best contrived of any in the kingdom for convenience, safety, privacy and expedition of driving into and out of the sea . . .

Wishing success . . . to the town of Margate, and to the bathers, I am, etc.

PHILOMARIS

27. *A carpenter, 1736, and a Quaker, c.1750, as pioneer innovators in the early history of Margate sea bathing.*

At Margate sea bathing comfortably preceded the medical publicity of the mid-eighteenth century (see Doc. 23). Usually the introduction of bathing machines was followed by the opening of sea-water baths, but not so at Margate where a sea-water bath was the pioneering innovation of a local carpenter in 1736, followed by extensions and improvements through to 1740.

(a)   [*The Kentish Post, or Canterbury News Letter*, 17 July 1736]

Whereas Bathing in Sea-Water has for several Years, and by great Numbers of People, been found to be of great Service in many Chronical Cases, but for want of a convenient and private Bathing Place, many of both Sexes have not cared to expose themselves to the Open Air: This is to inform all Persons that Thomas Barber, Carpenter, at Margate, in the Isle of Thanett, hath lately made a very convenient Bath, into which the Sea Water runs through a Canal about 15 Foot long. You descend into the Bath from a private Room adjoining to it. N.B. There are in the same House convenient Lodgings to be Lett.

(b)   [*The Kentish Post, or Canterbury News Letter*, 27 April 1737]

His Bath (which was advertis'd last Year) not [being] large enough for the Number of People which came there to bathe in the Sea Water, [he has erected] another Bath much larger and more commodious, so contriv'd, that there is a sufficient Quantity of Water to bath in it at any Time of the Tide, . . . [with] Lodging Rooms, Dressing Rooms, and a handsome large sash'd Dining Room, . . . [plus] a Summer House, . . . which affords a pleasant Prospect out to Sea.

(c)   [*The Kentish Post, or Canterbury News Letter*, 14–17 May 1740, 24–28 May 1740]

As a great many Gentlemen and Ladies have been deterr'd from coming to Mr. Barber's Sea Water Bath at Margate, by thinking it was expos'd to the open Air; I have therefore thought it necessary to inform the Publick, that 'tis quite enclos'd, and cover'd by a handsome Dining Room; and that there is a neat Dressing Room, and Dresses, adjoining to the Bath; and as the House fronts the Sea, there is a most delightful Prospect; and the Number of People that have received Benefit from Bathing, sufficiently demonstrates its Usefulness.
N.B. There are good Lodgings and Entertainment at my House, which adjoins to the Bath, and a good Coach-House and Stabling.
     THO. BARBER, at Margate, in the Isle of Thanett.

> Benjamin Beale, a Margate Quaker (c.1717–1775), assumed at the time and long since to have been the inventor of the famous Margate bathing machine, in 1753, is the second and more widely publicized innovator in the early days of sea bathing at Margate. During May 1759 Mr and Mrs Mount undertook a tour into Kent, which included a quick visit to Margate.

(d)   [Ed. F. Hull, 'A Tour into Kent, 1759', *Archaeologia Cantiana*, LXIX, 1955, or in Ed: M. Roake and J. Whyman, *Essays in Kentish History*, 1973, 188]

Wednesday 16.
One Beale a Quaker the first Inventor of the bathing Machines, and who keeps a Lodging House, was very Civil in walking with Us about the Town.

> What became in effect a myth in attributing the whole invention to

Benjamin Beale was perpetuated in guidebooks and other sources down the decades.

(e) [*The Margate Guide . . . In a Letter to a Friend*, 1770, 16]

This most useful Machine was the original Contrivance of Benjamin Beale, a Quaker, who seems to have undeniably the Right of a first Claiment to the Reward of his Ingenuity.

(f) [*The Gazetteer and New Daily Advertiser*, 19 May 1775]

The death was announced of Mr. Beale, one of the people called Quakers, the first person who erected a bathing machine at Margate.

(g) [G.W. Bonner, *The Picturesque Pocket Companion to Margate, Ramsgate, Broadstairs, and the Parts Adjacent*, 2nd Ed., 1831, 77–8]

The bathing machines were invented by Benjamin Beale, a native of Margate, and a member of the Society of Friends.

The refined bathing machine (see Doc. 28) evolved from bathing carts or chariots which were already in existence prior to the time, in 1753 or before, when Beale added a concertina like canvas canopy, so as to afford privacy to both male and female bathers. Better informed sources have seen him as a refining innovator rather than as a sole inventor.

(h) [*The Kentish Companion for the Year of Our Lord*, Canterbury, 1792, 120]

1753 – Bathing Machines, Beale, before which a tilted cart was used for bathing in the sea.

(i) [E.W. Brayley, *Delineations, Historical and Topographical, of the Isle of Thanet and the Cinque Ports*, I, 1817, 61–2]

Here it is recalled how Benjamin Beale's widow had remembered the first family that ever resorted to Margate for the purpose of bathing being carried into the sea in a covered cart.

(j) [*The Thanet Itinerary or Steam Yacht Companion*, 1819.]

The Bathers, from a door at the back of the vehicle, descend by wooden steps, until they reach the bottom, which is always composed of fine sand. Meanwhile they are entirely concealed from observation by an umbrella of canvas, covering the whole hinder part of the Machine. This screen was an invention of one, *Benjamin Beale,* . . . some of whose relatives still carry on the business of Bathers.

There were then at the lower end of Margate High Street six competing bathing rooms, including

Messrs T. Hughes and J. Beale.
A most elegant new Bathing Room, with marble baths, upon an improved plan, kept by Mrs Beale.

By means of a discreetly hooded modesty extension, in the shape of a canvas screen or umbrella, the famous Margate bathing machine was introduced by Benjamin Beale, sometime during the late 1740s or early 1750s. Bishop Pococke was certainly one of the first visitors to record its existence in 1754.

(k) [Ed: J.J. Cartwright, *The Travels through England of Dr Richard Pococke, during 1750, 1751, and Later Years, Camden Society,* II, 1889, 86]

They have the conveniency of cover'd carriages, at the end of which there is a covering that lets down with hoops, so that people can go down a ladder into the water and are not seen, and those who please may jump in and swim.

28. *Contemporary descriptions and assessments of the Margate bathing machine* (Illus. 4a).

The best description of the horse-drawn Margate bathing machine dates from 1793.

(a) [Zechariah Cozens, *A Tour through the Isle of Thanet and some other Parts of East Kent,* 1793, 3]

That sea bathing may be attainable with the strictest decency, there are near 40 machines employed in a season . . . In the course of more than 30 years experience, hardly any improvement has been made upon them: they consist of a carriage similar to that of a coach, but more simple, much stouter and considerably higher, that it may resist the waves in blowing weather; the wheels are high and strong, and . . . stand at right angles with the axles; in the front is a platform, from which you have admittance into the machine, which forms a neat dressing room, 6½ feet long, 5 wide, and 6½ high, with a bench on either side for the bathers to undress upon, the sides and top are framed, and covered with painted canvass; at the back opens a door, and, by means of a flight of steps attached to the machine, the bathers descend into the water, concealed from public view by a large umbrella of canvas stretched on hoops, which is let down by the driver, by means of a rope which comes to the front of the machine, until it touches the water, and forms a bath 10 feet long and 6 wide. There is a horse to each machine, and the proprietors employ very careful drivers, under whose guidance the machines are drawn out to the depth the bather may require: it is a pleasing sight to behold between 30 and 40 of these curious machines in a morning hovering on the surface of the water, . . .continually revolving in their course either returning with their cleansed guest, or going out with a freight of, perhaps, jolly citizens preparing to wash off the dust and care of a six months attendence to their counting houses.

> An early visitor to Margate was the famous bibliographer and antiquary Joseph Ames (1689–1759). While there he described the bathing arrangements and sketched a bathing machine.

(b)   [*Notes and Queries*, 2nd Series, VI, 1858, 163]

This town is much resorted to, . . . there being a fine sandy beach, and a flat shore, where at all times of the Tide the Machines or Bathing Waggons can drive a proper depth into the Sea for the accommodation of ye Bathers . . . The above is a view of the Machine to bath with; it contains a room to undress and dress in, with steps to go down into the Sea; will hold 5 to 6 People. There are Men and Women Guides, who, if desired, attend. The price is 4s. a week, or £1 1s. for six weeks, and you pay the Guide for every attendance. They drive into the Sea till it is about breast high, and then let down the Screen wch prevents being seen, under which you go down the Steps into a fine sandy bottom.

> The Rev. John Pridden provides also some very fine sketches of the bathing machine and 'The West View of the Harbour, Parade, and Bathing Rooms at Margate', dated 16 October 1781.

(c)   [Margate Public Library, the Rev. John Pridden, Ms. *Topographical Collections for a History of The Isle of Thanet in Kent*, II, 4]

Margate . . . has risen to a considerable degree of eminence by the resort of Company for the convenience of bathing; its Shore being level and covered with fine sand, is extremely well calculated for that purpose. On the wharf are seven bathing-rooms, which are large and convenient. Hither the Company resort to drink the Water, and from thence, in turns, they enter the Machines, which are driven out into the Sea, under the conduct of careful guides, often to the distance of two or three-hundred yards. The Number of Machines employed, on a fair Day, when the Sea is smooth, is so great that it appears like a floating Camp. These Machines are simple in their structure, but quite convenient; and by means of an Umbrella, the pleasures of bathing may be enjoyed in so private a manner, as to be consistent with the strictest delicacy. There is a door at the back of the Machine, by which the bathers descend into the Water, by means of a few Steps, and the Umbrella of Canvass is let down, which conceals them from public view.

(d)   [*The Margate and Ramsgate Guide in Letters to a Friend*, 1797, 12–13]

Every bathing-machine has a kind of canvas umbrella affixed to it, not much unlike the end of a waggon; that is let down to the water's edge, and forms a pleasing retired bath, happily calculated to preserve the modesty of the female sex in particular; very different from the marine watch or sentry-boxes of Brighthelmstone [Brighton].

> From its inception the Margate bathing machine appears to have undergone little alteration.

(e)   [G.W. Bonner, *The Picturesque Pocket Companion to Margate, Ramsgate, Broadstairs, and the Parts Adjacent*, 2nd Ed., 1831, 78]

Such were the perfection and simplicity of their original arrangement, that the lapse of half a century has produced no improvements in their construction . . . Soon after their first introduction, numbers were built at this place, and exported to the East and West Indies. By means of this very useful contrivance, both sexes may enjoy the renovating waters of the ocean, . . . without any violation of public decency, and . . . safe from the gaze of idle or vulgar curiosity.

29.   *Sea-water baths as an alternative to the bathing machine.*

> From the 1760s onwards sea-water baths formed an acceptable

alternative to open bathing in the sea. With the passage of time cold, hot and vapour baths, etc., were established, which became more elaborate as additional refinements and comforts were introduced. Among the Kentish resorts Margate led the field, followed within a few decades by nearby Ramsgate. During the 1760s at Margate a famous local hotelier, John Mitchener, effected a considerable improvement in bathing facilities, in the shape of warm salt-water baths.

(a)   [*The Kentish Gazette, 27–31 May 1769*]

JOHN MITCHENER begs leave to acquaint the Publick that he has carried every Accommodation for Bathing in the Sea to the highest Degree of Perfection; he has lately opened a Warm Salt-water Bath, for the Use of those to whom it might be inconvenient to venture into a Cold one; it may be brought in a few Minutes to any Degree of Heat which may be required, according to the Regulation of [a] Faxuhecto Thermometer, which has been provided for that Purpose. The same may occasionally be made use of as a Cold one, whenever the Sea may be so rough as to render bathing in the Machines unpleasant. Every Person that makes use of this Bath has the Pleasure of clean Salt Water each Time of Bathing.

(b)   [*The Margate Guide . . . In a Letter to a Friend*, 1770, 14–15]

Mitchener has lately erected two new Hot Salt-water Baths on a most excellent Construction. They are very elegant, and built at a great Expence; are cleared in a few Minutes, and are brought to any Degree of Temperature, which may be required, with the utmost Ease. It is not exceeding the strictest Line of Truth to say, that the Use of them has been attended with singularly good Effects.

(c)   [*The Kentish Companion for the Year of our Lord*, Canterbury, 1792, 160]

Mitchener's Hotel, Marble Salt Water Baths – ready for use every day.

One of the pioneering names of Ramsgate in this respect was Joseph Dyason.

(d)   [*The Kentish Gazette*, 27–30 April 1790]

RAMSGATE, ISLE OF THANET, KENT. MARBLE SEA WATER BATHS. J. DYASON respectfully informs the Nobility and Gentry, etc., that he has erected two HOT and one COLD SEA WATER BATHS, constructed on such principles as to have a Supply of Water in the most pure State, at any Hour of the Day. Very pleasant and convenient Waiting and Dressing Rooms adjoin . . . the Baths. *N.B.* The terms of Bathing may be seen at the Waiting Rooms, or of J. DYASON's, High Street, Ramsgate.

(e)   [*The Times*, 9 July 1800]

BATH HOUSE,
May 13, 1800.

Warm Sea Water Bathing, Ramsgate, Isle of Thanet . . . Warm Sea Water Baths are now open for the ensuing Season, . . . also a Sea Water Shower Bath. Letters (post paid) of enquiry after Lodging Houses, at Ramsgate, will be strictly attended to . . .

JOSEPH DYASON.

The Works of these Baths have been constructed at a very great expense, to obtain a sufficient quantity of pure Sea Water from every Tide (essentially necessary for Warm Bathing) and the Party may always, if they choose, have the opportunity of seeing their Baths filled.

Insofar as Joseph Dyason maintained a register of lodgings accommodation he continued a tradition already noted in earlier advertisements of 1754, relating to the provision of bathing machines at Broadstairs, Ramsgate and Deal. Dyason continued in business throughout the Napoleonic Wars and his efforts and achievements were praised in a guidebook which was published in 1816.

(f)   [*The New Margate, Ramsgate and Broadstairs Guide*, 6th Ed., Margate, 1816, 94]

Mr Dyason, of the bath-house, has erected four baths for warm sea-water, also a plunging and shower-bath, which are so contrived as to have a continual supply from every tide; attached to them are very convenient waiting and dressing-rooms; the whole are completed on such a plan as to be much approved and recommended: and we sincerely hope that they will well reward the proprietor for the great care and expense necessarily attendant on so extensive and beneficial an establishment.

The previous season's opening had been announced in a long advertisement in one of the Kentish newspapers.

(g) [*The Kentish Gazette*, 28 and 31 March 1815]

ROYAL WARM SEA WATER BATHS, AND SHOWER BATHS, RAMSGATE, Isle of Thanet, JOSEPH DYASON, the Proprietor, most respectfully informs the Nobility, Gentry, etc., that his Baths are now opened for the Summer Season, . . . and assures them it always has been his most earnest wish, as well as the call of gratitude, for the support and recommendation these Baths have received from many of the first Characters in the Kingdom, to omit no means in his power in causing them to be attended and conducted so as to give satisfaction to those who use them as a pleasurable preserver of health, or as efficacious in removing or relieving those complaints for which they are so recommended . . . He has visited many of the Warm Baths in England, also those at Boulogne, Paris, Perronne, Valenciences, etc. in France and Flanders, to see if any improvement could be made in the construction or mode of conducting the Warm Baths at Ramsgate, and the Nobility and Gentry who may visit Ramsgate this ensuing Season, may rely that the Attendants both for Ladies and Gentlemen, will most carefully observe every thing recommended by the Faculty and by the Proprietor, that their long experience at these Baths deems requisite for the comfort of the person bathing . . .

Cards of the Terms, and further particulars may be had at the Baths, where attendance is constantly given from 7 in the morning until 9 at night.

Letters of enquiry after Lodgings, addressed (post-paid) to J. DYASON, at the Baths, will be immediately answered.

Meanwhile, Broadstairs too had acquired the comforts of warm sea-bathing.

(h) [*The New Margate, Ramsgate, and Broadstairs Guide*, 5th Ed., Margate, 1809, 100]

Warm baths have lately been erected here upon a good construction, by *Mr Barfield*.

Immediately after the Napoleonic Wars Ramsgate laid claim to the newest and most lavish warm salt-water baths, which were publicly opened on 10 June 1816, in competition with those of Mr. Dyason. They were fully described in a guidebook, the Introduction to which was written ten days later.

(i)   [*The New Margate, Ramsgate, and Broadstairs Guide*, 6th Ed., Margate, 1816, 94–6]

They are situated on the west cliff, and terminate the elegant range of buildings called the Paragon. The front is placed towards the sea, the space between it and the cliff being laid out as a promenade; an elegant saloon forms the centre compartment, having the baths and dressing rooms in each wing. All the baths are formed of white marble, and of the dimensions of the celebrated warm baths of Naples; to allow of invalids using the friction brush so conveniently as not to expose any part of their bodies above the surface of the water, they are placed in a room lighted and ventilated from the ceiling; the dressing rooms which communicate with them are of an ample size and fitted up with everything that can administer to the comfort and pleasure of the bathers; the saloon is furnished with the daily papers, reviews, and other periodical publications; and commands delightful views of . . . Pegwell Bay, Deal, Dover, and the coast of France from Dunkirk to Boulogne. The shower-baths are also placed in rooms lighted from the ceiling, and the dressing rooms attached to each are of the same dimensions, and fitted up in the same manner as the others. Vapour baths are also included in this establishment, and constructed to produce *medicated vapour* if required. A horizontal funnel, in which the tide ebbs and flows, has been excavated in the chalk rock, and runs under the building until it joins with the vertical funnel containing the pumps and pipes, which raise the water to the reservoir on the top, from which it is conveyed by pipes to the boilers and other parts of the buildings. The pumps are worked by horses, and are so placed as always to get their supply at high water.

Considerable inconvenience often having been experienced by invalids using the warm bath, in consequence of the unequal temperature of the apartment, and the currents of cold air acting on some part of the body, great attention has been paid to obviate this objection to the mode of heating these buildings in general; this has been accomplished by adopting steam as the heating power, and the heat is so equally diffused over the whole building, that in the coldest days it has all the delightful warmth of a day in summer. Each warm bath is charged 3s. 6d. – cold bath, 2s. – cold shower-bath, 1s. 6d. – warm shower-bath, 2s. 6d.

Three years later it was claimed in

(j)   [*The Thanet Itinerary or Steam Yacht Companion*, 1819, 66]

Perhaps there is no other town in Great Britain, which can equal *Ramsgate* in point of its superior accommodation for Warm Bathing. In addition to the four baths erected by Mr *Dyason*, the *Isabella Baths*, built after the plan of the celebrated warm baths of Naples, were opened to the Public on the 10th June, 1816 . . . The centre compartment forms a noble Saloon, which is constantly furnished with Newspapers, and Telescopes. Here also are *Shower Baths* and *Vapour Baths* of superior construction . . . One of the chief advantages arising from the construction of these splendid baths, is, that means have been adopted to prevent currents of cold air from passing into the dressing rooms; which has been effected by a very ingenious method of warming them by steam, instead of stoves, so that an equal temperature is preserved, and a general warmth diffused through the whole building.

> The pumping of sea water, steam heating and a primitive kind of central heating were far removed from the very simple bathing arrangements of the 1750s. The latter had been considered adequate in their day, but with the passage of time greater attention was given to the comforts of bathing and merely lounging visitors. Ramsgate's new baths of 1816 were indicative of a nineteenth-century move towards greater lavishness. Margate maintained an overall lead over Ramsgate, in having a greater number of bathing machines and a finer bathing beach (see Doc. 33k), but having the latest in luxury bathing placed Ramsgate in a strong position to rival Margate, until the famous Clifton Baths were constructed during the 1820s (see Illus. 18b). This immense undertaking was begun in 1824 and involved a heavy capital outlay in coastal excavation and sea defences, such as to attract favourable comment in contemporary guidebooks.

(k)   [G.A. Cooke, *A Topographical and Statistical Description of the County of Kent*, New Ed., 1830, xxx–xxxii]

These works and subterraneous excavations were in progress upwards of three years; they are the plan and undertaking of an individual; and are equally novel and extraordinary, . . . the projector being possessed of the land opposite to a good sand, and where the sea-water is remarkably pure.

At the commencement of the work, the cliff was cut down to within about six feet of the level of the sea-shore; and the part so left (being a hard rock-chalk) was cased with brick-work . . . A tunnel has been cut into the solid chalk, and arched over, so as to form a roadway of the length of about 130 feet, for bathing machines to pass up and down, as the tides should render necessary . . . An immense excavation of chalk has been made in a circular form at the bottom . . . The whole interior is cased and supported by brick-work, and by eight arches, which diverge from the centre in exact distances and proportion . . . Through each arch, further excavations are made, so as to be capable of holding from 20–30 machines. Besides this, another archway is cut from the top of the cliff, so as to enable the machine horses and small carriages to pass up and down from the sea-shore; and another entrance, with a handsome flight of 34 steps for foot passengers, has also been made.

Communicating with the upper entrance, a very good porter's lodge has been built, with three . . . rooms, for the residence . . . of a toll gatherer, or of those who take care of the property; and last of all, a waiting or lounging room is building . . . The total quantity of chalk excavated and removed is computed at 40,000 cubic yards.

> By 1831 the waiting or lounging room had been completed, in association with a terrace walk, and the individual who was responsible for this costly investment could be revealed.

(1) [G.W. Bonner, *The Picturesque Pocket Companion to Margate, Ramsgate, Broadstairs, and the Parts Adjacent*, 2nd Ed., 1831, 83–4]

The Clifton Baths solicit particular attention, not because they are superior to similar establishments in the High Street, for the purpose of bathing, but because they are of a curious character, and are placed in a novel and interesting situation, . . . on, or rather in, the Fort . . . Baths, with large and convenient dressing rooms, and a spacious reading room, [have] been constructed; and in front of the latter we find an extensive promenade, which has been formed by lowering the cliff, where the company may sit or walk, and revel in all the pleasures which the ocean can afford . . . While it may be considered by the curious observer, as a remarkable instance of the flights of humour and fancy, . . . its proprietor, Mr Boys, a solicitor of Margate, . . . with very commendable humility, has not suffered his name to appear upon the tablets, which are placed upon these expensive and elaborate works, completed at his individual cost.

> Serving the needs of numerous houses built on the Fort they came to be advertised thus.

(m) [*Pigot & Co's National, London, and Provincial Commercial Directory, for 1832–3–4*, 5th Ed., 851]

Clifton Baths, vapour, shower, and general bathing establishment.

> By the 1840s bathing provisions both at Margate and at Ramsgate were extensive, ranging from the simple bathing machine to baths replete with every novelty and luxury.

(n) [*The Visitor's Guide to the Watering Places*, 1842, 168–9, 179–80]

MARGATE – Here are warm, shower, or sulphur baths, and baths en douche. Machine bathing may likewise be had on the shore under Buenos Ayres, towards the Infirmary, [while] in the Fort there is an extraordinary erection, or perhaps, excavation would be a more correct term, called THE CLIFTON BATHS, being built in the solid chalk, rising in a circular form, surmounted with a dome 33 feet high. Two chimneys, to represent pyramids, crown the structure. The buildings consist of a waiting or subscription room, 40 feet long, fronting the sea, opening on to a terrace 100 feet in length, in which alcoves and seats are introduced at convenient distances. Twenty bathing-machines stand under the former, 10 feet above high-water mark, whence there is an easy access to the sands . . . There is a plunging bath, 80 feet by 40, for females and children, and all kinds of medicinal baths . . . The place is altogether well deserving of a visit . . . Upwards of 12,000 persons have visited the Clifton Baths in a single season.

RAMSGATE – SEA-WATER BATHS have been erected facing the Sands, where vapour, tubular, shower, and baths-en douche, may be had from six in the morning till ten in the evening. In point of accommodation evidently no pains or expense have been spared . . . For the accommodation of invalids, slipper and hip baths are sent out with hot water of the temperature required . . . [The] ROYAL KENT BATHS AND READING ROOM, *Paragon, West Cliff, Ramsgate*, . . .

consist of warm and cold sea-water, shower, vapour, and medicinal pumping baths.

Terms: Warm bath, 3s.; eight ditto, 21s.; vapour bath, 6s.; four ditto, 21s.; pumping bath, 3s. 6d.; warm shower bath, 2s.; cold shower bath, 1s. Hip baths and slipper baths to let.

Here . . . the invalid may command all the different varieties of bathing that fancy or necessity may direct, while the healthy and luxurious may revel in their delights. . . . The subscription to the Reading Apartment is 10s. 6d. the season or 4s. monthly. To each bath is appropriated a cheerful dress-room, . . . and the rooms are kept up at a proper temperature by means of steam . . . The water . . . is pumped direct from the sea, and is free from all soil of the town. For the accommodation of subscribers, a spacious and elegant saloon, commanding a delightful prospect of the Royal Harbour, the Downs, the neighbouring coast, and the coast of France, forms part of the establishment, and is furnished with a liberal supply of morning, evening and weekly papers, the magazines, and other interesting publications. Telescopes are also provided . . .

Other machines, of a humbler appearance and at reduced charges, belonging severally to Messrs Lucas, Pearce, and Marshall, attend on that part of the sands nearer Broadstairs.

Similar entrepreneurial initiative, although not necessarily on such a lavish scale, was displayed in the other resorts of Kent. By 1790 hot sea-water baths had been constructed in Dover, judging from the personal observations of the Hon. John Byng.

(o) [Ed: C. Bruyn Andrews, *The Torrington Diaries*, IV, 1970, 161]

Tuesday, Sept. 21 . . . We walk'd upon The Beach. Viewing the new Hot and Cold Salt Water Baths.

(p) [*The Dover and Deal Directory and Guide*, Dover, c.1792, 2]

The new bathing machines are stationed higher up the bay, and are kept by Messrs. Kennett, Hawker, Iggleden, and Austin [also see Doc. 32i], and have also every convenience for bathing, particularly the addition of excellent hot-baths, which are heated at any time at the shortest notice; or, in stormy weather, when it is impossible to go into the open sea, they are used with the greatest convenience as cold baths, and the sea water shifted for each bather.

(q) [W. Batcheller, *A New History of Dover, to which is Added a New Dover Guide*, Dover, 1828, 352]

Three new and commodious hot, cold, and shower baths, comprising every accommodation for the infirm, or healthy, are erected on the parade; and machines are in constant readiness for sea-bathing. A handsome room is attached to each of the baths, where the visitor may sit and enjoy an extended view of the ocean, and of the numerous vessels that are continually passing the channel.

> At Deal the Royal Adelaide Baths, built at a considerable cost in 1835–6, had a chequered history. In 1841 they were auctioned as a freehold, offering fine views and with two 'Machines for Sea Bathing'.

(r) [*The Dover Telegraph and Cinque Ports General Advertiser*, 22 May and 12 June 1841]

The In-door Baths are now in full operation. The Season for the Sea Bathing is about to commence, with every prospect of increased success.

On Tuesday the Royal Adelaide Baths and Reading Room were sold by public auction for the small sum of £1,000 including the furniture, fixtures, books and machines. About five years ago this building was erected by a Company for over £3,000, and has never returned 1s. in the shape of profit.

> Jacob Vile was running this establishment in 1847, as

(s) [S. Bagshaw, *History, Gazetteer, and Directory of the County of Kent*, II, Sheffield, 1847, 355, 364]

THE ROYAL ADELAIDE BATHS AND READING ROOM, Beach-street, established in 1835, and so called by the express permission of Her Majesty, consists of spacious reading room, library, and baths, comprising warm, shower, and cold baths, and a plunging bath in the basement. There are also a number of bathing machines on the beach belonging to the same proprietor.

> At Folkestone the erection of warm salt-water baths by 1806 was associated with Mr Gill who, as a local medico, had pronounced on the efficacy of the chalybeate spring at nearby Foord or Ford in 1776 (see Docs. 32h, 40k).

(t)   [*A Guide to all the Watering and Sea-Bathing Places*, 1806, 228]

BESIDES the bathing-machines, which are like those of other places, here are bathing-rooms in Pent-street, near the sea, under the direction of Mr Elgar, and in Dover-street others conducted by Mr Gill, a medical practitioner of respectability. This gentleman has also erected warm salt-water baths, at a considerable expense, and the situation of his house and bathing-rooms is remarkably pleasant and salubrious.

(u)   [*The Hythe, Sandgate and Folkestone Guide*, Hythe, 1816, 107]

The hot bath is in Queen's Place; and several commodious bathing machines at the Western side of the harbour.

Of Sandgate it was noted in 1815.

(v)   [*A Guide to all the Watering and Sea-Bathing Places*, New Ed., 1815, 423]

Here are many bathing machines, besides capital warm baths.

(w)   [*The Hythe, Sandgate and Folkestone Guide*, Hythe, 1816, 30]

In addition to the convenience of numerous bathing machines which are fitted up with peculiar neatness, and the old bathing rooms, a commodious warm salt-water bath has been recently built.

It was also the nineteenth century which brought the provision of baths to Herne Bay, Sheerness and Gravesend.

(x)   [By a Lady, *A Picture of the New Town of Herne Bay*, 1835, 9]

There are two establishments for bathing, each with several machines, and good and obliging guides, at the east end of the bay. The same proprietors have also warm baths kept constantly ready for use, and convenient apartments for dresssing and resting.

At Sheerness,

(y)   [*Pigot & Co's Royal, National and Commercial Directory*, 1840, 361]

The warm and cold sea-water baths established by Mr Court have added another attraction to those previously existing.

Of Gravesend it could be claimed in the early 1840s that

(z) [W.H. Bartlett, J.D. Harding, T. Creswick and Others, *The Ports, Harbours, Watering-Places and Picturesque Scenery of Great Britain*, I, c.1842]

The bathing-establishments are on a large-scale, admirably constructed, and managed with great punctuality and attention. Adjoining the Clifton Baths [see Doc. 32k] is a delightful pleasure ground, agreeably varied with walks and seats, and ornamented with trees, shrubs and flowers. From this eminence, which overhangs the Thames, a charming prospect is open at all times to the groups of visitors by whom it is frequented.

Gravesend possessed two bathing establishments in 1842.

(aa) [*The Visitor's Guide to the Watering Places*, 1842, 3, 5]

ALBION BATHS. – These baths are in the proprietorship of Mr Prentice, and are pleasantly situated near the basin of the 'Thames and Medway Canal'. . . . The building is neat, and the baths are fitted up for convenience and comfort. The rooms have a complete view of the river and the adjacent country. The charges are very reasonable.
CLIFTON BATHS are adjoining the Clifton Hotel, on the bank of the river, at the west end of West-street: they are in the proprietorship of a company. The building is in the Oriental style, and forms a pleasing object from the water. The baths are fitted up with every accommodation, such as writing, dressing, and reading rooms. They comprise warm, cold, vapour, shower, and swimming baths. The machines for bathing in the river are commodious, with awnings in front, and stand immediately under the house-bath establishment.

It must have been the Clifton Baths, which were described in the following terms in *A Journal of an Excursion round the South Eastern Coast of England*, in 1834.

There are hot baths close by, and the building forms a very pretty object from the river. There is a tasteful garden for loungers attached to the baths.

30. *The bathing room and bathing charges.*

Holidaymakers of the 1790s who were intent on bathing in the sea were advised to proceed as follows.

176

(a) [*The Margate and Ramsgate Guide in Letters to a Friend*, 1797, 8–13]

I get up generally about *seven*, and the first thing I do every morning, let the weather be what it may, after leaving my chamber, is to go to the bathing or waiting-room, to have my name put down among the company who bathe, of whom there are frequently not less than one hundred, and sometimes more, in the height of the season.

The bathing or waiting rooms, from *seven* till *nine*, are generally full of persons of all ages; men, women, and children, waiting till their turns come up to go bathing, according as their names appear on the slate, one being kept at each room for that purpose. 'First come first served', is the invariable rule, and I think a very proper one; no distinction is made between the rich and poor, old or young, noble or ignoble . . . Every one, when their turns come, go without further delay . . .

Sometimes the tide is down at the time of bathing, when the machines are obliged to be drove . . . on the sands before they come to a proper depth for bathing; at other times, when the tide is in, they are not drove out above five or six yards from the bathing rooms; this naturally occasions a great difference as to the time of persons waiting to bathe . . . The principal inquiry of every one is, 'Is it my turn? or how long will it be before my turn comes?' There are young women appointed at each bathing-room, to take down the names of the company as they come, and see that none go out of their turn; but as the bathing machines will hold *six* persons, sometimes *three* or *four* go together; the *women* bathers are, in general, very . . . well behaved *young* women, very different from the clumsy old women guides at Bright-helmstone . . .

The conversation of such a mixed company . . . is very miscel-laneous, and often made up of what is generally styled, *small talk*, particularly among the females; such as, 'How do you do, Miss, this morning? How do you like bathing? Is it of service to you? Do you design to drink the water this morning? If it is agreeable, I will go with you in your machine to bathing, for it is quite tiresome waiting so long', etc., etc.

When I go to the bathing-room, which is generally between *seven* and *eight* o'clock in the morning, there are frequently twelve or fourteen names before mine, who have not bathed; consequently, I have often to wait till near *nine* before my turn comes, during which time, my principal amusement is to observe the dresses, behaviour, and con-versation of the gentlemen and ladies in waiting around me. The bathing-rooms are generally opened about six o'clock every morning, during the season.

Indeed I can compare the bathing-room, from seven till nine in the morning, to nothing better than a exchange for *ladies* . . .
August 1.

I have been bathing this morning with two young gentlemen, and find it very comfortable and refreshing, as the weather is very warm now; it is the custom to bathe *before* breakfast, in general; but I find little or no difference whether I bathe before or afterwards; only this rule, . . .not to go into the sea with a full stomach; an hour or two after breakfast, I apprehend is as good a time as before it.

As there are generally several machines in the water at one time, and often near to one another, it is no little diversion to hear the vociferous exclamations of some of the more timorous and fearful of the *female* sex, just before they are manuducted into the briny deep.

Those gentlemen that can swim, enjoy bathing most of any; those who cannot, are generally attended by a guide of their own sex, for which they pay threepence extra each person, otherwise it is for every man in company without a guide, sixpence each. Very few, if any, *ladies* go without one.

For my part I want no guide, as I frequently swim out from under the umbrella several yards . . . I bathe more for *pleasure* than health . . . It is accounted most serviceable to stay but a minute or two in the water . . . After bathing it is recommended to take a walk, to keep the blood in a proper circulation.

> Nearly all of Margate's sea bathing took place at the back of the High Street, where the bathing rooms were situated (Illus. 13a). From these rooms there was access to the machines, and to the sands, steps leading down to the latter from the galleries behind them. (Illus. 4a). While the procedure described above survived beyond the Napoleonic Wars, Margate's bathing rooms became more lavish and developed also as social centres, where visitors could meet their friends and where, for a small subscription, the daily and weekly newspapers could be consulted. Some acquired coffee rooms which remained open after bathing hours, and amateur concerts were held in the evenings.

(b)   [*The Thanet Itinerary or Steam Yacht Companion*, 1819, 39–40]

The names of those wishing to bathe are inserted upon a slate, and everyone is compelled to wait his regular turn; for which purpose convenient waiting rooms are provided, where there are grand piano-fortes, newspapers, and telescopes, for the use of Subscribers. Frequently of an evening, these rooms are filled by a respectable assemblage of visitors, who amuse themselves by amateur playing singing and dancing.

Contemporary wits wrote amusingly about the scene inside a bathing room and about the hopes of those who were intending to bathe in the sea.

(c) [George Keate, *Sketches from Nature, Taken, and Coloured, in A Journey to Margate*, 5th Ed., 1802, 49–53]

THE BATHING-ROOM

On entering one of the bathing-rooms, where people assemble and converse till such times as their turns come to take the machines, I was agreeably surprised to find a face or two among the company which I had three years before often seen in the same place . . . It is a pleasing circumstance to *invalids* to meet after a considerable absence; their hopes are mutually fortified, being thereby induced to conceive there is not so much mortality in their complaints as they may have suspected.

My lean carcase was complimented on being plumped out since we had last seen each other. I returned as gracious a salute to the billious gentleman who had the civility to tell me so . . . A poor crippled figure, with an eye of languour, was commending the improved looks of a lady, whose face wore the colour of an INDIAN pickle, which was strongly confirmed by a nervous gentlewoman, who sat in the next chair, shaking like a CHINA Josse . . .

Most of the company had talked over their own case, which *invalids* are particularly fond of doing, and all had given a judgement on the sea, but in general so contradictory, that [it] amounted nearly to this – it thinned and it thickened the blood – it strengthened – it weakened – it made people fat – it made them lean – it braced – it relaxed – it was good for everything – and good for nothing.

It will wash you all clean, however, says a grave gentleman in the gallery, if it does nothing else. I had, from my first coming into the bathing-room, observed the person who threw out this observation, sitting close to the balustrade. He was in a night-cap, . . . wrapped in a great coat, with a silk handkerchief tied round his neck . . . As soon as the machines had gradually carried off the company, I accosted him with the trite question of, Sir, don't you bathe?

Bathe, Sir! – no truly, not I – 'tis diversion enough to see others do it. Wet, or dry, none will be out of the fashion. I see all the folks here, young, or old, take to the water as naturally as the Duck. They seem to me to make a Popish Saint of the sea. What a cackle did yonder women keep about its miracles . . . By what one hears in these places, if it were not for broken limbs, all our hospitals might be shut up.

The virtues of sea-water, said I, may be overrated, but I still think it an instrument of health to many. You are happy to have no *demand* on it.

I beg your pardon for that, replied my gentleman, presenting me such an enriched full face, as had not obtained its colouring at a small expense. If I have no *demand* Sir, my physician has sent me for three months from LONDON on a fool's errand . . . I follow his rules . . . He prohibits me my *morning whet*, denies me good sauce and CAYENNE *pepper* with my fish, drenches me with salt water and mutton broth, and obliges me to sit and walk two hours every morning by the sea side, and as many after dinner, in order to *smell the sea mud*. As it was a high tide today, I took my station in this gallery, but I believe (looking at his watch) I . . . shall now go to the coffee-house to breakfast.

The terms of or charges for sea bathing at Margate in 1809 and 1819 and at Ramsgate in 1833 were as follows.

(d) [*The New Margate, Ramsgate, and Broadstairs Guide*, 5th Ed., Margate, 1809, 55; *The Thanet Itinerary or Steam Yacht Companion*, 1819, 40; *Picture of Ramsgate, or A Guide to the Various Amusements, Public Libraries, Building Improvements, etc. of that celebrated Watering Place*, Ramsgate, 1833, 33]

Lady taking a machine, guide included	1s 3d.
Two or more ladies, guide included	1s 0d.each
Child taking a machine, guide included	1s 3d.
Two or more young children, guide included	9d.each
Gentleman taking a machine, guide included	1s 6d.
Gentleman bathing himself	1s 0d.
Two or more gentlemen, guide included	1s 3d.each
Two or more gentlemen bathing themselves	9d.each

Warm bath 3s. 6d. each time, or Seven times for One Guinea (1809 and 1819, Margate).

To the Reading Room for the Season, 3s. 6d. (1819, Margate).

No bathing on Sundays after 10 o'clock (1833, Ramsgate).

31. *Aspects of sea bathing which attracted favourable, amusing or adverse attention.*

> There were naturally occasions when sea bathing had to be cancelled on account of bad weather as at Margate on Sunday morning, 23 September 1804.

(a) [*The Times*, 25 September 1804]

The unfavourable keenness of the breezes keep the West India fleet still in the Margate Roads, . . . about to sail . . . This morning was discovered a brig, laden with stones for Dover, driven aground on the Nayland Rock, . . . by the violence of the weather . . . Today the bathing machines are not allowed to go out, on account of the turbulence of the waves and the boisterousness of the winds, to the no small mortification and grief of numbers, who raise 'the voice of complaint in the streets', and deplore this unexpected deprivation of the '*benefit*' of *salt water*. The stormy weather seems to have been all the better for the Theatre, as two performances have had, on Friday and last night, very crowded benefits.

> While there is little information concerning capital investment in the bathing business, the cost of a new bathing machine in 1834 was about £60. A life expectancy of about 30 to 40 years was anticipated, depending on treatment and wear and tear. The rate of depreciation was such that after two years a machine would fetch 40 guineas, and after 30 years it might fetch only 4 guineas. [*General Sea Bathing Infirmary, Margate Committee Minute Book, 1811–37*, 15 July 1834, KAO, MH/T1/A3]. There were occasions when bathing machines failed or were damaged, with some risk to the lives of their occupants. 1801, so far as Thanet was concerned, appears to have been a notably sensational year in this respect.

(b) [*The Morning Chronicle*, 25 September 1801]

A bathing machine was on Sunday blown over at Ramsgate, with a Lady in it; the horse was killed, but the Lady escaped unhurt . . . On

Monday a bathing machine was blown down, with two Gentlemen in it, while bathing. The Machine was totally demolished, and the Gentlemen lost . . . all their clothes, themselves escaping with difficulty. In a state of trepidation and perfect nakedness, they trembled up the steps into the bathing room where sat some two dozen Ladies. Each Lady held her fan or gown to her eyes; but some, if they lifted their clothes to hide their faces, exposed some other parts, being too fashionably dressed to have petticoats. Such shrieking . . . and fainting, and scampering and roaring and crying never before occurred in the place.

(c)   [*The Morning Chronicle*, 29 September and 1 October 1801]

Had it been two Ladies instead of two Gentlemen, who were bathing a few days since at Margate, when the old crazy machine broke down and overturned, they must inevitably have been drowned.

The late incident of the bathing machine at Margate has hurt the delicacy of some *gentlemen* so much, that they are determined to go into the water with their *cloaths on*. Unfortunately, the present style of *female dress* does not admit of this precaution.

> Sometimes it was the horse and not waves or wind which caused a memorable mishap.

(d)   [*The Times*, 18 September 1805]

The bathing machines, with the canvas umbrella . . . are not contrived for strength or velocity. A sudden exertion of the horse snapped the pole of one of them, the carriage fell, and two gentlemen, with some difficulty, extricated themselves, and plunged into the water. They were dressed, and were returning from bathing. After this second immersion, they passed through the streets, in a condition which occasioned some clamourous merriment.

> Measures were adopted to overcome a perfectly natural fear of drowning.

(e)   [*The Times*, 10 September 1804]

Some [Margate] bathers have been, lately, using an apparatus of cork, which enables them to swim with ease, and is an effectual protection against the dangers of drowning. The seafaring people here call it the seaman's friend.

Two years later an important publication was announced, compiled by Dr. Benjamin Franklin, which, having been printed for J. Callow, 10 Crown Court, Princes Street, Soho, was selling for 1s.

(f) [*The Times*, 18 July 1806]

DIRECTIONS for LEARNING to SWIM; by attending to which a person who has never been in the water may escape being drowned.

The subsequent demand for this instructive manual was such that it was incorporated into a London guidebook of 1809, entitled *Picture of Margate, being a Complete Guide to all Persons visiting Margate, Ramsgate and Broadstairs*. In 1856, in his *Social History of the People of the Southern Counties of England in Past Centuries*, George Roberts, observed how 'when machines were unknown . . . one was obliged to undress on the beach' (p.550). Sea bathing in its infancy has been described as 'free and primitive'. Often no clothes were worn, there were no bye-laws for bathing and spy glasses were focussed as much on sea bathers as on fishing vessels.

(g) [*The Observer*, 14 September 1800]

The indecency of numerous naked men bathing in the sea close to the ladies' bathing machines, and under the windows of the principal houses at most of the watering places, has long been complained of, but in general has not been . . . redressed.

To prove the point the famous caricaturist James Gillray (1756–1815) sketched the following bathing scene in Margate in 1807.

(h) [D. Hill, *Mr. Gillray The Caricaturist*, 1965, 136–7]

Scene ye Machines in Muddy water, dead dogs, Fish Guts, Greens and filth swimming about – naked men among ye machines – Bathing women entering from one Machine to ye other, young Ladies looking thro' Telescopes at ye Naked Figures in ye Water. High Wind. John Bull & Family waiting on ye Stairs of Bathing House.

In the context of such a setting embarrassments were inevitable, as and when a venturesome swimmer mistook his own bathing machine. Although what follows is pure fiction, it might well in real life have marred a holiday and a personal reputation.

(i)   ['Peter Splitfig's Trip to Margate', *The Thanet Magazine*, November 1817, 217–9]

As I was walking down the High-street, a very civil little man enquired in the most humble manner if I chused to take a cold bath? I consented to go in one of the Machines, but having been very fond of swimming in my youth, I crept out from under the umbrella, and took a long turn round the bay. On my return it puzzled me much to conjecture which was my own Bathing Machine; at length however, feeling tolerably certain that I had found the right [one], I lifted up the canvass, and to my utter astonishment found myself in the midst of five beautiful nymphs, who were sporting in . . . naked simplicity. Four of them it is true had a sort of flannel garment round their waists, but the fifth wanted even this inefficient covering to conceal her pre-eminent loveliness. The streaming hair hung floating at their backs, and their exquisitely formed bosoms crested the briny waves. . .

The moment my head appeared, the naked sylph ran up the stairs into the Machine, and immediately banged to the door; the other ladies attacked me with all the violence of language and action . . . It was in vain that I apologized . . . It was utterly impossible to convince them that my intrusion was wholly unintentional. . .

Smarting under the effects of this disagreeable [experience], I fortunately happened to find out my own Machine, the driver of which had become exceedingly impatient at my long delay in the water. Having dressed myself and drove up to the block, I was accosted on leaving the vehicle by a fierce looking naval officer, who demanded my name and address, adding, that he expected to have the *pleasure* of exchanging shots with me before twenty-four hours had elapsed; as he was determined to wash out the insult which his sister had just received, in the blood of her brutal assaulter!!!

> Naked sea bathing comfortably outlived the arrival of the eighteenth-century bathing machine, added to which there were quiet spots where such facilities did not exist, away from the public gaze, as Samuel Taylor Coleridge could point out in a letter to James Gillman, written from Ramsgate on 20 August 1819.

(j)   [Ed: E.H. Coleridge, *Letters of Samuel Taylor Coleridge*, II, 1895, 700–1]

The tide comes up to the end of the lane, . . . and exactly a hundred of my strides from the end of the lane, there is a good, roomy, arched cavern, with an oven or cupboard in it, where one's clothes may be put free from the sand.

One of the private and quiet spots which can be identified in the 1830s was Dumpton Bay, lying between Ramsgate and Broadstairs.

(k) [*Picture of Ramsgate, or A Guide to the Various Amusements, Public Libraries, Building Improvements, etc. of that celebrated Watering Place,* Ramsgate, 1833, 47–8]

Near this place is Dumpton Stairs, the retired and favourite bathing place of the inhabitants and visitors who prefer a plunge into [the] open sea without the use of machines.

Bathing from the beach at Dover but with costumes caught the eye of John Crosier, as recorded in 1782 in his diary.

(l) [Quoted in C. Willett and Phillis Cunnington, *Handbook of English Costume in the Eighteenth Century,* 1957, 404–5]

The Ladies in a morning when they intend to bathe, put on a long flannel gown under their other clothes, walk down to the beach, undress themselves to the flannel, then they walk in as deep as they please, and lay hold of the guides' hands, three or four together sometimes.

Then they dip over head twenty times perhaps; then they come onto the shore where there are women that attend with towels, cloaks, chairs, etc. The flannel is stripp'd off, wip'd dry, etc. Women hold cloaks round them. They dress themselves and go home.

Gillray was right to stress the filthiness of the water in and about Margate harbour in 1807, one possible cause of which was subsequently removed.

(m) [*The New Margate, Ramsgate and Broadstairs Guide,* 6th Ed., Margate, 1816, 69]

The sewer, which heretofore emptied itself into the harbour, and which, from its filthiness and [faeces], was so generally complained of, is now conducted through the cliff at the Back of the Fort: the small shops too, which were on the Parade, are also taken down: [so] we may venture to assert, that this improvement will not suffer in comparison with the greatest that have been made at any other watering-place whatever.

But all was still not perfect to judge from a further and later observation of the 1840s.

(n) [J.H. Curtis, *Observations on the Preservation of Health in Infancy, Youth, Manhood and Age*, 1842]

Margate . . . is a very lively, bustling place . . . There are several places used for sea-bathing; but by far the best is near the Clifton Baths, away from the town. The place most frequented, in the neighbourhood of the bathing-houses, owing to the number of bathers and the circumstances that horses are employed for drawing the machines into the water, which do not, as may readily be supposed, add to its purity, [is] much inferior to the former . . . I should as soon think of going to bathe in the Mechanics' Bath at Lambeth, as of going into the water at this spot. The warm baths, however, are very good, and fitted up with great convenience.

32. *Dating the introduction of sea bathing to Kentish resorts other than Margate.*

The fame of the Margate bathing machines spread far and wide. It was from the Margate model that a bathing machine was introduced to Deal in 1753, and to Ramsgate and Broadstairs for the commencement of the 1754 season.

(a) DEAL [Ed: J.J. Cartwright, *The Travels through England of Dr. Richard Pococke, during 1750, 1751, and Later Years, Camden Society*, II, 1889, 91; *The Kentish Post*, 11–15 May and 18–22 May 1754]

Dover, Sept 12, 1754.
I went by Old Deal, and in a mile from it came to New Deal, which is a town chiefly supported by the shipping that lye in the Downs. Company also resort to this place to bathe.

At DEAL in Kent is the Original NEW-INVENTED MACHINE for Bathing in the Sea. The Machine moves on 4 Wheels, on which is erected a commodious Dressing-Room, furnished in a genteel Manner. This Machine is so contriv'd, that the Persons who bathe descend from out of the above Room into a Bath, which forms itself in the natural Sea

7 Feet in Length and 5 Feet in Breadth; all inclosed and railed, which renders it both secure and private.

The Machine, during the last Season, met with general Approbation; and, in order to make it still more useful, the Proprietors have this Season provided an additional Machine, with proper Conveniences for Bathing at all Times.

All Gentlemen and Ladies, who are desirous of making use of this Machine, are to apply to Mr. John Dixon, at the East India Arms in Deal, from whom they may hear of good Lodgings in the Neighbourhood, pleasantly situated, on reasonable Terms. N.B. A proper Woman is provided to attend the Ladies if required.

(b)   RAMSGATE [*The Kentish Post*, 22–25 May 1754]

At RAMSGATE in the Isle of Thanet is lately built, a large and convenient MACHINE for the Purpose of BATHING in the Sea. And at the same Place Gentlemen and Ladies may be accommodated with very good Lodgings, at reasonable Rates.

(c)   BROADSTAIRS [*The Kentish Post*, 1–5 June 1754]

At BROADSTAIRS, in the Isle of Thanet, Is a New-invented MACHINE for Bathing in the SEA.

The Machine moves on 4 Wheels, on which is erected a commodious Dressing-Room. This Machine is so contriv'd, that the Persons who bathe, descend from out of the above Room into a Bath which forms itself in the natural Sea 10 Feet in Length and 5 Feet in Breadth; and being an even smooth Bay, may go in at any Time of the Day, both secure and private.

All Gentlemen and Ladies who are desirous of making use of this Machine are to apply to Mr. John Jones, from whom they may hear of good Lodgings in the Neighbourhood pleasantly situated to the Sea. May be had one, two or three Rooms ready furnished, or whole Houses, if desir'd, and at reasonable Terms. . .

This Place affords all Kind of Fish in its Season, . . . and all Kind of Provision, very reasonable.

> Within fourteen years bathing machines on the Margate model were being publicized in Dover and Whitstable and as with the above advertisements some of the other essentialities of an embryonic resort were being stressed.

187

(d)   DOVER [*The Kentish Gazette*, 15–18 June 1768]

CORNELIUS JONES, near the Rope Walk, Dover, Begs Leave to inform the Public that he has lately provided a MACHINE upon the same Plan as those at MARGATE.

(e)   WHITSTABLE [*The Kentish Gazette*, 28 May–1 June and 1–4 June 1768]

HOCKLESS's Bathing Machines, now in full Perfection, ARE ready for the Reception of Ladies and Gentlemen, at his House at the BEAR and KEY. Good Accommodation with the best of Wines, etc. T. HOCKLESS.
N.B. Lodging, Coach-house, Stabling, etc. and Horses to any Part of England. A good Turnpike Road from Whitstable to Canterbury.

From the mid–1770s there are references to sea-bathing at

(f)   HERNE BAY [C. Seymour, *A New Topographical, Historical, and Commercial Survey of the Cities, Towns, and Villages, of the County of Kent*, Canterbury, 1776, 457, 459]

HERNE, six miles from Canterbury . . . is an agreeable recess in the summer season, on account of its vicinity to the sea; it consists chiefly of a long street . . . *Herne Bay* is about two miles distant from the street; here is a public-house, with good decent accommodations for private families, who come here in the summer season for the benefit of bathing in the sea. This Bay is frequented by small vessels and colliers from Sunderland. Two hoys go to and from London every week from thence; one of them is commanded by Captain William Amis, a skilful, obliging, and civil man. Passengers pay 2s. 6d.

> Here was Margate in miniature. (On 'The Old Margate Hoy', which by this time was very well established, see Docs. 4,5). Herne Bay remained small and relatively undeveloped until well into the nineteenth century.

(g)   HERNE BAY [Zechariah Cozens, *A Tour through the Isle of Thanet, and some other Parts of East Kent*, 1793, 452]

A bathing machine is now kept at this place, and good accommodations are to be met with at the two inns.

(h) SANDGATE too was noted as a sea bathing place during the 1770s [C. Seymour, *A New Topographical, Historical, and Commercial Survey of the Cities, Towns, and Villages, of the County of Kent*, Canterbury, 1776, 387, 389, 390–1]

Several pretty dwellings have been lately erected on this spot for the conveniency of bathing in the sea.

FOLKESTONE, in spite of having 'some neat houses facing the Church-yard, which have the advantage of a fine prospect', had failed to seize the initiative.

At a place called Foord, ¼ mile West from Folkestone, is a fine salubrious spring of water, which has all the virtue and efficacy of the chalybeate, being impregnated with iron in a degree equal to the Tunbridge water. It has been proved with success by Mr. Gill, operates by urine and perspiration, and is of infinite service in cold chronical distempers, weak nerves and bad digestion. If a subscription was opened by the inhabitants of Folkestone and the Gentlemen of the vicinity, to make this place convenient for public resort, it would greatly contribute to the benefit of the town.

By 1792 Folkestone and Hythe had joined the other Kentish resorts in providing bathing machines, apart from Gravesend which followed the fashionable trend four years later, with Margate and Ramsgate well out in front.

(i) [*The Kentish Companion for the Year of Our Lord*, Canterbury, 1792, 153, 156, 158, 159, 160, 162]

Margate – Upwards of 40 (Bathing Machines) employed in the season from April to November.
Ramsgate – a great number are employed in the season, which begins in April and ends in November.
Deal – Bathing Machines by Pitcher & Co., N. Mocket & J. Wood.
Dover – Bathing Machines in the Season by B. Gardner and Iggulden, Austin & Hawker.
Folkestone – 2 Bathing Machines.
Hythe – Bathing Machines and Lodging-houses, in the season.

(j) GRAVESEND [Edward Hasted, *The History and Topographical Survey of the County of Kent*, III, 2nd Ed., Canterbury, 1797, 320]

Proper machines have lately been established here, with every requisite accommodation for sea bathing.

Their introduction, as in so many other instances from Margate, was explained as follows.

(k) [R.P. Cruden, *The History of the Town of Gravesend in the County of Kent*, 1843, 449]

On the 18th of May, 1796, forty-nine inhabitants of Gravesend joined in a subscription of five guineas each, for the purpose of founding a Bathing Establishment; and they purchased a machine at Margate, to begin with, which was used for the first time on the 27th of the following month. There are now nine machines employed, at the same spot where they were first used, on the west side of the town; and the establishment is now called the Clifton Baths.

It is almost certain that Gravesend's first bathing machine of 1796 was consigned from Margate on one of the old Margate hoys (see Docs. 4, 44o).

33. *How the facilities for sea bathing at particular resorts were interpreted at different times.*

(a) GRAVESEND, 1834 [*A Journal of an Excursion round the South Eastern Coast of England*, 1834]

The river is a mile in width . . . There are several bathing machines and at high water a salt bath may be enjoyed. The shore, which is chalk or rock, and was rough, has been cut smooth, with much labour, at the bath place.

(b) GRAVESEND, 1842 [*The Visitor's Guide to the Watering Places*, 1842, 3]

BATHING here is rendered as pleasant as the situation will admit, although it is not equal to some other watering places; yet, from its vicinity to London, it attracts a considerable number of visitors. Much prejudice has existed against the river bathing here, from the occasional turbid state of the water, forgetting, or probably not knowing, that the very sediment which occasions it, is particularly recommended by several of the principal medical practitioners in the metropolis, as very efficacious in all cutaneous disorders. It is taken in pails, and other vessels, to be applied to medical purposes. Experienced dippers attend the machines, and boats are in constant readiness, to prevent accidents, from the too-venturesome inexperienced bather.

(c)   WHITSTABLE, 1789 [*The Kentish Gazette*, 23 June 1789]

It is an exceeding good shore, and the water allowed to be very pure.

(d)   HERNE BAY, 1835 [By a Lady, *A Picture of the New Town of Herne Bay*, 1835, 9]

The shore is so clear from mud, and so level, as to permit a safe bathing in all states of the tide.

(e)   HERNE BAY, 1847 [S. Bagshaw, *History, Gazetteer and Directory of the County of Kent*, II, Sheffield, 1847, 219]

The facilities for sea bathing are superior to those offered at many of the watering places on the coast. The shore is so free from mud and weed, and so gradual in its inclination to the sea, that safety is insured at all times of the tide. St. George's Baths are on the parade, and there are two establishments near the Ship Inn, which are amply furnished with convenient apartments and bathing machines.

(f)   MARGATE, 1780 [*The Margate Guide*, 1780, 12–13]

Margate is the Resort of a great deal of very genteel Company in the Summer, who come either for the Enjoyment and Advantage of its very fine and pure Air, or for the Benefit of Sea-bathing, for which no Place is so well adapted, the Shore being level and covered with Sand. On the Wharf are several bathing Rooms, which are large and commodious. The Company resort to them to drink the Water, and thence in turns, enter the Machines, which are driven into the Sea under the Conduct of careful and experienced Guides.

(g)   MARGATE, 1797 [*The Margate and Ramsgate Guide in Letters to a Friend*, 1797, 9, 10]

There are five bathing or waiting-rooms to accommodate the great number of persons who come here to bathe, and they are kept by *Phillpot* [Illus. 13a]. *Surflen, Sayer, Wood* and *Hubbard* . . . Each of them employ five or six machines for bathing every morning . . . From twenty to thirty machines are often seen in the water together at one time, and a pretty sight it is, as they much resemble an *aquatic encampment*, the chief of them being painted white . . . [compare Illus. 4a, 10a].

The sands where the company bathe are almost as level and smooth as a bowling green for near half a mile from the bathing-rooms, which makes it greatly preferable to Brighthelmstone, where the descent into the water is within a few yards from the beach, and in some parts covered with gravel.

(h) BROADSTAIRS, 1803 [*A Guide to all the Watering and Sea-Bathing Places*, 1803, 123]

In the harbour, and off its mouth, is the Bathing-place. The machines and rooms are on the same principle and terms as those at Margate and Ramsgate.

(i) RAMSGATE, 1776 [C. Seymour, *A New Topographical, Historical, and Commercial Survey of the Cities, Towns, and Villages, of the County of Kent*, Canterbury, 1776, 653]

Ramsgate has a very convenient place for bathing, on a clean sand, remote from public inspection; there are several bathing machines for the accommodation of the company.

(j) RAMSGATE, 1790 [*The Kentish Traveller's Companion*, 3rd Ed., Canterbury, 1790, 260]

The bathing place is under the cliffs on the east side of the harbour; the bottom is of chalk, covered with sand, and is continually improving from the sand daily thrown out of the habour into the sea, which being driven upon the shore by the tide, makes an excellent bottom for bathing [Illus. 3].

(k) RAMSGATE, 1797 [*The Margate and Ramsgate Guide in Letters to a Friend*, 1797, 32–3]

Many genteel families come to this town for bathing, as there are similar machines and attendants as at Margate, but nothing like so numerous. There are but *two* bathing-rooms here, and not more than *twelve* machines in use during the season. The sands on the outer side of the pier are not so level nor extend so far as at Margate, but the town is more agreeable to those who come more for health than pleasure, being more retired . . . and fashionable than the latter.

(l)   RAMSGATE, c.1804 [*Maritime Guide*, c.1804, 39]

The bathing place, which is furnished with machines, guides, and all other accommodations, is under the cliffs on the east side of the harbour, and has every advantage that can be desired.

(m)   RAMSGATE, 1809 [*The New Margate, Ramsgate and Broadstairs Guide*, 5th Ed., Margate, 1809, 81, 88]

Since sea-bathing has been found indispensably necessary, and indeed the only possible remedy in various diseases, Ramsgate has been much resorted to, during the summer season . . . The place for bathing is on the sand at the back of the pier, where the machines ply after the same manner as at Margate.

(n)   RAMSGATE, 1833 [*Picture of Ramsgate, or A Guide to the Various Amusements, Public Libraries, Building Improvements, etc., of that celebrated Watering Place*, Ramsgate, 1833, 32–3]

One of the many advantages afforded to the town of Ramsgate from the building of the pier has been the improvement of its sands, which from being narrow and of small extent, is become very considerable, and affords every possible facility for the accommodation of the numerous machines which crowd it during the season; and many hundred yards of a space, formerly rocky and rugged, has since the erection of its extensive harbour, been made level and sandy, affording a delightful parade for the company upon leaving the machines after bathing. Upwards of twenty machines are employed every morning during the season, and several convenient waiting rooms have been built where the company resort, to take in their turns the benefit of the invigorating bath. The proprietors Messrs. Barling, Wells & Co. have warm, cold, and shower baths, and pay every possible attention to such visitors who honour them with their support, providing for their use cleanly and comfortable machines, with careful and experienced guides, under whose protection the most delicate and timid may bathe in safety.

Direction posts are placed on the sands, to prevent persons bathing openly from approaching the machines or offending the decency of those who use them, and to ensure a certain extent of promenade for them after bathing.

The references to sand building up on the eastward side of Ramsgate Harbour arose from the ingenuity of that celebrated eighteenth-century civil engineer John Smeaton who constructed in 1779 an inner basin as a backwater to cleanse the outer harbour which was silting up, by means of a cross wall, in which were two sluices, 'the operations of which were amazingly powerful', such that 'they entirely cleared away the sullage from it down to the chalk, besides carrying out of the harbour's mouth great quantities of sand' [E. Hasted, *The History and Topographical Survey of the County of Kent*, X, 2nd Ed., Canterbury, 1800, 393].

(o)   DEAL, 1832–4 [*Pigot & Co's Commercial Directory*, 1832–4, 797]

The pebbled gently sloping beach forms an agreeable promenade. The bathing here is excellent, and there are several good machines [Illus. 7b].

(p)   DOVER, 1817 [*Horn's Description of Dover*, Dover, 1817, 23]

It is impossible to conceive a situation better adapted for the purpose of bathing; as the water is extremely strong and pure, and the beach at all times perfectly clean.

(q)   DOVER, 1828 [W. Batcheller, *A New History of Dover, to which is Added a New Dover Guide*, Dover, 1828, 349, 352]

The cleanness of the pebbles on the shore, and the transparent clearness of the water, invite to the pleasing refreshment of the cooling waves . . . The sea-bathing at Dover, on account of the clearness of the water, and the convenience of the shore, has obtained a decided preference to any other watering place on the coast [Illus. 20a].

(r)   FOLKESTONE, 1810 [*A Guide to all the Watering and Sea-Bathing Places*, 1810, 244]

The gentle declivity of the shore, and being well sheltered from the wind, renders the bathing not only safe, but pleasant in any state of the wind or tide.

(s) SANDGATE, 1816 [*The Hythe, Sandgate and Folkestone Guide*, Hythe, 1816, 29]

The beach which is of gravel, and slopes boldly from the houses to the water's edge is always free from humidity, and affords an agreeable walk, eastward as far as Folkestone, unless when the tides are very high; and in an opposite direction far beyond the town of Hythe [Illus. 12a].

(t) HYTHE, 1816 [*Ibid.*, 23]

Machines for the convenience of bathers are kept in that part of the town which borders upon the sea side, between which and the principal street, the military canal . . . runs in a parallel line, and its green banks afford on either side, a pleasant walk.

(u) HYTHE, 1840 [*Pigot & Co's Royal, National and Commercial Directory*, 1840, 314]

During the bathing season it has many visitors, for whose accommodation there are several machines on the beach.

34. *Sitting or lazing on the beach.*

References to paying for sitting on chairs on the beach at Ramsgate date from 1829.

(a) [*MS Journal of an Excursion to Ramsgate in July and August 1829*, Tyler Collection (Ramsgate Scrapbook), Cathedral Library and Archives, Canterbury]

Wednesday, July 22.
Went with Mrs. B—— to market and thence to the Beach where we each took a chair for half an hour, thence returned to our lodging. . .
Paid for sitting on Chairs on the Beach   2d.
Saturday, August 1.
After Breakfast went to Market with Charlotte and thence to the Beach when we took a chair for an hour. . .
Chairs on the Beach   2d.

Ramsgate may well have been one of the first seaside resorts to provide visitors with seating facilities on the beach, as the forerunner of the twentieth-century deckchair.

(b) [By a Valetudinarian, *Sea-Side Reminiscences: A Few 'Odd Thoughts' on Our Fashionable Watering Places*, c. 1835, 15]

I must not omit to notice Ramsgate Sands. For the accommodation of visitors, a number of chairs (some hundreds) have been placed on them, to a considerable distance. The charge being only 1d., per day, for each person, rends this accommodation mutually beneficial. A SUBSCRIPTION MARQUEE has also been erected, facing the sea. Here, even in wet weather, the visitors may sit and enjoy the pure sea-breezes, without experiencing any inconvenience. To complete the accommodation, flies and vehicles of every description are always in readiness to convey people home, without the misery of getting wet feet. In conclusion, no place equals Ramsgate for general accommodation.

> This was high praise indeed from someone who felt that in Broadstairs 'a more unsocial spot does not exist', whereas at Margate 'visitors and donkies are now looked upon here as public property', while 'HERNE BAY and the Ague are now synonymous terms' (*ibid.*, 16, 18, 21). The marquee mentioned above is confirmed for 1833–4, and for 1842.

(c) [*Pigot & Co's National, London and Provincial Commercial Directory, for 1833–4*, 856]

In proportion to the increase of visitors, various establishments for their convenience and pleasure have sprung up . . . Messrs. BARLING, FOAT & WELLS, opposite the pier gates, . . . have a splendid *marquee* upon the bathing sands, furnished with the London and other journals, and approved periodicals.

(d) [*The Visitor's Guide to the Watering Places*, 1842, 179]

THE SUBSCRIPTION MARQUEE, on the Bathing Sands, where five London papers are taken daily, and the most approved periodicals, is a pleasant lounge. The *Times*, *Herald*, *Morning Post*, and *Chronicle* arrive in Ramsgate the same evening of publication.

Terms of Subscription to the Marquee:

For the season	. . . . . . 9s.	For one month	. . . . . . 3s.
For two months	. . . . . . 5s.	For one week	. . . . 1s.

Chairs are placed on the Bathing Sands for the sole use of subscribers, and an attendant to remove them to any situation.

The hiring of penny chairs, portrayed so well in W.P. Frith's famous painting of Ramsgate Sands, in 1854, continued to be a sound business proposition.

(e) [MacKenzie Walcott, *A Guide to the Coast of Kent*, 1859, 112–3]

Near the pier, the visitors who fill the houses in the terrace and crescent ... do congregate, seated for their customary three hours on their penny chairs; the ladies working or reading their well worn novels.

What was introduced as the modern Margate beach scene was described graphically in 1845, one year before waves of visitors began arriving on the South Eastern Railway.

(f) [Mrs. Stone, *Chronicles of Fashion*, II, 1845, 299–303]

How shall we give the picture of today? We cannot do it: we will offer the materials, and our readers will combine them at pleasure. Look at these Sands! They appear one indiscriminate moving mass of cabs, cars, carts and carriages; horses, ponies, dogs, donkies, and boys; men, women, children, and nurses; and, the least and the biggest – babies and bathing machines. Imagine of course all proper associations and accompaniments: little boys with spades; nurses with babies; mammas with sewing; young ladies with novels; young gentlemen with Byron, canes, and eye-glasses; older ones with newspapers, sticks, and spectacles. Then the hawkers are a most noisy, important, and persevering fraternity here; such opportunities for 'cheap bargains'; nothing in the world that you may not buy.

Oh!, but how the scene changes when a shower comes and then disappears.

Nurses, and babies, and donkies, and boys, are all huddled together under the awnings of the bathing-machines, by this time drawn up in order ... Some amphibious animals, with lots of legs and arms, very scanty trousers, and jackets, scamper about, ... collecting stray gloves, books, parasols, scissors and thimbles, which have been dropped in the hurry of the retreat; and just as all these arrangements are satisfactorily completed, the rain drops cease, the cloud has passed over, the sun comes out bright and brilliant ... Chairs resume their 'native' positions, ... and the sands, which three minutes before were 'full of desolation', are again ringing with life and merriment.

While Charles Dickens at this time much preferred the retirement of Broadstairs to the bustle of Margate, his correspondence shows how he enjoyed nevertheless any excuse for sitting or lazing on the beach, as he revealed in a letter which he wrote on 13 September 1841 to his friend and biographer, John Forster (1812–76).

(g)   [Ed: M. House and G. Storey, *The Letters of Charles Dickens*, II, O.U.P., 1969, 380]

I am in an exquisitely lazy state, bathing, walking, reading, lying in the sun, doing everything but working.

On other occasions, again through his correspondence (*ibid.*, II, 83, 383], he admitted to being

as brown as berries,
[or] hideously lazy – always bathing, lying in the sun, or walking about.

35.   *Diversions on or about the beach.*

Guidebooks intended for a middle and upper class readership stressed the natural curiosities and antiquities of their areas, at a time when some of their readers at least were showing an increasing interest in natural, archaeological and local historical discoveries. One good illustration of this dates from 1819.

(a)   [*The Thanet Itinerary or Steam Yacht Companion*, 1819, 11]

A person who has the least taste for geological research will find much amusement during a ramble along the sands, in observing the peculiar manner in which the great mass of chalk [cliffs] is divided into separate layers or *strata*. At times, during hard frosts in winter, large proportions of the cliffs fall away, and form innumerable romantic caverns, or grotesque projections; and, upon such occasions, many antient coins and implements have been found among the rubbish.

Visitors, irrespective of drinking sea water or bathing in the sea, found much to fascinate them on the beach, along cliffs or in the simple pleasures of collecting shells or sea weed. Initially the seaside was a novelty, as at Deal, on Thursday, 17 May 1759.

(b) [Ed: F. Hull, 'A Tour into Kent, 1759', *Archaeologia Cantiana*, LXIX, 1955, or in Ed: M. Roake and J. Whyman, *Essays in Kentish History*, 1973, 189]

After Dinner walkt on the Beach . . . Hunt and Goodwin ran a Race on the beach which was almost knee deep in Stones. Gathered Sea Weed and past an hour or two in such Amusements.

(c) [C. Seymour, *A New Topographical, Historical, and Commercial Survey of the Cities, Towns, and Villages, of the County of Kent*, Canterbury, 1776, 558]

At low water, many persons go on the sands to collect shells, pebbles, sea weeds, which are deemed objects of curiosity by those who live far from the Sea.

Walking was particularly recommended after sea bathing as in Thanet's first guidebook of 1763.

(d) [John Lyons, *A Description of the Isle of Thanet, and particularly of the Town of Margate*, 1763, 17]

When the tide is ebbed, many persons go on the sands, to collect pebbles, shells, sea-weeds, etc. which, altho' of no great value, are esteemed as matters of curiosity by those to whom such objects have not been familiar. Some of these weeds, when spread on writing paper, extended with a needle, and pressed down, form an infinite variety of landscapes, in the most beautiful colours. Many of them are to be met with in and about *Margate*; but the most beautiful collection I have ever seen, of this kind, was executed by a very ingenious young lady who lives in the place.

(e) [*The Margate and Ramsgate Guide in Letters to a Friend*, 1797, 14]

Many young ladies often amuse themselves, when the tide is out, in picking up, on the sands, sea-weed, which is in great quantities, and of different colours, thrown up by the tide, and curious shells, to form into landscapes, and grottoes. Among the rocks are often found crabs, lobsters, and perriwinkles; the latter are as large as snails, and are fine eating when boiled.

Two instances of shell gathering can be quoted from holidays which were spent in Thanet at the end of the 1820s.

(f) [*MS Diary of Mary Figgins, 30 August–21 September circa 1828*, Margate Public Library, Local Collection, YO60. 41]

September 3 [Margate].
We all went to market and afterwards for a walk on the sands. Vincent took a sketch while we strolled about and picked up shells.

(g) [*MS Journal of an Excursion to Ramsgate in July and August 1829*, Tyler Collection (Ramsgate Scrapbook), Cathedral Library and Archives, Canterbury]

Friday, August 7.
Hired a boat by which we, i.e. Mrs. Benham, myself and our little one, Mrs. Hunt and 2 of her daughters, viz: Ann and Anise and our Nursery Maid Betsy Thornton were conveyed to Shellness near Sandwich. Drank tea at the Red Lyon on the Sandwich Road . . . On our return landed to pick up shells of which we collected a great number but none curious. Got to Ramsgate Harbour at 8 o'clock all pleased with a charming excursion.

> Two years later shell gathering was recommended as a family amusement.

(h) [G.W. Bonner, *The Picturesque Pocket Companion to Margate, Ramsgate, Broadstairs, and the Parts Adjacent*, 2nd Ed., 1831, 86]

With the visitants and their children, the search after shells is a fashionable and daily amusement; here [Margate] there are no splendid specimens of conchology, but shells may be found of such exquisite smallness, that many hundred may be stored in a very small bottle.

> Seaweed, pebbles, shells and a search for antiquities all came together on a visit to Herne Bay in 1835.

(i) [*MS. Journal of a Visit to Herne Bay in 1835*, KAO, U2491]

We turned and bent our way to the town whence after the purchase of a fowl for dinner and a basket for any discoveries, we roamed along the shore far on the way to Reculver. We were soon laden with pebbles and lovely seaweed which is here in greater variety than I have remarked at other places on this coast, but time forced us to shorten our ramble and we returned from a delightful walk to a comfortable habitation and a savoury meal.

[On another occasion] we wound our way down to the beach, . . . and toiled our way along the sea side – the tide was fast retiring, and . . . I looked for curiosities with all my eyes. I was just bewailing and sighing for a coin be it ever so small when we seemed all at once to have arrived at a new order of things. The cliffs now became steep, rose abruptly with their sandy precipices from the beach, while close to the shore the stones had almost universally a beautiful reddy tinge and glowed brilliantly in the sun. I put it all to the account of iron, and sure enough on groping I found quantities of pyrites, and what appeared to me to be iron ore . . . The shells also partook of the general reddish tinge and were dyed of an orange colour. They also became more plentiful. But with great pleasure I stumbled on a mass of clay covered with impressions of shells of all kinds. It was too heavy to move and I had no hammer, but with a large flint, assisted by despair, I broke off a few fragments . . . I staid to collect and grub among these eccentricities of nature.

The author had been told by a local inhabitant of how people not only found coins and hardware on the high tides but her father had sometimes dragged up deer's heads and antlers – *great* elephants' teeth and other things. We trudged homeward ecstatifyed with our adventures.

Beach entertainments were provided at Margate at least from the 1780s onwards.

(j)   [*The Morning Herald and Daily Advertiser*, 23 August 1781]

Our *Master of the Ceremonies* very politely went round to the *first families* in the place yesterday morning to acquaint them in *due form*, that the *usual diversions* would take place in a few days on the *sands*, consisting of *Jack-ass races*! – *Men jumping in sacks*!

(k)   [*The Times*, 14 September 1805]

Margate, September 12.
The humours of the evening on the sands were the antient, honourable, and royal amusement of *Bob Lemon*, and a pig race.

Nineteenth-century Broadstairs, however, achieved renown as a family resort, which Charles Dickens (1812–70) helped to advertise in his famous article on 'Our Watering Place', in August 1851.

(1) [*Household Words*, No 71, 2 August 1851, 435]

So many children are brought down to our Watering Place that, when they are not out of doors, as they usually are in fine weather, it is wonderful where they are put: the whole village seeming much too small to hold them under cover. In the afternoons, you see no end of salt and sandy little boots drying on upper window-sills. At bathing-time in the morning, the little bay [Viking Bay] re-echoes with every shrill variety of shriek and splash – after which, if the weather be at all fresh, the sands teem with small blue mottled legs. The sands are the children's great resort. They cluster there, like ants: so busy burying their particular friends, and making castles with infinite labour which the next tide overthrows.

36. *Two popular attractions of the 1800s: the Margate Grotto and a camera obscura.*

The discovery of a grotto at Margate caused it to become an enduring attraction from the 1800s onwards and it has remained so ever since.

(a) [*The Times*, 26 September 1804]

There is at Margate, though known to a very few persons, a curious grotto, concerning the construction and real date of which nothing is certainly known. It is on the premises and behind the house of Mr. OLDFIELD, . . . most plentifully adorned with valuable shells of various kinds and sizes. It is only within a short time that it has been discovered.

In 1809 Margate's camera obscura was a major attraction.

(b) [*The New Margate, Ramsgate, and Broadstairs Guide*, 5th Ed., Margate, 1809, 52]

An admirer of those admirable scenes and engaging objects which are beheld from the Pier, would much regret his leaving the spot without re-enjoying a sight of them in the Camera-obscura, which, from its very extensive scale, and peculiar situation, may be said to equal if not surpass every thing of the kind. Mr. Cuthbert, the late proprietor, styled it *The Beauty of all Beauties*: we presume, from the marked attention of his numerous visitors, who never failed to express their

202

approbation of the ingenious apparatus, and of that obligingness which for many years distinguished him as a favourite of the public.

Ten years later this attraction was housed in 'a little circular wooden building' and was reached by a flight of steps leading from the Pier up to the Fort.

(c) [*The Thanet Itinerary or Steam Yacht Companion*, 1819, 41–2]

The Proprietor could not have chosen a more favourable situation as his revolving glasses can here command a most beautiful variety of objects.

Forty years after it was first publicized the Margate Grotto was visited by some holidaymakers in 1844.

(d) [*MS Journal compiled by S. Daniele in 1844*, KAO, U2666 F1, 37–8]

[It is] very large and intirely composed of shells found on the Kentish coast, arranged in the most singular and elegant patterns. The walls are divided into compartments and every one is differently ornamented. The shape of the cave is a circular passage . . . The entrance is a Gothic doorway. About the middle is a dome, which rises very much above the arch of the other part of the passage, and it was by the falling of the earth through this dome that the grotto was discovered, exactly in the same state of preservation as it is now shown. The date of the work and the name of the ingenious person who did it are both a profound mystery as there is no record of it in any of the Kentish chronicles . . . Since it has been known a circuitous passage has been cut in the rock to descend into it, and at the further end a large room has been excavated and similarly ornamented.

37. *Marine excursions and regattas.*

Sailing and fishing excursions soon developed as popular forms of outdoor amusement.

(a) [John Lyons, *A Description of the Isle of Thanet, and particularly of the Town of Margate*, 1763, 18]

In fine weather, many parties put off to sea, for the diversion of fishing, or to go on board the ships, which lie at anchor in the Roads.

(b) [*The Margate Guide*, 1780, 17–18]

[In addition] as there are established Pacquets regularly passing between Margate and Ostend, . . . the Company will be able with great Safety, and at an easy Expence, to take a View of the most remarkable Places in the Netherlands, Holland, or France. – The Proprietors, for whom Mr. Hall, of the Circulating Library is Agent, have provided Vessels extremely well calculated to render the Passage agreeable and pleasing. The Distance is only twenty Leagues, which with a fair Breeze, they run in nine or ten Hours. Several very pleasant Tours may be performed in Flanders, Holland, and France, within a short Time . . . An Excursion to the Continent for ten or twelve Days would afford great Entertainment to Persons desirous of seeing those Countries.

In that Time, Bruges, Ghent, Brussels, the Hague, Leige, the Spa, Cambray, St. Omer's, etc., may be visited with infinite Ease. A particular Description of those Places, with a very accurate Account of their Distances from each other, the best Routes, and other Articles of useful Information, is to be found in a small Book just published, entitled the Traveller's Vade Mecum through the Netherlands, Holland, and France, which may be had at Mr. Hall's.

Instances of this route actually being used in 1780 can be quoted, beginning with a bachelor traveller, Sylas Neville (1741–1840).

(c) [Ed: B. Cozens-Hardy, *The Diary of Sylas Neville 1767–1788*, O.U.P., 1950, 263]

Got up at 5 in the morning to look out for the land, could see none, but about 7 was gratified with the sight of the white cliffs of my country and at 8 landed at Margate after a peragrination of near three years, in which I have gratified my curiosity much and increased my knowledge not a little, but at the expence of being exposed to many dangers and difficulties.

Margate; rather disappointed, thought this famous bathing place was something better than a collection of new huts upon the cliffs; the Assembly room [is] however a plain and elegant building very conspicuous at sea.

(d) [Ed: Lord Herbert, *Henry, Elizabeth and George (1734–80) Letters and Diaries of Henry, Tenth Earl of Pembroke and his Circle*, 1939, 558–9]

June 5 [1780]. For my passage from Ostende to Margate, drink money, etc. 81 French L.

	£	s.	d.
June 6 Bill at the Hotel at Margate, Waiter, Maid, etc. included.	1	8	5
For a Chaise and pair, and one Saddle Horse, Post-boys, Ostlers, etc., etc.	6	6	0
June 13 Landing and bringing the baggage at Margate to the Custom House and Inn, Customs House Officers, Duties, etc.		17	6
To the Post boy at the Hotel.		1	0
Turnpikes from Margate to Town.		4	1
A Servant, Trunk and Portmanteau's passage in the Stage from Margate to London.	2	6	6

Most visitors contented themselves with local and shorter excursions on the water, such as along the coast to the Reculvers and back, or with fishing in mind.

(e) [*The Times*, 1 September 1804, 4 September 1804]

The fineness of the weather occasions excursions every day, both by land and sea.
Aquatic parties are daily formed.

(f) [*The Morning Chronicle*, 8 September 1810]

Those visitors who are fond of the water frequently pass some hours on the sea in the novel amusement of fishing and frequently return loaded with those delicious whitings for which this coast has been so deservedly celebrated.

(g) [*The New Margate, Ramsgate and Broadstairs Guide*, 6th Ed., Margate, 1816, 58]

In fine weather, parties are frequently made upon the water by the company; some merely for the purpose of sailing, and others for that of fishing, who frequently catch considerable quantities of excellent whitings, thornbacks, and other fish. Excursions are also made to ships at anchor, as well as to Dover, Deal, and other places on the coast; and in peaceable times are extended to the Netherlands, Holland and France.

(h) [*The Thanet Itinerary or Steam Yacht Companion*, 1819, 43]

There is no want of public amusements in *Margate*; but besides these, there are constantly parties of pleasure formed among the visitors, who either go to the tea Gardens at *Minster*, or embark from the *Parade* in neat little pleasure boats, for the purpose of enjoying an excursion upon the ocean.

(i) [G.A. Cooke, *A Topographical and Statistical Description of the County of Kent*, New Ed., 1830, xxxiv–xxxv]

Margate abounds in amusement: besides those afforded by the place itself, water-parties are frequently formed to Deal and Dover, and almost daily to Broadstairs and Ramsgate; between which places and Margate there is an hourly interchange of company.

> Two sets of holidaymakers of the later 1820s recorded sailing trips from where they were staying, respectively in Margate and Ramsgate, circa 1828 and in 1829.

(j) [*MS Diary of Mary Figgins, 30 August–21 September circa 1828*, Margate Public Library, Local Collection, YO60.41; *MS. Journal of an Excursion to Ramsgate in July and August 1829*, Tyler Collection (Ramsgate Scrapbook), Cathedral Library and Archives, Canterbury]

Tuesday, September 20 [Margate].
. . . It was a beautiful day. We went for a sail with Mr. Dunnet, a young lady and a little girl. It was very pleasant indeed. Rose and the young lady were sick.
Thursday, July 30 [1829, Ramsgate].
. . . Took a boat and were rowed out of the Harbour for an hour . . . [Illus. 11b, 23a]. Boat hire – one hour   2s.

> From Ramsgate boat excursions were run to the notoriously dangerous Goodwin Sands where cricket matches were sometimes held.

(k) [*The Visitor's Guide to the Watering Places*, 1842, 184–5]

These far famed banks . . . have swallowed up more shipping than the whole British Navy, immense as it is, is worth . . . Parties are often made up from Ramsgate, etc., to proceed to the Sands when the tide admits, which are so perfectly firm, when uncovered at low water, that cricket matches are even occasionally played on them. The men on the [Trinity Company] vessels, too, are glad to have the monotony of their occupation relieved by occasional visits from the land, and freely supply such refreshments as they can command, for a very moderate gratuity. The skill and civility of the boatmen, and their moderate demands, make this excursion a very pleasant one. As an additional inducement, the reader may be reminded that, when there, he has an excellent opportunity of viewing the French Coast.

Regattas which occurred off the Thanet coast attracted numerous spectators from an early date. An early regatta at Margate took place on 8 September 1789, on the very day that 'Lady Jemingham and her elegant daughter set off [from Margate] for Ostend, in the Yacht'.

(1) [*The Maidstone Journal, and Kentish Advertiser*, 15 September 1789]

The sailing match this morning afforded a most beautiful spectacle to a great concourse of people of all ranks – assembled upon the pier, cliffs, and Bathing Houses.

About 20 sailing boats started exactly at 1 o'clock, after manoeuvering near an hour, for the Reculvers; the prizes were 2 guineas, 1 guinea, ½ guinea and so low as a crown. White was the favourite, and is the winner of the principal prize.

Margate's 1841 regatta appears to have been no less appealing.

(m) [*The Dover Telegraph, and Cinque Ports General Advertiser*, 4 September 1841]

This Regatta came off on Thursday [2 September]. The weather was fine, and a large concourse of persons assembled to witness the sports. Likewise in 1842.

(n) [*The Dover Telegraph, and Cinque Ports General Advertiser*, 27 August 1842]

This Regatta took place on Wednesday last [24 August], and was witnessed by nearly 6,000 spectators. The first race was by 6 oared galleys, and was won by the Comus, of Margate.

1826 saw the first annual Pegwell Bay Regatta. Prior to the 8th Annual Regatta, which took place on Thursday, 21 August 1834, the following advertisement was placed in a Kentish newspaper in the hope of attracting a considerable custom.

(o) [*The Kentish Observer*, 14 August 1834]

Belle Vue Tavern, Pegwell Bay.
John S. Cramp most respectfully acquaints his friends and the public who may honor him with their support on the REGATTA DAY, . . . that every attention shall be paid to their commands, and they may rely on the most reasonable charges. The tables prepared for Cold Dinners, Luncheons, etc., will be accompanied with a printed Bill of Fare, annexed to which the charge for every variety of refreshment.

> The patrons of the event for that year included the Earls of Guilford and Darnley, J.P. Powell Esq. and Moses Montefiore Esq., the outstanding Jewish philanthropist of the nineteenth century who for £5,500 had purchased East Cliff Lodge in 1831, as a substantial marine villa occupying a fine site between Ramsgate and Broadstairs. The success of the event was reported thus.

(p) [*The Kentish Observer*, 28 August 1834]

The company began to arrive long before the commencement of the gala and such an influx poured into the little village as we have rarely before witnessed, there being 5,000 persons present. The line of road . . . and fields adjoining were densely filled with splendid equipages of the gentry . . . The lawn of the Belle Vue boasted a numerous and fashionable assemblage of nearly 1,000 – the pleasure ground (overlooking the Bay) of Sir William Garrow's Marine Villa, was graced with a numerous and select party, by invitation . . . H.R.H., the Princess Sophia Matilda, now sojourning at Broadstairs, commanded a donation of £5 to be presented in aid of the funds . . . The whole arrangement was under the direction of the Ramsgate Galley Club [Illus. 16b].

> Pegwell Bay's annual regatta was being keenly anticipated once again at the very beginning of August 1835.

(q) [*The Dover Telegraph, and Cinque Ports General Advertiser*, 1 August 1835]

This annual aquatic festivity, which is now looked forward to as the most attractive occurrence during the season, in the Isle of Thanet, is shortly to take place. H.R.H. the Duchess of Kent, who with the Princess Victoria intend sojourning at Ramsgate, it is expected will be present; as well as the numerous noblemen and gentlemen, the patrons of the regatta. Exclusive of the Royal Kent Cup, there are three others of silver to be contested, and much sport is anticipated from the determination of the Deal boatmen to win the first named prize.

There was keen rivalry between competing towns and much excitement at the Ramsgate Regatta of 1841.

(r) [*The Dover Telegraph, and Cinque Ports General Advertiser*, 11 September 1841]

Shortly after 1 o'clock a large concourse had assembled from the town and places adjacent, among whom were the Earl of Guilford, the Hon. H.H. Lindsey, M.P., Sir Joseph Douglas, etc. The greatest exertions were made by the boatmen of Ramsgate, Margate and Deal, but it was evident they had no chance against the Folkestoner, who again came off victorious.

Marine excursions were no less recommended from the other resorts of Kent as they developed and expanded.

(s) GRAVESEND [*The Visitor's Guide to the Watering Places*, 1842, 3, 20]

BOATS FOR HIRE, for pleasure parties, may be had on application at Mr. Waite's, and other hotels situated on the banks of the river, and at the Town and Terrace Piers. The prices are regulated by the Watermen's Company of London.
PLEASURE BOATS. – Gravesend is, perhaps, better provided with conveniences for sailing, than any other watering-place. The sailors are, for the most part, an obliging sort of people, and if well paid, will point out the prettiest and most attractive objects.

(t) [Anon., *The Pictorial Guide to Gravesend and its Rural Vicinity: A Holiday Handbook*, 1845, 30–1]

Those who like exercise can hire a wherry, and pull along the Thames and Medway Canal to the entrance of Higham Tunnel, a gigantic excavation through the chalk hills, $2\frac{1}{2}$ miles long, that has its termination at Stroud. – A railway is now forming along the towing path, which will afford a rapid communication between Gravesend and Stroud, and thence to Rochester and Chatham.

Ten years previously *The Gravesend and Milton Journal*, 30 May 1835, had carried the following advertisement.

CANAL TAVERN AND TEA GARDENS. B. GARDENER – Pleasure Boats ready at all times for excursions on the Thames and Medway Canal.

(u)   HERNE BAY [By a Lady, *A Picture of the New Town of Herne Bay*, 1835, 10, 19]

The sea, here, and the evenness of the shore, afford better opportunity than any where else on the coast, for rowing and sailing, free from danger of rocks or cliffs . . . Clean, well-conditioned boats, may . . . be had at a moment's notice. A favourite excursion in them is to the Reculvers (four miles), for those who prefer the sea. Another, and of longer duration, is up the east Swale, round the Isle of Sheppey, from Queenborough fall into the Medway, and pass Sheerness in the way back. Either of these are delightful trips for persons fond of the water.

(v)   [*The Visitor's Guide to the Watering Places*, 1842, 200]

PLEASURE BOATS, for water excursions, to the Isle of Sheppey, Sheerness, Queenborough, Margate, etc., can be hired on reasonable terms.

(w)   [S. Bagshaw, *History, Gazetteer and Directory of the County of Kent*, II, Sheffield, 1847, 219]

Pleasure boats are kept on the beach for those who are fond of aquatic sports, and who love to inhale the invigorating and healthful breezes of the ocean in their native purity.

(x)   DOVER [W. Batcheller, *A New History of Dover, to which is Added a New Dover Guide*, Dover, 1828, 356]

[There are] pleasure boats for excursions on the water.

Although Dover held a regatta in 1841, warnings of the need for more amusements in the resort were issued in that and the following year.

(y) [*The Dover Telegraph, and Cinque Ports General Advertiser,* 11 September 1841, 10 September 1842]

There can be no doubt that these, and such like amusements tend very materially to benefit the town. Visitors naturally expect some kind of amusement to be going forward, and if they cannot find it in one town they will go to another. [Compare 1842] Never was Dover more full of company than it has been this season and yet no exertions have been made to render it attractive by amusements . . . Ramsgate, Margate, Hastings and Tunbridge Wells have their regattas and [other] amusements. We trust [that] efforts will be made to put Dover upon a par with the other places to which we have alluded.

(z) HYTHE [*Pigot & Co's Commercial Directory 1832–4,* 832]

One possible excursion for visitors, under 'Conveyance by Water', was

To APPLEDORE, a *Passage Boat,* by the Royal Military Canal, every morning (Sunday excepted) at half-past ten, performing the distance in two hours and a half, and forwarding passengers, etc., by *Van* to RYE and HASTINGS.

38. *Getting out and about within and beyond the Isle of Thanet.*

Eighteenth and nineteenth-century holidaymakers were often more energetic and adventurous than some of their counterparts today. Sea-bathing and sitting on the beach occupied relatively little time, compared to exploring the neighbourhood, on foot, or by horse, donkey or carriage (Illus. 13b, 17a). Getting out and about soon developed as an important feature of seaside social life. Visitors made their presence felt in the hinterlands of resort towns, where amenities and amusements were opened up and where, in neighbouring villages, new sources of business were promoted. Where to go from Margate was clearly spelt out as early as 1763.

(a) [John Lyons, *A Description of the Isle of Thanet, and particularly of the Town of Margate,* 1763, 17–23, 25–7, 34–5, 66]

The places most frequented for this purpose [walking] are the Parade, the Fort, and the Rope Walk . . . Having mentioned walking on the sands as an amusement [see Doc. 35d], it may be proper to give you some little account of them. They extend, for some miles, along the shore, quite smooth and dry, at low water, and may be passed with safety, six hours in the day. The ocean on the one hand, and the caverns and grottos every where worn in the high chalky cliff, on the other, form together, a scene most beautifully romantic. To prevent being overtaken by the tide, for want of knowing the time of its return, you will do well to carry with you one of *Lyon's Tables*, which are calculated with all possible exactness for that purpose; they are printed on a card, and may be understood in a moment. . .

Before I quit *Margate*, I will give you a short account of such places in its parish, as are taken notice of by strangers.

Nash Court was formerly a Gentleman's Seat, but now much gone to decay. Its situation is pleasant; having more trees about it than are usually found here. Many resort hither for tea-drinking, or an evening walk. . .

Draper's is an endowed Hospital, with a Meeting-House for Quakers. This Hospital was built A.D. 1709 . . . The gardens are pleasant, and are frequented for the same purposes as *Nash Court*.

Dandelion is the ruin of a fine old Mansion-House; . . . little of it now remains, but a curious gateway, . . . built of bricks and flints, in rows, with . . . battlements at top. . .

There are few persons who have carriages, or horses, but do every day, when the weather will permit, take an airing over some part of the island . . . The air of the *North-Foreland* is so fresh, that you will hardly complain of the want of appetite when you return . . . You will observe, that what are called here *Gates*, or *Stairs*, are no other than slope-waggon-ways, which are cut through the high perpendicular cliff to the level of the water's edge. Through these are drawn up sea-weed, for manure of the land, flint, gravel, chalk, pebbles, and other articles of the like nature.

King's-gate is in *St. Peter's* parish, situate on a small but beautiful bay. Here are two pretty houses, one of which has been lately hired by a person of great distinction . . . Near to this place, are those venerable monuments of antiquity, the banks of *Hacken-Downe*, or field of Battle-Axes. There are two *Tumuli*, or *Barrowes*, of earth, the tombs of some of the chief officers, killed in a bloody battle, fought on this spot, between the *Saxons, English*, and the *Danes*, in . . . 853. . .

Still keeping along the coast . . . is the Light-House, which is a strong octagon building of flint, on . . . the *North-Foreland*; a fire of coals is kept blazing all night on the top of it, for the direction of Mariners. As many parties resort hither for dining, tea, etc., two booths are built for their reception, and attendance is given by the Light-keeper.

Not far from hence is *Broad Stairs*, a small Sea-Port, remarkable for fine lobsters . . . The ruins of an old gate [York Gate], formerly fortified by a portcullis, to prevent the inroads of privateers, still remain . . . A very pleasant room has lately been built here, in an house of good accommodation facing the Harbour, for the entertainment of strangers who are fond of sea prospects.

Opposite to this place, at the distance of somewhat more than two leagues from the shore, lie the *Goodwin Sands*, which . . . are visible at low water. They are of so voracious and ingurgitating a property, that ships which strike on them, very rarely escape, being usually entirely swallowed up. . .

Still going on, with a full view of the *Cliffs* of *Calais* on your left, you will pass through *Dumpton* to *Ramsgate*, a very neat sea-port town, with many good houses . . . The new Pier, now building there, attracts the admiration of all strangers . . . It is built chiefly of white *Purbeck* stone, and extends itself into the ocean near eight hundred feet, before it forms an angle. Its breadth at top is twenty six feet, including a strong parapet, which runs all along the outside of it . . . This is intended as a place of refuge for ships to flee to in hard gales of wind. . .

At *Manston*, in this parish, is a very large cavern, cut out of the chalk, and supported by pillars of the same. It being esteemed curious, many strangers think it worth a visit.

You will probably return through the village of *St. Peter's*, where the only thing which deserves your notice, is a very neat and beautiful Church. The summit of its tower commands as delightful and extensive a prospect, by sea and land, as the imagination can form. This tower is a sea-mark . . . I think I have now mentioned everything worth your notice on this side the island. . .

Going out at the upper end of the town [Margate], and keeping the coast on your right hand, you will pass through *Galenge* [Garlinge], a very pleasant village, over a fine fertile country to *Birchington*. You will be tempted to spend an hour or two here, which you may do very agreeably . . . The Mansion-House still bears the name of Quekes [Quex], its former proprietors . . . At *Quekes*, King *William* the third used to reside, while he waited for winds to carry him to *Holland*. His room, and the crimson damask bed in which he lay, are still shewn. . .

I think your enquiries are all answered now, except the last, which respects a more extensive tour along the coast. It is generally made by the ruins of *Richborough Castle, Sandwich,* and *Sandown Castle* to *Dover;* from thence it is not unusual to go to *Canterbury,* and round that way back again to *Margate...*

I have now, I think, performed the task you enjoined me, and hope it will induce you to spend much of your time among us.

> Someone who spent some time in the area in 1777 was John Baker. Accompanied by Mrs. Woodington he stayed in Margate between 11 September and 14 October, during which time several local excursions were undertaken.

(b) [Ed: P.C. Yorke, *The Diary of John Baker,* 1931, 418–21]

September 12, 1777 ... Went out in chaise to King's Gate (Lord Holland's) consisting of variety curious buildings – £900 a year left to Charles Fox by his father – they say he lets it go to decay...

September 15, 1777. Afternoon rode out, through a pleasant village, good church and good houses called St. Peter's; then on to S. E. to Broad Stairs, a tolerable village, close by sea-side.

September 17,1777. Afternoon went out again; fresh dispute with postillion at door, and on road he still grumbling; went to Birchington, good, pleasant village. Stopt to give horses some water at a publick house by the churchyard [The Powell Arms]; hay cider – Mrs. Woodington but just tasted it – was afraid to drink it having pain in stomach.

September 18, 1777. After dinner went to Mount Pleasant, a public house, so-called, where a horse race – given out to be at 4, but a scheme to bring custom to the house, [as] the first heat began at 6.

September 26, 1777. Went afternoon to Draper's Hospital ... Bought 4 pair of garters, 2 white at 2s., Mrs. W. and self, one purple and white to Charles at 1s. 3d., and one red for Sally at 1s. [Charles being the postillion and Sally Matthews the maid].

October 7, 1777 ... Drove through Broadstairs. The coachman complained his horses thin by working every day...

October 8, 1777 ... Went at 8 o'clock thro' Acol and turned up to St. Nicholas; thought to breakfast there but only one public house and that scrubby, so got into carriage again and a mile further to Halfway House at Sarre, where you enter the Isle of Thanet, and breakfasted; ate toast and butter and drank tea with such a relish, as had done neither this month past. Home through Monckton, Minster and Manston Court.

214

While some of the excursion recommendations of 1763 were taken by this holidaymaker in 1777, as well as by many others who came after him, John Baker seized on two opportunities which were publicized in 1770.

(c) [*The Margate Guide . . . In a Letter to a Friend*, 1770, 25–6, 44]

At this place [Kingsgate], situated on a small but pleasant Bay, stands the delightful seat of the Right Hon. the Lord Holland, built on a very different plan from any other house in the Kingdom; the whole being intended to resemble an Italian villa. The Saloon of Neptune and other . . . apartments are very fine . . . On the front of the house, facing towards the Sea, is a noble Portico of the Doric order. The wings are faced with flint, of curious workmanship . . . Here are, likewise, a great number of antique marble Columns, Statues, Busts, Vases, etc., which were purchased in Italy, at a very considerable expense. The towers and other buildings of Grecian and Roman architecture, which appear at a distance from the house added to the several Edifices of Gothic antiquity, form an appearance, at once so singular and so beautiful, that they seldom fail to excite the admiration of Strangers. . .

At a small distance from hence [Ramsgate] is Mount Pleasant, a little Public-house, built on an Eminence, and much admired for its beautiful Prospect.

In its issue of 28 May to 1 June 1768 *The Kentish Gazette* noted how 'last week the Rt. Hon. Lord Holland arrived at his Seat at Kingsgate, near Margate, from making a Tour through France, Italy, etc'. Having been Paymaster General of the Forces during the Seven Years War (1756–63), the first Lord Holland, out of wealth acquired from office holding, established between Margate and Broadstairs one of the earliest and finest marine residences, complete with numerous follies, in eighteenth-century Kent, involving a total expenditure of possibly £100,000, the neighbourhood of Kingsgate being landscaped and embellished with a sham castle, abbey and convent. Long after his death the Kingsgate estate was one of the sights to be visited in Thanet.

(d) [*The European Magazine*, August 1787, 94–6]

KINGSGATE is in the vicinity of Margate, [where is] the delightful seat of the late Lord Holland, afterwards of the honourable Mr.

Charles Fox . . . The design never fails to excite the wonder and frequently the censure of the spectators . . . The Castle serves the family for coach houses, stables, etc. The gate or passage to the sea has the remains of a portcullis . . . There is also a public-house erected by Lord Holland, which had for its sign the head of Capt. Digby . . . The house serves for a place of entertainment for the visitors of Margate.

(e) [By an Inhabitant, *The Margate Guide, A Descriptive Poem, with Elucidatory Notes*, Margate, 1797, 106]

[At] the sign of the *Noble Captain Digby*, . . . the tenant, Mr. *Herbert*, exerts every attention and assiduity to accommodate his guests who, during the season, are very numerous from the above mentioned places [Margate, Ramsgate and Broadstairs].

(f) [*The Margate and Ramsgate Guide in Letters to a Friend*, 1797, 27–8]

You wish me to proceed in my account of Margate and its environs, . . . of the places of public resort in and near this town.

The late *Lord Holland's* seat at Kingsgate, about three miles from this place, is much resorted to of an afternoon, it being either a pleasant ride or walk to it, through an open country, and a very good road.*

> *Many go from Margate to Kingsgate, on the sands, when the tide is down, and a very pleasant ride or walk it is; but rather a longer way than through the fields.

. . . A range of buildings, called the *Convent* . . . consists of several small houses in a row, with arches before each, and crucifixes in them: Poor women live here all the year round, one of whom provides tea, etc. for company, at eight-pence each.

> Nor was it only the Kingsgate estate which raised opportunities for making money from holidaymakers out to see the sights. Eight old ladies who occupied the Quakers' almshouses, known as Drapers, soon took to entertaining Thanet's visitors to tea, while selling to them haberdashery and other small souvenirs, including pin cushions, and the garters purchased by John Baker, on 26 September 1777.

(g) [*The Margate Guide*, 1780, 20]

At Drapers . . . the Company frequently form Parties, and go to drink

Tea at some of the Apartments, in all of which a great Degree of Neatness and Simplicity is to be found.

(h) [G. Keate, *Sketches from Nature, Taken, and Coloured, in a Journey to Margate*, 5th Ed., 1802, 82]

As most of the women employ themselves in knitting garters, laces, pin cushions, etc. they have every day visitors and customers.

New generations of visitors confronted changes both at the North Foreland Lighthouse and at Dandelion.

(i) [By an Inhabitant, *The Margate Guide, A Descriptive Poem, with Elucidatory Notes*, Margate, 1797, 106]

Between Kingsgate and Broadstairs is the North Foreland Lighthouse, which being fitted up on the new construction of patent lamps, with large magnifying lens, will repay the curiosity of the stranger; as from the summit he may command a considerable part of the island, with the ocean on one side, as far as the eye can reach.

(j) [Z. Cozens, *A Tour through the Isle of Thanet, and some other Parts of East Kent*, 1793, 29]

DANDELYON fitted up as a place of entertainment, [with] a delightful bowling green and pleasure gardens, [is] much resorted to, during the summer season, by the company from Margate, Ramsgate, Broadstairs, etc., especially every Wednesday morning, when there is a public breakfast.

One visitor who indulged in the delights of Dandelion on 22 August 1804 was the famous topographical artist and diarist Joseph Farington, R.A. (Illus. 5d).

(k) [Ed: J. Greig, *The Farington Diary*, II, 1923, 277–8]

At one o'Clock went in a Chaise with Miss Glover to Dandelion to a public breakfast. John and Wm. Offley rode. There was much company, who breakfasted in boxes, etc., at long tables on one side of a space of ground like a bowling green. A stage for dancing was also laid and a small band of music in a circular orchestra [Illus. 4b]. Several young people and children danced under the direction of Mr. Le Bas, master of the ceremonies at Margate and Ramsgate. The first dance was led off by a beautiful girl Lady Diana Herbert daugr. of Lord Pembroke, who with her brother, Lord Herbert, were there with their grandmother the Dowager Countess of Pembroke . . . There was much fashionable company. The dance was made up of a very mixed party, many citizens children being of the number, and it was agreeable to see the different ranks partaking of the amusement. I met S. Boddington there [Samuel Boddington from 7, Bedford Square, London, a West India merchant], who came with S. Rogers [the banker poet].

> Public breakfasts at Dandelion, and at other tea gardens which were opened up subsequently, were reported on in national and local newspapers. One such report, following Joseph Farington's return to London, arose out of a well supported benefit on behalf of Charles Le Bas, who occupied the important social post of Master of the Ceremonies at both the Margate and the Ramsgate assembly rooms for over twenty years.

(1)   [*The Times*, 18 September 1804]

Dandelion was yesterday the great scene of fashionable attraction. Margate, Ramsgate, and Broadstairs poured forth their hosts of visitors, and the road was occupied with a string of coaches, post-chaises, barouches, sociables, curricles, gigs, saddle horses, and all the other modes of conveyance. Near 700 persons were in the garden, and the amusement continued an hour longer than usual. There was a most enchanting exhibition of female beauty and elegance, [including] one of the daughters of Prince CASTLECIBERT, the Neapolitan Ambassador, . . . and Lady DIANA HERBERT. Among the Company were the Neopolitan PRINCE and PRINCESS, with all their family, Lady CHOLMONDELEY, with a number of her friends, Miss BENTINCK, daughter of Lord EDWARD BENTINCK, Lord PEMBROKE, Lord COLERAINE, Lord RODNEY, several Officers of the Herefordshire Militia, . . . with some Naval Officers. The Band of the Herefordshire (which is a very capital one) attended, and executed many beautiful airs, in addition to the usual band of the place. This . . . was for the benefit of Mr. LE BAS, the *Maitre des Ceremonies* of Margate, Ramsgate, and Broadstairs. MITCHENER contracts for the entertainment, . . . and pays *Le Maitre des Ceremonies* 80 guineas, so that the business was no losing concern.

> Equally popular both in the 1790s and in the 1830s was an

excursion to Pegwell Bay, and particularly to the Belle Vue Tavern which was renowned for its fine shrimps (Illus. 16b).

(m)   [*The Margate and Ramsgate Guide in Letters to a Friend*, 1797, 33–4]

About a mile from Ramsgate is a fine large bay called *Pegwell Bay*. There is a beautiful prospect of the coast of France, the Downs, etc. from a house entitled *Bellvue*, lately fitted up in this place, for the accommodation of parties to dine or drink tea.*

> *The finest shrimps I ever saw are caught here, and with bread and butter are a favourite regalement during the season.

Many come here for this purpose both from Margate and Ramsgate, during the season, and there are public breakfasts here every Monday upon the same terms as at Dandelion, at which time the Margate band are engaged to attend.

(n)   [G.W. Bonner, *The Picturesque Pocket Companion to Margate, Ramsgate, Broadstairs, and the Parts Adjacent*, 2nd Ed., 1831, 172–3]

PEGWELL BAY, from its proximity to Ramsgate and Margate,. . . is admirably calculated to attract the visitors of those places. The scenery in the neighbourhood is delightful and engaging; and, therefore, parties are continually arriving at [the] BELLE VUE INN to enjoy the views, and to regale themselves upon the shrimps caught in this bay, which are large, fine and high flavoured. The fishermen in this hamlet are well repaid for their labours.

A delightful account of such an outing to Pegwell Bay dates from 18 August 1828.

(o)   [*MS Journal of a Holiday in Ramsgate in 1828 including Visits to Broadstairs and Margate*, KAO, U2446 F1]

This morning after Emily had taken her bath we hired a little boat to go to Pegwell . . . It is celebrated for shrimps and all the Margate 'hoy' people go there in abundance. We saw 8 or 10 flocks of them. After a pretty tossing voyage, which made Mary and Emily look rather queer, of more than an hour's length (as the wind was completely ahead) we embarked on some rocks covered with sea-weed, about $\frac{1}{4}$ of a mile from the Inn. Mary stepped up to her ancle in mud, but the rest of the party made pretty good progress. We enjoyed our luncheon most heartily, having partaken of three plates full of shrimps and divers slices of bread and butter, . . . both white and brown, and a jug of indifferent ale. We paid 4s. 3d. for the repast, which was 1s. 1d. for the three others and 1s. for myself, having the daintiest appetite of the four. The water was so shallow when we returned to the beach that we could not get the boat within 30 yards of us, so the boatman, Sutherland and myself tucked up our trowsers to the knee, and waded up to the boat. Sutherland and the man having procured a board carried Mary and Emily, as we used to call 'in a sedan', and then we, having pushed the boat some 10 or 12 yards further out, jumped in, put on our shoes and stockings and sailed home. Mary and Em. were highly delighted with the adventure, although they were not quite well enough to enjoy their laugh at it on the way home, in consequence of an untimely swell on the surface of the ocean, which made it difficult for them to abstain from pale lips and wry faces. However we *reached* the habour (don't think I meant any pun) without any serious accident, and having made a most *hearty dinner*, . . . are now reposing in the drawing room, rather exhausted with the fatigue which our *jaws*, hands and limbs have undergone in the course of the day.

> A very different mode of conveyance which developed during the 1800s took the form of riding on asses, with Margate being the first seaside resort in which donkey-rides became a familiar and popular amusement (Illus. 13b).

(p)　[*The Thanet Itinerary or Steam Yacht Companion*, 1819, 42–3]

Within the last 12 or 15 years, it has become the fashion at most of our watering-places, but especially at *Margate*, for the Company to amuse themselves by riding on Asses, for the hire of which, a certain sum (generally 1s.) per hour, is paid to the owner together with a trifling gratuity to an attendant boy. The Ladies are the chief encouragers of this exercise, though for the sake of the frolic, they are generally accompanied on these excursions by their male friends. The principal *Asinarium* or *Donkey Stud* in this town is kept by a notoriety and eccentric named BENNETT in *High Street*.

> From Margate it was made known on 11 August 1810 in *The Morning Chronicle* that here there were 'asses . . . to be let . . . , to bear ANGELS by day, and SPIRITS [an obvious reference to smuggling] by night'. During a two month stay at Margate in 1812

Mrs. Pilkington engaged donkeys for local excursions on two occasions.

(q) [Mrs. Pilkington, *Margate!!! or Sketches Amply Descriptive of that Celebrated Place of Resort*, 1813, 47–8, 99–100]

The anticipation of a promised ride upon the animal which our saviour selected for its humility and patience, so completely occupied the thoughts of Fitzmaurice, that he awoke before 6 o'clock . . . A few minutes before the hour fixed upon for their departure, four very nice donkeys . . . walked up, and become stationary before the door . . . The young party immediately mounted, and . . . proceeded to Dandelion . . . As they entered their ears were saluted by the band of the Westmeath Militia, part of which was stationed at Margate, playing one of their national airs. . .

The party met a lady of their acquaintance, who had just arrived from Ramsgate . . . After the first salutation was over, Mrs. Simpson, who was remarkably fond of children, kindly declared her intention of making Fitzmaurice a present . . . 'I should *like* a ride upon a donkey better than anything, Madam', replied Fitzmaurice, 'That liking you shall immediately have gratified; and as I did not come to Margate solely for the pleasure of seeing your mamma and Mrs. P., you shall ride to the Infirmary' [The Margate or 'General Sea Bathing Infirmary', at Westbrook, founded in 1791, as a charitable hospital for poor people suffering from scrofula or tuberculosis – see Doc. 46]. It was therefore determined that as soon as Mrs. S. had taken some refreshment, the whole party should accompany her to the Infirmary, and message was dispatched to Mr. BENNET's, to order 2 donkeys . . . When the party arrived at Westbrook, they were delighted with the spot which had been judiciously selected for the erection of the Infirmary, not only from its elevation, but from its contiguity to the sea.

On another occasion when Fitzmaurice associated going to Drapers with a ride upon a donkey he was disappointed [pp. 76–77].

You will not *ride* to Draper's, because it is a distance we can all *walk*, without inconvenience; and as I came to Margate for the sole purpose of *restoring health* to your dear brother Francis, I do not mean to spend a single farthing unnecessarily . . . I shall waste no money in idle gratifications – if you cannot *walk*, you must remain at home with Mrs. Williams.

One holiday which did involve a number of excursions was undertaken by Mr. and Mrs. Benham to Ramsgate in 1829. During their stay there, they enjoyed several varied outings, the details and costing of which Mr. Benham recorded with meticulous detail.

(r) [*MS Journal of an Excursion to Ramsgate in July and August 1829*, Tyler Collection (Ramsgate Scrapbook), Cathedral Library and Archives, Canterbury]

Saturday, July 25.
. . . After Tea hired a carriage and taking up Mr. Hunt by the way we were conveyed to Birchington, whose Church containing some old Brasses and monuments we went into, but there was not sufficient time to allow of my copying anything. Took a glass of sherry wine at the Powell Arms on account of the coldness of the evening. . .

Paid:	s.	d.
1 Pint Bottle of Sherry Wine	2	6
Biscuits at Birchington		2
1 Pint of Ale for the Man		4
Paid the Ostler		2
The Sexton for Viewing the Church	1	0
The Carriage	5	0

9s. 2d..

Tuesday, July 28.
. . . After Dinner at ½ past 2 joined Mrs. Hunt and her 8 children and proceeded to Shallows Tea Gardens near St. Peters where we enjoyed ourselves until ½ past 6 playing and swinging with the children. . .

Paid:	s.	d.
1 lb. Lump Sugar 10d. and ¼ lb. Tea 1s. 9d. for the Shallows	2	7
Bread, Butter and Water and the Use of Table, etc., in the Shallows Gardens, 6 Adults @ 8d. and 8 children @ 4d. each	6	8

For attendance at the Shallows tho' not demanded   1   0

                                               10s. 3d.

Thursday, August 6.

... At ½ past 11 proceeded in the Carr we had yesterday (which we hired for the day) through Cliffsend and Minster to Monkton and copied the following Inscriptions in the Church ... From Monkton proceeded to St. Nicholas and put up at the Bell where the host furnishing us with plates and knives and forks and a clean Table Cloth, and supplying us with Bread and excellent Ale, we enjoyed the cold mutton with which we were already provided, and our appetites exceeding our provision a few slices of excellently flavoured Ham boiled, although cut rather clumsily, enabled us to complete a hearty dinner. That done went to the Church where the Monuments were so numerous that I was obliged to content myself with tracings of the Brasses that were at all curious and such other memorials as a very hasty visit would permit ... Continuing our intended Tour we proceeded to Birchington where at the Powell Arms we were regaled with Tea, doubly grateful to us on account of the warmth of the weather.

Paid:	£.	s.	d.
Carriage for the Day		14	0
Driver		2	6
Entrance into Monkton Church and for getting the Key		1	2
7 Currant Buns			6
For accommodation at St. Nicholas		5	0
For attendance do.			6
Entrance into St. Nicholas Church			6
Tea at Birchington		4	0
Man do.			8½
Attendance			3½
For getting into Birchington Church		1	6

                                           £1   10s.   8d.

39. *Post-Napoleonic tea gardens in Thanet and Gravesend.*

Tea drinking at Drapers and public breakfasting at Dandelion prior to 1815, as well as similar excursions elsewhere, have already been noted (see Docs. 38a, b, g, h, j, k, l). The popularity of tea gardens increased markedly during the 1820s, 1830s and 1840s. Dandelion went out of existence to be replaced by other places of public resort.

(a) [*The Thanet Itinerary or Steam Yacht Companion*, 1819, 49–50]

Until within these few years, Dandelion was laid out as a public Tea Garden [Illus. 4b], where the visitors of *Margate* used to resort for the purpose of amusing themselves by dancing, or swinging, or walking under the shade of the noble grove of trees which grow at that place; but as this did not yield sufficient to satisfy the Proprietor, it has lately been sold, and has now become the seat of the gallant Sir Thomas Staines, a Post Captain in the Royal Navy.

It was there that he died on 13 July 1830. In the meantime,

(b) [*The Kentish Gazette*, 10 April 1829]

The Isle of Thanet is to be adorned by a striking resemblance of that magnificent place, the Tivoli, at Rome. The spot selected is near Margate . . . About 30 workmen are now employed on the grounds in forming the garden, which will consist of different flowering shrubs, . . . cascades, fountains, temples, Swiss cottages, statues, and a handsome rotunda or concert room, with a café for French wines and refreshment. This property has lately been purchased by J. Sinclair Esq., the celebrated vocalist, who has resided some years at Rome. It is expected that a great part will be finished by August, to be opened this summer under the superintendance of Mr. T. Cramp.

The following year it was noted,

(c) [G.A. Cooke, *A Topographical and Statistical Description of the County of Kent*, New Ed., 1830, xxix]

Le Jardin de Tivoli,
formerly called *Shady Groves*, is situate in a valley about ½ mile from Margate, forming by Nature one of the most beautiful and romantic spots in Thanet, interspersed with sheets of water, groves of oak, elm,

ash, poplar, etc. JOHN SINCLAIR, esq., of the London theatres, has
fitted this place up with infinite taste, contriving to make it rival the
most favoured resorts on the Continent. The grounds contain magic
chairs, rocks, banks, and Chinese arbours; jets-d'eau, promenades,
alcoves, and conservatories. It possesses a concert room, 75 feet long by
45, of unique and elegant architecture. The right wing of the tavern is a
coffee room in the Parisian style; the left is a Cosmorama, with accurate
representations. In the rear are Swiss cottages, ice-wells, etc., with a
large enclosure for the exhibition of the ancient and elegant science of
archery. The gardens contain a chalybeate spring.

Press reports show these gardens to have been well patronized.

(d)   [*The Kentish Observer*, 17 July 1834]

On Saturday evening last, the grand gala at Tivoli took place, under
the most flattering auspices, both as regards the weather, and the high
quality of the distinguished visitors, . . . [including] the Marquis of
Granby, Col. Horace and Miss Seymour, the Marquis of Hertford, Sir
Robert and Miss Wilson, Lady Parker [and] we also observed J.P.
Powell Esq., of Quex Park, John Slater Esq., Admiral Sir Thomas
Harvey, Lady Neale Campbell.

(e)   [*The Dover Telegraph, and Cinque Ports General Advertiser*, 18 July
1835]

G.H. PHILPOTT informs the public that a *Grand Gala* will take place
every Tuesday and Saturday during the season, on which occasion the
Gardens are brilliantly illuminated, [with] a Splendid Display of FIRE
WORKS, by Messrs D'Ernst & Duffell of Vauxhall. Concert 6 o'clock
and dancing in the Concert Room.
   Admission 2s. Children 1s.
The Gardens are open every day. A Band attends at 4 o'clock for
dancing and a musical mélange during the evening. Admission 1s., for
which refreshments to the amount are given, except on Gala Nights.
Dinners, Luncheons and every kind of Refreshment provided for
Private Parties, on the shortest notice, and most moderate terms.
Good Stabling.
The first Public Breakfast will take place on Monday, July 20, and be
continued every Monday during the season. . .
On Tuesday 28th July the first Grand Masquerade.

By 1830 the village of St. Peter's close to Broadstairs had also acquired two tea gardens.

(f) [G.A. Cooke, *A Topographical and Statistical Description of the County of Kent*, New Ed., 1830, xxviii–xxix,xxx]

Since the conversion of the once celebrated *Dandelion* into a private mansion, Mr. NEWBOLT has fitted up a large piece of ground at St. Peter's, about 2 miles from Margate, where public breakfasts are given twice a week, and nearly 1,000 persons have been known to visit it in one day. The price of admission to the breakfast is 2s. 6d. each person: tea, coffee and cold collations are furnished. On other days, visitors are admitted at 1s. each, for which refreshment to the amount is furnished. A platform is raised for dancing, and an excellent band is provided; the dancing generally continues from 4 till dusk. A well-levelled bowling-green is divided from the other parts of the garden by a row of flowering shrubs, where cigars may be smoked in the open air, which is not permitted in the other parts of the garden.

Shallows . . . is on a smaller scale; parties may bring their own tea and sugar, and 8d. each is charged for the other accompaniments of the tea-table. This place is a favourite resort with juvenile parties [see Doc. 38r].

By the 1840s the former gardens had been considerably embellished and were being well patronized.

(g) [*The Dover Telegraph, and Cinque Ports General Advertiser*, 9 July 1842]

RANELAGH GARDENS, ST PETER'S, ISLE OF THANET.
Messrs CRAMP acquaint the Nobility, Gentry and Public that on the 14th the REFRESHMENT DEPARTMENT shall have their best attention. All Viands and Wines of the first quality. A Quadrille Band will be in attendance.
The Gardens are open every day from 9 a.m. Promenade Band at 4 p.m. Singing and dancing in the new and elegant SALON DE DANCE, which will be splendidly illuminated.
Cosmorama, Dioramic Tableau, Bowling Green and a variety of amusements.
Breakfasts, Luncheons, Dinners, Tea, Coffee, Suppers, etc. provided with a due regard to comfort and economy.

Admission 1s., Juveniles 6d., for which refreshments to the full amount will be given.

(h) [*The Dover Telegraph, and Cinque Ports General Advertiser*, 6 August 1842]

We feel pleasure in informing our readers that these delightul gardens continue to prosper under the able management of Messrs. Cramp. On Monday last, there was an excellent attendance of visitors, it being a gala night . . . The quadrille band, under the direction of Mr. T. Pitcher, of Ramsgate, is the most efficient orchestra we have heard in these gardens . . . The illuminations were splendid . . . We must not forget to compliment Messrs. Cramp on the complete success of their efforts to please the public, and cordially wish they meet that encouragement they so justly merit.

Visitors to Thanet in the early 1830s could also visit tea gardens other than those mentioned above.

(i) [*Picture of Ramsgate, or A Guide to the Various Amusements, Public Libraries, Building Improvements, etc., of that celebrated Watering Place*, Ramsgate, 1833, 71, 75–6]

THE WILDERNESS, on the side of the Hill near the Mills, leading to Northdown, is another Pleasure Ground, thickly studded with trees, forming delightful walks, alcoves and bowers, ornamented with statues, busts, etc.
MINSTER . . . At this place are two pleasant Tea-gardens, one kept by W. Buddell, and the other by J. Moore; once in the week during the season a band of music is provided for dancing. The price of admission is 1s. each person, which entitles the bearer to the value in refreshments.

Gravesend too had its Tivoli Gardens which were improved prior to the opening of the 1835 season.

(j) [*The Gravesend and Milton Journal*, 18 April 1835]

W. KILBE begs leave to inform the Inhabitants and Visitors of Gravesend, that he has at great expense beautified and embellished the [Tivoli] Gardens which will be re-opened for the ensuing Season on *Good Friday* . . . During the Season, the Gardens will be the scene of

227

constant and varied amusements. The GALA NIGHTS will be on a most extensive scale.

The Victoria Gardens opened several weeks later.

(k)   [*The Gravesend and Milton Journal*, 23 May 1835]

R. ROUSE has taken the [Victoria] Gardens and they will be opened for the Season on Monday, June 1st, with a Gala and Firework Display. The evening will conclude with a Ball. Admission 1s.

Both these and other gardens were recommended in 1842.

(l)   [*The Visitor's Guide to the Watering Places*, 1842, 6, 14, 19]

THE TERRACE GARDENS are situated on the north side of the Terrace, and afford a delightful place of resort for visitors at a very small charge; they are laid out on a gentle acclivity, commanding a fine view of the river, and the opposite coast, with Tilbury Fort. As they front the Terrace Pier, persons may be amused, whilst they sit in some sequestered part, by viewing the hurry of embarkation and landing. The grounds are planned and executed with taste and neatness, exhibiting a great variety and profusion of shrubs and flowers. The walks are led under the road, thus forming several dry arches, beneath one of which is the ice well. Seats are placed in every direction, both by the sides of the paths and on the grass, and during the heat of the morning sun, many nooks may be selected, where the visitors may fully enjoy the salubrity of the breeze, the perfume of the flowers, and the beauty of the surrounding scenery. The expense of the land on which these gardens are formed amounted to the sum of nearly £9.000.
THE ESPLANADE fronts the Terrace Gardens, of which it commands a view. It reaches from the Terrace Pier to Customs Bridge. Here the beach is pleasant for a promenade, and seats are placed to accommodate visitors.
TIVOLI GARDENS AND HOTEL are on the west side of the hill. They are very generally resorted to by visitors, for whose amusement ample provision is made. 'Mine host' will be found indefatigable in his endeavours to please *in doors*, while his company are furnishing themselves with an appetite *out* of *doors*. The grounds adjoining the house are laid out with much taste. Some amuse themselves with the bow – some at trap ball – while others enter the 'swing' and soar aloft . . . In short, this place is looked upon as the 'Paradise' of Gravesend.

VICTORIA GARDENS AND HOTEL, situate about a quarter of a mile to the right of Tivoli, are on a scale *approaching* to that of Vauxhall, the fireworks, etc. being little inferior to those of the celebrated D'Ernst and Southby. Balls, assemblies, etc., are held here constantly throughout the season, and are numerously attended.

> The famous Rosherville Gardens are noticed elsewhere (see Docs. 40 a, b). From all accounts it was a pleasant experience to sit in the Terrace Gardens in 1845.

(m) [Anon., *The Pictorial Guide to Gravesend and Its Rural Vicinity: A Holiday Handbook*, 1845, 15]

[They are] as agreeable as any portion of any watering-place within easy reach of London. A seat in the Terrace Gardens, or upon one of the piers, affords . . . an opportunity which few spots in the World can equal – for here, within eye-shot, passes the commerce of the mightiest of commercial cities. The visitor who needs amusement may find it in learning a few facts about the various vessels as they pass, fleet after fleet, along this busy watery highway.

40. *Getting out and about from Gravesend, Herne Bay, Dover, Folkestone, Sandgate and Hythe.*

(a) GRAVESEND [*The Visitor's Guide to the Watering Places*, 1842, 5–6, 7, 11–13, 16–17, 20]

COBHAM-HALL, situate five miles south-east of Gravesend, to the right of the road to Rochester, is the seat of the Earl of Darnley, . . . in an extensive, well wooded, and diffusely watered park, stocked with deer . . . The house is of the Elizabethan style, being of red brick . . . The state rooms are shewn once a-week (Friday), from eleven till four o'clock; tickets of admission two shillings, to be had at Mr Caddel's library only . . . [a]
CRICKET GROUND, . . . in a large meadow, on the north side of the Dover-road, . . . is hired for this purpose by Mr Hodgkins, of the Fountain Tavern. Cricketing here forms a very important source of manly recreation during the summer months. . .
GAD'S HILL is situated on the road to Dover . . . Its summit commands a very extensive and beautiful view over the counties of Kent and Essex. . .
ROSHERVILLE NEW TOWN, . . . between Gravesend and North-

fleet, . . . and the Kent Zoological and Botanical Gardens . . . The watering-place of Gravesend has hitherto been signalized by its lamentable deficiency of any public place affording instructive amusement . . . The gardens occupy a space of about seventeen acres . . . The animals are disposed in situations most consistent with their natural habitats – the eagles and other mountainous birds being chained to ledges of the cliff, whilst other creatures have their dens excavated in it . . . A variety of plants from different foreign countries may be seen growing within a short distance from each other . . . The directors have constructed a labyrinth, and also a curious contrivance, . . . called 'The Fairy Towers' . . . There is also a romantic dell, consisting of about four acres, called the 'Pic-nic Garden', intended for those visitors generally styled 'Gipsy Parties', who may prefer taking their own viands . . . One of the most prominent eminences of the garden is occupied by a *camara obscura*, erected by Mr Youle, practical optician, Leadenhall-street: the site selected is, from its elevation and aspect, particularly adapted for its exhibition, as the reflections command considerable portions of the beautifully diversified scenery of the Thames [and] adjacent country. . .
RURAL WALKS – There are several in the neighbourhood of Gravesend and Milton. . .
WATER CRESS GROUNDS at Spring Head . . . Visitors may . . . walk in the gardens contiguous, by making a purchase of the cresses or fruit, both of which are particularly fine. . .
WINDMILL HILL . . . is a place of great resort, on account of its commanding an extensive . . . prospect, reaching as far as the Hampstead and Highgate hills, on the north-west [and] to the Nore on the east . . .

Almost all watering places are alike. Their chief amusements consist in reading, walking, riding, driving, and sailing. All these may be enjoyed in Gravesend to perfection. Horses, gigs, ponies, chaises, etc., may be hired at a minute's notice; indeed, every thing may be commanded, provided a person has the means of paying for it.

(b) [Anon., *The Pictorial Guide to Gravesend and Its Rural Vicinity: A Holiday Handbook*, 1845, 16–19, 22–5]

The charms of Gravesend are not all within it. Pleasant rural villages are thickly dotted round about . . . *Windmill Hill* – the view from the hill top is very fine . . . The old mill, which gave its name to the spot, is preserved for the amusement of holiday-gazers, who, climbing its wooden stairs, enjoy the far spread view from an upper gallery . . . Wherries over to *Tilbury Fort*, [open on] Tuesdays, Thursdays and Saturdays for the admission of visitors, or we may take the ferry boat, . . . every ¼ hour, by which the fare across to Tilbury is only 3d. . . . [The] *Gardens of Rosherville* [are] the *beau ideal* of all that a 'ruralizer' can desire . . . *Springhead* [is] a favourite resort of Gravesend visitors, . . . celebrated for its watercress plantation, nourished by a stream which meanders along some ¼ mile of fruit and flower garden ground . . . Visitors here congregate in great numbers, not only for the purchase of watercresses, but to feast on strawberries and other dainties throughout the summer months. . .

(c)   HERNE BAY [By a Lady, *A Picture of the New Town of Herne Bay*, 1835, 9–10, 19]

On leaving the bathing machines, you are irresistibly prompted to take salutary exercise by the view of the high grounds immediately before you, which command, in front, the expanse of the majestic ocean, and, on all sides, fields waving with crops; . . . in short, a landscape of the most bewitching character for all tastes and humours. On these high grounds seats are placed at certain distances, for the feeble, or the contemplative pedestrian. This is the foot road to Reculver, a walk of between three and four miles . . . [Illus. 24].

Those usual appendages of a bathing-place, donkey and pony chaises, are in abundance at Herne Bay, and seem to perform their tasks well.

A visitor to Herne Bay in that year was sufficiently impressed by the walk described above to liken it to Torbay.

(d)   [*Ms. Journal of a Visit to Herne Bay in 1835*, KAO, U2491]

We first discovered a sweet and natural green path along the downs leading on to the Eastern cliffs, . . . strewn with benches, commanding a fine sea view, and it put me in mind tho' I can't tell why of the lovely promenade fields at Torbay.

(e)   [S. Bagshaw, *History, Gazetteer and Directory of the County of Kent*, II, Sheffield, 1847, 219]

The *Walks and Drives* are numerous and pleasant [and] in every direction the vicinity abounds with verdant undulations.

Excursions featured prominently in a holiday which was partly spent at Herne Bay in 1844.

(f)   [*MS Journal compiled by S. Daniele in 1844*, KAO, U2666 F1, 9–24, 24–6, 27, 29–30]

Saturday, August 31.
We started directly after breakfast in a fly for the City of Canterbury which is 9 miles from Herne Bay. The road lay through a prettily diversified country . . . [There they visited the Cathedral and attended the afternoon service, the Dane John, the Norman castle, St. Augustine's Abbey and St. Martin's Church].

Monday, September 2.
We again bathed, and took a short walk; after dinner watched a rowing match for sometime, and then started in a donkey chaise for the village of Herne, which is about 2 miles from the Bay. Herne is a very ancient place, [and] the church is particularly interesting . . . We went to the top of the tower which commands a nice view of the neighbourhood and sea . . . After having some cake and milk at a cottage, we walked home. . .

Tuesday, September 3.
Had a very early dinner and then started for the Reculvers. They are about 4 miles distant from Herne Bay, if you walk by the cliff. The Reculvers are two square towers, the remains of a church and monastery . . . There are a few scattered houses, and a station of coastguards here, but owing to its exposed situation it has a desolate appearance. After looking at everything that could be seen, and purchasing some stones and crystallized water which is found here sometimes when the cliff falls, we returned homeward, and by the time we reached Herne Bay were quite damp and tired, for owing to the roughness of the wind and water the spray had reached us as we walked on the top of the cliff.

(g)   DOVER [*A Guide to all the Watering and Sea-Bathing Places*, 1815, 276]

The ride over the Cliffs to Folkestone, and Sandgate, is the grandest in England, if it can be equalled in the world.

Besides its castle and busy harbour, Dover was well known for its 'delightful situation' and 'romantic and beautiful views' (*ibid.*, 271), which attracted favourable comment from William Cobbett (1762–1835), when he visited the town on the evening of Wednesday, 3 September 1823.

[William Cobbett, *Rural Rides*, I, 1930 Ed. 226–7]

The town of Dover . . . is a most picturesque place, to be sure. On one side of it rises, upon the top of a very steep hill, the old Castle, with all its fortifications. On the other side of it there is another chalk hill, the side of which is pretty nearly perpendicular, and rises up from 60 to 100 feet higher than the tops of the houses, which stand pretty nearly close to the foot of the hill.

I got into Dover rather late. It was dusk when I was going down the street towards the quay. I happened to look up, and was quite astonished to perceive cows grazing upon a spot apparently 50 feet above the tops of the houses . . . I went up to the same spot, the next day, myself: and you actually look down upon the houses, as you look out of a window, upon people in the street. The valley that runs down from Folkestone is, when it gets to Dover, crossed by another valley that runs down from Canterbury . . . It is in the gorge of this cross-valley that Dover is built. The two chalk-hills jut out into the sea, and the water that comes up between them forms a harbour for this ancient, most interesting, and beautiful place.

(h) [W. Batcheller, *A New History of Dover, to which is Added a New Dover Guide*, Dover, 1828, 349–50, 356]

The constant intercourse with the continent is another never failing source of amusement to the visitor at this place. Since the establishment of steam packets, the time of their arrival and departure may generally be estimated within a few minutes. As it draws near, hundreds are seen bending their way towards the harbour to witness from the platform on the piers, or from the several quays, the bustling scene that is to ensue. Then, horses, suspended from gigantic cranes, are reluctantly swung from or to the vessel, while their heads, hung down, and their extended limbs, betray their terror . . . Heavy carriages, nicely poised, are removed in a similar manner. Passengers are seen taking a temporary farewell of their friends, while others stepping on shore, seem to forget the inconvenience of a sea voyage, in their joy to revisit the land that gave them birth. And foreigners pass in review, in every variety of costume, from . . . the Parisian dandy [to] the turbaned merchant of Morocco. . .

Fly Chariots, Donkey Chaises, etc. are in constant attendance for short excursions, in the town and neighbourhood . . .

> Among the more obvious places to visit nearby were St. Margaret's at Cliffe, a 'retired and healthy situation . . . contiguous to the shore' and the South Foreland Lighthouse (*ibid.*, 365).

The views from these towering and almost perpendicular cliffs, with the sea nearly four hundred feet below their summit, and sometimes dashing against their bases, are truly grand and impressive. As the stranger passes along the footpath . . . [to] Dover, with ˙ . . . the venerable castle just before him, he cannot fail to feel emotions, such as his own language can hardly express.

> The situation of Folkestone and a walk along what is now 'The Leas', were equally appealing to a visitor who was there in 1809.

(i)   FOLKESTONE [*MS The Kentish Portion of an Anonymous Tour of 1809*, KAO, U2402 F1]

Sunday, 10 September.
Part of the Town lays on the Edge of the Sea, but other parts, together with the Church, are placed on high Cliffs . . . It is perpetually up and down Hill [Illus. 16a]. . . . There is a most beautiful walk along the Cliffs to Sandgate about 2 Miles and from it being Sunday I was delighted with the appearance of the Inhabitants of Folkestone. The females were *all* cleanly and neatly dressed with a sufficient appearance of Fashion to show a variation from old costume . . . All had an appearance of Decorum and Modesty . . . The Martello System of Defences here commences and continues all along the Coast between Folkestone and Romney. There are near thirty.

Monday, 11 September.
. . . On the summit of the Cliffs to Sandgate, . . . having left Folkestone Church, on the right [I] observed on one of the lofty Hills which I descended in coming from Canterbury (and which I then remarked) the appearance of a large Camp which on Enquiry I found was a right Conjecture as it is still called Castle Hill, probably therefore was Roman and Castrum is now become Castle. When near Sandgate I descended into that small Place.

(j) [*A Guide to all the Watering and Sea-Bathing Places*, 1810, 245]

The walk on the Cliffs to Sandgate is generally frequented, and certainly is one of the most delightful in the country. The bold and romantic scenery on the land side, the charming marine prospect, the view of the . . . French coast, . . . with the stately fleets passing in 'silent grandeur,' give particular animation to the scene.

(k) [*The Hythe, Sandgate and Folkestone Guide*, Hythe, 1816, 98–101]

WALKS AND RIDES.

The most frequented walk is that which passing the church runs along the edge of the cliff towards Sandgate . . .

Another pleasant walk will be found from the northern side of the town leading through the small village of *Foord*, in which, close to the side of the public road, is

A CHALYBEATE SPRING,

which only requires to be more generally known in order to rival others of a similar class . . .

Passing along the *Vale of Folkestone*, rich in verdure and fertility, and arriving at the foot of the hills which are its northern boundary, . . . a romantic spot presents itself . . . Here in the rudest stile of simplicity stands a cottage half hidden amongst the fruit trees, which have occasioned it to be called

THE CHERRY-GARDEN.

. . . The fine valley opening before it interspersed with woodlands and hop gardens offers a charmingly varied landscape in which the town of Folkestone and its church, the Martello towers, the white cliffs toward the south-east, and the wide expanse of sea, are only a few of its numerous and interesting pictures. The cottage . . . is fitted up as a house of refreshment, and is much visited in the summer season [from] Folkestone, Sandgate, and the neighbourhood . . . It is not unusual for . . . young persons to enjoy [a] sprightly dance upon the turf in the cool of evening. . .

Near the Cherry Garden, and occupying the summit of a lofty eminence, . . . is CASTLE HILL,

which is described by *Camden* to have been originally a Roman fortification.

(l) SANDGATE [*A Guide to all the Watering and Sea-Bathing Places*, 1815, 423]

The Cliffs on the land side are highly romantic, and all the walks and rides round this place are captivating.

> There were many possible excursions which could be enjoyed equally from Folkestone, Sandgate and Hythe, as was emphasized in 1816.

(m) [*The Hythe, Sandgate and Folkestone Guide*, Hythe, 1816, 30, 36–8]

WALKS AND RIDES.

The vicinity of Sandgate to HYTHE as well as FOLKESTONE renders the walks which lie commodiously for either of those places, common to them all.

In the immediate neighbourhood, besides the beach the fine smooth well-gravelled and firm foot-path which borders the turnpike road to Hythe is pehaps the most frequented. It commands a full view of the sea and its vessels on the left, with the fine sweep of coast bordered by Martello Towers. . .

There is another walk which ascending the lofty hill eastward of SANDGATE commands a most enchanting prospect of the environs of the village, the charming residence of Lord Darnley [an elegant villa, . . . built on a considerable elevation, which overlooks the houses of the village, the sea and the ships with which it is almost constantly studded], the artillery barracks at Shorncliffe [Illus. 12a], . . . the church and other buildings at Folkestone, . . . the sea [and] the white cliffs towards Dover. . .

(n) HYTHE [*ibid.*, 39]

In the immediate neighbourhood of HYTHE there is a pleasant walk called the Marine Grove, leading to the sea-side, and another denominated Sir William's Wall, where both visitors and the inhabitants frequently form agreeable promenades (especially in the summer evenings), and to which the refreshing coolness of the sea-breezes are extremely inviting. Others resort to the heights above the town [Illus. 17b].

(o) [*Pigot & Co's Commercial Directory, 1832–4*, 830]

The vicinage of Hythe abounds with romantic scenery, and affords numerous pleasing walks and rides.

41. *Assembly Rooms.*

On 17 July 1787 *The Maidstone Journal and Kentish Advertiser* observed how 'the Masters of the Ceremonies at the different Watering-places are now looking out their summer silks and their dancing pumps, with great alacrity'. Looking backwards from the 1850s George Roberts, in his *Social History of the People of the Southern Counties of England in Past Centuries*, 1856, page 553, argued that 'the Assembly Rooms were the great source of delight', where 'persons penned up in uncomfortable lodgings spent the evening regularly twice a week in society, played at cards, and danced'; in addition, 'many took their tea and coffee there every night'. Indoor and outdoor amusements and entertainment soon formed an important and growing part of the social apparatus of an expanding and popular resort. This was true alike for the older inland spa towns, such as Bath or Tunbridge Wells, and the newer seaside resorts of the later eighteenth century. Indeed, the latter modelled their social life on that of the former, by providing assembly rooms, balls, masters of ceremonies, theatres or play-houses, and circulating libraries. These facilities developed along lines which had been familiar in the older inland spas, and their existence was taken for granted by visitors drawn from the ranks of the aristocracy, the gentry and the clergy. The building of assembly rooms was as natural to eighteenth-century seaside resorts as it was to inland spas. Both types of watering place appealed to the upper classes, who craved for the formality and organized social life of assembly rooms, circulating libraries and theatres. In Margate the erection of permanent assembly rooms and an adjoining hotel in Cecil Square represented the resort's first major building venture at the end of the 1760s, whereas for Ramsgate it was left to *The Maidstone Journal, and Kentish Advertiser,* of 17 July 1787, to announce that 'new rooms . . . are to be begun on immediately: equal, if not superior to Margate'. Rivalry between these two resorts was clearly in the air by the 1780s but some thirty years previously the fact that neither town possessed permanent assembly rooms did not detract from the holding of assemblies or balls, which were, more generally, a prominent characteristic of eighteenth-century social life.

(a) [*The Kentish Post, or Canterbury News Letter*, 2–5 January 1754]

An Assembly at the Black Horse at Margate on Thursday next, at which time a Subscription will begin.

(b) [*Ibid.*, 29 May – 1 June 1754]

RAMSGATE

GEORGE VANDAM, Dancing Master, Gives a Publick Ball for Gentlemen and Ladies on Tuesday 4th June at the RED LYON at Ramsgate, in the Isle of Thanet.

There will be good Company. 2s. 6d. Tea and Coffee included. Tickets to be had at the Red Lyon.

> Margate's Black Horse inn changed its name to the New Inn in 1761, following its purchase by John Mitchener (also see Doc. 18f). It was this inn which pioneered assembly room activity and social life within Margate in its early days as a rising seaside resort. Yet again the enterprising proprietorship of John Mitchener is all too evident in the guidebooks and newspapers of the 1760s.

(c) [John Lyons, *A Description of the Isle of Thanet, and particularly of the Town of Margate*, 1763, 16–17, 68]

Amusements. Assembly-Rooms.

The Assembly-Room is a part of the New-Inn; it stands on the *Parade*, and commands a fine view of the Harbour and Roads. This prospect is exceedingly pleasant, especially when it happens that a large fleet is lying there, waiting for spring-tides to carry them up the River. This room, without any pretensions to magnificence, is perfectly neat and commodious, being seventy feet in length, and twenty in breadth, with a gallery for Musick. Publick breakfastings have not been usual, probably, because they would interfere too much with the hours of Bathing. Eighteen or twenty couple dance very conveniently. On Card Assemblies there are generally eight or ten tables; and at other times, seldom less than four or five. There are two Card Rooms adjoining, but they are seldom used as such, except on the nights of Dancing Assemblies. Those who have no particular engagements often drink tea here, in the afternoon, and either spend the remainder of the evening at cards, or ride, walk, or go to the Play as their inclinations lead them. A good harmony prevails, for the most part, among the company, and I have never seen a public place, where people are less on form, or more free from any disagreeable restraints. You receive inclosed the Subscriptions, Rules, etc. The number of Subscribers, last year, amounted to 429...

SUBSCRIPTIONS *and* RULES *for* MITCHENER'S ASSEMBLY-ROOM. *Margate* 1763.

	s.	d.
Subscriptions to the Room for the season to each Gentleman or Lady,	5	0
Dancing Assembly on *Monday* night, (Tea inclusive), each Subscriber, Gentleman or Lady,	2	6
Each Non-subscriber	5	0

CARD-ASSEMBLY, on
Thursday night.

	s.	d.
Whist, etc. each table	6	0
Lottery-table	12	0
Each Non-subscriber for admission, (Tea inclusive,)	1	0

BREAKFASTING.

To Subscribers	0	8
To Non-subscribers	1	0

TEA *in the* AFTERNOON.

To Subscribers	0	6
To Non-subscribers	1	0

COFFEE-ROOM

Subscriptions for the Coffee-Room, to each Gentleman for news-papers, extra post, pens, and paper.	2	6

(d) [*The Kentish Gazette*, 27–31 May 1769]

The number of Subscribers to his [Mitchener's] Assembly amounted in the last year to 500.

(e) [*Ibid.*, 24–28 June 1769]

Dancing Assembly at the New Inn and Assembly Room every Friday, John Mitchener, proprietor.

> By now Mitchener's assembly room days were numbered, with Margate's new and permanent assembly rooms in Cecil Square having already opened in a blaze of publicity.

(f) [*Ibid.*, 24 May 1769]

As it is impossible to give a personal Invitation to the Nobility and Gentry who frequent this Place, I am requested by the Proprietors of the New Assembly Rooms to take this Method of presenting their Compliments to the Nobility and Gentry, and to acquaint them that the said Rooms will be opened on Monday the 5th of June, with . . . a Ball in honour of his Majesty's Birth-day, when they shall esteem it as a Particular Favour to be honoured with their Company. The greatest endeavour to render every Thing agreeable shall be employed.

J. WALKER, M.C.

Mr. FOX, from St. Alban's Tavern, having taken the above Rooms, with the late Mrs. Omar's House adjoining, which is made into an elegant Tavern, . . . hopes to have the Honour of the Nobility and Gentry's Commands, as he has taken care to have a good Cook, and the best of Wines. He will make it a particular Study to oblige and spare no Pains to accommodate those who shall please to favour him with their Orders, and is their most dutiful and obedient Humble Servant.

JAMES FOX.

On 7 June 1769, through the medium of *The Kentish Gazette*, Mr. Fox returned 'his Dutiful Thanks to the Nobility and Gentry who did him the Honour to be at the opening of his Room and Tavern on Monday last', hoping that 'every Thing was to their Satisfaction', and promising to 'take the greatest Care to provide the best for their Accommodation, having prepared Bedchambers for the Reception of the Company, till they can suit themselves with Lodgings'. At the same time it was announced that the rooms would 'be open Every Day; Ball-nights every Monday; Publick Tea-drinking on Thursdays and Sundays in the Afternoon', while 'a very good Billiard Table will be set up next Week', and 'the Coffee-house is ready for the reception of Company'. So it was that Margate acquired permanent assembly rooms, which were over seen by a Master of Ceremonies from 1769 onwards. Mr. Walker remained Margate's first M.C. until he was succeeded almost twenty years later by Charles Le Bas in 1788 and, having opened successfully on 5 June, the habit of holding public breakfasts commenced at the end of July 1769.

(g)   [*The Kentish Gazette*, 29 July 1769]

At Mr. Fox's New Assembly Room, by the particular Desire of the Nobility and Gentry, Mr. Noel proposes on Saturday morning next, at Eleven O'clock, to have a Public Breakfasting . . . [A] Band of Music will play . . . and afterwards [he will] perform several Concertos, Solos and Select Pieces, upon that celebrated Instrument called The Pantaleon. After the Entertainment, Country Dances, N.B. The Piece of Music for Clarinets and French Horns, called 'The Echo', [is] composed by Mr. Noel. Tickets 3s. 6d. Each, which include the Breakfasting, to be had at Messrs. Silvers' and Halls' Circulating Library.

The first guidebook to describe the new assembly rooms was published in 1770.

(h)   [*The Margate Guide . . . In a Letter to a Friend*, 1770, 13–14]

It is admirably designed, and as well executed. The great Ball-room is 87 feet in length, and 43 feet in breadth, of a fine Height, and richly ornamented. It fronts towards the Sea. The Apartments for Tea and Cards join to it, and are spacious and perfectly convenient. . . . The Ground-floor consists of a fine Billiard-room, and a large Apartment, for the Use of public Entertainments, which belongs to, and communicates with Fox's Tavern, together with Hall's circulating Library and Toy-shop, the great Coffee-room, and a large Piazza, which extends the Length of the whole Building. The Number of Subscribers to these Rooms, the last Season, amounted to 930 at 5s. each. It is not supposed that any public Place in the Kingdom could boast of more. The Diversions are regularly conducted under a Master of the Ceremonies, who is a very worthy, prudent Man, and has been hitherto very happy, in not having made himself a single Enemy.

Of John Mitchener's New Inn it was noted how, *ibid*., 14,

Assemblies were held [here] before the Building of the present Rooms.

Over succeeding decades readers of guidebooks were introduced to many flattering assessments of the Margate assembly rooms.

(i) [*A New Display of the Beauties of England: or, A Description of the most elegant or magnificent PUBLIC EDIFICES . . . in different Parts of the Kingdom*, I, 3rd Ed., 1776, 207]

[In Cecil] square is a noble and commodious assembly-room, finished with great elegance and taste, . . . supposed to be the largest in England . . . The number of subscribers to these rooms have amounted to near a thousand in a season. The amusements are conducted with great regularity by Mr. WALKER M.C., who has the happiness to give general satisfaction.

(j) [*The Margate and Ramsgate Guide in Letters to a Friend*, 1797, 19]

The subscription is . . . half-a-guinea to the assembly-room for the season. [It] is a noble building indeed; one of the largest and most elegant rooms of the kind I ever saw; it has two rooms adjoining it, in which the company play at cards; underneath it is a piazza the whole length of it, which is eighty feet, where the company frequently walk in wet weather. Balls, during the season, are twice a week, with public tea-drinking, every Thursday: A band of music attends and plays, every day, Sundays and Wednesdays, excepted, from twelve till one in the assembly-room, for the entertainment of the subscribers.

(k) [E.W. Brayley, *The Beauties of England and Wales; or Delineations Topographical, Historical and Descriptive*, VIII: *Kent*, 1808, 959–60]

The *Assembly Rooms* [form] a handsome building of the Ionic order, with Venetian windows . . . On the ground floor is a good Billiard, and a Coffee-room, several Dining-parlours, and a Piazza supported by a range of duplicated Doric columns. On the first-floor are the Tea and Card-rooms, and the Ball-room: the latter is a very elegant apartment . . . The walls are tastefully ornamented with various stuccoed compartments, and festoons of flowers encircling . . . mirrors; at the west end of the room is a handsome orchestra, with wings for the accommodation of spectators; and five large and elegant glass chandeliers are suspended from the ceiling [Illus. 8]

Margate scenes: (a) The bathing rooms and (b) an obstinate donkey on the beach, c. 1820.

Illus. 13

(a) Samuel Bettison's library at Margate, 1820.
(b) A view of Folkestone, 1822.

Illus. 14

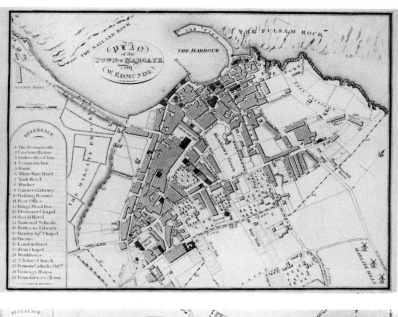

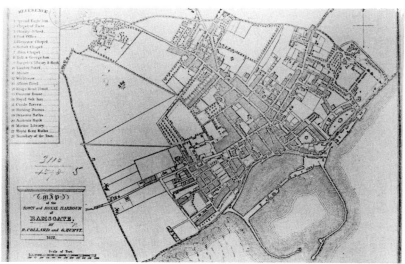

Plans of (a) Margate in 1821 and (b) Ramsgate in 1822.
Illus. 15

(a) A view of Folkestone, 1825–6.
(b) The Pegwell Bay regatta, 1828.

Illus. 16

(a) The Marine Terrace at Margate, 1828.
(b) The barracks and town of Hythe, 1829.

Illus. 17

Baths at (a) Gravesend in 1828 and (b) Margate in 1829.

Illus. 18

(l) [G. W. Bonner, *The Picturesque Pocket Companion to Margate, Ramsgate, Broadstairs, and the Parts Adjacent*, 2nd Ed., 1831, 71–2]

The entrance to the assembly room is at the west end of the colonnade, from where by a long and lofty vestibule, we arrive at the staircase, which conducts us to the card, tea, waiting and ball or assembly room, which is a magnificent apartment, . . . fitted up with elegant taste. In the pediments of the chimney-pieces are excellent busts of his Majesty George III, and the late Duke of Cumberland, which are considered to be good and expressive resemblances of those royal and distinguished individuals. . . . Weekly concerts, and several other lively amusements, may be enjoyed in these rooms, and on Sunday evening, the company may enjoy a selection of Sacred music

> While the décor might have been lavish, the existence and the conduct of the assembly rooms did not meet with universal approval.

(m) [*Letters of Momus from Margate; Describing The most distinguished Characters There, and The Virtues, Vices and Follies to which they gave occasion, in what was called the SEASON OF the Year 1777*, 1778, 2–3]

Margate, September 1, 1777.
I go to the rooms, where an insipid, and almost a fashionable dullness prevails. . . . The M.C. has a strange predilection for haberdashers, manteu-makers, and miliners, and takes every opportunity of setting them above the wife or daughter of a merchant who hath left off trade; of a quack-doctor; of a dentist; of a Lincoln's-Inn lawyer; of a doctor in divinity, or an M.P. . . . In the anxious and corroding silence of the card room an invalid coughed in a note like that of a pig; the astonishment it occasioned made the man ashamed to own his infirmity. Some referred it to evil spirits, and the clergy were desired to go home for their prayer-books. . . . Being reduced to difficulties they started the supposition that the noise was made by a ventriloquist.

> 'Some moral reflections on cards, and dancing in public' were voiced in the fifth Letter of

(n) [*The Margate and Ramsgate Guide in Letters to a Friend*, 1797, 23, 38]

[While] I would not have you to suppose . . . that I am an enemy to an innocent game at cards among friends in private, or an occasional

dance, among young people, in the presence of their relatives or friends,
. . . I think either of these, in *public* rooms and among promiscuous
company, should, in general, be dispensed with, as no real *benefit* or
advantage can possibly accrue from them; but real *harm* often has, and
may, to both sexes, particularly the younger part of the *female* sex. . . .

The theatre and assembly-rooms are not so numerously attended as
might be expected, in a town so devoted to gaiety and dissipation,* . . .
the master of the ceremonies not being altogether approved of† . . .

> * Margate, as well as other public watering-places, during the *summer*
> season, is visited as much, if not more by the votaries to *pleasure*, as
> the inheritors of *disease*. . .

> † Since the above letter was written, Mr. Walker, the master of the
> ceremonies, has resigned, and a Mr. *Le Bas* unanimously chosen in
> his room, who appears much more likely to give general satisfac-
> tion.

> Charles Le Bas succeeded Mr. Walker as M.C. at both the
> Margate and Ramsgate assembly rooms in 1788 and occupied that
> post for twenty six years until 26 September 1814.

(o) [*The Morning Post*, 26 September 1814]

Our Arbiter Elegantiarum, Mr. LE BAS, after wielding the sceptre for
[over] twenty years, abdicates his throne, . . . in favour of an officer in
the York Militia . . .
Mr. LE BAS is to receive from Captain CLOUGH £200 per annum by
way of annuity. The former does not quit his post altogether, until the
latter is formally inducted, and generally acknowledged throughout the
Island.

(p) [*Ibid.*, 30 September 1814]

Margate, September 27.

An Important Era.
Yesterday the Isle of Thanet witnessed a scene, which excited a great
sensation! – We allude to the formal abdication of the *Monarch* of the
Graces, Mr. LE BAS, after swaying the sceptre for the space of 26 years.
At 9 o'clock p.m. the ceremony took place in the Assembly-room when
Captain CLOUGH's election followed.

The Annual Ball,
on this occasion, excited more interest than any since the period when
the late Duchess of DEVONSHIRE honoured it with her presence.
When the election was over the dancing began. It is at the M.C.'s Ball
that all the beauty and fashion of the vicinity appear; and last evening
was a *proud one* in the annals of gaiety. Carriages *innumerable* arriving ere
the hour of ten, Captain CLOUGH directed the band to strike up.

(q) [*Ibid.*, 1 October 1814]

Margate, September 28.
The Ball on Monday night still continues the topic of general conversation; there were present 653 persons of *ton* [fashion].

> As hinted at above, the M.C.'s prime responsibility was to
> regulate social life and to uphold decency and gentility in stan-
> dards of dress and behaviour. He exercised in effect social control
> over a variety of indoor and outdoor amusements (also see Docs.
> 35j; 38k, l; 47f). While he endeavoured to introduce himself
> personally to known families of importance, visitors for their part
> were encouraged to subscribe to the room and to introduce
> themselves to the M.C. What was involved was made quite clear
> to visitors in a guidebook of 1809.

(r) [*The New Margate, Ramsgate and Broadstairs Guide*, 5th Ed.,
Margate, 1809, 59–62]

The season begins on the 4th of June, and terminates the last ball night
in October. . . . The following equitable Regulations, formed for the
pleasure and advantage of the visitants, are enforced with the greatest
politeness by Mr. *Le Bas*, Master of the Ceremonies, with such
attention to the company, as highly deserves every mark of public
approbation.

MARGATE ASSEMBLY-ROOMS.
Rules and Orders for Admission.

I.   That every person, to be entitled to walk and play at cards in the
rooms, during the season, do subscribe 10s. 6d. and none but subscribers to be admitted into the card-room of a morning.
II.   That on Mondays and Thursdays, subscribers do pay 1s. 6d.

admittance, and non-subscribers 4s. Tea, at Ten o'clock, 1s. each.

III. That on Sundays, subscribers do pay 6d. admittance, and non-subscribers 1s.; each person to pay 1s. for tea, if called for.

IV. That all persons playing at whist, quadrille, commerce, or loo, do pay 11s. for two packs of cards; 7s. for a single pack; and lottery-tables to pay 15s. No other games to be played in the rooms, without the permission of the Master of the Ceremonies.

V. That no person be permitted to play with cards which have been left by another party.

VI. That no person be admitted into the gallery without a written order, signed by the Master of the Ceremonies; and no servants to be admitted up stairs on any account whatever.

> N.B. After two o'clock, subscribers, or non-subscribers, to pay 6d. an hour so long as they continue to play at cards, whether ball-night or not.

As the utmost decorum is necessary to be observed in all public assemblies, the Master of the Ceremonies requests of the company a strict compliance with the following regulations:

I. That on ball-nights no ladies be admitted into the great room in habits, nor gentlemen in swords, boots, or pantaloons; military gentlemen excepted.

II. That the balls do begin at eight o'clock and finish at twelve, precisely, even in the middle of a dance.

III. That after a lady has called a dance, when it is finished, her place in the next dance is at the bottom.

IV. That all ladies who go down a dance do continue in their places till the rest have done the same.

> N.B. As a deviation from this rule gives universal offence, the Master of the Ceremonies will pay the utmost attention possible, to see it strictly observed.

V. That ladies, whether of precedence or not, do take their places at the bottom after a country-dance is begun.

VI. That the balls be on Mondays and Thursdays, and that they both be considered as undress balls. Cotillons and reels will be danced on Monday nights.

VII. That the rooms be open on Sunday evenings for a promenade.

VIII. That two sets for country-dances be not formed, till upwards of twenty couple stand up, to be then equally divided, and no person to change from one set to another.

IX.   That no lady do permit another to stand above her, after she has taken her place in a set.

The Master of the Ceremonies entreats those ladies and gentlemen whom he has not the honour of knowing personally, to afford him an early opportunity of being introduced to them, as it will not only in a certain degree be a means of preventing improper company from coming to the rooms, but will enable him to pay every individual that attention, which it is not less his inclination than his duty to observe.

CHARLES LE BAS, M.C.

It is necessary to observe here, that Mr. *Le Bas* some time since published a Letter, addressed to the company frequenting Margate, Ramsgate, and Broadstairs, to which we would particularly refer our readers.

That Charles Le Bas was efficient in his duties and was highly thought of during the 1800s is reflected by the decision of the editor of the guidebook, just referred to, to set alongside the title page an engraving of 'CHARLES LE BAS ESQ. M.C.', which was justified as follows.

(s)   [*Ibid.*, vi] (Illus. 10b)

The Editor feels great pleasure in having it in his power to prefix the portrait of Mr. LE BAS, M.C. to this Fifth Edition of the Margate, Ramsgate, and Broadstairs Guide, to all of which places he is equally, in his official capacity, attached. He considers it highly appropriate, from the circumstances of his being Master of the Ceremonies; but more so from the very able and conciliatory manner with which he has conducted himself in this arduous and difficult situation. It is now upwards of twenty years since Mr. LE BAS succeeded Mr. WALKER as M.C. and from that period to the present, the testimonies of approbation from the Subscribers to the Margate and Ramsgate Assembly-Rooms, have been constantly increasing. That he may long enjoy the fruits of his indefatigable exertions, is the sincere wish of his and the Public's faithful and obedient humble servant,

L.S.

Margate, July 1809.

> The same 'Rules and Orders for Admission' applied in 1816 under 'Charles Clough Esq. M.C.', *ibid.*, 6th Ed., Margate, 1816, 66–8. Although it was costly to patronize the assembly rooms, the strict rules of dress and behaviour enjoyed the approbation of the aristocracy, clergy and gentry, particularly since promenading, tea drinking, card playing and dancing were manifestations of genteel social life in England's provincial county towns as well as its spas and seaside resorts. There were occasions, however, when the assembly rooms were relatively empty while at other times they were full of company.

(t) [*The Times*, 6 September 1804]

Margate, September 4.

The Promenade at the Rooms on Sunday evening was very full, and rather shewy, the Ladies being for the greater part dressed in very good taste. There were many symptoms displayed of the early steps in the progress of love, or of court-ship at least, and there seems little reason to doubt, that this Autumn will ripen a very full *matrimonial* harvest. . . . [However] the Assembly last night did not keep pace with the Sunday's promenade. . . . SILVER had a numerous audience . . . BETTISON's was crowded with beauty . . . Mrs. JORDAN [at the Theatre Royal] drew as full a house as has been known since her arrival . . . She was received with great applause . . . Several fashionables were in the boxes, among whom were Lady ESSEX, Lady FRANKLAND, etc. . . . Miss DUNCAN, the favourite Heroine of Margate, is re-engaged by the Manager for eight nights.

> The above report is but one illustration of how the assembly rooms had to complete vigorously with Margate's Theatre Royal and the circulating libraries in the provision of entertainments, a point which did not escape the attention of the compiler of a 1797 guidebook.

(u) [*The Margate and Ramsgate Guide in Letters to a Friend*, 1797, 38]

The owners of the libraries reap the benefit, . . . as their shops are resorted to by all ranks every day but Sunday, when they are entirely shut up; [they are] generally crowded of an evening.

There was much on offer to amuse the holidaymaker.

(v)   [*The Times*, 6 September 1804]

[At Margate] the votaries of pleasure are provided with a very ample bill of fare for the rest of the week:- *Two* masquerades, one at the *Theatre* tomorrow, and another at the *Rooms* on Friday, . . . besides the Plays, the Libraries, and twenty other things, all wonderfully well adapted for lightening the pockets of a Citizen, and putting him in mind, in due time, of his counting-house or his shop.

> With so much on offer, remembering too that fine weather could militate against indoor entertainments, it is not surprising that attendances fluctuated at all functions.

(w)   [*The Times*, 10 September 1804]

Margate, September 7.
Last night there was a Ball at the Assembly Rooms, which was tolerably well attended, but was not remarkably distinguished for its splendour. There were upwards of 200 persons, with an ample proportion of young masters and misses . . . Miss SCOTT sings [however], with great applause, in the evenings, at BETTISON'S [library], to very numerous audiences . . .

September 8.
Last night the second Masquerade for this season was given at Kidman's [Assembly] Rooms. . . . Public chit-chat had promised much diversion, but there was a lamentable falling off from our expectations. Not 150 persons attended, of whom there might, perhaps, [have been] 20 characters, a dozen masks. . . . The rooms were prettily illuminated; there was a tolerable band in the gallery; and to do the Ladies present justice, though they were not dressed for a Masquerade, they were elegantly dressed for an assembly, [but] the appearance of many of the Gentlemen was careless and slovenly to excess. . . . There were wag-goners, flower-girls, a bathing woman, a fisherman, a ballad singer, a Hebrew conjurer [and] a Sultana, [but] there was little dancing. The whole broke up shortly after 2 o'clock.

> Masquerades at this time were attracting moral censure.

There is much talk today about an advertisement from the Society for the Suppression of Vice, in which the Margate Masquerades are particularly censured: they are considered as great nuisances. Those who have seen the Masquerades given this season, will find some difficulty in discovering any very crying evil in their present state; for really they have all been very ill attended, and possess so very few attractions, that he who has been once, will scarcely be drawn again. There have been but four of them in all (admission 4s.), two at the Theatre, and two at the rooms.

With all submission to the Society, the inhabitants and the visitors of Margate contend, that if the propriety of allowing or suppressing public amusements bear any relation to the facility with which they may produce good or evil effects, the Masquerades of London should be stopped rather than those of Margate. They think that the *metropolitan* society should take the beam out of their own eye, before they meddle with the mote in their brother's.

> Ten years later masquerades were still being put on at the Margate assembly rooms, one of which was attended by 400 people, according to *The Morning Post*, 13 September 1814. In 1819 it was made clear that Sunday evenings in the Margate assembly rooms were given over to sacred music,

(x) [*The Thanet Itinerary or Steam Yacht Companion*, 1819, 34–5]

when several able performers are procured at a great expense from London, and the celebrated Mr. WEIPPERT generally plays some of his delightful Solos on the Harp. A military band is introduced to occupy the time, during the pauses which are necessarily made by the Singers and Musicians in the Orchestra.

> One instance of the popularity of these occasions was reported as follows during September 1805.

(y) [*The Times*, 18 September 1805]

Notwithstanding the full attendance on the Parade to a late hour, the company at the Rooms exceeded 500. Several pieces of sacred music were performed, and the anthem of 'God Save the King' was heard with that enthusiasm the subject naturally inspires in a . . . loyal nation.

> The ground-floor billiard room was also well patronized that season.

(z) [*Ibid.*, 17 September 1805]

The elegant and scientific game of billiards has occasioned a large influx of the friends of the sport at KIDMAN'S. During two days a match has been played between EVANS, . . . one of the most skilful persons in the kingdom at this diversion, and a gentleman from Canterbury . . . of 21 games EVANS obtained 16.

Elegance continued to grace the Margate assembly rooms right up to the close of the Napoleonic Wars.

(aa) [*The Morning Post*, 7 October 1814]

The general dress is of white satin, [with] diamonds in profusion.

(bb) [*Ibid.*, 11 October 1814]

The fashionable population of the Isle of Thanet mustered strong . . . last evening. Indeed we never recollect to have witnessed except upon some very *important* occasion, so great a concourse of rank and beauty as graced the Assembly Rooms . . . Cecil Square was filled with carriages and four from Ramsgate, Broadstairs, and even Dover. It was a most flattering encouragement in every respect.

Two days later it was also noticed, *ibid.*, 13 October 1814 that 'the *Libraries* have not been *so crammed* at night as we have been accustomed to see them'. After 1815 competition intensified notably with the bazaars of the 1820s (see Doc. 44), but even so the assembly rooms continued to be highly recommended.

(cc) [*The Thanet Itinerary or Steam Yacht Companion*, 1819, 33–4]

In an account of the public amusements of Margate, the Assembly Rooms are certainly entitled to the first and highest recommendation. . . . The entertainment provided in them is superior to anything of the kind, which this town, or perhaps any other watering place in *Great Britain*, can afford.

Two visitors were singularly unimpressed by what they encountered when they paid a chance visit to the Royal Hotel and Assembly Rooms.

(dd)   [*MS Diary of Mary Figgins, 30 August – 21 September circa 1828*, Margate Public Library, Local Collection, YO60. 41]

On our road home we went into the Royal Hotel to see the fancy fair but, as it was so empty and there was such an awful stillness, . . . we soon came out. . . . Two base viols were practising their parts.

> Had their visit been of an evening they might have come away with a different impression.

(ee)   [*Picture of Ramsgate, or A Guide to the Various Amusements, Public Libraries, Building Improvements, etc of that celebrated Watering Place*, Ramsgate, 1833, 69]

The Rooms open for the season the first week in July, and the last ball night is in October. . . . Every Thursday evening the Rooms are appropriated to an Evening Promenade and Concerts.

Several London vocalists of eminence perform at the Concerts, and the instrumental department is ably conducted. On Sundays selections of Sacred Music are performed. On the ground floor . . . are elegant dining rooms, a billiard room, and coffee room.

OCTAVIUS SCOTT, Esq., Master of the Ceremonies.

> For the same year Ramsgate's assembly rooms were presented as follows.

(ff)   [*Ibid.*, 38]

At the Albion Hotel and East India and American Coffee-house there is an elegant and spacious assembly room, with good card rooms adjoining, ornamented and finished in a very superior style, which commands an extensive prospect of the Downs, a part of East Kent, and the Coast of France; Mrs. Bear (widow of the late Henry Bear), the proprietor, is very attentive to the accommodation of the nobility and gentry who frequent them. . . . Subscription to the assembly rooms, 10s. 6d. each person during the season.

Lieut. Col. Clarke, C.B., our polite master of the ceremonies regulates the sprightly dance with much attention, and his pleasing urbanity and conciliating manners peculiarly qualify him for the distinguished situation of directing the elegant amusements of the ball room, in which he has been placed by the nobility and gentry, subscribers, visiting and residing at Ramsgate; their numbers are very considerably increased since the election of Lieut. Col. Clarke, C.B.* Printed rules and orders for admission may be seen at the rooms.

   * At the Memorable Battle of Waterloo Colonel Clarke commanded the Scotch Greys.

   What had long been the custom whereby Margate and Ramsgate shared the services of one M.C. had been abandoned by the 1830s. Back in 1797 the Ramsgate assembly rooms were still relatively new.

(gg) [By an Inhabitant, *The Margate Guide, A Descriptive Poem, with Elucidatory Notes*, Margate, 1797, 98]

The Assembly Room is situated near the harbour, and is a neat structure, with the conveniences of coffee, tea, and card rooms: the amusements are under the direction of *Charles Le Bas*, Esq., Master of the Ceremonies, at Margate.

   By 1809, as if not to be outshone by Margate, a billiard room had been added to the facilities and, although less pretentious and slightly cheaper than the Margate rooms, those at Ramsgate were nevertheless governed by similar 'Rules and Orders, for admission, etc.', being likewise 'under the direction of Mr. *Le Bas*, the Master of the Ceremonies'.

(hh) [*The New Margate, Ramsgate and Broadstairs Guide*, 5th Ed., Margate, 1809, 86]

RAMSGATE ASSEMBLY ROOMS.

I.   That every person, to be entitled to walk and play at cards in the rooms, during the season, do subscribe 7s. 6d.

II.   That the balls be on Tuesdays, the card assemblies on Mondays and Fridays, and on Sundays the rooms to be open for tea.

III.   That there be no dancing whatever in the rooms on the nights of the card assemblies.

IV.   That on Tuesdays subscribers do pay 2s. 6d. admittance, and non-subscribers 5s. and on Mondays, Fridays, and Sundays, subscribers do pay 1s. admittance, and non-subscribers 1s. 6d. Each person calling for tea, at ten o'clock, to pay 1s.

V. That all persons playing at whist, quadrille, commerce, or loo, do pay 10s. 6d. for two packs of cards; 7s. for a single pack; and lottery-tables to pay 15s. No other games to be played in the rooms, without the permission of the Master of the Ceremonies.

VI. That no person be permitted to play with cards which have been left by another party.

> Ten years later it remained the case that at the Ramsgate assembly rooms,

(ii) [*The Thanet Itinerary or Steam Yacht Companion*, 1819, 67]

the regulations for dancing and card playing are the same as at *Margate*. M.C. Mr. Clough.

> Indeed, when he made his entrée at a ball held there in October 1814, it was noted that

(jj) [*The Morning Post*, 15 October 1814]

the Assembly Rooms were full of company of the *first-class* – an unprecedented event.

> Broadstairs was too small to possess its own assembly rooms, prior to the 1830s. Its visitors subscribed to either the Margate or the Ramsgate rooms, or to both, while joint subscriptions applied equally to those holidaymakers patronising either Margate or Ramsgate. One visitor who felt able to comment on the contrasting social life and atmosphere of the three Thanet towns in 1804 was Joseph Farington, R.A. (Illus. 5d).

(kk) [Ed: J. Greig, *The Farington Diary*, II, 1923, 273–4]

AUGUST 11 – ... In the evening we went to Ramsgate to the Assembly Room, where Madame Bianchi sang several songs to a Pianoforte and Meyer played on the Harp. At $\frac{1}{2}$ past 9 the music was over. 7s. 6d. was paid by each person for admittance. A Ball then commenced. At Eleven we came away. There was much company, and among them, Lady Augusta Murray and her Son, and Sister: [also] Lady Hamilton [Nelson's Emma] with Mrs. and Miss Nelson, – Lord Essex and many officers of the Herefordshire Militia which he commands, stationed here. His Lordship spoke to me . . . Lord Cholmondeley was also there and also Lord Keith, who commands the fleet in the Downs. – Lady Augusta Murray has a very singular-shaped face.

The Lower part from the Nose falling as if shaved off. Her Sister still more plain. I thought them coarse and confident looking women. She has entered Herself in the subscription book at Ramsgate *Duchesss of Sussex.* We saw Her Son, a fine boy of 11 or 12 years of age seemingly, and very like the Royal Family. He is said to be called the *Prince.*

Some of the names mentioned above need identifying in order to make this reference more meaningful. Madam Bianchi as Miss Jackson, a popular singer, had married Francesco Bianchi, the famous Italian composer, who had settled in London in 1793. Philip James Meyer, born in Strasburg, settled in England in 1784, as the first musician to play the pedal harp in this country in 1772. Lady Augusta Murray, the second daugher of the fourth Earl of Dunmore, was wide open to gossip, for having married in Rome, on 4 April 1793, Augustus Frederick, Duke of Sussex. The King, under the Royal Marriage Act of 1772, had declared this union void in August 1794.

AUGUST 14 – At one o'clock rode to Margate, 3 miles, with J. and Wm. Offley and saw the Library, the Assembly-rooms and the Bathing Houses. – Lord and Lady Cholmondeley, Miss Seymour, – Lord Essex and several other fashionable persons were there. Margate is *a very public place.* I much prefer the quiet retirement of Broadstairs.

Public Margate might have been, but Broadstairs offered only 'The Dreary Round'.

AUGUST 15 – The company at Broadstairs has increased in number, but all are in parties, there does not appear to be any association. The English reserve is fully expressed. Card tables are set every even'g in the Library, but as yet there are no players. We dined and passed the even'g as usual. We breakfast abt. $\frac{1}{4}$ past 9, – dine at 4, – tea $\frac{1}{2}$ past 6, – light supper at 9 – and retire between 10 and 11.

Ten years previously at the end of September 1794 when Mary and Agnes Berry were staying at Prospect House, near Broadstairs (Illus. 2b), they were content to stay at home in the evenings.

(ll) [Ed: W.S. Lewis and A. Dayle Wallace, *Horace Walpole's Correspondence with Mary and Agnes Berry*, XII, New Haven, 1961, 112]

We are so far from the two metropolises of Margate and Ramsgate, that having as yet had no inducement strong enough to take us out 3 miles in cold dark nights, we have spent every evening at home and alone, except last night [27 September], when we dined at Broadstairs, our nearest town, with a Scotch Lord and Lady Balgonie.

Broadstairs appeared to be very quiet to a valetudinarian of the 1830s.

(mm) [By a Valetudinarian, *Sea-Side Reminiscences: A Few 'Odd Thoughts' on Our Fashionable Watering-Places*, circa 1835, 16–17]

BROADSTAIRS is a pretty little village, little more than 2 miles from Ramsgate. I have passed many a pleasant hour there, in solitude – for company there is none. A more unsocial spot does not exist. . . . Being born with an enquiring disposition, I asked one of the inhabitants, why so few persons visited the place? He informed me that none but serious, sedate and quiet people, ever came there; and that music (unless sacred?), raffles, assemblies, and things of that nature, were held, by the generality of visitors, in great abhorrence. 'Billiards', he added,

'were tolerated though disapproved of, for the sake of reconciling the young men, who must, of necessity, in some cases, accompany their papas and mammas to the "solemnity of the village".'

Notwithstanding all these drawbacks to the general visitor, Mr. HALE has opened a very excellent library, and is determined that, on his part, nothing shall be wanting to promote comfort.

Indeed, of the two Broadstairs libraries, kept by Mr. Barnes and Mr. Hale, it was pointed out in 1831 that

(nn) [G.W. Bonner, *The Picturesque Pocket Companion to Margate, Ramsgate, Broadstairs, and the Parts Adjacent*, 2nd Ed., 1831, 187]

both . . . command a view of the Downs, and contain a large collection of books; while the respective proprietors strive by assiduity and unremitting attention, to deserve the support of their friends and summer visitors. Here are also assemblies for dancing and cards, which are held alternately, during the season, at the library of the former, and at the new rooms lately erected by the latter, and adjoining the library.

The absence of assembly rooms as such in Broadstairs did not prevent balls and other social functions from occurring in such venues as the circulating libraries of the town. Considerable indignation was expressed over suggestions that balls were poorly attended in Broadstairs in 1814.

(oo) [*The Morning Post*, 5 October 1814]

Broadstairs, October 3.
It has been reported that the Balls here are not well attended. The report is untrue – 'a weak invention of the enemy'. On Friday night an Assembly was held at Nuckell's Great Room, which was attended by nearly 100 fashionables of *consideration*, all carriage company! Dancing commenced at 9 o'clock. . . . Refreshments of a superior description were provided and distributed at midnight. Dancing was kept up until 1.30 . . . Captain CLOUGH officiated.

> Sandgate, sandwiched as it was between Folkestone and Hythe, was in a somewhat analogous position to Broadstairs (also compare after jj above).

(pp) [*A Guide to all the Watering and Sea-Bathing Places*, 1806, 230]

The New Inn is the usual place of entertainment, but there is neither a ball nor assembly-room.

> In a New Edition of *ibid*., 1815, 423, the comment was added that

these luxuries may be enjoyed by the lovers of dancing, either at Hythe, Folkestone or Dover, within accessible distances.

> Retirement too was the keynote of Sandgate in 1816.

(qq) [*The Hythe, Sandgate and Folkestone Guide*, Hythe, 1816, 28]

That which has been eloquently said of another place of fashionable resort may, with at least equal propriety, be applied to SANDGATE.

> 'It has cheerfulness without noise, tranquility without dullness, and facility of communication without the disturbance of a public road'.

> In 1806 Hythe was accustomed to holding an occasional assembly.

(rr) [*A Guide to all the Watering and Sea-Bathing Places*, 1806, 230]

An assembly is held here occasionally, in a room belonging to the Corporation.

Ten years later *The Hythe, Sandgate and Folkestone Guide*, Hythe, 1816, 25, referred to occasional balls being held 'particularly in the bathing season'. The amusements of Folkestone in 1806 were described as follows.

(ss) [*A Guide to all the Watering and Sea-Bathing Places*, 1806, 229]

THE amusements of this place are but few, when compared to some of its neighbours. Here is, however, a small theatre, which is only occupied in the winter. Besides an assembly-room called the Apollo, here are two billiard-tables.

Assembly rooms were operating on a regular basis in Dover by the 1790s.

(tt) [*The Dover and Deal Directory and Guide*, Dover, c. 1792, 21]

The influx of a number of most respectable families, as summer-visitors, has occasioned the erection of a new assembly-room and theatre. At the assembly-room there are regular public breakfastings, card-assemblies and balls; it commands a fine view of the sea, the coast of France, etc.

Horn's Description of Dover, Dover, 1817, 23, refers to 'regular card assemblies and balls' being held in the assembly room in Snargate Street. Under the heading of 'MUSICAL PROMENADES, etc.', it was noted of Dover, in 1828,

(uu) [W. Batcheller, *A New History of Dover, to which is Added a New Dover Guide*, Dover, 1828, 352]

Musical Evening Promenades and other fashionable amusements, such as are usual at other watering places, continue, during the season, at the King's Arms Assembly Rooms.

Although Deal possessed assembly rooms, they clearly lagged behind those of Dover in the 1840s.

(vv) [S. Bagshaw, *History, Gazetteer and Directory of the County of Kent*, II, Sheffield, 1847, 355]

THE ASSEMBLY ROOMS, Lower-street, is a plain brick building of which Mr. Thomas Hayward is the proprietor. Assemblies are occasionally held during the season, and are numerously attended by the fashionable circles of the neighbourhood.

In the developing Herne Bay of the 1830s assembly rooms were looked upon as an essential asset.

(ww)   [By a Lady, *A Picture of the New Town of Herne Bay*, 1835, II]

In this line of buildings [on the Parade] is an assembly room of magnificent dimensions.

Gravesend too did not lose out in the business of providing amusements, following the introduction of steamboats in 1815.

(xx)   [*Pigot & Co.'s Commercial Directory*, 1832–4, 816]

In proportion to the increase of visitors, preparations have been made for their accommodation, including baths, a theatre, assembly-rooms, libraries and reading-rooms.

Among Kentish seaside resorts, and with the possible exception of Dover, Margate above all, followed by Ramsgate, led the field in the provision of assembly rooms, measured both by the magnificence of the building erected and the scale and order of entertainments provided. Herne Bay to some extent shared with both Broadstairs and Sandgate a much greater degree of tranquility and retirement.

(yy)   [*The Visitor's Guide to the Watering Places*, 1842, 196]

A degree of tranquillity, unknown to Margate in the bathing season, may, undoubtedly be found at Herne Bay.

42.   *Circulating libraries.*

Compared to the provision of assembly rooms, Kentish resorts other than Margate and Ramsgate fared rather better in the erection of circulating libraries. Along with assembly rooms and theatres they were essential to the social life of eighteenth and early nineteenth-century spas and coastal watering places. They also became a familiar amenity in the county and principal market towns of Georgian England. In a highly developed form they combined under one roof the reading of newspapers and magazines, the reading and borrowing of books, shopping for stationery and other goods, promenading and socializing, and the provision of indoor entertainment. The libraries of well-developed resorts offered to their customers much more than newspapers or books. They sold through their attached shops a variety of stationery, fancy goods, trinkets, Tunbridge ware, curiosities, etc., which were bought as souvenirs or gifts. As with the bathing rooms they were centres for socializing and lounging. They were venues of entertainment, offering their patrons gambling, musical concerts, and evening assemblies. They advertised and sold tickets for other forms of entertainment, including the local theatre or playhouse. They functioned as accommodation agencies. Their proprietors were often well informed about the locality and what it had to offer. Finally, they were places where local guidebooks were sold and even published. Librarians, who had their own printing works, produced and published maps and guidebooks of their locality, drawing often on a good personal knowledge of the antiquities and topography of their own areas. There is no mention of circulating libraries in the first guidebook to Margate which was published in 1763. Indeed, specific mention of them in guidebooks is delayed until the mid–1770s.

(a) [*The Kentish Traveller's Companion*, Rochester, 1776, 120]

When the weather is windy or wet, [there] are two circulating libraries, . . . well stocked with books for the amusement of the company within doors.

> The history of Margate's libraries centres around four names: Joseph Hall, Samuel Silver, William Garner and Samuel Bettison. Three famous circulating libraries developed in the resort, situated in areas which became fashionable and were well patronized by visitors, namely the Parade, and Cecil and Hawley Squares. Joseph Hall was the first Margate librarian to announce his appearance during February 1766.

(b) [*The Kentish Post, or Canterbury News Letter*, 1 February 1766]

JOSEPH HALL, Bookseller, begs leave to acquaint the Nobility, Gentry, and others, that he has fitted up a commodious Shop near the Parade for a Circulating Library consisting of a large Collection of new and entertaining Books. Each Subscriber to pay 10s. 6d. per Year or 3s. per Quarter. All Sorts of Stationery at the most reasonable Rates, viz: Writing-papers, Shop-books, Copy-books, Spelling-books, Bibles, Common-prayers . . . Books neatly bound, and Gentlemen's Libraries repaired; a great Variety of Paper-hangings as cheap as in London.

In those early days there was no mention of providing entertainment or selling fancy articles. His premises were next door to a bathing house when John Baker visited Margate in September 1777. His diary gives one insight into the demands exerted by an early holidaymaker.

(c)   [Ed: P.C. Yorke, *The Diary of John Baker*, 1931, 417, 418, 420]

11 September.
. . . Mrs. Woodington went out and got lodgings at Hall's the bookseller, next door to Bathing House. Went thither and had dinner sent from hotel . . . Mr. Hall brought his book and I subscribed 5s. . . .

16 September.
. . . Read the two volumes of Vicar of Wakefield from Mr. Hall's library.

1 October.
. . . Returned this afternoon to the shop Lewis's Hist. and Antiq. of Isle of Thanet.

Joseph Hall was a Margate librarian for twenty nine years until he was afflicted by bankruptcy in 1795, having moved from the waterside in 1786 to his new Hawley Square library erected by Crofts, a Margate builder. It attracted both praise and censure from a local guidebook compiler of the 1790s. Zechariah Cozens, as one of the leading inhabitants and architects of Margate, having a hand in the designing of many Margate properties, may have designed the new Hawley Square library, but the final result from the builder did not meet with his full approval.

(d)   [Z. Cozens, *A Tour through the Isle of Thanet, and some other Parts of East Kent*, 1793, 25]

Hall's elegant shop and library [is] much the largest of any in the town, and finished in an expensive manner: it consists of two compartments; the first containing a curious assortment of jewellery, toys, Tunbridge Wares, muslins, etc. . . . A row of handsome columns . . . separates the shop from the library, composed of a well chosen collection of amusing books, in various languages . . . [While] the building is pleasing to the cursory inspector, [it] would have given more pleasure to the informed architect, if the builder had confined himself to a strict observance of the Orders; as such a departure from them, as is observable in almost all our modern buildings, will be a proof of the declining taste of this extolled age.

> By now there were two other librarians who were operating successfully in Margate.

(e) [*Ibid.;* 25, 28]

Silver's Library [Cecil Square] containing a good assortment of books, and a comfortable room behind the shop, calculated for the accommodation of the company in reading, etc.

Garner's Library [at the bottom of the High Street] pleasantly situated at the waterside, thereby having the peculiar advantage of a most delightful sea prospect; . . . furnished with upwards of 3,000 volumes, chiefly in the English language, comprizing an excellent selection of History and Antiquities.

> Samuel Silver, originating from a Sandwich circulating library family, had moved by May 1771 into Cecil Square, under the assembly rooms, both of which had been completed by 1769. Joseph Hall, having established himself as already noted in 1766, and Samuel Silver, from 1771, became great rivals in the Margate circulating library business.

(f) [*The Margate Guide*, 1780, 15]

There are two circulating Libraries, having a very good Collection of Books in all Languages, which the Company read at a very trifling Expence. One is pleasantly situated near the Pier, and kept by Mr. Hall, and the other under the New Rooms by Mr. Silver.

> Samuel Silver, having also a long reign as a circulating librarian, extending over thirty nine years, was the first of the Margate librarians to expand on a really large scale. In 1782 he began the

construction of a new library on the east side of Cecil Square, occupying the site of the present General Post Office. He moved from under the colonnade of the assembly rooms to his new library during March 1783, where he remained in business until February 1808, ending his career likewise as a bankrupt. The stocks which he carried were both enormous and expensive. *The Kentish Gazette* of 24–28 July 1773 relates how when his shop was broken into he was robbed of 2,000 pairs of silk stockings and gloves valued 'to a considerable amount'. Fourteen years later his 1787 catalogue listed over 5,000 volumes, offering to the reader a wide choice of books, covering 'History, Antiquities, Lives, Memoirs, Voyages, Travels, etc.'

A New
CATALOGUE
of
SILVER'S CIRCULATING LIBRARY,
(formerly under)
now removed opposite
The Assembly-Rooms, Margate.

Consisting of many Valuable Books, among which are the following, viz.

Antiquities of Glo'stershire
———— Herculaneum
———— the Isle of Thanet
Astley's Voy. & Trav. 4,v.
Brookes's Nat. Hist. 6 vol.
Chesterfield's Miscel. 2 vol.
————'s Letters, 4 vol.
Clarendon's Rebellion, 6 v.
Churchill's Poems, 2 vol.
Cooke's Voyages, 4 vol.
Cooke's last Voy, to 1781.
Cox's Russian Discoveries
Gibbon's Rom. Empire, 3 v.
Gray's Poems and Letters
Hume's Hist. of Eng, 8 vol.
Justamond's Indies, 5 vol.
Journey to the Glaciers
Life of Petrarch, 2 vol.

Life of Garrick, 2 vol.
Life of Alfred the Great
Miller's Gardener's dict.
Medicinal Dict. Jame's, 3 v.
Melmoth's Cicero, 3 vol.
Pliny's Letters, 2 vol.
Robertson's America, 2 vol.
————'s Charles V.
Smollett's Hist. of Eng. 16 v.
Swift's Work's, 22 vol.
Sully's Memoirs, 6 vol.
Stern's Works, – 24 vol.
Sheridan's Sweden
Trusler's South Sea Islands
Tyburn Chronicle, 4 vol.
Thicknesses Journey, 2 vol.
Trials of Keppel, etc.
Universal History, 21 vol.

Where may be had a general Assortment of Books, Stationery,
Perfumery, Silver and Plated Goods, Jewellery, Pearls, Cutlery,
Hard-Ware and Toys; Hats, Hose, Gloves, Purses, Fans, Pieces for
Ladies Shoes, Umbrellas, Bathing-Caps, Whips, Canes, Walking-
Sticks, Inlaid Tunbridge-Ware, Pocket-Books, etc.

The same as at the most Capital Shops in London.

N.B. Books Bound in the Neatest Manner.

LONDON:

Printed by J. Walter, at the Logographic Press,
Printing-House-Square, Black-Friars.

1787

He prefaced his Catalogue as follows, apologizing for having to
charge sixpence for it.

To The
LADIES AND GENTLEMEN
Who Honour The
LIBRARY
With Their Subscriptions.

THE PROPRIETOR of this LIBRARY, which has been established, and received the Support of the Public for so many Years,
replete with Gratitude to his numerous and respectable List of
Subscribers, begs they will accept this Testimonial of his most sincere
Thanks, and an earnest Solicitation of future Favors; as under their
Protection he presumes to hope, by Diligence and Attention, to render
his Library an useful and entertaining Repository of Literature: strictly
attending to select such Books as shall be inductive to the Cause of
Virtue, serve as a Solace to enliven the Mind, and a continual Mentor
for the Improvement of the Understanding.

As the Publishing this new catalogue is attended with Considerable
Expence, he humbly hopes SIXPENCE will not be thought too much
for it.

This Shop is conveniently situated not only for those Ladies and Gentlemen who frequent MARGATE, but also for the Inhabitants of the following Villages in the Neighbourhood, viz. St. Laurence, Ramsgate, Broad Stairs, St. Peter's, Lord Holland's, Cleve, Birchington, Daun De Lyon, etc.

> N.B. S. SILVER is also Agent to the Royal Exchange Assurance Fire-Office, London.

> As was the case with assembly rooms, so certain charges and conditions of procedure were laid down by circulating library proprietors. In Samuel Silver's case his 1787 Catalogue dealt with these matters on pages 5–6, immediately following his Preface.

CONDITIONS
of
SILVER'S Circulating Library,

1. The Sum of Five Shillings for each Person to be paid at the Time of Subscribing.
2. Subscribers are to give in their Names and Place of Abode, and if required to deposit the Value of the Books they take away, and are to engage not to lend any of the Books to Non-Subscribers on the Penalty of paying a double Subscription.
3. To prevent disappointments, Subscribers are requested to send a List of eight or more Numbers of such Books as they wish to read.
4. If any Book is wrote in, torn, or damaged while in the Custody of a Subscriber, that Book, or (if it should belong to a set,) that set of Books to be paid for.
5. Every Subscriber will have the Privilege of reading any Book in the Catalogue, at the Library, where also the Morning and Evening Papers may be read every day.

** Constant Attendance will be given at the Library, (Sundays excepted.)

It was the Hawley Square library, however, which most impressed the compiler of a 1797 guidebook.

(g) [*The Margate and Ramsgate Guide in Letters to a Friend*, 1797, 17–18]

[It contains] a noble room . . . upon a much superior plan, respecting size and elegance, being large enough to contain between three and four hundred people: It has a dome in the fore part of the ceiling (not in the middle, as it ought to have been), from whence is suspended an elegant glass chandelier, which, when lighted up, is a truly brilliant spectacle: In the front and on the side of this room is a noble piazza with seats for the use of the company.

> The fame of Joseph Hall and Samuel Silver was surpassed by that of William Garner and Samuel Bettison, both of whom enjoyed extremely long reigns as Margate librarians, being men of tremendous initiative and personality. In his 1827 *Miscellaneous Recitations or Whims of the Loo Table*, William Garner claimed to have been a Margate librarian for 44 years. His association with Margate's Marine Library dated from 1789.

(h) [*The Kentish Gazette*, 12 June 1789]

Garner . . . most respectfully acquaints the Nobility and Gentry, frequenting Margate, that he has [taken] the Shop, late Mr. Hall's, near the Water Side.

> He acquired and rebuilt what had been Margate's first circulating library, belonging to Joseph Hall before the latter moved to the new Hawley Square library in 1786. What soon became well known as the Marine Library acquired popularity from two causes.

(i) [*The Margate and Ramsgate Guide in Letters to a Friend*, 1797, 18]

Mr. *Garner* has also opened an elegant library and toy-shop, at the bottom of the High-street, the back of which fronts the sea; which makes it greatly frequented for the marine prospect it affords, and no less for the polite behaviour of the proprietor; who is celebrated for acting the part of *Shylock*, in the Merchant of Venice, little inferior to *Macklin*; as well as several other characters, which he generally does in the course of the season, at the particular request of numerous friends.

> William Garner's career as a librarian was punctuated by misfortunes. In 1808 he was threatened with complete ruin following the great storms of that winter when his library and house were washed out to sea (Illus. 10a). His stock had been destroyed and

his library was wrecked, but because he was popular among Margate's visitors, as an amateur actor, whose name appeared on the boards of the Theatre Royal, his plight attracted widespread public sympathy. Following the great storm of January 1808 he moved temporarily into fresh premises in the High Street, and quickly rebuilt his old library, struggling bravely to retrieve his fortunes. When over 70 years of age he was described as 'the senior Librarian and one of the oldest inhabitants of *Margate*'.

(j)   [*The Thanet Itinerary or Steam Yacht Companion*, 1819, 36]

His whole life [nevertheless] has presented nothing but a continued series of unforeseen and unmerited misfortunes. The terrific storm, 1808, entirely washed down his *Library*, and spread a large proportion of his property adrift upon the waves. Still as he possessed good friends and unshaken credit, he was enabled to rebuild his *Library* upon a plan which has constituted it a handsome ornament to the town, [but] unhappily the Builder's expenses so far exceeded his estimate, that Mr. Garner was compelled to sell off all his effects, and to become a Tenant in that House of which he should have been Proprietor. Ever since that time, he has been using his utmost endeavours to retrieve his affairs.

The Marine Library in 1819 (Illus. 13a) offered a delightful sea view, looking towards Birchington, Reculver, etc., by means of [*ibid.*, 37]

a shaded Gallery, [which] projects over the Sea, where there are telescopes and seats provided for subscribers. . . . [Moreover] every evening there is a small *Card Loo* drawn here, in which the Prizes are articles taken from the shop [jewellery, plated goods, cutlery or toys]. These loos are decided about 9 or 10 o'clock, when the crowd of fashionable company is very great.

Five years later William Garner faced bankruptcy, resulting from all the problems mentioned above, coupled with advancing age, and an intense competition, both in entertainments and the sale room, from the increasingly popular bazaars of the 1820s (see Doc. 44). He was succeeded at the Marine Library in 1824 by W.G. Bettison junior. Samuel Bettison senior represents the fourth great name among Margate's circulating librarians. After fifteen years beginning in the High Street in 1785, he acquired from Thomas Ware the Hawley Square library, which he re-opened on 31 May 1800.

(k) [*The Kentish Gazette*, 27 May 1800]

Samuel Bettison returns thanks for the support he has received for the last fifteen years at his shop in [the] High Street. He is leaving that situation, having engaged that extensive Library in Hawley Square (late Ware's) where he hopes for continued support.

N.B. The Library will be regularly kept open during the ensuing winter, with good fires and every other necessary accommodation for the benefit of yearly subscribers.

> Following Joseph Hall's bankruptcy the Hawley Square library had stood vacant during much of 1795, Thomas Ware commencing business there in January 1796 and finishing in April 1800. Samuel Bettison ran this library for 38 years until 1838. Like William Garner he had to contend during the 1820s and 1830s with increasing age and rivalry from popularly acclaimed bazaars. In 1838 he also shared the same fate of bankruptcy as the other library proprietors whom he outlived.

(l) [*The Kentish Gazette*, 4 September 1838]

Samuel Bettison, Librarian, Stationer, Dealer, and Chapman, has been declared a bankrupt. A Ball for the benefit of Mr. Bettison Senior (now in his 80th Year), who has been in business 58 years in Margate, will be held at the Assembly Rooms, on Monday 10th September.

> He was approaching 90 years of age when *The Kentish Gazette* on 20 April 1847 announced his death in Boulogne. Four notable bankruptcies resulted from the establishment and embellishment of three famous circulating libraries in Margate. These bankruptcies arose from a combination of factors. To begin with, as noted at the outset, they were multifunctional businesses. During the course of his career, Joseph Hall, for instance, combined the businesses of librarian, bookseller, stationer, wine merchant and postmaster and by 1780 was an agent for passenger vessels plying between Margate and Ostend, Holland or France, quite apart from acquiring various property interests in Margate. Like librarians all over the country he combined the business of running a library with a modicum of publishing. He produced and published in 1790 *Hall's New Margate and Ramsgate Guide: containing a Description of the Libraries, Theatre, Assemblies, New Buildings, Accommodations, Mode of Bathing, Lists of the Coaches, Diligences, Hoys, etc., with the*

Time of their Going out and Coming in and a general Account of the Isle of Thanet: to which is prefixed a Map of the Island, taken from an actual Survey. A second edition followed in 1792. The following observations concerning the business side of circulating libraries date from 1797.

(m) [*The Margate and Ramsgate Guide in Letters to a Friend*, 1797, 18–19; By an Inhabitant, *The Margate Guide, A Descriptive Poem, with Elucidatory Notes*, Margate, 1797, 55]

Each library has also a shop connected with it, furnished with all kinds of Tunbridge ware, curious trinkets, pocket books, and nicknacks, particularly for *ladies*, which are continually put up in raffles, from one shilling to ten shillings and sixpence each person, according to the price of the article; there are sometimes above sixty persons in one raffle. Many of the shops also about the town get off their different goods by this method.

At each library there are suitable accommodations as well as ample matter for reading; books of all kinds and the public papers being taken in and kept for the use of the subcribers, of which there are generally some hundreds in the season.*

* The subscription is five shillings each person.

Viable circulating libraries required a number of Subscribers [both] considerable and sufficient . . . to reward the proprietors for their heavy expence and attention.

. From an investment point of view typical seaside circulating libraries and shops called for substantial inputs of both fixed and working capital. The fixed capital was represented by extensive and lavish premises, which had to appeal to the upper classes of society, on a scale that was greatly in excess of the everyday needs of the local population. Partly because their subscribers' reading interests were so diverse they had to carry enormous stocks of books, as well as stationery and shop goods, involving a large outlay in working capital. The introduction of gambling, lotteries, raffles and auctions called for additional stock. Such were the heavy capital outlays in impressive well-stocked buildings that *The Kentish Gazette* of 7 April 1795 informed its readers that Joseph Hall's Hawley Square library and stock in trade would be auctioned on 5,6,7 and 8 May 1795, followed by his furniture and plate on 9,11,12 and 13 May. Bankrupt circulating librarians confronted unlimited liability. The heavy capital demands made by this line of business are clearly demonstrated in a sequence of advertisements relating to the auction of Mr Thomas Pallister's business in Cecil Square, Margate, during 1815. This was the business founded by Samuel Silver who, as a bankrupt, had sold out to Bousfield and Pallister in 1808. With this partnership ending in 1812, Mr Thomas Pallister then assumed sole proprietorship until 1815.

(n)　[*The Kentish Gazette*, 10,14,24,28, and 31 March and 11 April 1815]

MARGATE
TO BE SOLD BY AUCTION, . . . all that genuine and excellent STOCK in TRADE, belonging to the Library, comprising several thousand volumes of books, and a splendid assortment of JEWEL-LERY . . .

All persons having any Books in their possession belonging to the Library are requested to return them immediately that they may be lotted for sale.

Moving on to the end of March:

To Booksellers, Jewellers, Hardwaremen, and Others,
TO BE SOLD BY AUCTION,
By Mr GILES GRAINGER,
(On the Premises)
PALLISTER'S LIBRARY, CECIL-SQUARE, Margate.
On MONDAY the 3rd day of April, 1815, and following days,
The Valuable LIBRARY and Excellent STOCK IN TRADE; the Library comprising nearly 4,000 Volumes; the Stock in Trade consisting of an elegant assortment of jewellery, gold chains, pins, broaches, lockets, purses, necklaces, both coral and amber, set in gold, . . . fruit knives, caddie spoons, . . . variegated tortoise shell and silver snuff-boxes, nutmeg graters, butter knives, . . . a variety of beautiful work boxes, . . . broach boxes [and] dressing boxes in Tunbridge Ware.
　MOROCCO GOODS.
Writing desk, dressing cases, drawing desks, cotton boxes, writing boxes, flute cases, backgammon, cheese boards . . .
　IVORY GOODS.
Handsome chess men, backgammon ditto in bone, ivory, ebony . . .

HARDWARE.

High polished scissors, pen knives, boot hooks, cork screws, patent and common nut crackers, . . . razors, . . .

Also a bagatelle board, 9 feet long, 3 feet wide compleat [and] . . . several maps.

The Sale of Books will commence on the first day.

The Sale will commence on each day at eleven o'clock . . . Catalogues 1s. each . . . may be had on application to the Auctioneer, Margate, or at the place of sale. To be viewed on Saturday preceding the sale, and on the morning of sale.

During April the library was advertised for sale or letting on lease.

All that extensive Premises in Cecil Square, Margate, . . . where for many years an extensive business has been carried on in the Jewellery, Stationery, and Bookselling Business; as also a Circulating Library and Musical Promenade, for which it is better adapted, than any other premises, and in point of situation stands unrivalled for that or any other business; consisting of a Shop and Library 75 feet long, and a good proportionable width, with parlour adjoining; six rooms of good proportion on the first floor, and eight on the second, with two good kitchens; large garden and numerous other conveniences. For Particulars apply (post-paid) to Mrs NEWTON, Cecil Square, Margate, or to Mr Hodgson, Bookseller, Wimpole-street, London.

Other factors to be borne in mind in the success or otherwise of this line of business, apart from entrepreneurial acumen, or failure through age, included the seasonality of operations, the fact that there were both good and bad seasons, and changes in fashion, with profits having to be maximized during the summer holiday-making months, not forgetting too the intensification and competitiveness involved in providing amusements from the 1790s onwards, involving rivalry with assembly rooms, theatres and bazaars (also see Docs. 41, 43, 44). Some idea of the amusements and entertainments which were provided can be gleaned from the newspapers.

(o)   [*The Times*, 1 September 1804]

There was a Masquerade here the other evening at BETTISON's [Hawley Square Library] which was attended respectably enough in point of *numbers*, but had to lament a deficiency in *characters*. Indeed, a good Masquerade seems to be a thing not practicable in Margate.

(p) [*The Morning Chronicle*, 27 September 1810]

This lively town [Margate] still continues the centre of every fashionable amusement . . . At Garner's Loos we laugh in the evening at the sprightly wit, [with music at]
Bettison's magnificent Room and at Bousfield's and Pallister's [Cecil Square library].

(q) [*The Maidstone Journal and Kentish Advertiser*, 9 September 1817]

On the 1st. inst. there was a Ball at Bettison's Library, Margate, and before 11 o'clock, it was ascertained that upwards of 190 persons were present . . . A large assemblage of beauty honoured the library with their presence, and a number of fashionables from Ramsgate and Broadstairs added much to the splendour of the rooms.

> By 1816 Samuel Bettison had completed fifteen seasons at the Hawley Square Library, having made 'very considerable alterations, and fitted it up in the most tasteful manner' (Illus. 14a).

(r) [*The New Margate, Ramsgate, and Broadstairs Guide*, 6th Ed., Margate, 1816, 71]

An excellent shop and library [form] together a square of 42 feet, of a proportionable height, with a spacious dome in the front department, giving light and ornament to the whole structure, from the centre of which is suspended a beautiful glass chandelier . . . Nearly across the centre of the room is a range of Corinthian columns, which not only support the roof, but are designed to separate the shop from the library. On the cornice of each of the bookcases are busts of the poets. The side walls and ceiling are most richly ornamented with figures and flowers . . . The library contains a good selection of many thousand volumes; the reading of which, together with the privilege of walking in the room, the use of the newspapers, and other periodical publications, are on very reasonable terms.

> The Cecil Square library had also undergone improvements during the proprietorship of Thomas Pallister,

THE EARLY KENTISH SEASIDE

(s) [*Ibid.*, 72]

having in the year 1811 been enlarged by the addition of a handsome music and reading room, . . . [forming] from the entrance at the shop, to the end of the reading room, a pleasing lounge or promenade of 80 feet in length . . . The reading room, owing to its distance from the shop, has the advantage of being completely retired from the bustle occasioned by the general routine of business peculiar to such establishments, and is agreeably enlivened by overlooking a large garden . . . The present proprietor [Mr Purday from 1815] has rendered this establishment complete, by the addition of a handsome and well constructed billiard room.

Within fifteen months of taking over and restocking these premises Purday too was declared a bankrupt. By 1831 Margate's Cecil Square library had ceased to function as such, but the number of libraries in the town had increased to four.

(t) [G.W. Bonner, *The Picturesque Pocket Companion to Margate, Ramsgate, Broadstairs, and the Parts Adjacent*, 2nd Ed., 1831, 68–70]

Bettison's Library [Illus. 15a],
. . . [a] beautiful and handsome structure, . . . in Hawley Square . . . It is a spacious and ornamental building, with a broad paved colonnade, supported by handsome pillars in front . . . The present proprietor and his family are courteous and obliging.
W. Bettison's Library,
. . . at the bottom of High-street, is a handsome and convenient building, consisting of a shop and circular saloon, from the ceiling of which hangs a brilliant cut-glass chandelier: there is a balcony in front, which commands an extensive sea and land view, in which the company may sit at high water, and, while enjoying the cool and delightful marine breezes, behold all that is going on upon the pier and in the harbour. The Library contains an excellent collection of books, and is kept by Mr WILLIAM BETTISON, whose unceasing endeavour is to oblige and gratify his numerous subscribers.
   The Libraries of
Mr WITHERDEN,
of the Marine Parade, and also that of
Mr BROWN,
on the Marine Terrace, are well supplied with the usual periodicals, etc., etc.

The Margate evidence rather suggests that there were few season-al seaside trades where the potentiality for bankruptcy was greater than with the circulating libraries of the late eighteenth and early nineteenth centuries. Some had floundered through personal misfortune, or because ambition tempted them to overreach themselves financially, but equally there were causes of failure which were peculiar to their line of business. Successive bankrupt-cies did not deter new enterprise, and there were circulating library proprietors, who displayed considerable initiative in the neighbouring resorts of Broadstairs and Ramsgate. Indeed, the Isle of Thanet closed the eighteenth century with eight circulating libraries, which were sufficiently close to each other to promote competition and to attract any of the Island's inhabitants and visitors. An interval of ten years elapsed between the opening of Margate's first circulating library by Joseph Hall in February 1766 and the emergence of an early Ramsgate library when it was announced in *The Kentish Gazette*, 14 August 1776, that 'a Circulat-ing Library is opened by Miss Croux, Linen Draper, near the King's Head, Ramsgate.' Visitors to Ramsgate in 1797 could choose between two libraries.

(u) [By an Inhabitant, *The Margate Guide, A Descriptive Poem, with Elucidatory Notes*, Margate, 1797, 98]

Near the Market, in the High Street, is *Burgess's* Circulating Library, well furnished with books, and has attached to it a commodious shop, stored with stationery, toys, etc. The Proprietor has for many years filled this situation with much credit, and to the ease and emolument of the company and inhabitants.

Lower down, in the same street, is a smaller Library and Toy-Shop, kept, and managed with assiduity and attention by Mrs *Witherden*.

Broadstairs likewise by this time possessed two circulating librar-ies.

(v) [*Ibid.*, 104]

Delightfully situated is *Nuckell's* Circulating Library, Post-Office, and Toy-Shop, furnished with books, stationery, etc.; and from the exten-sive views which it commands is well calculated for the ease and amusement of the subscribers . . . Lower down in the same street, is

Barfield's Library, which fronts the Rose Inn [see Doc. 19b] and from the back windows commands a fine view of the ocean with the Downs, and French coast.

In 1816 the same firms as named in 1797 operated both in Ramsgate and Broadstairs, thereby indicating that there were some circulating library proprietors who enjoyed stability and financial solvency. Mrs Witherden, however, had moved from Ramsgate High Street to a new library on Sion Hill, employing her upper rooms as a boarding house.

(w) [*The New Margate, Ramsgate, and Broadstairs Guide*, 6th Ed., Margate, 1816, 93–4, 109–10]

Ramsgate.
Mrs WITHERDEN has lately erected a most elegant and spacious library in Cliff-street, Sion Hill, which commands an uninterrupted view of the Downs and French Coast: the extensive rooms over this library are appropriated as a boarding house, for a limited number, which we have noticed are very select, and of the most respectable description . . . The assiduous attentions of Mrs Witherden to her numerous subscribers and Boarders are too well known to need any comment [also see Docs. 22k, 1]
    BURGESS's valuable and extensive library is in [the] High-street, near the Market, and has attached to it a good shop, well supplied with stationery, jewellery, toys, etc.

Broadstairs.
Opposite to [the Rose Inn] stands BARFIELD's Library, desirably suited for business, which has a good collection of books, and is well furnished with stationery, toys, etc. The library and reading room front the sea . . .
    There are many other good houses in this place, the principal part of which are situated on the cliff towards the pier, among which is NUCKELL's Library, Post Office, and Toy-shop, which has a valuable collection of books, stationery, etc., and has a very fine view of the Downs and French coast.

As in Margate these libraries had become venues for other forms of entertainment.

(x) [*The Morning Post*, 19 October 1814]

Ramsgate, October 16.
A brilliant concert was given last evening, at Mrs. WITHERDEN's Library, which was attended by 250 fasionables.

(y) [*Ibid.*, 20 September 1814]

Broadstairs, September 16.
Last evening Mr FORSYTH, of [Pierremont] House, gave a grand Ball at Barfield-rooms, on the Marine Parade, which was attended by about 100 fashionables, many of whom came from Ramsgate. The Ball-room was brilliantly illuminated by chandeliers . . . At midnight the company partook of a Sandwich supper, set out with much taste; the wines were of the best vintages. At 2 o'clock the party broke up.

By the 1830s the Burgess family of Ramsgate had gone into partnership with Hunt, while the Sion Hill library had passed into the hands of Messers Sackett and Fuller.

(z) [*Picture of Ramsgate, or A Guide to the Various Amusements, Public Libraries, Building Improvements, etc. of that celebrated Watering Place*, Ramsgate, 1833, 31]

Messrs Burgess and Hunt's, in the Market Place, and Messrs Sackett and Fuller's, on Sion Hill, have been established for many years, having very extensive collections of valuable books, in the selection of which, much care has been taken. The Reading Rooms are large and handsomely fitted up, and well furnished with the best authors; to which a Printing Office and Book-binding business is attached. At Messrs Sackett and Fuller's musical saloon concerts, promenades and balls are held in the season. The extensive rooms over [this] library are converted into a boarding house, under the proprietor's own care.

Sackett's proprietorship and enterprise can be traced back to 1822.

(aa) [*The Morning Post*, 22 August 1822]

Ramsgate, August 20.
. . . Our amusements, though few, are very well supported; the Evening Music Promenade at SACKETT's Marine Library is really good in every respect, and well managed.

Six years later during September 1828,

(bb) [*The Maidstone Journal and Kentish Advertiser*, 9 September 1828]

Our Libraries here [Ramsgate] boast a very brilliant assemblage every night.

A year later Mr Benham and his family took a holiday in Ramsgate, where there are references to their having both business and social contacts with the Hunts of Burgess and Hunt's circulating library, beginning on Monday, 20 July 1829, the day of their arrival (see Doc. 12).

(cc) [*MS Journal of an Excursion to Ramsgate in July and August 1829*, Tyler Collection (Ramsgate Scrapbook), Cathedral Library and Archives, Canterbury]

After having given my friend Hunt of Burgess's Library a call and taken some refreshment we retired to rest greatly fatigued by the day's exertion.
Tuesday, July 21.
N.B. William Alexander Hunt born 15th. Jan. 1789 at Ostend now of Burgess's Library, Ramsgate.
Wednesday, July 22.
At ½ past 12 to 1 called on my friend Hunt and bought red ink, pencil and rubber . . .

	£ s. d.
Paid	
Red Ink 6d., Indian Rubber 3d.,	
Blacklead Pencil 9d.	1 6

Mr Benham was keen on sketching and copying church monuments and inscriptions, hence the purchases referred to above. Excursions taken in association with the Hunt family occurred on Friday, 24 July, Saturday, 25 July, Tuesday, 28 July and Friday, 7 August (see Docs. 35g, 38r). Contacts with the Hunts on other days were as follows.

Thursday, July 30.
. . . At 12 walked to Mrs Hunt's at Effingham Place . . . At 5 went to Mr Hunt's and drank tea with him and his family.
Tuesday, August 4.
. . . Walked with Mr Hunt to the Library, staid till 8 when Charlotte [his wife] called for me and we returned to our Lodging . . .

Paid:	£	s.	d.
A Memorandum Book		1	0
Copy of Burgess and Hunt's Ramsgate Guide		2	0

Thursday, August 6.

Paid:	£	s.	d.
Drawing Paper ½ quire			9
Leather for the Tracings			2

Sunday, August 9.

. . . In the evening heard Mr Goldsmith at Zion Chapel, after which called on Mr Hunt and bade him and his family farewell.

> The Benhams returned by steamboat to London on Monday, 10 August 1829 (see Doc. 12). Apart from the two libraries of Messrs Burgess and Hunt and Messrs Sackett and Fuller, Ramsgate could also offer in the way of libraries and stationery shops three other choices in 1833.

(dd) [*Picture of Ramsgate, or A Guide to the Various Amusements, Public Libraries, Building Improvements, etc. of that celebrated Watering Place*, Ramsgate, 1833, 31–2]

Mrs Fowler has also a well furnished library stocked with a good assortment of toys, trinkets, stationery, perfumery, etc., pleasantly situate near the new Custom House, Goldsmid Place, where may be had on hire Pianofortes and Music for sale.

Mr Jarman has also a shop with well selected articles in books, prints and fancy stationery, with Printing Office and Bookbinding attached, also engraving and copper plate printing, Albion Street.

Mr A. Goldsmith's Printing Office and shop for miscellaneous stationery, adjoin[s] the High Street, near the Theatre.

> Broadstairs at this time still retained two circulating libraries, the proprietorship of both having changed since 1816.

(ee) [*Ibid.*, 48–9]

LIBRARIES are kept by
Mr HALE and Mr BARNES.
These Libraries have reading, card and assembly rooms attached to each, commanding extensive sea views; [they] contain a large assort-

ment of the best books for general reading, with a variety of London daily and Kentish newspapers; also a large stock of useful and fancy articles for sale.

A card party every evening, and
BALLS AND CONCERTS
ONCE A WEEK,
[are] alternately held at either assembly room, under the direction of Lieut. Col. Clarke M.C. [As] great pains are taken to render these parties attractive and select, they are consequently in high repute [also see Doc. 41 nn]

> Deal possessed by the 1790s a public room which doubled up as a library.

(ff) [*The Dover and Deal Directory and Guide*, Dover, c.1792, 43]

A public room has lately been opened by Mr Richard Long, bookseller, with a good library, where the London and provincial papers are taken in for the use of the subscribers; and it is but justice due to the proprietor to say, that neither expence nor pains have been spared to make it both neat and commodious.

> Almost half a century later better library and reading facilities formed part of a package of improvements in Deal.

(gg) [*Pigot & Co's Royal, National and Commercial Directory*, 1840, 271]

The town has of late years received many improvements. The most prominent of these is an elegant esplanade, in the formation of which, with the contiguous grounds, upwards of £4,000 have lately been expended. The Royal Baths [see Docs. 29r,s] are also a great ornament; they are fitted up in the best taste, and possess every requisite convenience, together with a well-furnished library and reading rooms: the baths are situated on the beach, adjoining the Royal Hotel [see Doc. 19hh].

> By the 1790s there were two circulating libraries in Dover.

(hh) [*The Dover and Deal Directory and Guide*, Dover, c.1792, 21]

There are two circulating-libraries in Dover, both well calculated for furnishing amusements to the inhabitants and the numerous visitors of the place in their leisure hours. The Apollo library is situated in

King's-street, at a short distance from the bathing-machines, and has a handsome public reading-room, where the London and country news-papers are every day taken in for the use of subscribers to the library. The reading-room is likewise furnished with music and musical-instruments, particularly a fine-toned harpsichord, and the library contains a good collection of entertaining books. This library is kept by Mr J. Horn, and is everyway calculated for an agreeable lounge.

The proprietor of the Albion library is Mr C. Ledger. It is situated in Snaregate-street, and is fitted up in a very handsome modern stile; this likewise possesses a good collection of books, and the London and country news-papers are also regularly taken in for the use of subscri-bers.

It was J. Horn who compiled and published one of the famous guidebooks to Dover in 1817.

HORN'S
Description of Dover
CONTAINING A
CONCISE ACCOUNT
OF THE
CASTLE, HEIGHTS, HARBOUR,
AND TOWN,
ALSO OF THE
Plan for its Improvement and Enlargement.
LIKEWISE
SOME USEFUL INFORMATION TO TRAVELLERS,
Respecting the Custom House, Passage Vessels, etc., etc., etc.,

———

EMBELLISHED
With an accurate coloured View
Of Dover Castle and the Town

———

DOVER:
PRINTED FOR AND BY J. HORN,
Military and Commercial Printing-office,
KING'S STREET, MARKET PLACE;

and Sold By
MESSRS. LONGMAN, HURST, REES, ORME AND BROWN:
PATERNOSTER ROW, LONDON; LIKEWISE BY ALL THE
BOOKSELLERS IN THE KINGDOM.

1817.

Dover's two circulating libraries at this time were J. Horn's Apollo library and C. Ledger's Albion library, which were described on page 24 in almost identical terms as above. From his King's Arms Library, William Batcheller printed and published in 1828 his *New History of Dover, to which is Added a New Dover Guide*, where, on pages 341–2, he describes the three circulating libraries of the town, two of which had been built during the 1820s. The oldest was the Albion Library, built by G. Ledger in 1782, which by 1828 was being run by Z. Warren, who was conducting also the Marine Library, which had been erected in 1823 by Mr Bonython. William Batcheller himself had been responsible for constructing the King's Arms Library, near the Parade, in 1826.

It contains upwards of 5,000 volumes, [with an] assembly room over the shop and library, where promenades are held during the summer, and quadrille and card assemblies in the winter [also see Doc. 41uu]

William Batcheller was obviously a successful librarian, printer and publisher bringing out in 1838 the 4th Edition of his *New Dover Guide*, this particular guidebook having been first published in 1829. Dover's three circulating libraries of 1838 were introduced on pages 119–20 as follows, beginning with his own.

THE KING'S ARMS LIBRARY, No. 1, Snargate-street, near the Parade, was erected by W. Batcheller in 1826 [Illus. 22b]. The circulating library contains 5143 volumes, embracing every branch of English literature; and new publications are continually adding to the number. A handsome room is fitted up for the accommodation of subscribers; and the table is constantly supplied with six daily, and thirteen weekly and provincial papers, besides magazines, reviews, etc. Adjoining the library is a stationery shop, furnished with a large selection of books, prints, fancy stationery, music, drawing materials, etc. Over the shop is an assembly room. Here are occasional balls, concerts, and other amusements; and musical promenades, or quadrille and card parties, during the season. A selection of pianofortes, harps, guitars, etc. constantly on sale or hire.

THE MARINE LIBRARY, pleasantly situated on the Marine Parade, was built by Mr Bonython in 1823, and is now conducted by Mr Warren. It is a handsome stationery shop, and is well furnished with books, prints, fancy articles, music, drawing materials, etc. The shop is also used as a reading room and circulating library, which has a good selection of modern publications, and the London and county papers, reviews, magazines, etc. are taken in. A selection of pianofortes and guitars are also on sale or hire.

THE ALBION LIBRARY, 86, Snargate-street, was built by the late Mr G. Ledger, in 1782, and is now conducted by Mr Hendrey. The London and county papers, reviews, magazines, etc. are taken in for the use of subscribers, and a handsome room, well furnished with library books, is fitted up for their reception. The adjoining stationery shop contains a good selection of the articles usually sold in that department.

BOOKSELLERS, etc.
In addition to the libraries there are other respectable booksellers, viz. T. Rigden, 66, Snargate-street; T. Williams, 145, Snargate-street; J. Cleveland, Last-lane; and J. May, King-street, Market-place.

The last location seems to fit in with what had been Horn's Apollo library. Folkestone possessed one circulating library by the 1800s.

(ii) [A Guide to all the Watering and Sea-Bathing Places, 1806, 229]

LIBRARY, etc.
HERE is a good Circulating Library, in the High-street, kept by Mr RODEN. It contains an extensive collection of books, and new works of merit are constantly added to it. At this library there is also a reading room, furnished with the London daily papers, magazines, reviews, and other periodical publications. In addition to the bookselling business, the proprietor has established a printing office.

Mr Roden's library was considered to be 'one of the principal amusements' of Folkestone in 1810.

(jj) [*A Guide to all the Watering and Sea-Bathing Places*, 1810, 244–5]

This library is regularly furnished with the London and provincial papers, magazines, and other periodical publications, and it is well supplied with new books. Like all other libraries on the coast, a general assortment of stationery, music, perfumery, and all the fashionable fancy articles are constantly kept, and his REPOSITORY forms a most agreeable lounge every Tuesday and Friday evening, during the season, and is well attended; much credit is due to the proprietor for the accommodation afforded to its visitors.

By 1816 there were two circulating libraries in Folkestone.

(kk) [*The Hythe, Sandgate and Folkestone Guide*, Hythe, 1816, 108]

The town contains two libraries, the principal one in High-street, where the London and provincial newspapers are taken in, for the use of subscribers; and the other, on a smaller scale, at the corner of Rendezvous-street.

> For the 1830s *Pigot & Co's Commercial Directory, 1832–4*, page 815, merely lists under the 'Miscellaneous' trades, 'Boxer John, watch maker, stationer, subscription reading rooms, etc., Butcher-row', Folkestone. Visitors to Sandgate at this time could resort to Thomas Purday, bookseller, stationer and reading room, *ibid.*, 863, whose proprietorship of a circulating library can be traced back to the 1800s.

(ll) [*A Guide to all the Watering and Sea-Bathing Places*, 1806, 230]

Purday keeps a small circulating library, adjoining to which is a billiard room.

(mm) [*Ibid.*, New and Improved Ed., 1815, 423]

There is a good circulating library, conducted by Mr PURDAY with great spirit, [adjoining] to which is a billiard-room. There is another billiard-table, kept by Mr Woore.

(nn) [*Ibid.*, 1823, 29; 1829, 29]

Here is a good circulating library, conducted with great spirit by Mr
PURDAY, who possesses a taste for music.

> Thomas Purday's opposite number in Hythe, according to *Pigot &
> Co's Commercial Directory, 1832–4*, page 831, was William Tiffen,
> 'porter merchant, bookseller and library', who, like William
> Batcheller of Dover, published a famous seaside guidebook which
> passed through several editions.

THE
HYTHE,
SANDGATE AND FOLKSTONE
GUIDE:
CONTAINING
AN ACCOUNT OF THEIR
ANCIENT AND PRESENT STATE,
AND
A DESCRIPTION
OF THE
PRINCIPAL OBJECTS WORTHY OF ATTENTION
IN THE NEIGHBOURHOOD.
To which is subjoined,
A BRIEF
HISTORY OF THE CINQUE-PORTS.

HYTHE:

PRINTED, PUBLISHED AND SOLD BY
W. TIFFEN, AT THE LIBRARY.

SOLD ALSO BY MR. PURDAY, SANDGATE; MR. MAYSTON,
FOLKSTONE; MR. LEDGER, AND MR. HORN, DOVER; MESS.
ROUSE AND CO; COWTAN AND COLEGATE, AND WOOD
AND CO., CANTERBURY; MR. PURDAY, MARGATE; MESS.
WICKHAM AND CUTBUSH, MAIDSTONE; MR. ELLIOTT,
ASHFORD; AND MISS BALDWIN AND CO., 47,
PATERNOSTER-ROW, LONDON.

1816.

This publication, pages 7 and 24, makes reference to

a subscription reading room and an excellent public library . . . The *Subscription-room* connected with the *Library* is the principal place of resort for conversation and politics; and is much frequented by the gentry of the neighbourhood as well as the principal military and naval officers, and visitors of the place.

In 'A New and Improved Edition, 1815', of *A Guide to all the Watering and Sea-Bathing Places*, page 428, Hythe was credited with two circulating libraries.

At this place are two good Libraries, where are to be found the periodical publications and newspapers, and much intelligent company in the season.

It was inevitable that Herne Bay, as a rising resort of the 1830s, would follow closely in the footsteps of other Kentish resorts.

(oo) [*Pigot & Co's Commercial Directory, 1832–4*, 829]

Heading the list of 31 'SHOPKEEPERS & TRADERS', under 'HERNE BAY, AND HERNE STREET' was

Banks, Mrs Maria, stationer, perfumer, and circulating library, Herne Bay.

She was also the Post Mistress and was one of five people who had 'LODGING HOUSES' in Herne Bay, offering board as well as lodging if required. A little more is learned of her in 1835.

(pp) [By a Lady, *A Picture of the New Town of Herne Bay*, 1835, 16]

The old circulating library of, perhaps, twenty years' standing, is next to the Ship at the east end of the town, and is kept by Mrs Banks. It seems to have shared the fortunes of the town in rising to eminence. This is also the post office. Letters are delivered from 8 to 10 in the morning, and are received till 6 in the evening.

In addition there was a new circulating library on the Parade, *ibid.*, 11, among

an assemblage of extremely handsome shops, built on the site of 230 feet frontage taken on the beach. They are of the height of one story only, to prevent their intercepting the view of the sea and the pier under them, to the company residing in St. George's Terrace. These shops are spacious, and are finished in a superior style and elegance . . . [Here] is also an assembly room [see Docs. 41ww] . . . and under the same proprietor, Mr Bonython, of Dover, a suite of baths, constructed by an eminent engineer, . . . said to be matchless in their machinery. Mr Bonython has, in addition, reading and billiard rooms.

Reading rooms and two libraries held good for 1842 in Herne Bay.

(qq) [*The Visitor's Guide to the Watering Places*, 1842, 199]

On the Parade . . . is an elegant Assembly Room, attached to which are Reading-rooms, Billiard-rooms, etc. There are also two Libraries, one situated near the Pier, and the other on the Marine-terrace.

(rr) [S. Bagshaw, *History, Gazetteer and Directory of the County of Kent*, II, Sheffield, 1847, 221–2]

Marine-terrace, Banks Maria, stationer, news room and circulating library.

William-street, Napier Misses, stationers, fancy repository, news room, and circulating library.

Libraries were certainly on the list of Gravesend's amusements, on page 16, of the 1845 *Pictorial Guide to Gravesend and Its Rural Vicinity: A Holiday Handbook*. Indeed, three were listed in a commercial directory of the 1830s.

(ss) [*Pigot & Co's Commercial Directory, 1832–4*, 818]

Gilbee John, New road.
Penny William (and reading rooms), Milton place.
Richardson Caroline and Son (and stationers), Parrock place.

Of these one was singled out for special mention, *ibid.*, 816.

The establishment conducted by Mr Penny, in Milton-place, may be mentioned as one of considerable attraction, from its pleasing situation, and the judicious selection of the journals and other literary works with which it is furnished.

As the 1835 season began to develop he announced that

(tt)   [*The Gravesend and Milton Journal*, 25 April 1835]

PENNY'S LIBRARY.

. . . The Evening Promenade and Reading Room, in Milton-Place, is open for the Season every evening with Music and Singing.

In the very same issue the opening of a new library was advertised on the front page.

ROYAL LIBRARY,
West-Street, New Pier, Gravesend.
Messrs. TALBOT & CO. – opening of new and extensive premises on Saturday, 2nd May, next.

The final word on this subject ends on a general note in Gravesend in 1842.

(uu)   [*The Visitor's Guide to the Watering Places*, 1842, 18]

LIBRARIES. – The chief attraction of a watering place, say what you will, is the Library. This . . . is sure always to be patronized. Here you will find not only an abundant supply of newspapers, periodicals, etc., but all the new novels, travels, historical works. etc.

43.   *The coastal theatres of Kent.*

Theatre building was restricted much more to the larger resorts of Kent. Theatres were costly to build, their working capital requirements were substantial and they had to offer attractive programmes in order to compete effectively with the entertainments offered by assembly rooms, circulating libraries and the popular bazaars of the 1820s, a decade when some theatres were established on a more permanent footing. Not all theatres were fully operational during the height of the season when holiday making visitors were most in evidence. Dover provides but one instance of the latter fact.

(a)   [*The Dover and Deal Directory and Guide*, Dover, c.1792, 21]

The theatre usually opens the latter end of the summer, and is occupied by a company of comedians of very considerable merit under the management of Mr Barnard, late of the theatre royal Covent-garden.

(b)   [*A Guide to all the Watering and Sea-Bathing Places*, 1806, 214]

The theatre opens at the close of the summer, and possesses generally a respectable company of performers.

(c)   [*Horn's Description of Dover*, Dover, 1817, 23]

The theatre usually opens in November, and generally closes in April or May.

(d)   [W. Batcheller, *The New Dover Guide*, 4th Ed., Dover, 1838, 117]

THE THEATRE. This building was erected in 1790, by a company of gentlemen who advanced the money in fifty pound transferable shares. It is situated in Snargate-street, and is usually open as a play-house, from September till nearly April. There are occasional balls and masquerades.

> Ten years previously Dover's theatre was the summer venue only for 'occasional card and dancing assemblies', according to W. Batcheller's, *New History of Dover, to which is Added a New Dover Guide*, Dover, 1828, 340. One of the first visitors to comment on its presence in 1790 was the Hon. John Byng during his 'Tour into Kent'.

(e)   [Ed. C. Bruyn Andrews, *The Torrington Dairies*, IV, 1970, 162]

Tuesday, September 21.

. . . Alone – and at mine Ease, I strolled back thro the Town (observing a newly erected mischevious Play House).

> Small theatres were in existence both in Folkestone and Hythe before 1820.

(f)   [*The Hythe, Sandgate and Folkestone Guide*, Hythe, 1816, 108]

There is a theatre under the management of Mr Dowton [Folkestone; also see Doc. 41 ss].

(g)   [*Ibid.*, 25]

[At Hythe] there is a neat Theatre under the management of Mr Trotter, who spares neither pains nor expense to afford entertainment to the public by engaging an excellent company of performers.

Pigot & Co's Commercial Directory, 1832–4, 830, describes it as being 'small but neat'. Although theatrical enterprise never graced the smaller resorts of Sandgate, Deal and Walmer, Broadstairs, or Herne Bay, they were within reasonable driving distance of the theatres of Hythe, Folkestone, Dover, Thanet and Canterbury, whose theatre dated from 1790. The years 1786–7 were important for the promotion and opening of a permanent theatre in Margate, which was the only Thanet resort to acquire this facility before 1815.

(h) [*The New Margate, Ramsgate, and Broadstairs Guide*, 6th Ed., Margate, 1816, 69–70]

At the East corner of Hawley Square stands the Theatre Royal, which was erected in the year 1787, at the expence of nearly £4,000. It is an unornamented brick structure, totally divested of exterior decoration, [but] its inside is fitted up in a handsome though chaste style, something after the plan of Covent-Garden; and is possessed of a complete wardrobe, as well as some excellent scenery, painted in a bold and masterly manner by Hodgins.

The present proprietors, who exert their abilities in the selection of performers, and in the management of the Theatre during the season, spare neither cost nor pains to render their efforts for the public amusement worthy support; good actors are retained at great salaries; and the acting manager by his frequent introduction of the most favorite performers from the metropolis, shows himself by no means inattentive to give satisfaction, and to ensure the approbations of the visitors and inhabitants of this fashionable summer resort. The house is open only during the season, being limited to that time by its licence.

The whole history of theatrical activity in Margate, both before and since 1787, is well documented by Malcolm Morley in his 1966 study of *Margate and its Theatres 1730–1965*. This work combined with numerous advertisements and announcements in both the national and local newspapers produce a considerable literature on this single aspect of Margate's rise as a seaside resort, and especially on the plays which were performed and by whom. Theatrical enterprise in Margate originated before 1787, and predated boarding houses (1770) [see Docs. 18; 22] and circulating libraries (1766) [see Doc. 42b]. Initially theatrical activity was spasmodic and originated from places outside Margate. The increasing presence of visitors inspired companies of players to come to Margate for a season, so that in the summer of 1752, for instance, Mr Perry from Sittingbourne arrived with his troupe of comedians. For several summers beginning in 1754 William Smith and his company from Canterbury entertained Margate's early visitors. Smith offered greater comfort in 1761, when he provided Margate's first playhouse, in a converted barn close to the centre of the town, complete with boxes set apart for the *élite*, admission to which was 2s. for each person, with a pit at 1s. 6d., a gallery at 1s., and a top gallery somewhere under the roof at 6d. There he opened his summer season during July with Benjamin Hoadley's *The Suspicious Husband* and Samuel Foote's *The Minor*. For another seventeen years Smith dominated the Margate scene and controlled the well-known Canterbury Circuit, which extended out also to Dover, Deal, Maidstone, Faversham and Rochester.

(i)   [John Lyons, *A Description of the Isle of Thanet, and particularly of the Town of Margate*, 1763, 17]

We have a Play-House, where a Company of Comedians from *Canterbury* peform three times in the week, [but] if you expect to see great elegance in the house, scenes, and decorations, or any extraordinary degree of theatrical merit in the Actors, you may be disappointed, [even though] they meet with encouragement, which they do their utmost endeavours to deserve.

> Such an honest admission was more than echoed fourteen years later in the critical reaction to a double performance of a Margate visitor of 1777.

(j)   [Ed: P.C. Yorke, *The Diary of John Baker*, 1931, 419]

September 23, 1777.

To play-house [for] the 'Wonder' and 'Irish Widow' [Comedy by David Garrick], a vile house and vile acting.

> Much was to change after another ten years once parliamentary approval had been secured for a permanent theatre in Margate, but not before other and rival theatrical companies had sought to entertain Margate's visitors, following William Smith's decision of 1768 to relinquish control of the Canterbury Circuit, whereupon

Thomas Burton from Faversham seized the opportunity of taking over Margate's playhouse.

(k) [*The Kentish Gazette*, 27–31 May 1769]

[He is] fitting up the house in a most elegant taste; it has a new ceiling, . . . all new painted, with new front boxes; and the scenery entirely new . . . He has engaged a very good Company of Comedians, who intend to open soon after his Majesty's birthday.

Performances were advertised for a longer period than in any former season from June until October, but despite having 'lately received some improvements', *The Margate Guide . . . In a Letter to a Friend*, of 1770, page 20, felt that 'the present Playhouse is but an indifferent one.' Following Burton's death in 1771, Margate's first playhouse fell into disuse, but its equipment was acquired by two Canterbury men, William Brown, a currier, and John Richardson, a tailor. They transferred their operations to a stable at the rear of the Fountain Inn. Richardson soon left the partnership, but Brown continued until 1778. Although in July of that year Margate theatre-goers saw for the first time Oliver Goldsmith's 1773 dramatic masterpiece *She Stoops to Conquer*, it was acted out in what John Baker in 1777 had considered to be 'a vile house'. In the meantime the Dover Circuit had been formed to concentrate on the coastal towns of East Kent and appeared in Margate for the first time in 1779. Originating from a playhouse in Dover, it was owned by an eccentric Charles Mate, who had given up a maritime career to pursue theatrical management. He found in Margate an important ally in Francis Cobb, who was influential both as a flourishing brewer and as Town Deputy to the Mayor of Dover, Margate being a non-corporate limb of the Cinque Port of Dover. Cobb owned the Fountain Inn, at the back of which stood the Margate playhouse, which Mate proceeded to enlarge by adding an adjoining stable, rented from Mr Cobb at £20 per season. A new playhouse effectively resulted from £200 which Mate spent upon reconstruction, with seats in the boxes now having doubled to 4s. On 9 July 1779 Richard Sheridan's famous comedy *The School for Scandal* had its first performance in Margate. Six years later in 1785 a formidable opponent appeared in the remarkable person of Mrs Sarah Baker, the first female theatrical manager in England and dubbed by Malcolm Morley 'the governess-general of the Kentish drama'. Having gained command of the Canterbury Circuit, she confronted opposition from Francis Cobb. That fact notwithstanding she opened up in opposition to Charles Mate in a wooden playhouse costing £500. Visitors to Margate now had the benefit of two playhouses. Intense rivalry ensued between Charles Mate and Mrs Sarah Baker, as illustrated by very competitive front-page advertising in *The Kentish Gazette* through July, August and September 1785. Price cutting and frequent changes of programme were involved in the competition which intensified as the season progressed.

(1)   [*The Kentish Gazette*, 6–9 and 9–13 September 1785]

Mrs Sarah Baker's New Theatre.

13 September, never acted here, the Comic Opera of *The Castle of Andalusia*, with the Farce of *Who's the Dupe?*
14 September, never acted here, the Comedy of *Which is the Man?*, with never acted before, the Comic Opera of *The Son in Law*.

Mr Charles Mate's Old Theatre.

13 September, the Comedy, *She Stoops to Conquer, or the Mistakes of a Night*, to which will be added a Farce, called *Miss in her Teens*. The Part of Fribble by a Gentleman for his Amusement.
14 September, The Tragedy of *Alexander the Great*, to which will be added the Farce, called *The Quaker*.

Mate lost not only money weekly, but the energy and determination to continue. Indeed, so powerful was the opposition from Sarah Baker that he was compelled to close down. There is no doubt that this short term bout of rivalry stimulated local desires for a permanent theatre, which would be more rigorously controlled. The prospect that Sarah Baker would be left in complete possession of Margate met with particular disapproval from the Town Deputy, Mr Cobb, who summoned local residents to a meeting where he proposed the founding of a permanent theatre. Sarah Baker's monopoly could be annulled if the townsfolk were to sign a petition which Mate had prepared for a royal patent. A royal charter would license Mate as the patentee with authority to outlaw Mrs Baker's Company from the town. The effect would be to banish any intruding company from Margate. Mr Cobb undertook to use his influence towards securing the necessary charter for a new and permanent theatre. Thomas Robson, a former singer at Covent Garden who was living in Margate, came forward to help Mate, and with such prominent backing the petition was enthusiastically received. It cost £550, but attracted over 900 signatures. Messrs Mate, Robson and Cobb approached Sir James Watterall, one of the Members of Parliament for Dover. Through his efforts the petition passed through both Houses of Parliament, and the royal patent was secured. The petition was introduced to Westminster as the Margate Playhouse Bill.

(m) [26 Geo. III c. 29]

An Act to enable His Majesty to license a Play House within the Town and Port of *Margate*, in the Isle of *Thanet*, in the County of *Kent*, under certain Restrictions therein limited.

The preamble to this Private Act of 1786 drew attention to the need for rational amusement in a rapidly expanding seaside resort.

WHEREAS the Town and Port of *Margate*, and several of the Villages within the Vicinity of the same, have of late Years, greatly increased both in Buildings and Inhabitants, owing to the numerous Resort of Persons who frequent the same on account of the Convenience of Bathing and Salubrity of the Air, . . . the Inhabitants of the said Town and Port, in order to contribute to the rational Amusement of the Company so resorting thereto, are desirous of having a licensed Playhouse there.

The Act sought

Letters Patent . . . for establishing a Theatre or Play House, . . . from the Fifteenth Day of *June* to the last Day of *October* in every Year.

The Bill passed through the House of Commons without a dissenting voice, but it faced opposition in the House of Lords, where it received its first reading on 26 April 1786. A petition from twenty one Margate inhabitants was lodged against the Bill.

(n) [*Ms Petition of Several Persons, Inhabitants of the Town of Margate against the Margate Playhouse Bill and Preying to be heard by Counsel against the Same*, 1st May 1786, House of Lords Record Office]

Your petitioners observe the growing Dissipation and Licentiousness which daily extend their baneful Effects among the Inhabitants at large, most of whom are Mariners, Artificers, and others dependent on their Labours, and are apprehensive that such a Licence will be very pernicious in its Consequences, as it may render the Inhabitants less active in their industrious Occupations, and more relaxed in their Morals . . .

The parochial Rates are at present very high, and [are] considered by your petitioners as a very heavy, tho' necessary Burthen . . . The Introduction of a number of indigent Strangers, who by a Licensed Theatre may gain Settlements in, and become chargeable to the Parish, must of course increase the number of the Poor, and consequently increase the Rates.

> The counter-petitioners hinted at an element of corruption in the proceedings so far.

The Petition to the Honorable the Commons in support of that Bill is . . . subscribed by some Persons who do not reside at Margate, others who are not Housekeepers, and many who have since been convinced of the pernicious Consequences of the Bill and have therefore changed their Opinions.

> They were not opposed to theatrical activity in Margate; indeed, Dramatic Exhibitions . . . have been hithertoo performed at Margate during the Season for Bathing there without any Interruption or Restraint, the performers at such plays in case of misconduct or the desire of the Inhabitants. [being] subject and amenable to the Laws in those Respects and [being] with ease removed from the Town, but should a Licence be granted to perform Plays at Margate, Such performers, tho' they should misbehave, and the Inhabitants of Margate should find the Playhouse very injurious to them, cannot be restrained from playing or removed from the Town without great difficulty, if at all, and then at a very heavy Expence, as there is no Police established in the Town, [nor] any Magistrates to apply to for Redress nearer than Dover, which is upwards of 20 miles from Margate.

> Margate's dependence on Dover which was some 21 miles away meant that justice was administered only by overcoming difficulties of time and cost. An attempt in 1785 to secure a charter of incorporation was foiled by opposition from Dover. A further 72

years had to pass until Margate was made a Borough under a Charter of Incorporation granted on 29 July 1857. The only really significant local government and judicial changes so far as Margate was concerned involved the establishment of Improvement Commissioners in 1787 (27 Geo. III c. 45), followed twenty years later, in 1807, by a Court of Requests for the recovery of small debts (47 Geo. III c. 7) and the appointment of two resident Magistrates for the town under an Act of Parliament passed in 1811 (51 Geo. III c. 36). Despite all opposition, the royal assent to the Margate Playhouse Bill was secured on 22 May 1786. Armed with a legal monopoly of theatrical entertainment in Margate, Charles Mate and Thomas Robson re-opened the playhouse in King Street during the summer of 1786 under the name of the Theatre Royal. The Lord Chamberlain made an order for suppressing Mrs Baker's wooden theatre, whereupon she moved her operations to Faversham. Mate and Robson were drawn into a closer partnership, it being reported at the conclusion of the 1786 season,

(o)   [*The Morning Chronicle and London Advertiser*, 16 September 1786]

the new Manager at Margate, Robson, has had a very profitable season; and his troop of comedians have conducted themselves with great propriety.

In the meantime plans to erect a new and better theatre were proceeding apace. A site at the north-east end of Hawley Square was purchased for £610, and newspapers widely reported the laying of the foundation stone on 19 September 1786.

(p)   [*Ibid.*, 26 September 1786; *The Maidstone Journal*, 3 October 1786]

Margate, September 20.

Yesterday the first stone of the intended new Royal Theatre was laid in this town, by Mr Robson, manager of the Company, who spoke an address to the town, amidst the acclamations of near 5,000 people . . . The address stated:

'The motive of the present undertaking [is] to offer a source of entertainment, at once rational and elegant to the town of Margate, on a more regular plan, and with the sanction of his Majesty's authority'.

Length of building 97 feet by 41 feet.

In less than nine months a permanent Theatre Royal had been completed. Over £3,000 had gone into its construction and like most theatres of the eighteenth century it was of square box-like design. It opened on Wednesday, 27 June 1787, with the much acclaimed comedy of *She Stoops to Conquer* as the main attraction of the evening, followed by Isaac Jackman's *All the World's a Stage*. It contained inside boxes, a pit, a gallery, a box office and a treasury. The prices of admission were set at 4s. for the boxes, 2s. for the pit and 1s. for the gallery. The 4s. admission to the boxes represented a return to the 1779 charges, or a rise of 1s. since the days of Mrs Sarah Baker in 1785. The theatre could hold 700 people, and at full capacity gross takings amounted to £60 per night. With the passage of time proprietary shares changed hands, and were sold and resold. The following information was conveyed to Margate's visitors in 1797, ten years after the theatre had opened.

(q) [By an Inhabitant, *The Margate Guide, A Descriptive Poem, with Elucidatory Notes*, Margate, 1797, 83]

The present Proprietors are Messrs. *Grubb, Shaw* and *Wells*, who exert their abilities in the selection of performers and in the management of the Theatre during the Season; in short, no expense in spared to give satisfaction and to insure the approbation of the visitors and inhabitants of this fashionable retreat. The house is open only during the Season, being limited to that time by the Licence.

Partners were attracted from Covent Garden/Drury Lane and this dual control ensured that many of the plays which were staged had the hallmark of those London theatres. Mr Grubb, as one of the proprietors of Drury Lane, had acquired Charles Mate's partnership interest for £2,200. Talented young actors were introduced to Margate, at the same time as good and well-established old favourites were retained. Two of the most famous actresses of their time, Mrs Sarah Siddons (1755–1831), 'the greatest tragedienne of the British stage', and Mrs Dorothea Jordan (1762–1816), 'the most celebrated comedienne of her day', performed at Margate's

Theatre Royal, as well as at Covent Garden and Drury Lane in London. The dramatist and poet Bertie Greathead (1759–1826) returned to Margate while Mary and Agnes Berry were staying at Prospect House, near Broadstairs, during the autumn of 1794.

(r) [Ed: W.S. Lewis and A. Dayle Wallace, *Horace Walpole's Correspondence with Mary and Agnes Berry*, XII, New Haven, 1961, 129]

Monday, 6 October 1794.

We are going tomorrow to the play at Margate with the Greatheads to see *Hamlet* acted by gentlemen, and very gentleman-like acting I dare say it will be . . . Mrs Siddons left . . . the very day after we called upon her.

> In fact Mrs Siddons had returned to London so as to be able to make her first appearance for the season at Drury Lane on Saturday evening, 4 October. Top performers were expensive to hire.

(s) [*The Observer*, 3 September 1797]

Mrs Jordan commenced her engagement with the Managers of the Margate Theatre on Wednesday night, when she played *Miss Peggy* in the *Country Girl* . . . She is to have £300 for six nights; and the price of admission to the Theatre has been raised to defray this extraordinary expense.

> Professional performances, ably directed by men with well known London experience, which attracted some of the country's leading performers, at fees reaching up to £50 a night, were far removed from the rustic companies of players and comedians who had operated the circuit system of the 1750s and 1760s. There was much buoyancy in the Theatre during the 1804 season.

(t) [*The Times*, 14 September 1804]

Mrs JORDAN left this place on Sunday last, having netted, including her benefit and her extra night, £208 by her eight evening performances.

(u)   [*Ibid.*, 18 September 1804]

The Theatre was as full as it could hold on Friday, it being the [benefit] night of the Manager [Robert Copeland], who is deservedly a great favourite . . . The House [took] upwards of £80.

> At the end of that season it was local people who were aspiring to fame as actors.

(v)   [*Ibid.*, 25 September 1804]

Mr JARVIS eminent *surgeon* of this place, and GARNER, the *Librarian*, have been acting parts.

> William Garner was a favourite among the amateur actors of Margate (also see Doc. 42i).

(w)   [*The Morning Chronicle*, 8 September 1810]

On Saturday next there will be a play at the Theatre for the benefit of the amiable widow and family of our late regretted worthy manager, Mr Willmott Wells. Mr Garner, of the Library, whose excellence in the part of *Shylock* is deservedly celebrated, has kindly offered his assistance.

> Another great favourite among the professional actresses of the 1800's was Miss Duncan (Mrs Davison), 'an effervescent comedienne' and 'the favourite Heroine of Margate' (also see Doc. 41t), where she performed during the seasons of 1804 and 1805.

(x)   [*The Times*, 12 September 1805]

Margate, September 10.

The principal attraction was the Theatre, where the Benefit of Miss DUNCAN had been announced for the evening. The merits of this Actress are so well known in the Metropolis, [that] the House overflowed in every part, . . . and the receipts . . . exceeded £100.

> Following the Napoleonic Wars Margate's Theatre Royal was still the only theatre in Thanet, but it was highly praised in 1819, and 1830.

(y)　[*The Thanet Itinerary or Steam Yacht Companion*, 1819, 35]

The Managers certainly exert themselves in a surprising manner to render it attractive. The distance from *London* being small, and, since the establishment of *Steam Packets*, the passage to and fro being rendered both pleasant and certain it induces almost the whole of the distinguished Metropolitan performers, in succession, to exhibit their talents here for a few nights, in some of their most esteemed characters. By this means, the visitors from *London* are afforded convenient opportunities to judge more accurately of the respective excellencies of their favourite actors; as it is admitted by the best judges of dramatic effect, that a moderate sized building is better adapted for this purpose than the immense structures of *Covent Garden* and *Drury Lane*.

(z)　[G.A. Cooke, *A Topographical and Statistical Description of the County of Kent*, New Ed., 1830, 297]

The Theatre Royal . . . is a neat structure, unornamented on the exterior, but handsomely disposed within. Some of the favourite performers on the London boards usually add to the annual attractions of this place of rational amusement, [added to which] Hawley Square has been recently improved by plantations of evergreens and flowering shrubs [Illus. 14a] which afford a promenade to families residing in the contiguous houses.

> In the meantime Ramsgate had acquired a theatre of its own which was destroyed by fire on 30 November 1829, soon after that evening's performance had finished. Between 1820 and 1840 Mr Faucit Saville not only managed Margate's Theatre Royal but also branched outwards to Ramsgate, and revived the fortunes of Gravesend's theatre.

(aa)　[*Picture of Ramsgate, or A Guide to the Various Amusements, Public Libraries, Building Improvements, etc. of that celebrated Watering Place*, Ramsgate, 1833, 37]

A small but very neat Theatre was erected in the year 1826, by Mr Faucit Saville, the very intelligent acting manager of the Margate Theatre, – for this purpose an Act of Parliament was obtained, by which this Theatre is permitted to be opened from the beginning of October to the end of January, on every week day evening except Saturday.

This provision was obviously amended at some point prior to 1828.

(bb)   [*The Maidstone Journal and Kentish Advertiser*, 9 September 1828]

The theatre has been crowded during the last three nights. The magnet [is] the lovely Foote, . . . [a] highly gifted actress . . . Ramsgate is filling very fast; and the company, as usual, [is] very select.

The fire of November 1829 while it demolished the theatre did not destroy the ambitions of Mr Faucit Saville.

(cc)   [*The Gentleman's Magazine*, XCIX, Part II, December 1829, 555]

From the combustible nature of the interior of the building, the flames raged with appalling force: and as soon as a vent was obtained by the falling in of the roof, they illuminated the sky for miles round and the sea, glowing with fiery tints in the darkness of the night, presented a spectacle worthy of admiration. Long before day light the whole of this fine property, with all the scenery, decorations, dresses, etc. were consumed. The theatre is the property of Mr FAUCIT SAVILLE, and it is understood to be insured, but to no amount sufficient to cover the loss.

(dd)   [G.W. Bonner, *The Picturesque Pocket Companion to Margate, Ramsgate, Broadstairs, and the Parts Adjacent*, 2nd Ed., 1831, 159]

The neat little theatre at Ramsgate, which was built in the year 1826, by that indefatigable individual Mr FAUCIT SAVILLE was unfortunately destroyed by fire in 1829, but nothing daunted by this calamity, by which Mr SAVILLE suffered severe pecuniary loss, because the building was not insured, that persevering gentleman raised the present structure, which continues to be a source of considerable amusement to the visitors of Ramsgate, and which will, we sincerely hope, be productive of increasing gain to its very spirited proprietor.

Gravesend's somewhat chequered theatrical history up to 1842 reinforces many of the points which have been made in this documentary section.

(ee)   [*The Visitor's Guide to the Watering Places*, 1842, 14–15]

THE THEATRE is situated on the south side of the New-road, at the corner of Garrick-street. Theatrical companies visited Gravesend several years before a regular theatre was built. It was at length accomplished by F. Trotter, Esq., of Worthing, in the year 1808, and under his judicious and spirited management proved a very lucrative concern for several years, but was shut up for a considerable period when the above gentleman retired from the profession. It was again opened in the year 1822 by Mr Faucit Saville, of the Margate Theatre, who conducted it with considerable success. Gravesend Theatre boasts of its boards having been trod by a Cooke, an Emery, a Kean, a Knight, an Incledon, and others of first-rate talents, from the metropolis. The house is small but neatly fitted up.

44. *Auctions, dice, loo, lotteries, raffling and post-Napoleonic bazaars and boulevards.*

Margate was a highly organized resort by the 1830s in every respect.

(a) [*Pigot & Co's National, London, and Provincial Commercial Directory, for 1833–4*, 5th Ed., 849]

The baths, hotels, libraries, reading rooms, bazaars, assembly rooms, theatre, promenades, etc. are unrivalled in their efficiency.

(b) [*Pigot & Co's Royal National and Commercial Directory and Topography, November 1839*, 339]

The baths, hotels, libraries, reading rooms, assembly rooms, theatre, bazaars, promenades, etc. surpass those of most other places on the coast.

1839 was the year when Margate was minutely observed by John Poole.

(c) [John Poole, 'Margate', *The Amaranth*, 1839, 70–1]

The *manufactures* of Margate consist chiefly of eau de Cologne, . . . and French perfumery in general. French artificial flowers, and the lighter articles of French millinery, from Paris, are also made here in great abundance. But Margate does not aspire to the making of French watches and clocks, or of French jewels and trinkets: these are the produce of Birmingham and Sheffield. Its French work-boxes, dressing cases, and toys, it derives from Tunbridge; whilst Worcester has the honour of supplying it with all its French porcelain . . . All these articles are purchased in great quantities by the visitors from the metropolis.

The *commerce* of Margate is comprised under the preceding head; and I am not aware that the place is remarkable for its *natural productions* – if we except shrimps, cockle-shells, bathing women, and a few other marine curiosities . . . The *accidental* population of Margate (the visitors), at the height of the season, must be utterly incalculable . . . Margate is the classical resort of the citizens of London – the Baiae of Cockney-land, . . . a very pleasant retreat from the close alleys and crowded thoroughfares of the vast and sleepless city it is.

> The above account is interesting for indicating what people could take home with them from holidays spent in Margate; likewise in 1833.

> (d) ['Amusements at Margate', *Chambers's Edinburgh Jouranl*, 1833, 155–6]

MARGATE, as a bathing place, might be imagined a retired spot, to which invalids resorted for the benefit of their health, and therefore conclude it presented one vast hospital or receptacle of human misery. Far otherwise. There are . . . many who delight in [the] opportunity for care-killing – many whose happiness consists in escaping from a crysalis state in London, to flutter a butterfly at Margate. To these is the place indebted for the visits of nearly 100,000 persons in the course of a season . . .

Some of the *fortunates* at the dice box will become possessed of a great number of tickets, for which, at their departure, the amount may be received in trinketry or trumpery. . . Every lure is set, every trap is baited, to catch the contents of the Cockney's purse. Step into the bazaars, they appear as if the Boulevards of Paris had emptied all their fiddle-faddles, sweet scents, and nonsense, to attract.

> Stepping back in time the attractions of dice, loo and various kinds of gambling were already well established, judging from the following censorious letter written by 'An OLD BATCHELOR', and addressed 'To the Editor of the Lady's Magazine', in 1815.

(e) [*The Lady's Magazine*, 1815, 458–60]

Margate, Sept. 5, 1815.

Mr Editor,

Though a man, who has been nine and twenty years secluded from the world in a country village, and in one of the most northern counties of England, can scarcely hope to be considered as an entertaining correspondent either by yourself or any of your fair readers, yet having been informed that your publication is open to persons of every description, I shall unhesitatingly disclose my sentiments . . .

As the vicar of the parish, in which I reside, had some business of importance in the Isle of Thanet, little persuasion was required to induce me to become his companion. Margate I had been taught to consider as the focus of attraction for *invalids* of every *description*. Judge then, sir, what must have been my astonishment at beholding its inhabitants decorated with as many flowers and feathers as would have formed a *May garland*. It is not merely the *heads* of these *valetudinarians* which actually seem to bend under the load of finery, but their whole figures [are] decorated out for the purpose of exhibiting their various talents . . .

A knowledge of *music* seems no longer to be acquired for the gratification of *friends* and *parents*, but for the itinerent loungers of a public bathing-room . . . I have seen young ladies actually stalk up to the instrument, and, uninvited, begin playing in the presence of *fifty strangers!* . . . Another practice, which appears to me [to be] perfectly *un-feminine*, is the fashionable dice-box, and the public game of loo, in which, the sexes indiscriminately combine at the libraries, with the *eagerness* of complete gamblers . . .

These practices, Mr Editor, appear to me of a most dangerous tendency, and seem to *unsex* the *sex*, if I may be permitted to make use of such a term; for as *Nature* evidently designed that a distinction should be placed between them, I have no idea of having her *rights infringed upon* by the authority of *Fashion* . . . As the *sick* and *healthy* alike resort to this much-frequented bathing place, it doubtless is politic in the inhabitants to furnish them with a variety of amusements, but . . . the *dice-box* and the *loo-table* I consider as having a more dangerous tendency . . . May not frequent success at these libraries engender a fondess for still more seductive and hazardous pursuits? The frequent association with men . . . may have incalculable mischiefs.

An infectious spirit of gambling, by means of cards, dice, raffles and lotteries, first gripped Margate during the 1780s. *The New Margate and Ramsgate Guide in Letters to a Friend*, 1789, 15, associated raffles and lotteries not only with circulating libraries but also with many of the shops of Margate (also see Doc. 42m). In addition, the circulating library proprietors instituted petty auctions, these being the precursors of the famous Margate bazaars of the post-1815 steamboat days. In a poem describing a visit to Margate, 'written in the year 1805', William Robinson, Esq. referred to the prevalence of gambling at that time.

(f)   [William Robinson, *A Trip to Margate*, 1805, 20, 21, 22, 23]

Where'er you turn, you find the rage for play,
More properly for gambling every way,
Completely gratify'd. [Of] cards, or dice,
Or billiards, almost ev'ry street supplies.
In each of these no want is ever found
Of betting company who stand around,
Each bett they'll take, propose it as you may . . .
    To try their luck at *Garner's* some will go,
By cutting cards, the high against the low.
The highest fixes who shall win the stake,
[And] aces there they always highest make . . .
    For recreations of another sort
Margate is well provided. There's the sport
Of *Silver's* auction. A most curious man
That *Silver* surely is. Beat him who can . . .
It is the vogue most useless things to buy,
And trifles from mere sport to run up high . . .
Papa must mind to overbid the throng;
And if a pretty work-bag please the mother,
No price must let it go to any other . . .
Silver dwells longest on plated goods, the rest he sells
For half their value, if you will believe . . .
''Tis your's – to you I gladly knock it down' . . .
'Tis strange to see such numbers faint and sweat,
Enduring all th' extremities of heat,
Within a crowded room, for scissars, knives,
And netting-boxes coveted by wives;

Morocco-folding purses, amber-beads . . .
Old papas embrace
With eagerness a handsome tooth-pick-case,
To make believe they've teeth efficient left . . .
Thus *Silver* traffics six nights out of seven,
And twice on Sundays seeks the road to heav'n.

> Raffles and lotteries were destined to have a chequered history.
> Shortly after William Robinson's observations the latter were
> prohibited by legislation, and this interference was greatly regret-
> ted by an 1809 guidebook.

(g) [*The New Margate, Ramsgate, and Broadstairs Guide*, 5th Ed.,
Margate, 1809, 67]

The Raffles, or the Subscriptions, were generally for some article of
jewellery, Tunbridge-ware, etc and were so numerous, that many
goods were disposed of in an evening, at the Libraries, by this means.
The brilliancy of the company which attended them was astonishingly
great; for as they here enjoyed some of the pleasures of the ball-room,
without being under the restrictions which are necessarily observed in
an assembly, not only the generality of the visitants, but those of the
highest rank, were found partaking of the amusements which these
rooms afforded. An act of parliament, not long since passed, called
'The Little Go Bill' has put a stop to this sort of lottery. We cannot
avoid lamenting this, as the smallness of the sum subscribed certainly
rendered it an innocent recreation; and we hope that the Legislature
may yet in its wisdom, repeal so much of this bill as relates to raffling.

> The circulating libraries were driven to devote added effort and
> resources to their musical entertainments and evening prom-
> enades (also see Docs. 42p, q), but in so doing they confronted
> direct competition from both the assembly rooms and the Theatre
> Royal. Ten years later card loos remained as one popular attrac-
> tion on offer of an evening at the Margate circulating libraries (see
> Doc. 42j); likewise at Ramsgate in 1828.

(h) [*Ms. Journal of a Holiday in Ramsgate in 1828 including Visits to
Broadstairs and Margate*, KAO, U2446 F1]

11 August.

. . . I went to the library the other evening with four shillings in my pocket to try my luck at the loo, which goes on every evening. It is the same as at Brighton only instead of 8 chances there are 6, and we use dice instead of cards. I won *the 3 first times*, and the 4th I only lost by a number or two (A miss as good as a mile, N.J.). I took one 6 shilling ticket and the other 12 I laid out in shares for a workbox and inkstand. I hope I may be successful in one or the other.

12 August.

. . . I went last evening to the Library and threw one of my chances for a musical workbox. I threw 33 in 3 throws 3 dice each time, but 39 was thrown almost directly afterwards so that *that* chance is gone. I have another which I mean to try to-night . . .

14 August.

. . . I went to the library this morning and threw my remaining chance for the musical box. I threw 40 – the highest was 42 so I lost it! My two chances for the inkstand fared the same luck . . .

21 August.

Last night we went to the Library and I tried my luck in several loos, but was not at all successful.

> Surviving also from about this time is the holiday diary of a very ordinary family, whose stay in Margate was dogged by poor weather, as was indeed the Ramsgate holiday referred to above (see Doc. 50). While the Margate diary makes no mention of bathing, it is very informative about raffling. Here were three single people, Mary, Rose and Vincent who enjoyed themselves in the libraries and bazaars of the town, at a time when the former were having to compete against the attractions and mounting popularity of the latter (also see Doc. 42).

(i) [*MS Diary of Mary Figgins, 30 August – 21 September circa 1828*, Margate Public Library, Local Collection, YO60. 41]

August 31.

. . . Vincent proposed going and seeing all that was to be seen for nothing. The first place was the Boulevard which was crowded. They have made an addition by which you can go through to Cecil Square. The new room is very prettily fitted up, and there is a lady plays the piano and a boy the harp, they play very well indeed . . . The centre of the room is filled with loo tables. We saw Mr and Mrs Obbard and 3 daughters. He had given them sixpence to raffle, and they had won a two shilling ticket. We then proceeded to the French bazaar which was much the same as the other, raffling but no music. After that we went to the temple of fancy and then to Betterson's Library, but the music at both places was far inferior to that at the Boulevards, but they were all crowded alike. Vincent thinks that for sight seeing Margate is a very cheap place.

September 1.

. . . After dinner we went for a walk on the Pier. . . . On our road home we went into the Boulevards, etc., but they were not as crowded owing to there being a juvenile fête at Tivoli (see Docs. 39b–e).

September 2.

. . . After dinner we went for a saunter but found it so windy that we went to the Boulevards. We then went to the fancy fair where I and Vincent took two chances in a raffle. Vincent played at loo at Jolly's and won 2s. After supper we went to enquire when the raffle would take place and heard that it would be settled the next evening at 10.

September 3.

. . . In the afternoon we went on the pier where we saw the Misses Collins. We then came home and did not go out again till 9 when we went about the raffle and had to saunter about the bazaar an hour. However, it repaid us for our pains for Vincent won the musical workbox which was the chief prize.

September 10.

. . . Rose tried her luck in a raffle and lost. . . . We met Mr Wilson [their fellow lodger] and his party. We joined them and went to all the different places of amusement. Rose raffled and lost. Mr, Mrs and Miss W. likewise. With chances in raffles we returned to supper with them. Afterwards [we] went to see about the raffle, but there was such a set of noisy young men there that we came home. I enjoyed being out, it was such fun . . . We went to bed at ½ past 11 monstrous late.

Thursday, September 15.

. . . We went into Jolly's. I won 2 shillings. . . . In the evening we went on the jetty and pier. I won a chance in a raffle.

Friday, September 16.

. . . We dined at quality hours and afterwards went for a saunter on the jetty, but it began to rain and we went into the bazaar, etc. At ½ past 9 we went to the raffle. Rose won a musical workbox – it was so provoking, I was only one number short.

> Jolly's Bazaar which is referred to in the above account was one of three Margate bazaars which were described at some length in a guidebook of 1831.

(j) [G.W. Bonner, *The Picturesque Pocket Companion to Margate, Ramsgate, Broadstairs, and the Parts Adjacent*, 2nd Ed., 1831, 79–81]

LEVEY'S BAZAAR,
in [the] High Street, is a very spacious long room, with a paved floor, which in summer renders it delightfully cool; it is lighted by windows in the roof, and is very tastefully and neatly fitted up. The length of this apartment is greatly relieved by arches thrown across it, and at the end is a splendid mirror, from which the busy scene going forward is reflected to our view. This Bazaar is approached through an elegant Grecian archway, with a circular lantern at the top, which, while it forms an ornament to High Street, is really a very pretty object, and does credit to Mr W. EDMUNDS, by whom it was designed, [he, as a native architect, having also designed Margate's new lighthouse of 1829]. Here may be purchased jewellery of all kinds, trinkets of endless variety, bijoutry, foreign china of great beauty and excellence, toys for the amusement of children, perfumery from the best manufactories, cutlery and other goods, from which we have made but a brief and faint selection. In the evening this room is lighted with gas [gas lighting having been introduced to Margate in 1824], and when crowded with company, presents an animated and lively scene, which it would be a vain attempt to describe, and which need only be visited to be enjoyed.

Mr LEVY allows the visitors of Margate to pass through this Bazaar into Cecil Square, by which they are . . . spared the bustle and noise of High Street.

JOLLY'S BAZAAR,

which last season was well supported, and as amply supplied as the rival establishment, which is only selected for more lengthened description because it is the parent institution. Indeed the success of Mr JOLLY's endeavours to please the visitors of Margate is sufficiently proved by the expensive alterations which he has made in his establishment, which we are certain, from what we have seen and heard, fully deserves, and will most certainly obtain, a continued and extended share of public approbation and support.

THE LONDON BAZAAR,

is likewise situate in High Street, and is of a very different character from the two already described, being a large plain building, approached through a passage, and divided into various departments, which are respectively occupied by females, who sell a variety of goods of the best quality, which it would be useless and unnecessary to describe.

The first mentioned bazaar was well known in 1833 as the 'BOULEVARD DE PARIS.'

(k) [*Picture of Ramsgate, or A Guide to the Various Amusements, Public Libraries, Building Improvements, etc. of that celebrated Watering Place*, Ramsgate, 1833, 70]

You enter by a splendid Arch and Dome in High Street. [It] rivals every other fashionable lounge in Margate.

Jolly's French Bazaar continued to flourish during the 1830s, being no less keen than circulating library proprietors to announce new innovations in entertainment, as in 1836.

(l) [*The Kentish Gazette*, 31 May 1836]

The Visitors and Inhabitants of the ISLE OF THANET are respectfully informed that the FRENCH BAZAAR is now open. This establishment will present an additional attraction the present season, Mr Jolly having purchased a self-playing instrument, the Euterpean. This instrument performs many of the finest overtures and concerto pieces with a correctness, power, and effect which are truly astonishing.

Two bazaars in the same street are merely entered by name in a Dover guidebook of 1838.

(m) [W. Batcheller, *The New Dover Guide*, 4th Ed., Dover, 1838, 120]

T. Squier and Son, 121, Snargate-street; and J. Reuben, 4, Snargate-street.

The Visitor's Guide to the Watering Places, 1842, 197, noted that Herne Bay contained 'several bazaars', while *The Pictorial Guide to Gravesend and Its Rural Vicinity: A Holiday Handbook*, 1845, 16, included among Gravesend's amusements Tully's Bazaar, which three years before was described in the following terms.

(n) [*The Visitor's Guide to the Watering Places*, 1842, 16]

TULLEY's BAZAAR is situated on the east side of Windmill-street. This attractive lounge has been ornamented at a very considerable expense. Here are promenade concerts, *à la Musard*, morning and afternoon; an exhibition of cosmoramic views, and vocal and instrumental performers every evening. No charge is made for admission during the day.

Of the shops generally in the town at this time it was noted, *ibid* 20,

SHOPS. – The town can now boast of some very excellent shops, which are furnished with every useful and ornamental article that can be required. Gravesend being so near to London, fresh goods are arriving almost hourly.

This last point must refer partly to the good water communications which existed between Gravesend and London and may be compared with the provisioning of Margate's shops in the 1760s.

(o) [John Lyons, *A Description of the Isle of Thanet and particularly of the Town of Margate*, 1763, 14–15]

There are several good [shops], and many very reputable Tradesmen. [Any] deficiency is, in a great measure, supplied by the numerous articles to be found in most of them, and by their ready and quick communication with *London* by the Hoys. Was it not for the assistance of these vessels, it would be almost impossible for *Margate* . . . to furnish . . . the vast numbers of people who resort to it.

Bazaars were only one type of shop which expanded in the growing seaside resorts of Kent.

45. *The patronage of the wealthy and the great: contemporary references to and lists of fashionable visitors.*

Evidence abounds to show that a substantial proportion of the visitors to all Kentish seaside resorts, prior to their social tone being lowered by the massive consequences of railways in promoting passenger travel and popular excursions, were drawn from polite society. In other words, they were people of good birth, of high social status and were either wealthy or of independent means as to income. Fellow travellers and holidaymakers noted the presence of other visitors of distinction in their letters, diaries or travel journals (see Docs. 38 k, 41kk). Holidaymakers of importance featured prominently in newspaper reports and visitors' listings. Their presence was very much welcomed by the writers of guidebooks. The overall evidence is more scanty for the less well developed resorts, such as Folkestone, Sandgate and Hythe, but even so, as in 1816, there are indirect pointers to fashionable patronage.

(a) [*The Hythe, Sandgate and Folkestone Guide*, Hythe, 1816, 7–8, 24, 30–1, 83, 107]

Folkestone – There are many lodging houses and the town is much resorted to by persons fond of the seaside, and lovers of retirement . . . A society for conversation and debate on literary and moral subjects is held weekly; and a book society monthly. Here are . . . respectable seminaries for youth.

Sandgate – Most of the requisites to constitute a reputed bathing place, and render it worthy of fashionable resort, are . . . already to be met with, . . . [including] several habitations capable of accommodating families of distinction.

Hythe – The shops for trade as well as the dwellings belonging to the superior classes of the inhabitants bespeak the opulence, respectability, and commercial importance of the place.

The social life of Hythe benefited not only from 'respectable and genteel' visitors but also from army officers of rank who were stationed in the local barracks. Resorts which were said to be retired or secluded invariably attracted by inference a more fashionable type of visitor.

(b) [Thomas Potts, *Gazetteer of England and Wales*, 1810]

Sandgate . . . is a small bathing-place, which has wholly grown up within the last sixteen or seventeen years, and is now much frequented by those who wish [for] quiet and retirement.

(c) [*The Kentish Traveller's Companion*, 4th Ed., Canterbury, 1794, 271]

With reference to the number of houses in Broadstairs,
the number is greatly increased within these few years, for the accommodation of strangers in the bathing season; where those who may not chuse to mix in the gaiety and pleasure of a more public place [a reference to Margate], will find this a retired and agreeable situation.

The exclusiveness of seaside resorts was influenced not only by royal patronage, as in Brighton from 1783 onwards, or in Broadstairs and Ramsgate during the 1820s and 1830s, but also by fashionable preferences, which could change from one season to another.

(d) [*The Morning Herald and Daily Advertiser*, 20 August and 24 August 1781]

[Southampton is] the place where they [the visitors] are most numerous and genteel. [Also] Margate, Ramsgate, Brighthelmstone [Brighton] Deal, etc. etc., . . . have attracted greater numbers this season than for some years past.

Brighton and Weymouth were ahead in popularity early in July 1786.

(e) [*The Morning Herald*, 1 July 1786]

The number of people of fashion who have left London within the last fortnight, must be immense, as it is scarcely credible the amazing difference that is visible in almost every street at the West-end of the town within that space.

Brighton is already become *cheerful*, and seems to bid fair to stand as the favourite *haven* in the calendar of the sons and daughters of pastime and pleasure, during their summer excursions.

Weymouth has her partizans and can sometimes produce more *honourable* visitors than all the other *bathing ports* together . . . *Margate* fills as usual – the *City dames* insist upon a trip in the *hoy*, as a matter of *right*, established by custom and usage.

> Lowestoft and some of the other east coast resorts were popular in fashionable circles during August 1797.

(f) [*The Observer*, 20 August 1797]

Lowestoft this year boasts a very numerous and fashionable company: Lord and Lady Dalkeith and family, . . . Lord Montagu and family [and] Lady Fann and family . . . Southampton is filling fast [but] Bath is nearly deserted; the company at present chiefly consists of valetudinarians . . . Southwold, Aldborough, Cromer and other places on that coast have more than their accustomed complement of visitors.

> One distinguished visitor who was quite clear about his preference for Margate in 1787 was Lord George Herbert, the future 11th Earl of Pembroke (1759–1827). Having on Sunday, 8 April 1787, married Elizabeth (1767–1793), the daughter of Lady Diana and Topham Beauclark, Margate was chosen a few months later as the place most likely to be beneficial to Elizabeth in her state of health, and so a house was rented there for two weeks at a cost of ten guineas towards the end of September, which prompted the 10th Earl of Pembroke (1734–1794) to write to his son in the following terms (Illus. 5a, b).

(g) [Ed: Lord Herbert, *Letters and Diaries of Henry, 10th Earl of Pembroke and his Circle*, 1950, 322, 360]
Wilton House, 21st Sept. 1787.

Dear George,

I was in hopes to have seen you and Elizabeth here . . . but I find you are going, if not gone, to Margate. I hope she has not miscarried again, which the name of a sea-bathing place makes me fear she has. Pray let me know.

Lord Herbert dutifully and immediately answered his father's query.

> Margate, Sept. 24th '87.

My coming to this place is not on Elizabeth's account. She is going on very well, but I myself like to get a month or six weeks bathing in the Spring and in the Autumn. Brighton is where I usually go in the Spring, but at this time of the year it rather overflows with Royalty and Weymouth is in my opinion a most detestable place, so I am come to try this.

> Margate, despite the socially lowering effects of cheap water transport (Docs. 5b-e), managed to attract some of the most respectable of visitors until well into the nineteenth century.

(h)   [*The Kentish Gazette*, 4–8 June 1768]

Much company is already gone down to Margate; and 'tis expected there will be more people of rank and fashion than has ever been known in one season.

(i)   [*A Short Description of the Isle of Thanet; Being chiefly Intended as a Directory for the Company Resorting to Margate, Ramsgate and Broadstairs*, Margate, 1796, 11, 13–14]

MARGATE [is] the capital of the Island [Thanet] . . . A great number of nobility and persons of fashion resort to Margate in the summer both for the enjoyment of its pure and salubrious air, and for the benefit of the sea water.

> This flattering assessment of 1796 applied, however, only to a portion of Margate's visitors. Indeed, a much wider cross section of society travelled to that resort in private carriages, public coaches, hoys, sailing packets and yachts before 1815, followed by steamboats after 1815, than went to Broadstairs or Ramsgate. In terms of respectable and fashionable patronage these two resorts, allowing for their smaller size, comfortably outpaced Margate. Thus, of Ramsgate it was claimed during the 1790s:

(j)   [*The Kentish Traveller's Companion*, 5th Ed., Canterbury, 1799, 285]

Buildings [have] continued to increase, notwithstanding the stagnation of public improvements in many other parts of the kingdom. The air, soil, situation and other local advantages possessed by Ramsgate, over almost any other watering place upon the sea coast, has induced the opulent to give it an encouragement far beyond any of its competitors: and the number of noble and distinguished families who have resided here not only for the bathing season, but [have] made it their constant residence for a number of years past, fully verify its pre-eminence.

As if to labour the last point in the mid–1770s:

(k) [C. Seymour, *A New Topographical, Historical, and Commercial Survey of the Cities, Towns and Villages of the County of Kent*, Canterbury, 1776, 653]

The Lord Viscount Coningham has here a summer residence, as well as the Earl Verney.

Mrs Pilkington in 1812 concluded that Broadstairs visitors were superior to those frequenting Margate.

(l) [Mrs Pilkington, *Margate!!! or Sketches Amply Descriptive of that Celebrated Place of Resort*, 1813, 189]

The company who frequent Broadstairs [is] more select, or rather more *fashionable*, [being] evident from the number of elegant equipages [which we saw] during [our] drive in the morning.

Lord Cholmondeley was a visitor to Thanet in 1786, and again in 1804, when his presence was noted on more than one occasion in the diary of Joseph Farington (see Doc. 41kk).

(m) [*The General Advertiser*, 29 September 1786]

Lord *Cholmondley* has lately left Kingsgate where he had been for some time; his stile of living was equal to his high rank; his deserts, upon an average, amounted to 15 guineas a week, which was furnished by the *fruitress* on the parade at Margate.

During the 1795 season it was reported on 1 September that

(n) [*The General Evening Post*, 1–3 September 1795]

The Lord Chancellor has a house at Ramsgate, where he bathes.

Subsequently he was summoned to Weymouth where the Royal

Family were in residence, *ibid.*, 12–15 September 1795.

The Lord Chancellor and Mr [William] Pitt are set off to Weymouth, where they are to be met by the other Cabinet Ministers; and this day at 2 o'clock a grand Council will be held with the King at Gloucester Lodge, on the present situation of affairs in Europe.

Two years later *The Observer* was full of the comings and goings of titled visitors at different resorts, beginning on 30 July 1797.

The Duchess of Newcastle is the present occupant of Lady Tancred's villa in the Isle of Thanet.

Lady Loughborough on Wednesday left London for the neighbourhood of Deal, where she is to be soon joined by the Chancellor for the summer.

The Duke and Duchess of York on Friday arrived at Broadstairs. Two houses in Chandos-row are laid into one for their accommodation.

A week later, 6 August 1797:

The Duchess of Devonshire returns to Bognor Rocks . . . The Duchess of Rutland and her lovely daughters form the great attraction of Lymington.

Two weeks later it was reported that

The Duke of York is returned to Town, from Broadstairs.

As late as 17 September 1797,

Lord and Lady Cholmondeley, Lord and Lady Holland, . . . are still at Ramsgate.

The Observer offered the following conclusion on that season in its issue of 6 August 1797.

We are told that the visitors at the watering places are so *select* this season that there is no room for the envenomed tongue of slander. We should suppose from this valuable piece of information that the visitors are pretty *even* with one another.

Ramsgate and Broadstairs were fashionably patronized during 1799.

(o) [*The Observer*, 18 August 1799]

Mrs Fitzherbert [privately married to the Prince of Wales, later George IV] is at Ramsgate and appears in excellent health and spirits. She has a new and gay equipage [facts noted also in *The Morning Post and Gazetteer*, 19 August 1799]. The Prince, according to the rumour at Ramsgate, is to be there in the course of the coming week. Lady Heathcote, with her lovely family, Lord Bruce, Lord and Lady E. Bentinck, and several others of distinction are amongst its present visitors . . .

Broadstairs has more to boast in the quality than the quantity of its visitors. – To those who admire dullness and retirement, this place has great attractions.

(p) [*The Morning Post and Gazetteer*, 21 August 1799]

Ramsgate promises to be one of the most fashionable *dipping places* this autumn.

(q) [*Ibid.*, 5, 7 and 9 September 1799]

At no preceeding season have the watering places in the Isle of Thanet so much abounded with company of the first fashion. Last week more than 1,500 persons breakfasted at Dandelion [see Docs. 38j–l]. The greatest number on any former occasion was 1,004 . . .

Lord ASHBURNHAM and family, Lady and Miss TWISDEN, and SIR FRANCIS BLAKE are just arrived at Ramsgate. That place has been a long time quite *full* . . .

Lady ANN and Captain HUDSON remain at Margate during the remainder of the month. – Lady GLENCAIRN is there for health only.

The Marchioness of DONEGALL lives in great retirement at Broadstairs.

The Countess of GUILDFORD and her sister Lady BURDETT are at Ramsgate. Lady CLANBRASSIL is at the same place.

> Fashionable visitors continued to be much in evidence during the seasons of the 1800s in all three Thanet resorts.

(r) [*The Morning Chronicle*, 4 September 1801]

A paper of yesterday says, that the DUKE of MANCHESTER is in the neighbourhood of Margate, sporting his elegant pleasure boat.

> He was in the same neighbourhood and at Dover during September 1798, according to correspondence emanating from Henrietta, Countess of Bessborough (1761–1821), daughter of John, first Earl Spencer and younger sister to Georgiana, Duchess of Devonshire (see v and ee below).

(s) [Ed: Castalia Countess Granville, *Lord Granville Leveson Gower (First Earl Granville) Private Correspondence, 1781–1821*, I, 1917, 223]

DOVER

Tuesday (September).

We have had all sorts of adventures . . . We stay tomorrow and go back Thursday with the D. of Manchester and Mr Smith, who take us in their boat first to Margate and then to London [Illus. 5c].

(t) [*The Times*, 31 August 1802]

Margate is now full in every part. Many Fashionables are there; among whom are the Machioness of BATH and her three Daughters, the Ladies THYNNE. Mr LITTLEDALE, the Dutch Banker, and family, are expected, and the Duke and Duchess of St ALBANS, To-morrow.

(u) [*Ibid.*, 16 September 1802]

Fashionable Arrivals at Ramsgate.

Lord and Lady Bessborough; Sir W. Farquhar and two Miss Farquhars; . . . Mr Conyngham; Rev. W. Tooke; . . . Col., Mrs and Miss Hartcup; . . . Marquis of Hartington; . . . Lord Paulet; Lord and Lady Sydney; . . . etc.

> Some of the above visitors subsequently attended the Ramsgate ball in honour of Mr Le Bas, Master of the Ceremonies (Docs. 41 o–s).

(v) [*Ibid.*, 25 September 1802]

Ramsgate, September 22.

The Ball last night for Mr LE BAS was attended by all the Fashion of the Isle of Thanet. It commenced at 9 o'clock by Lady H. Cavendish and Mr Townley. The others followed:-

The Marquis of Hartington	Hon. Miss Lambe
Lord Duncannon	Hon. Miss C. Lambe
Hon. Mr Lambe	Hon. Miss Fitzroy
Mr Conyngham	Miss Farquhar

Wright's York Hotel at Margate, 1829.

Illus. 19

(a) Dover from the beach, 1830.
(b) The proposed pier at Herne Bay, c. 1830.

Illus. 20

(a) The Royal Sea Bathing Hospital at Margate, 1831.
(b) A view of Folkestone, 1831.

Illus. 21

(a) The completed pier at Herne Bay, c. 1835.
(b) The King's Arms library at Dover, 1838.

Illus. 22

(a) The West Cliff at Ramsgate, 1839.
(b) A view of Sheerness, c. 1840.

Illus. 23

Two views of Herne Bay in 1842–4.

Illus. 24

The Duchess of Devonshire gave the company a most elegant entertainment. Also present were the Duke and Duchess of St. Albans, Lord
and Lady Melbourne, Lord and Lady Brownlow, Sir Gilbert and Lady
Heathcote, the Earl and Countess of Jersey, Duke and Duchess of
Manchester, Lady Southampton, etc.

Moving into 1803.

(w) [*Ibid.*, 18 July 1803]

Margate is beginning to fill. Among the principal houses taken for the
season are the following: the Castle at Kingsgate, Lord Viscount
CHETWYND; Lord Holland's House [see Docs. 38b–d,f], General
JONES; North Down House, the Duke of MONTROSE; Chapel Hill
House, Lady ARABELLA WARD; the Fort House, Mr AGAR.

(x) [*Ibid.*, 20 August 1803]

Margate, August 17.

Within these few days, the general appearance of this place is much
altered, and the arrival of numerous visitors, among whom are many of
the most fashionable, has already so cheered the inhabitants, that they
have no doubt of a good season.

(y) [*Ibid.*, 28 and 30 September 1803]

Margate, Sunday Evening, September 25.

. . . This morning the Pier (the favourite promenade by day) was much
crowded, and was honoured by the presence of the Duchess of St.
ALBANS, Lady HEATHCOTE, Miss MANNERS, Colonel PLUNK-
ET, and many others of distinction and respectability.
Margate, Tuesday Evening, September 27.
. . . The Duke and Duchess of St. ALBANS, Lady HEATHCOTE and
the MANNERS'S still remain.

Meanwhile over in Broadstairs the launching of a vessel from Mr
Thomas White's famous ship yard, at about the time the Whites
became firmly entrenched in the Isle of Wight having purchased a
second shipyard at Cowes, was the scene for a fashionable
gathering.

(z) [*Ibid.*, 25 August 1803]

Broad-stairs, though not full of company, is gay and cheerful beyond expectation. A fine new ship was last week launched from WHITE'S Yard. After the launch, a very numerous and fashionable company breakfasted in an elegant tent erected for the purpose on the lawn, in front of – CALVERT's Esq. house (the owner of the vessel): after which country dances commenced. Amongst the company present were, her Grace the Duchess of RUTLAND, who presided at the table; also, Lord and Lady MOLESWORTH, Lady ARABELLA WARD, Sir WILLIAM CURTIS, General and Mrs CROSBIE, General RAINSFORD, Lady CUNNINGHAM, the Hon. Miss BURTON, Sir WILLIAM and Lady PENNYMAN, etc. The Company, who breakfasted on the occasion, amounted to about 200.

> Yet another social occasion in the Thanet calendar centred around the annual visitation of directors, medical men and well wishers to the Margate or 'General Sea Bathing Infirmary' which, as a charitable hospital, had opened its doors during 1796 at Westbrook. What was a weekend visitation provided an opportunity for the London directors, members of the London Medical Board and Life and Annual Governors to join with the Margate Committee and local physicians, surgeons and Governors in inspecting the fruits of their benevolence. On the Sunday morning anniversary sermons, given by invited clergymen of some prominence, were preached in the local churches and chapels which had as their primary object the collection of funds for the institution. These collections were boosted socially as well as financially by the élite of society handling the collections at the doors of the respective churches and chapels. Monday was taken up with a visit to and inspection of the Infirmary, followed by an Annual General Meeting in Margate and a dinner. Thanks were very much the order of the day for voluntary services rendered at the Annual General Meeting which, for 1803, was held in Margate Town Hall on 19 September.

(aa) [*General Sea Bathing Infirmary, London Committee Minutes*, Court of Directors, Extraordinary, 12 March 1804, 76–7, KAO, MH/T1/A2]

The Minutes of the [Meeting] at Margate of Sept. 19th . . . were read as follows . . .

FRANCIS COBB Esq. reported that the several sums collected yesterday, at the different places of worship, amounted to £227 11s. 9d. . . .

Resolved, That the grateful Thanks of this Meeting be given to Her Grace the Duchess of St. Albans, Her Grace the Duchess of Montrose, the Countess of Glencairn, the Vicountess Molesworth, Lady Edward Bentinck, Lady Arabella Ward, Lady Heathcote, the Hon. Mrs. Gould, the Hon. Miss Agar, the Hon. Mrs Cornwall, the Hon. Miss Burton, Mrs Duff, Mrs Townley, and Miss Manners; for their very distinguished and kind attention to the Interests of this Institution, by giving their personal attendance at the Doors of the several places of public Worship yesterday, to receive the contributions of the respective Congregations, and that the Ladies named in this Resolution be requested to permit us the Honour of enrolling their Names as Patronesses of this Institution: and that Mr Forsyth, V.P. be requested to communicate to the several noble and honourable Ladies named in the preceeding Resolution.

Resolved [also], That the Thanks of this Meeting be given to Her Grace the Duchess of Rutland, the Countess of Pomperet, Lady Dacre, Lady Mary Singleton, Vicountess Chetwynd, and Lady Curtis, who were obliged on account of ill-health to decline the invitation of assisting in collecting at the Church Doors.

Margate's Theatre Royal attracted a highly fashionable audience on the night of 28 September 1805.

(bb)   [*The Times*, 1 October 1805]

We had an enchanting and magnificent display of beauty and fashion, . . . among whom we observed Lord KEITH, and a numerous body of Naval Commanders [Admiral Lord Keith was then residing at East Cliffe Lodge between Broadstairs and Ramsgate as Commander in Chief of all the warships stationed in the Downs]; the Earl of MANSFIELD, and many other Military Officers [N.B. how holidaymaking and the season went on as usual despite the Napoleonic Wars]; the Countess of MANSFIELD, Earl and Countess of LIMERICK, Lady BROOKE, Lady HALES, Lady GLYNN, etc. There was such a throng of carriages, that in the absence of the customary precautions of the capital, it was very difficult to avoid accidents, and impossible to prevent confusion . . . The brilliant circle of hereditary distinction is daily increasing, but the pleasant humours of what is called Hoy Fair are on the decline.

An important factor encouraging the patronage of the upper classes and the wealthy from the 1790s through to 1815 lay in the Revolutionary and Napoleonic Wars which impeded their ability to travel to and from the Continent. They had to seek solace from waters nearer at home, and so the fashionable seasons continued through to 1814.

(cc)   [*The Morning Chronicle*, 16 August 1810]

Lady MULGRAVE [has] left Tunbridge Wells . . . for Broadstairs, where she is expected to remain about a fortnight, previous to the family going into Yorkshire.

(dd)   [*The Morning Post*, 8 August 1814]

Lord WELLESLEY is at his seat at East Cliff Lodge, Ramsgate.

Once the Napoleonic Wars were over the aristocracy could resume travelling uninterruptedly to and from the Continent, at the same time as holidaymaking along English shores came within the reach of ever increasing numbers of middle class and trading folk, not only because steamboats brought increasing numbers of visitors to Margate and Ramsgate but equally as a social consequence of expanding national wealth, itself a product of sustained economic growth. What had long been a tendency for Margate in particular to attract holidaymakers from all classes became increasingly pronounced from 1815 onwards. Nine years later *The Times* was quick to seize on this social change.

(ee)   [*The Times*, 28 September 1824, quoting from *The Kent Mercury*]

What an entire change has taken place in the character of our visitors within twenty or twenty five years. In those days, the Duchess of Devonshire (mother of the present duke), Lady Duncannon, Lady Bessborough, Lady Elizabeth Foster, the Duke of St. Albans, Earl Thanet and his brothers, the Tuftons, Sir H. Man, and all the leading nobility of Kent, were residents during the season, . . . and occasioned Margate to be a powerful rival of Brighton, although his present Majesty [George IV, formerly the Prince of Wales] was even then its patron. Margate subsequently became unpopular with the fashionable world, but continues more or less the summer retreat of the 'London citizens'. [While] the introduction of steamboats has given the whole coast of Kent, [and] the Isle of Thanet in particular, a prodigious lift, . . . the visitors to Margate are composed of the inhabitants of eastern London during the early part of the season almost entirely. The company at present [late September, however,] are far more select and respectable than they have hitherto been: some of the most opulent merchants, East India Directors, and bankers, are now here, [plus] a few who may be denominated a portion of the fashionable world. Sir Gilbert Heathcote has engaged Capt. Cotton's House, in the neighbourhood of Margate, for one month, at the high rate of 200 guineas, the Captain himself having gone to the Highlands to shoot grouse.

Some of the longest lists of fashionable arrivals at the Thanet resorts were published between June and September 1817 in a local magazine.

(ff)   [*The Thanet Magazine*, 1817, 39–40, 88–90, 132–4, 171–3]

FASHIONABLE ARRIVALS IN JUNE 1817.

MARGATE	RAMSGATE	BROADSTAIRS
The Right Hon. Lord Sondes	Sir John and The Hon. Lady Palmer	Sir George and Lady Anson
General Montresor	Lady Wright and Miss Trower	Lieut. Col. and Mrs. Booth
The Right Hon. Lady Sondes	Sir Peter Pole	Rev. James and Miss Beresford
Hon. Miss Watson	Dean of Lichfield	
Hon. George Watson	Mr and Mrs Curtis	Mr and Mrs Henry Rowles
Hon. Henry Watson	Mr and Mrs C. Knight	Mr and Mrs Crowther
Rev. Mr Jones	Cpt. V. Bennett	Mr Todd
Col. and Mrs Murphy	Mrs and Miss Parkers	Mr J.B. Price
Rev. Dr. Nantz and family	Mrs George	Mr and Mrs Fairbone
Mrs Manton and family	Mr and Mrs Sharwood	Mr and Mrs Brough
Mr Lewis and family	Mr and Mrs A. Ryder	Miss West
Mr Hazard and family	Mr and Mrs Sedgwick	Mr and Mrs A. Morton
Mr and Mrs Amplett	Mr and Mrs Layard	Mr and Mrs Prickett
Mrs Burns	Mrs Pembroke	Miss Clarke
Mr and Mrs Stewart	Mr and Mrs Peckham	Miss Oakley
Mr and Mrs Read	Rev. T. Barne	Mrs Mackmurdo
Mr Millard	Rev. Charles Pettingal	Capt. Morton
	Rev. Henry Hale	

MARGATE	RAMSGATE	BROADSTAIRS
Capt. Robinson		
Capt. Wallace		
Mr and Mrs Field		
Mrs and Miss Rooke		
Mrs Gibbs and family		
Mr Hurst and family		
Mrs Finucane and fami-		
ly		
Capt. and Mrs Young		
Dr. Bancroft and family		
Mrs Bowker and family		
Mr and Mrs S. Brooke		
Mr and Mrs Storeham		
Mr Peacock		
Mr Matthews		
Mr Carlos		
Mr Little and family		
Mr and Mrs Johnstone		
Mr Brown and family	*KINGSGATE*	
Mr Graham and family		
Lieut. Howgrave	Colonel Allen	
Mr Moon	Capt. Cotton	
Mr Valentine		
Mr Musgrave and fami-		
ly		
Mrs Freeman	*BIRCHINGTON*	
Mrs Sharp		
Miss Brown	Admiral and Mrs Wat-	
Mrs and Miss King	kins and family	
Mr and Mrs Prickett		
Mr Savory and family		
Mr Hedges and family		
N.B. Mr Briscoe from the		
Continent		
N.B. Mr Ross and friend from		
the Continent		

FASHIONABLE ARRIVALS IN JULY 1817.

MARGATE	RAMSGATE	BROADSTAIRS
Lord Cochrane	Dowager Countess	Earl and Countess
Colonel Allen	Dunmore and Lady	Delawar
Capt. Vernon	Virginia Murray	The Hon. Lady Dering

MARGATE	RAMSGATE	BROADSTAIRS
Mr and Mrs Austin and family	Viscount and Lady Bernard	The Rev. F. Mandy
Mr and Mrs Cooper and family	Lord Winchelsea	Mr R. Bell
Mr and Mrs Watson and family	Lady Augusta D'Ameland	Colonel Elford
Mr Steward and family	Lady Whitcombe	Mr and Mrs Hallan
Mr Bacon	Sir William and Lady Wake and family	Mrs Pringle
Mr Bowles and family	Sir William and Lady Fraser and family	Mr Dean
Mr Taylor and family	John Round Esq. MP	Mr Gregory
Mr Dalrymple	Admiral and Mrs Vashon	Rev. E. Gregory
Rev. Mr Robinson	Rev. James Vashon	Lieut. Col. Boger
Rev. Mr Owen	Col. Buckland	Mr and Mrs Boger
Mr Snodgrass	Col. Blunden	Miss Lake
Mr King	Capt. Boys R.N.	Mr Ashworth
Capt. Wyndham	Capt. Champain	Mr Hodges
Mr Carr	Capt. Simeon, R.N.	Mrs Jacomb
Capt. Sherwood and party	Capt. Bathurst, R.N.	Dr. de Courcy Luffan
Mr and Mrs Dearsley and family	Major General Foveaux	Mr Madocks
Mr and Mrs Van and family	Major Halford	Mr de Lassence
Mr Bullock	Major Brace	Mr E. King
Colonel Abernethy	Capt. Newton	Miss Thompsons
Mr Oliver and family	The Rev. W.A. Armstrong	Mr and Mrs Prickard
Mr Bird and family	The Rev. W. and Mrs Clarke	Mrs and Miss Atkinson
Mr Edmunds and family	Dr. and Mrs Grey	Rev. Mr and Miss Tayler
Mr Beskett and family	Mr R. Filmer	Mr Reid
Major Light and family	Mr and Mrs Barrett	Mr Northcote
Mr Austen and family	Mr and Mrs Prescott	Mr Middleton
Mr Wright and family	Mr Collings	Mrs E. Hoper
Mr Parnell and family	Mr Gundry	Miss Chalié
Mrs and Miss Riggs	Mrs Woodhouse	Mrs Forsyth
Mrs More and family	Mr and Mrs Cadogan	Miss Mortin
Mr Shrewbridge and family	Mr Yarde	Miss Bankers
Mr Perrier	Mr and Mrs Kymer	Mrs Taunton
Mrs Hales and family	Mr and Mrs Pepys	Mrs Gourdez
Mrs and Miss Bertram	Mrs Corbett	
Mr Barton and family	Mr and Mrs Jackson	
Mr Baskerville and family	Mrs Macvicar	
Mr Warrington and family	Mrs Mocatta	
Mr Mortlock and family	Mrs Lewis	
	Mr and Miss Finch	
	Miss Fitzgerald	

MARGATE	RAMSGATE	BROADSTAIRS
Mrs and Miss Sparrows	Mr and Mrs Newton	
Mr and Mrs Bagley	Mr Gordon	
Mrs Samuel and family	Mr Freeling	
Mr Isaacs and family	Miss Shaw	
Capt. Crawley	Mrs Hodges	
Mr Ricardo	Mr Williams	
Capt. Gardner	Mrs Brandrick	
Mrs Graham	Miss Smith	
	Mr Barnes	
	Mrs L. Wilson	
	Mr Gostling	

For August and September 1817 the style of presentation was strictly according to rank.

FASHIONABLE ARRIVALS IN AUGUST 1817.

MARGATE	RAMSGATE	BROADSTAIRS
Sir Edward and Lady Hales	*Countess* Egremont	*Sir* W. and Lady Taunton
Baroness de Beaufain	*Sir* J. and Lady Earle	Maria, *Lady* Anstruther
General Lightburne	*Sir* J. Wynne de Bathe	*Capt.* Kelly
Colonels:-	*Major-Gen.* Armstrong and lady	*Messrs:-*
Charitie and lady	*Dr.* Strachey	Cockburn and lady
Carey	*Lieut-Gens:-*	Stevenson and lady
Burslam	Bligh	Larkins and lady
Crane	Tryon	G. Enderby and lady
Majors:-	*Majors:-*	H. Larkins
Lipper	De Bathe	Hall and family
Dyson	Scott Waring and lady	Delafield
James	*Captains:-*	Hodges and family
Aubrey and lady	Fraser	T. Gray and lady
Courtenay	Gurney and lady	Smith and daughter
Captains:-	Grace and lady	Richards
Damant	*Hon.* Mrs J. Bennett	J. Coggan and lady
Doyle	*Reverends:-*	Martin and lady
R.N. Hanmer	D. Ruell	W. Roots
Barlow	T. Mitchell	E. Hanmer
Lieut. Kidd	A. Downes	Tullock
Doctor Brown	Mr Easter	Tattersall
Messrs:-	J.S. Becker	Dax
Simpson	W. Boughton	Atkinson
Hull	*Messrs:-*	Murray and lady
Priddy	Mallory	*Mesdames:-*

MARGATE	RAMSGATE	BROADSTAIRS
Carter and family	Prescot and lady	Collins
Boncock	Curling	Rees
George	Bryant	Jarvis
Symondson	Winn	Trelawny
C. Parr	Smales	Parsons
W.H. Durham	R. Mackmurdo	Mowbray
Robinson	Gosling	two Sinclairs
J. Brown	Hamilton	Hamilton
Rixon and lady	Spurling	A. Noyes
Crawford	W. Heath	*Misses*:-
W.T. Brown	Goddington	Kelly
Lee and lady	Carlen	Wagstaff
Joyce	Smith	
Harrison	Saunders	
Fetherstone	Edwards	
W. Cobham jun.	W. Rutter	
Horne	Brodrick	
Davies	Bullock	
Elwyn	Gillett and family	
Devis	P. Smith	
W. Baker	Hammond and lady	
Martyn and lady	Earle	
Fermer	Conyers	
Cloves	Fermor	
Cock	Newte	
Maund and lady	T. Hawley	
Setwell	F. Maitland	
Tukes	Bligh	
Mackenzie	Askew and lady	
Hanmer and lady	Pickard	
Raymond and lady	Kirkpatrick	
Dowrick and lady	E. Perceval	
Langton and lady	Law and family	
Loot and family	Cornfield Fraser	
Neve	Bullock	
Vaughan and lady	T.W. Mercer	
Morley	Thompson	
Delaval	Harris	
Dehamy	Reade	
Serle	Fielding	
Bradley	Divett and lady	
Hart	Percival	
Dixon	Caley	
Butcher	Flanagan	
Clarke	Prior	

MARGATE	*RAMSGATE*	*BROADSTAIRS*
Richer	Washington	
Ewing	Rogers	
Green	Gutteres	
Thweng	Samler	
Baker and lady	R. Byng	
Munns and lady	Eade and lady	
Mesdames:-	Munro and lady	
Maubert	Elliott	
Neve	Harrison	
Chapman	Bassil	
Duncombe	E. Lawes	
Furrance	Crafter	
F.A. Branston	Thackthwarth	
Horwood	D. Ricardo	
Harman	Brickwood and lady	
Stoddart	Vardon and lady	
Abbott	Powell	
Evans	J. Taylor	
Hobson	Harris	
Hayland	Inglis	
W. Watson	Matthews	
Metcalfe	Walton and family	
Stewart	*Mesdames:-*	
Thackery	Morton	
Kirkup and family	Hunter	
Gompertz	Chalmers and family	
Montefiore and family	Moody	
Treacher and family	Stanley and daughter	
Bowman	Turner and family	
Hon. Mrs Leesom	Seymour	
Misses:-	R. Dawson	
Moorman	Moulton	
Belsey	Whish	
Fitzgerald	Jaffray	
Skipper	Button	
	Robinson	
	Halliburton	
	Lenox and daughter	
	Hodgson	
	Alexander and	
	daughter	
	Craig	
	Palmer	
	Misses:-	
	Rolleston	

MARGATE	RAMSGATE	BROADSTAIRS
	two Bridges	
	two Hargoods	
	Armstrong	
	Smith	
	Long	
	Knivett	
	Arthur	
	Pearson	
	Hill	

FASHIONABLE ARRIVALS IN SEPTEMBER 1817*.

*It is the Editor's intention to discontinue this list until the commencement of the next season [*The Thanet Magazine*, however, did not survive into 1818].

MARGATE	RAMSGATE	BROADSTAIRS
Sir Edward and Lady Hales	*Lord* William Fitzroy	*Sir* Isaac Heard, *Garter King at Arms*
Lieut-Gen. Stevenson	*Sirs*:-	
Colonel Harris	William Curtis	*Baron* Wolff
Captains:-	George Prescott	*Messrs*:-
Romilly	Francis Ford	Cuppage
de Rippé	*Baron* Wolff	Cobb
Paget	*Hon.* Edward Perceval	Saumarez and lady
The Hon. Mrs Robert Leesom	*General* St. John	Beltz
Messrs:-	*Lieut-Gen.* Thornton	Wyatt and lady Ablett
Bragg and lady	*Major* Rowan	Bynon
Monday and lady	*Captains*:-	Pullen and lady
Heathcote	De Starck, R.N.	Wiggen and lady
Lloyd	Bourchier	Richardson
Hepworth	Evelyn	Savile
E.H. Robins	Hurrock	Miller
Cooper	Douglass	Luxmore
Randall	*Lieutenants*:-	Nottidge and family
Lister	Hutchinson	Chalié
Green	Boyce, R.N.	Temple and family
Lewis Goldsmith	Mr. Serjeant Manley	Kemble and lady
Curtis and lady	*Doctors*:-	Taunton
Two Macklins	Canderleath	*Rev.* C. Wakeman and lady
Richardson and family	Strachey and family	Burn
Ramsden	*Ladies*:-	*Mesdames*:-
Elmslie	Jemima Hay	Hopkins
	Hopkins	Ross
	Curtis	Franklyn
	Moore	

MARGATE	*RAMSGATE*	*BROADSTAIRS*
Roe	Blunt	Walker and family
Butcher	*Messrs:-*	Dermer
Goodwin	Jones and lady	Trower
Eades	Hall	Turner
Lewis	Wilkinson	Fletcher
Rev. James Rudge	Terry and lady	Oakley
Taylor	Langton	Hersley
Reynolds	Butler	Gipps
Rixon	Austen and lady	*Misses:-*
Montrion	J.B. Ince	Reid
Golding	Harris	Dermer
Hall	Alington	C. Hoper
Talmadge	Stone and lady	Kenrick
Buchan	Calverly	de Crispigny
Salter	Blagrave and lady	
Moorman	Robinson	
Knight	Walker	
Barnes	Green	
Williamson	Fry	
Latham	Benn and lady	
Halford	Page	
Franks and lady	Dyer	
Haywood and family	Kettlewell	
Power	Mackay	
Shepherd	Munro	
Bristow	Aubrey	
Kibblewhite and	Lindo	
family	Bryant	
Samuel and lady	Rivington	
Waymouth	Cookson	
Rev. Evan James	Costeker	
Simpson and family	Chamberlain	
Wiltshire	Wintle	
Carrick	Lenox	
Fentiman	Tillock	
Cartwright	Searle	
Bonde	Richards	
Holland	Smith	
Bridge	Kershaw	
Meredith	Snell and lady	
Phelps	Lexley	
Power and family	Fleming	
Morant	Stiff	
Skilbeck and lady	Turton	
Mesdames:-	Ironside	

MARGATE	RAMSGATE	BROADSTAIRS
Rogers	Frend	
Marchall	Judson	
Parker	*Rev.* R. Moore and	
Steers	lady	
James Robins	Mantell	
Furrance	Hay	
Wyett	Morriss and lady	
Neve	Wilson	
King	Shaw	
Baxter	Booth and lady	
Pott	Birch	
Felix	Dunlop	
Reyner	Smith	
Millington	Girdlestone	
Jefferson	Cameron	
Greenfield	Hodgson	
Porter	Winter and lady	
Bingley	Pellatt	
Myers	Sheen	
Misses:-	Crowther and lady	
Bone	J. Crowther	
Sutherland	Curling	
Wadham	Goud	
Lumley	Entwistle	
Brass	Lane	
Fox	Nixon	
Edwin	Young	
Maclellan	Rule	
Orlebar	Trant	
Cope	Morris	
	Nind and lady	
	Barclay	
	Gatty and family	
	Moon	
	Mills	
	Phelps	
	Trower and lady	
	Hammersley	
	Knyvett	
	Gordon	
	Allen	
	Rev. G. Curtis	
	Pepys	
	Rev. Henry Pepys	
	Amedroz and lady	

MARGATE	*RAMSGATE*	*BROADSTAIRS*
	Manley	
	Hughes	
	Bradley	
	Reed and lady	
	Mesdames:-	
	Walton	
	Walford	
	Lousada	
	Law	
	Fordyce	
	Benyon	
	Granger	
	Inglis	
	Morris	
	Spalding	
	Mackay	
	Hurrock	
	Andrews	
	Skelton	
	Cobbett	
	Raikes	
	Pope	
	Jacques	
	Broderick	
	Edwards	
	Misses:-	
	Curtis	
	Holman	
	Morland	
	Greaves	
	Collett	
	Dinwiddie	
	Blunt	
	Rennie	
	Campbell	
	Mylne	
	Lenox	
	Aldridge	
	Gibbs	

The above lists show that titled visitors, including nobility, along with gentry and clergy, flatteringly reckoned to be 'people of the first distinction' in guidebooks, were still evident among Thanet's post-Napoleonic holidaymakers, more so, however, in Ramsgate and Broadstairs than in Margate. These 900 or so entries represented only a proportion of the total number of visitors to the Thanet resorts, between June and September 1817. They do not indicate total arrivals and with a preponderance of males listed almost certainly underestimated women, wives and children. A seasonal peak for August and September is shown, confirming the 1824 observation above (see ee), that nineteenth-century seasons were more fashionable towards their close, during September, rather than during July, which was also true to some extent of the years before 1815. Although it was an aspect of gentility to be seen at the seaside for a prolonged duration, comparatively few of the 1817 arrivals stayed over two or more months, but among them were Sir Edward and Lady Hales and the Hon. Mrs Leesom, during August and September in Margate; or Dr Strachey, who spent those two months in Ramsgate. While the listings do not indicate why people were classified as 'fashionable', nor how they were listed as such, Ramsgate was the resort most preferred by titled people and the clergy. The 'fashionable arrivals' of Ramsgate nearly matched those of Margate in July and were way out in front for August and September. Ramsgate managed to continue attracting visitors of high social rank.

(gg)   [*The Morning Post*, 22 August 1822]

Ramsgate, August 20.

This place has certainly, this season, more nobly supported its character for respectable and numerous patrons. It never was known so full of respectable families so early in the year as at the present time, and the increasing demand for houses certainly indicates a most prosperous conclusion . . .

Among our latest arrivals we have to notice:- H.R.H. the Duchess of Kent and suite; the Danish Ambassador; the Earl of Hardwicke and Lord Caledon; Dowager Lady Astley, Dowager Lady Amherst, Lady Charlotte Ram, Sir William Heathcote, etc.

(hh)   [*The Maidstone Journal and Kentish Advertiser*, 5 August 1828]

This favoured Town [Ramsgate] begins to regain its summer gaiety. The influx of visitors daily increases, and its Promenades abound with fashionable company. The steamboats arrive well filled and we have every prospect of a good season; within a day or two the hotels have received a considerable increase of nobility, among whom may be named Earls Chesterfield, Castlereagh, Harborough, etc., with their several *suites*.

Three weeks later.

(ii)　[*Ibid*., 26 August 1828]

Ramsgate, August 21.

This place continues to be visited by the *haute-ton*. The Duke of Newcastle and family are about to occupy Albion House, Albion Place. Remain – the Duchess of Manchester, Lady Emily Montagu, Lady Bentinck, Countess Carnworth, Lord and Lady Dalgell, Lady Bromley and many other families of distinction.

> Dover too was the resort of fashionable visitors and, according to *The Dover Telegraph and Cinque Ports General Advertiser*, 1 August 1835, was filled with 'respectable families' much earlier that summer than on former occasions. The patronage of the wealthy and the great was soon, however, to be a social phenomenon of the past, since, in the words of Sir Walter Besant, *London in the Nineteenth Century*, 1909, 16, 'for the middle classes there was the fortnight or month at Herne Bay or Margate.'

46.　*An Important chapter in English medical and social history: the Margate or 'General Sea Bathing Infirmary', later the Royal Sea Bathing Hospital at Margate.*

When the Margate or 'General Sea Bathing Infirmary', intended for poor people suffering from scrofula or tuberculosis, opened its doors during 1796 at Westbrook, it was a pioneer in charitable medical specialization, its fame being national, early and unique. The history of this hospital is an important chapter in English medical and social history, because, in the words of Courtney Dainton, *The Story of England's Hospitals*, 1961, 93, it was 'the country's first hospital for tuberculosis.' It was early and unique in the sense that the founders of eighteenth-century hospitals lacked sufficient knowledge of medicine and surgery to think of specialization, in terms of setting aside specifically certain hospitals for the treatment of particular types of disease. All their foundations had been general hospitals with very few exceptions, general in the sense that they dealt with all types of diseases. It is also significant that the founding of a Sea Bathing Infirmary at Margate during the 1790s was not followed by any widespread provision elsewhere for the many tuberculosis sufferers of the late eighteenth and early nineteenth centuries. Its foundation during 1791 owed much to a famous eighteenth-century Quaker physician, Dr John Coakley Lettsom (1744–1815), who firmly believed that fresh air, sea water, sunlight and regular habits were essential to the treatment of many diseases, and espcially those of the chest and all tubercular troubles. Although by the twentieth century medical emphasis had changed from curing scrofula in the poor to modern methods of treating tuberculosis, one element of the originally prescribed treatment of the 1790s remained unchanged, namely exposing patients to the benefits of sea breezes on verandas in the open air. This phenomenon has been observed by countless generations of visitors to Margate. Dr Lettsom was greatly assisted in his endeavours by two philanthropic friends, the Rev. John Pridden and John Nichols who was editor and proprietor of *The Gentleman's Magazine*, and locally within Margate by the physician Dr John Anderson, who wrote about the virtues of sea bathing at Margate and the air of the Isle of Thanet (see Doc. 23c). Dr Lettsom reasoned the case for such a charitable institution in one of his many publications.

(a)　[J.C. Lettsom, 'Hints for Establishing a Sea-Bathing Infirmary at Margate for the Poor of London', *Hints Designed to Promote Beneficence, Temperance and Medical Science*, III, Section 6, 1801, 235–7]

Were a stranger cursorily to pass through the great streets of London [having by then a population of one million people], nothing would be more strongly impressed on his mind than the general appearance of wealth, health and plenty, [but] were he to quit the spacious streets and squares, and penetrate into the little alleys or courts, the scene would be dismally reversed in the contemplation of poverty, sickness and want, . . . aggravated by want of air and exercise . . . Among the poor, and particularly the children of the poor, there [is] a species of disease, for which no suitable aid had till lately been afforded, [viz] scrophulous diseases, . . . [for which] sea air and sea bathing are peculiarly requisite; and yet these remedies are procured with very little expense.

By the Thames, a cheap conveyance to sea-water is commanded . . .
Margate, or its vicinity, seems peculiarly adapted for this salutary
purpose.

Dr Lettsom envisaged a hospital in which patients could be
housed in 'solaria', open air shelters which offered access to sea
breezes and sunshine. His biographer, Thomas Joseph Pettigrew
in *Memoirs of the Life and Writings of the Late John Coakley Lettsom,
M.D., L.L.D., F.R.S., F.A.S., F.L.S., etc., etc., etc., With a Selection
from his Correspondence*, 1817, shows over two volumes how Dr
Lettsom worked extremely hard to effectively establish and sustain
the Margate Sea Bathing Infirmary from the 1790s through to his
death on 1 November 1815. The same conclusion emerges from
the excellent minute records of the Infirmary which have been
deposited in the Kent Archives Office. Indeed, the only holiday
which he allowed himself was an annual visit to Margate to attend
the annual general meeting of the Infirmary, for which purpose he
devoted 72 hours, travelling down to Margate on a Saturday
night, so as to arrive in time to hear the annual charity sermon in
the parish church (compare Doc. 45aa and before). The rest of
Sunday was partly spent in local courtesy calls. On the Monday he
visited the hospital, examined every patient himself and attended
the General Meeting of the Governors. At seven o'clock in the
evening he departed for London, where he arrived on the Tuesday
morning. When he was already 69 years of age Dr Lettsom paid
his customary visit to Margate taking the boat from London as his
diary makes clear.

(b)   [J.J. Abraham, *Lettsom His Life, Times, Friends and Descendants*,
1933, 286, 288–9]

28th August 1813.

At four o'clock in the afternoon sailed from Billingsgate in the packet,
and got to Margate at nine on the 29th. Attended the new chapel at
Ramsgate, where the Rev. David Garrow preached for the General Sea
Bathing Infirmary; the collection £86. Dined at Pegwell with Sir
William Garrow [he was Attorney General in 1813 and owned 'a neat
villa' adjoining to Pegwell Bay, his only daughter Eliza Sophie having
married on 6 April 1802 Samuel Fothergill Lettsom, Dr Lettsom's
second son], and returned to Margate with [William] Norris [who as a

London surgeon was a Consulting Surgeon to the Sea Bathing Infirmary]. In the morning visited the Infirmary, and made a report of the state of the patients. Afterwards dined at the Royal Hotel, Sir Wm. Garrow being chairman. The whole collection reported amounted to about £500, being a considerably larger sum than at any previous anniversary. Left Margate at nine in the evening of the 30th, and arrived in London by chaises at ten o'clock in the morning.

Below are part of the proceedings as minuted 'At The Annual General Meeting of this Institution held at the Royal Hotel, Margate, the 30th August, 1813'.

(c) [*General Sea Bathing Infirmary Margate Committee Minute Book, 1811–1837*, 19, 20, 21, 22, KAO, MH/T1/A3]

Present – Sir William Garrow, M.P., V.P. in the Chair.
Sir Horace Mann, Bart, V.P. [see Doc. 45 ee]
Hon. George Watson.
Sir Christopher Pegge.
Rev. D. Garrow.
Wyndham Knatchbull Esq.
Francis Cobb Esq., V.P.
and several other Gentlemen.

The Treasurer reported the Collections at the different places of worship yesterday to be as follows:

	£	s.	d.
Margate Church	101	7	2
St. Peter's Church	34	8	8
Ramsgate Chapel	86	15	0
Independent Meeting Ramsgate	13	9	7
Baptist Meeting Margate	9	0	0
	£245	0	5

The following Medical Report was read.

'Upon a careful inspection of the General Sea Bathing Infirmary, we find 120 Patients in the House, the greater part of whom are in a rapidly improving state of health.

Were we to notice individual cases, the most generally interesting

349

objects of recovery that excited our attention were Mary Allen, Elizabeth Fryer, Agnes Service, Ann Cook, John Marston, Isabella Robson, Ann Mitchell, Elizabeth Frome.

Several of these were afflicted with Abseses, Diseased Joints, with Shrinkened Ligaments, and Carious Bones, which are amongst the worst effects of that formidable disease Scrophula.

However, pleasing our former visits to the Infirmary may have been, we have the satisfaction to report, that the present instances of improvement have been still more gratifying.

These cases afford a very happy illustration of the good effects arising from cleanliness, temperance and proper diet, aided by medicine judiciously applied, assisted by sea air and sea bathing.

Beside those in the House, there are 80 Out-Patients who receive the benefits of Sea Bathing and Medicine.

It affords us additional pleasure, upon this occasion, to testify our full approbation of the judgement, humanity, and skill of the Physicians and Surgeons of the Institution.

(Signed) J.C. Lettsom,
William Norris.'

The Governors who inspected the Infirmary this day, Reported

'That they had gone through the different wards, and found every thing much to their satisfaction; the House very clean, the Patients thankful for the treatment and care taken of them: that Prayers were daily read in the respective Wards and that such Patients as were able attended Divine Worship on Sundays.'

They had examined the Provisions and found them good and wholesome and were informed that those which had been supplied were satisfactory to the Gentlemen of the Margate Committee.

'At the Anniversary Dinner, the same Day', the treasurer reported on donations, 'in addition to the Collections at the several Places of Worship amounting to £245 0s. 5d.,' which raised the total sum collected on that particular Anniversary to £454 8s. 11d., including ten guineas from the Rt. Hon. the Lord Sondes, £10 from Lady Burton, five guineas from the Hon. George Watson, finishing up with a 'Donation to the Permanent Fund Wyndham Knatchbull Esq. [an] additional £25.' The origins of the Infirmary can be traced back to an inaugural meeting held on 2 July 1791 at the London Coffee House on Ludgate Hill.

(d) [*The Original Minutes of the Margate Infirmary, 1791–1793*, KAO, MH/T1/A1)

Present, Dr Lettsom in the Chair, Mr Adams, Mr Beaumont, Dr Hawes, Dr Muller, Mr Deputy Nichols, Sir John Peter, Rev. John Pridden, Mr J.R. Syms.

The Chairman informed the above Gentlemen that he had requested their attendance to impart to them an Idea he had long formed of establishing a Receptacle for the Relief of the Poor whose Diseases required Sea-Bathing, that among the numerous places of resort on the Sea-coast none appeared to him, as well as to several others to whom he had intimated his design, so proper as Margate or its vicinity; the extreme salubrity of that part of the coast, and the ready and cheap conveyance thither [4s. by the hoy], giving that Place a decided preference to all others . . . In consequence of these superior Advantages, he had, together with Dr Anderson, of Margate, endeavoured for a considerable time to procure an eligible Spot of ground for the purpose of erecting a Hospital upon . . . He had lately been favoured with intelligence from Dr Anderson informing him that Ground convenient for the Purpose was offered for Sale . . . Considering these Circumstances, together with the important and increasing Use of Sea-Bathing, and the utter inability of the Poor to experience any Benefit from such a Remedy by the Expence attending a distant Residence from their Families and Occupations, he conceived no Opportunity so proper as the present for forming such an Institution for the Relief of the Poor and [so] therefore he submitted to their Judgements what Procedure would be most efficacious to expedite the Formation and Establishment of such a valuable and much wanted Institution.

Resolved, That the above Gentlemen together with John Milward Esq., Dr William Saunders, and Dr James Sims, form a Committee for managing the Affairs of an Institution to be called

THE MARGATE INFIRMARY,
For the Relief of the Poor
Whose Diseases require SEA-BATHING.

Resolved, That this Society consists of a Patron, a President, Vice Presidents, a Treasurer, a Secretary, Governors, a Collector and a Messenger.

Resolved, that Dr Lettsom be the Treasurer, and Rev. Mr Pridden be the Secretary to this Charity.

Resolved, That Dr Lettsom, Mr Deputy Nichols and the Rev. Mr Pridden be requested to view the Ground offered for Sale, as soon as they conveniently can, and if it appears eligible for the Purpose to procure the Same.

Resolved, That Subscriptions be solicited, and the following Address and Resolutions be printed for the Information of the Public

MARGATE INFIRMARY

THE great Importance of Sea-bathing having suggested to several Gentlemen the Propriety of erecting an Hospital on the Sea Coast for the Benefit of the Poor, . . . the following Resolutions [have been] unanimously agreed to:

1. That the great and increasing Use of Sea-bathing is a strong Proof of the Advantages derived from that Remedy to such whose Circumstances admit of their resorting to the Coast.
2. That many valuable poor Sufferers, who might be relieved by the same Remedy, are deprived of it . . .
3. That, notwithstanding the many Charitable Institutions already so well supported in Great Britain, it cannot be deemed on Intrusion on the Benevolence of the Publick to request their Attention to one for the sole Relief of such Objects of Compassion whose Diseases require Sea-Bathing.
4. That the Vicinity of the Town of Margate appears well calculated for such an Institution, on account of the well-known Salubrity of that Part of the Coast, the ready and cheap Conveyance thither, and the probable Residence, during the Summer, of many of the Subscribers who may inspect the Management of the House, and be satisfied concerning the proper Application of their Contributions.
5. That Ground, convenient for erecting such an Hospital, be forthwith purchased, and that a Committee be appointed in London, to correspond with another at Margate, to carry the Design into Execution.

6. That Subscribers of One Guinea, or upwards, annually, shall be considered as Governors, and have a Power of nominating a Patient whenever there is a Vacancy; and that Subscribers of 20 Guineas, or upwards, shall be Governors for Life.

7. That Subscriptions be received at the following Bankers: Baron DIMSDALE & Co. Cornhill; . . . Sir R.C. GLYN & Co. Birchin Lane; GOSLING & Co., Fleet Street; Sir R. HERRIES & Co., St James's Street; . . . PRESCOTTS & CO., Threadneedle Street [etc.]; by Dr. LETTSOM, Basinghall Street, Treasurer; and by the Rev. JOHN PRIDDEN, 61, Salisbury Square, Fleet Street, Secretary.

∴ Subscription Books are also left at the Public Rooms and Libraries at Margate, Ramsgate and Broad-stairs.

Read a *Letter* from Samuel WHITBREAD, Esq. offering a Subscription of 50 Guineas and further support if necesssary; also a Letter from a Lady inclosing a £10 note and desiring her Name to be concealed.

> The above was only the first of many appeals for funds. Dr Lettsom lost no time in going down to Margate as he made clear in a letter to Sir Mordaunt Martin Bart., dated 11 July 1791.

(e) [T.J. Pettigrew, *Memoirs of the Life and Writings of the Late John Coakley Lettsom,* . . . *With a Selection from his Correspondence*, II, 1817, 53]

I inclose a plan of a new Hospital and Infirmary, which I am endeavouring to establish at Margate, for the poor of London, whose diseases require sea-water. Last Wednesday I set out for this sea-girt town, staid two hours, and returned the same day, 144 miles in the day and night. I purchased two acres of land for the Structure, and formed a Committee at Margate to correspond with one in London . . . Often do I wish for new resources to alleviate the woe, which in this metropolis abounds, and will abound. I almost envied the wealth of the Dutchman Frehouven, whom I lately attended: what good might have been effected with his income of £17,000 a year!

> *The Original Minutes of the Margate Infirmary, 1791–1793*, show how on 6 July 1791 Lettsom, Nichols and Pridden purchased a site at Westbrook measuring 450x140 feet for £300, on which they paid an initial deposit of five guineas. Westbrook in those days although near to Margate stood detached from the town (compare Illus.

353

15a, 17a). It was left to the Rev. John Pridden, as an antiquary and amateur architect, to design the original building, provision being made for patients to sleep on verandas in the open air, which previously had been unheard of in hospital architecture. The laying of the foundation stone on Thursday, 21 June 1792, was an occasion for some considerable celebration.

(f)   [*The London Chronicle*, 30 June 1792]

The Gentlemen of the London Committee in the morning joined the Gentlemen of the Margate Committee at the Town Hall where the friends to the Institution were introduced to form a procession to the place, . . . which immediately took place, the bells striking up as the signal for it to commence, in the following order:

Two stands of colours.
A grand band of Music.
Gentlemen two and two, etc., etc.

The spot of ground being prepared, the stone was deposited in its place . . . The Inscription, which was engraved on a brass plate, was twice read by the Rev. Mr PRIDDEN, Secretary to the London Committee . . . The Plate being placed in a groove cut in the stone, was covered by a course of bricks, laid by Dr LETTSOM.

At Benson's [Royal] Hotel, 46 gentlemen sat down to a most sumptous entertainment.

The Infirmary which opened in 1796 was designed for 30 beds.

(g)   [*The Gentleman's Magazine*, LXVI, 1796, 608–9]

Margate, July 20th, 1796.

An erection is just completed here, for the reception of 30 poor persons from the hospitals, whose cases render sea bathing necesssary. The building is constructed in a very commodious manner; it is situated near the beach between Margate and Dandelion and the expense is defrayed by subscription. It will be fit to receive patients in a few days; they will have medical assistance, and a bathing machine has been built for their sole use.

Dr Lettsom's own figures indicate that few patients were admitted initially, no more than 16 during 1796 and 25 in 1797, rising thereafter to 48 in 1798, 62 in 1799 and 86 in 1800.

(h) [Lettsom, *Hints, op.cit.*, 251]

237 patients . . . have been admitted [over the first five years], many of whom have been restored to their families perfectly cured, and most of whom have derived considerable benefit by Sea-bathing . . . The Public will see . . . that the numbers admitted are annually increasing, . . . reflecting its great utility in restoring to health many poor objects by warm and cold Sea-bathing, where all other means are ineffectual.

The general policy of the Infirmary was laid down by a Board or Court of Directors, which met in London, who were advised by a Medical Board which functioned also in London, and by a local Management Committee in Margate, the latter casting an eye over the day to day running of the Infirmary. The Margate Committee maintained close contact with the Infirmary staff which on the census night of 7 June 1841 [P.R.O. H.O. 107/468/6] totalled 25 persons, 10 and 7 of whom were respectively nurses and housemaids, working alongside a steward, a matron, a resident surgeon, an assistant surgeon, a bath nurse, a male servant, a female servant and a cook, who in turn were caring for a much higher intake of patients than forty years earlier, viz: 128 males and 86 females, or 214 in total. In the 1800s the Margate General Sea-Bathing Infirmary was governed by a total of nineteen regulations, which included the following.

(i) [Lettsom, *Hints, op.cit.*, 246–7]

15.   No persons to be deemed objects of this Charity but such as are really necessitous and of decent character.
16.   The Physician, or other attending Medical Practitioner of the Charity will prescribe Medicines when necessary.
17.   The patients are to procure their own linen, except sheets. They must conform strictly to the rules of the Institution; regularly attend Divine Service; and, when cured, return thanks in the parish church. No patient to continue more than six weeks in the Infirmary without a renewed recommendation, unless the Faculty at Margate should deem it necessary.
18.   The patients are provided with food upon the terms of 5s. a week

for all above 12 years of age; and 2s. 6d. a week for children. A proper diet-table is prepared, under the direction of the Medical Gentlemen [see r below]

19. The Meetings of the Committees, both at London and Margate, being considered as open, the attendance of any Governor at the same will be esteemed a favour. And the Committee will feel themselves much obliged to any subscribing Lady, who will occasionally take the trouble of inspecting the female ward.

Holidaymakers to nineteenth-century Thanet were encouraged also to visit the Sea-Bathing Infirmary and while there to donate something to its financial support, as did a family party who were on holiday in Ramsgate in August 1829.

(j) [*Ms. Journal of an Excursion to Ramsgate in July and August 1829*, Tyler Collection (Ramsgate Scrapbook), Cathedral Library and Archives, Canterbury]

Wednesday, August 5.

. . . After dinner took a Chaise, and proceeded to Margate. Went over the Infirmary . . . Put into the Infirmary Box 10s. 0d.

Problems of finance were ever pressing throughout the nineteenth century so far as the hospital was concerned, so that every financial contribution, however small, was welcomed. According to *The New Margate Guide* of 1797 'the list of subscribers is truly respectable', and though 'many have been liberal, yet this charity still craves . . . patronage and benevolent assistance.' A list of 196 subscribers to the Infirmary in its early days included the following names.

(k) [*Subscription List to the Sea Bathing Infirmary*, KAO, MH/T1/FS1]

	£	s.	d.
John Anderson, M.D., Margate	5	5	0
Sir Joseph Andrews, Bart.	5	5	0
Mr J. Benson, Royal Hotel, Margate	3	3	0
Mrs Benson	1	1	0
Hon. Lieut. Col. Broderick, 3d.			
Regiment of Foot Guards	1	1	0
Mrs Bryan, Boarding School, Margate	1	1	0

	£	s.	d.
Archbishop of Canterbury	21	0	0
Elizabeth, Duchess Dowager of Chandos	5	5	0
Francis Cobb Esq. Margate	21	0	0
Francis Cobb Jun. Esq., Margate	5	0	0
Mr Alderman Curtis	10	10	0
Rt. Hon. Lord Eardley	50	0	0
Sir Walter Farquhar Bart, M.D.			
Great Marlborough St.	10	10	0
Dr Fothergill, Bath	1	1	0
William Garrow, Esq.	10	10	0
Lady Hales, Cavendish-square	1	1	0
Mr John Harrison, Preston	12	12	0
Sir John Henniker Bart.	5	5	0
2nd Subscription	15	15	0
Miss Horsman, Clapham	30	0	0
2nd Subscription	20	0	0
Mr William Hoyle, Chemist, Margate	1	1	0
John Coakley Lettsom, M.D.	21	0	0
John Miers Lettsom	10	10	0
Samuel Fothergill Lettsom	10	10	0
Pickering Lettsom	10	10	0
John Milward Esq., Artillery-place, Finsbury-square	21	0	0
Mr Deputy Nichols	3	3	0
Miss Nichols	1	1	0
Mr William Norris, Old Jewry	10	10	0
Sir John Peter	5	5	0
Rev. John Pridden, M.A.	2	2	0
Hon. Philip Pusey	50	0	0
Mr John Silver, Surgeon, Margate	2	2	0
James Sims, M.D.	5	5	0
Lord Southampton	1	1	0
The late Samuel Whitbread Esq.	105	0	0
Lady Worsley	1	1	0

Subscriptions were solicited sometimes from more than one member of the same family, from people from all ranks and in all walks of life, with a heavy emphasis both locally and in and around London but reaching also out to Bath, Preston or

Norwich. Institutions and corporate bodies were also encouraged to subscribe.

(l) [*The Times*, 16 July 1800]

Monday the Lord Mayor held a Court of Common Council at Guidhall. Sir William Leighton introduced a Petition from the Infirmary at Margate, for Sea-bathing, which being read, Dr Lettsom, Mr Blizzard, and other Gentlemen, spoke very favourably of this Institution, after which the sum of £100 was voted to it.

> In December 1850 *The Gentleman's Magazine*, always a good friend to the Infirmary in its fund raising, put out a 'Christmas Appeal', page 632.

Amongst charities which appeal to us for a word of recommendation we know no one that we can more safely commend to Christmas liberality than the GENERAL SEA BATHING INFIRMARY AT MARGATE, founded in 1796. The advantages of sea-bathing, pure air, and proper wholesome food to the poor who may be suffering under scrofula need not be insisted upon. Since its foundation no less than 22,000 persons have obtained relief through this charity, and, were its funds more ample, its usefulness might be considerably enlarged. Amidst the festivities of the memorable season which is now approaching, a mite to such an institution ought not to be forgotten.

> That the Infirmary was a truly national institution was strongly emphasized early in 1816.

(m) ['General Sea-Bathing Infirmary at Margate', *The Gentleman's Magazine*, LXXXVI, Part I, January 1816, 17]

From that period [1796] to the present 3,756 patients have experienced, in various degrees, the salutary effects of this establishment; numbers of whom have gone from the close and confined chamber of poverty and disease [which is their home], situated either in some lane or alley of a populous city; several from the poor-houses of out-parishes, the hospitals, and other charitable foundations, as well as many from various parts of the kingdom; the institution not being confined to any particular district, as its title 'General' testifies.

> Dr Lettsom was quite open in making publicly known the finances of the Infirmary in his capacity as its first treasurer.

(n)   [Lettsom, *Hints, op.cit.,* 250–1]

Receipts and Disbursements, from the origin of this Charity in 1791 to the beginning of 1801.

	£	s.	d.
Benefactions and Subscriptions			
received at Margate	1,348	5	8
Ditto in London	1,957	7	10
	£3,305	13	6
Expended in the purchase of ground to build on	325	1	8
Cost of the Building	1,766	10	9
Interest of Money advanced for the building	99	12	10
Furniture, Bedding, etc.	265	7	7
	£2,456	12	10

Paid servants' wages, and gratuities to
officers, and poundage to the Collectors   338   5   0

Sundry Articles for the Infirmary

	£	s.	d.			
In Coals, Soap,						
Candles, etc.	61	13	6			
Drugs	31	17	9	93	11	3

	£	s.	d.
Printing, Stationery and Advertising	175	15	10
Incidental Expences for 10 Years	201	15	7
	£3,266	0	6
Ballance in the Treasurer's Hands	39	13	0

The four first articles of expenditure may be considered as so much property belonging to the Institution; and the remaining sums (the charge of printing and advertising deducted), amounting only to £633 11s. 10d., comprize the whole of what has been really spent in conducting the business of the Charity, and in administering relief to 237 patients who have been admitted.

Patients were admitted on the recommendation of a subscribing Governor, after having been first examined by the Medical Board which operated from two addresses in London, the Court Room of the London Workhouse, in Bishopsgate Street, and St. George's Hospital at Hyde Park Corner. They were admitted only with a proper 'Form of Admission'.

(o)   [*Ibid.*, 248]

GENERAL SEA BATHING INFIRMARY AT MARGATE.

Recommended by
  [Life or Annual] Governor.
Examined, and found a proper Object, by
  Consulting [Physician or Surgeon]
Let the Patient be admitted,
  Treasurer, Waterman's-Hall.

N.B. No Patient can be admitted from London or its Environs without the Signature of a Governor, one of the examining Faculty, and the Treasurer.
To the Steward of the Infirmary.

Parishes, hospitals and other charities in London and elsewhere acquired the right to purchase so many beds in the Infirmary.

(p)   [*Royal Sea Bathing Infirmary Court of Directors Minute Book, 1826–1851*, KAO, MH/T1/A4]

Royal patronage was conferred by George IV in 1821.

12 April 1826.

Application from the Governors of the Poor of the Parish of St. Mary-le-Bone requesting the use of 2 beds during the ensuing Season – granted on the usual terms of £8 for each bed.

9 April 1834.

6 beds for the Use of the Radcliffe Infirmary, Oxford.

8 October 1834.

The Treasurer to entreat with St. Bartholomew's Hospital to the extent of 20 Beds or 2 distinct Wards.

13 April 1836.

Letter from the Radcliffe Infirmary to know the terms for extra beds for the season – use to be granted on the same terms as the Parishes in London, viz: £8 each.

On 11 December 1839 the Court of Directors decided to admit children at the age of five instead of six years, 'subject to the discretion of the Medical Board', and fixed ahead of the 1841 season, on 23 April, the 'Patients' Board per Week', at 4s. 6d. for adults, and for children under ten 3s. The Infirmary, as already noted above, was operational over the census night of 7 June 1841, when there were 214 patients who were receiving seasonal treatment within its walls [P.R.O. H.O. 107/468/6]. Children were clearly the main beneficiaries between the ages of 5 and 15. Children aged 15 and under constituted the bulk of the in-patients, accounting for 73% of males and just on 70% of females. The occupations of 43 male patients only were recorded, with a strong working-class composition, including three agricultural labourers, a bricklayer's labourer, two footmen, a gardener, two lightermen, a male servant, a medical student, a nurseryman, an ostler, two plumbers, a ploughman, two porters, three printers, three shoemakers, three tailors, a wheelwright and a wine porter. The ability of such people to benefit from sea air, sea bathing and coastal convalescence depended solely on the existence of a charitable institution like the Royal Sea Bathing Hospital. The Margate Committee kept a watching brief over the day to day running of the Infirmary.

(q) [*General Sea Bathing Infirmary Margate Committee Minute Book, 1811–1837*, KAO, MH/T1/A3]

17 May 1836.

The Committee went over the Wards and examined the Provisions, the Contracts appeared to give satisfaction. The Number of Patients reported as follows:

Men	38	Out-Patients	
Boys	10	Males	11
Women	19	Females	14
Girls	8		—
	—		25
	75		

31 May 1836.

In-Patients, 183.   Out-Patients 62.
It having been reported to the Committee the necessity of providing a
more convenient Chair for the removal of Patients in and about the
Infirmary and it appearing that a very suitable one belonging to Mr
Pain may be purchased for £5, . . .
Ordered, That the same be bought for the Use of the Institution.

14 June 1836.

The Contracts continue to be well served and the beer excellent.

28 June 1836.

In-Patients, 197.   Out-Patients, 137.
The attention of the Committee having been drawn by the Surgeon
[William Oliver Chalk] to the improper introduction of eatables, etc.,
to the Patients,
Ordered, That no Patients be permitted to purchase or receive any
outside food or other eatables but with the approval of the medical or
other officers of the Institution under liability of immediate discharge.

9 August 1836

The state of the House was reported by the Steward to have been
particularly orderly throughout the Season.
In-Patients, 194.   Out-Patients, 214.

25 October 1836.

The Margate Committee in recording their *concluding Report for the
Season* have to express their satisfaction with the conduct of the Officers
of the Charity, and the economy and management of the Infirmary,
together with their approbation of the uniformly creditable Manner in
which the Contracts have been fulfilled.

30 May 1837.

The Surgeon, Mr Chalk represented to the Committee the necessity of
his having a lock up Closet for the purpose of securing Medicine and
Bottles.

Resolved, That the same be provided upon the Understanding that the Expense shall not exceed £4 10s. as estimated.

The patients' diet at the beginning of the nineteenth century was made up as follows.

(r) [Lettsom, *Hints, op.cit.*, 252]

TABLE of Diet for the Patients in the SEA-BATHING INFIRMARY at Margate.
GENERAL SEA-BATHING INFIRMARY FOR ADULTS

	Breakfast	Dinner	Supper	General Allowance
Monday, Wednesday, and Friday	Milk-porridge one pint	½ lb. boiled mutton ½ lb. potatoes	Broth 1 pint	12 oz. of bread 1 quart of table beer
Tuesday, Thursday, and Saturday	Water-gruel one pint	½ lb. boiled beef ½ lb. potatoes	Rice Milk 1 pint	12 oz. of bread 1 pint of table beer 1 pint of porter
Sunday	Milk one pint	½ lb. roasted beef ½ lb. of suet pudding	Butter 2 oz. or cheese 2 oz.	12 oz. of bread 1 pint of table beer 1 pint of porter

FOR CHILDREN

Monday, Wednesday, and Friday	Milk porridge one pint	1 pint of broth ½ lb. suet pudding	Rice Milk 1 pint	10 oz. of bread 1 pint of table beer
Tuesday, Thursday, and Saturday	Water gruel one pint	6 oz. of boiled mutton or beef ½ lb. potatoes	Broth 1 pint	10 oz. of bread 1 pint of table beer
Sunday	Milk one pint	6 oz. roasted beef ½ lb. of suet pudding	Butter 1 oz. or cheese 1 oz.	10 oz. of bread 1 pint of table beer

Modifications and improvements to the diet were introduced during the nineteenth century. Despite financial stringencies the Infirmary was enlarged to house considerably more beds than when it had opened in 1796. Twenty years later the position was as follows.

(s) [*The New Margate, Ramsgate and Broadstairs Guide*, 6th Ed., Margate, 1816, 63]

Since the committees have been enabled to complete the deficient wing, it is become an ornament to the surrounding country ... It is now sufficiently large to contain about 90 patients, [and] we most sincerely hope that in a short time the funds may be equal to the house being kept open the whole year, and not merely during the summer, [being] fully persuaded that scrophula (the disease in which sea-air and sea-bathing are peculiarly, and indeed *specifically* useful) is never removed by the cursory visits of a few weeks.

> This hope unfortunately was not to be realized until 1858. Only then were the finances such that wards could be kept open during the winter months. Within fifteen years of 1816, however, the capacity of the Infirmary had more than doubled.

(t) [G.W. Bonner, *The Picturesque Pocket Companion to Margate, Ramsgate, Broadstairs and the Parts Adjacent*, 2nd Ed., 1831, 103–4]

This building has been from time to time enlarged, and is at present capable of affording accommodation to more than 200 scrophulous patients, who are admitted for the summer months . . . There are few public charitable establishments so extensively useful, or which afford so great blessings to the indigent sick; and when we consider the dreadful malady which sea air, and sea bathing, are alone calculated to relieve, we . . . easily understand why the wealthy, having themselves, perhaps, experienced their restorative power, should have kindly hastened to extend their sanative influence to the suffering and necessitous poor [Illus. 21a].

> It was about this time that what had long been regarded as a rather neat and simple building received a lasting embellishment, namely a monumental Doric four-columned portico. This was added to the front of the original hospital building and remains to this very day an impressive addition, when viewed from the Canterbury Road, the portico itself having once graced the front of the first Lord Holland's seat at Kingsgate (see Docs. 38b–d), now known as Holland House. Being in receipt of a legacy of £1000 3% Consols left by William Long Esq., the Court of Directors decided on 12 October 1836 that

a portion of the above Legacy . . . be sold out for the purpose of defraying the expenses of the Portico at the Infirmary.

47. *References to busy seasons and their economic and social consequences.*

The economics of present-day holidaymaking attaches importance both to the volume of holiday expenditure as well as to the fact that visitors' money is often turned over very quickly, to the benefit of providers of transport, accommodation, entertainments, provision retailers, guidebook publishers, patent medicine and luggage manufacturers, etc. These facts were no less true of spa towns and seaside resorts of the 1800s.

(a) [D. Macpherson, *Annals of Commerce, Manufactures, Fisheries and Navigation*, 1805, Appendix 4: 'A Commercial and Manufactural Gazetteer of the United Kingdom of Great Britain and Ireland']

BATH – a fashionable resort of invalids and others, whose expenditure circulates sufficient sums to support those who make it their business to provide accommodations and amusements for them.

BRIGHTHELMSTONE or BRIGHTON – The principal business is fishing and in time of peace an intercourse by packets with Dieppe; unless we reckon as more important, the entertainment of summer visitors, the place having become a fashionable resort since the Prince of Wales made it his occasional summer residence.

BUXTON – a town in the Peak Country . . . the chief business of the place [being] the entertainment of strangers, who visit it on account of the mineral waters, or for viewing the natural curiosities of the country.

DEAL – Though a maritime town, . . . the resort of . . . summer visitors makes [for] a brisk circulation of money.

DOVER – Being the nearest port to the Continent packets for Calais sail from it in peacetime, and the money spent by passengers is the chief support of the town, which has very little trade or manufactures, except shipbuilding, and the branches connected with it.

MARGATE – has a harbour for small vessels, and some coasting trade, particularly in shipping the corn of the island for London, [but] being [also] a fashionable bathing place, a good deal of loose money is scattered in it every summer.

TUNBRIDGE WELLS – a place of fashionable resort on account of its mineral wells, and also receives a good deal of money from the sale of Tunbridge Ware.

The tremendous difference which visitors made to Gravesend's economy in the space of less than forty years can be illustrated as between the 1800s and the 1840s.

(b) [*Ibid.*]

GRAVESEND – a town on the Thames chiefly supported by supplying necessities to the vessels, which, whether outward or homeward bound, generally anchor opposite it. Almost the only manufacture of the place is shipbuilding.

(c) [W.H. Bartlett, J.D. Harding, T. Creswick and Others, *The Ports, Harbours, Watering-Places and Picturesque Scenery of Great Britain*, I, c.1842]

The great facilities of communication with the metropolis, the salubrity of the air, the beauty of the surrounding scenery, and the public amusements by which it is enlivened, have all contributed to render Gravesend the most frequented town on the River Thames. The thousands of visitors, who here keep holiday during six or eight months of the year, have insured resources to the inhabitants more to be depended on than the fluctuations of trade. New houses, new streets, hotels, reading rooms, public baths, and pleasure gardens, have all appeared in succession since the introduction of steam on the river, and now present attractions rarely to be met with in any inland or maritime town of like size.

(d) [*The Pictorial Guide to Gravesend and Its Rural Vicinity: A Holiday Handbook*, 1845, 8]

GRAVESEND boasts three landing places . . . [There is] a general rush of holidaymakers. Long seats accommodate scores of invalids, wives, nursemaids and children – all on the look out for fresh air and familiar faces . . . Omnibuses, flys, coaches, watermen, pilots, seamen, and idlers of all sorts, throng the spot . . . The town has a bustling air, and seems to be in a kind of transition state – half sea-port, half watering-place. Go where you may, you are sure to find shrimps to sell and 'lodgings to let'.

The contrast as between Margate out of season and Margate in-season is very well illustrated over roughly the same time-span.

(e) [John Poole, 'Margate', *The Amaranth*, 1839, 70]

To see how Margate looked in the winter, I paid the place a visit . . .
All was closed!, not a living creature was to be seen!, not a sound was to
be heard, save the melancholy echo of my own footsteps as I paced the
desolate streets! . . . At the termination of one season, the resident
population are all packed up, and carefully put away somewhere, till
the commencement of another.

(f) [*The Times*, 13 September 1804]

We are now gathering in a most plenteous harvest. Ship and coach
loads of Cocknies are arriving every day, so that we are fuller than we
have been all this season, which is one of the fullest we have ever
known. Our lodging houses can with difficulty muster an extra bed for
a new visitor; and all the provisions in our market are bought up early
in the morning by the inn and boarding-house keepers. Our libraries
are filled with people . . . Our bathing machines are all in a state of
constant requisition; and it should be added our Doctors find the
number of their patients considerably on the increase . . .

A Sermon was preached on Sunday at the parish church, for the
benefit of the Sea-Bathing Infirmary. Divine Service was attended by
most of the respectable inhabitants and visitors of Margate; among
others, by the Bishop of ROCHESTER, whose Lady, Mrs DAMPIER,
held a collection plate at the south door, accompanied by the MAS-
TER of the CEREMONIES [Charles Le Bas]. The contributions
exceeded £60 (also see Docs. 45aa, 46c).

> References to busy seasons abound and they caused some discom-
> fort to visitors, as and when Mr and Mrs Mount and their party
> arrived in Margate on Wednesday, 16 May 1759.

(g) [Ed: F. Hull, 'A Tour into Kent, 1759', *Archaeologia Cantiana*,
LXIX, 1955, or in Ed. M. Roake and J. Whyman, *Essays in Kentish
History*, 1973, 188]

Hunt and Goodwin . . . found the party in the utmost Confusion at
Margate, occasioned by a Scarcity of beds, and at the Aspect of the
Landlord where they had applied. Goodwin proposed to leave their
Quarters and try elsewhere. Happily they were better, tho' indifferently
off at one Jewell's, who by the much Intreating of Mrs Jewell, took
Them in, upon the resignation of a bed by a Young Clergyman.

Valentine Jewell, who died on 19 August 1766, was landlord of the White Hart on the Parade at Margate, one of the old inns of the town, his name appearing in advertisements in *The Kentish Gazette* of that period. Subsequently the White Hart was to become one of Margate's leading hotels (see Docs. 19b, c,n). Pressures on accommodation were most acute at the height of the season, August and September being the peak months.

(h) [*The Morning Herald and Daily Advertiser*, 23 August 1781]

Letter from Margate, August 21.

We muster so strong at this *delightful* Summer retreat, [that] as to lodging, we are stowed of a night as thick as well packed *figs* in a *grocer's* cask!

(i) [*Ibid.*, 14 September 1781]

Margate and *Brighton* have been more successful lately than any other of the watering places; 40 families came away from Margate on Sunday and Monday last, but the importation of new visitors being equally rapid, they were hardly missed.

(j) [*The Morning Chronicle, and London Advertiser*, 24 August 1786]

Margate has more visitors this summer than ever was remembered; upwards of 1,000 subscribers to the rooms were in the book last week.

(k) [*The Observer*, 19 August and 26 August 1798]

Margate, Ramsgate and Broadstairs experience the fullest season that has been known for many years; particularly at the former.

Margate is unusually full; there is scarce an apartment in the town unoccupied; Muhener [Mitchener at the Royal York Hotel on the Parade] makes up 40 beds.

A year later almost to the day it was recorded that

(l) [*The Morning Post and Gazetteer*, 24 August 1799]

there has been many a wrinkled brow in the City, since Margate was reported so crowded as to oblige the visitors to lie *three in a bed.*

One week later, *ibid.*, 31 August 1799,

the visitors lounge away their time with tolerable satisfaction, and are eased of their money as *quickly as usual*.

Newspaper reports other than the one noted already (see (f) above) pointed to a good season during 1804.

(m)   [*The Times*, 1 September, 10 September 1804]

Margate, August 30.

This fashionable watering-place has not been so full of visitors for eight years past, as it is this season. Every *hoy* or, according to the modern term, every *packet* is literally *loaded*. The smallest of these vessels brought down 120 persons yesterday morning.

Margate, September 7.

Visitors to Margate have certainly no reason to be reproached for want of liberality in their expenses while here ... The weather remains extremely warm. Not a breath of air is to be felt, and the ocean is as calm as a lake ... A hoy came in loaded this morning ... Between comers and goers, we still strike a considerable balance in favour of our population, and still more in favour of our inn-keepers and boarding houses, our billiard tables, and bathing machines.

Six years later the picture was much the same.

(n)   [*The Morning Chronicle*, 4 September and 8 September 1810]

Notwithstanding the increase of accommodation within these few years, a bed is at present obtained with difficulty.

Margate, September 6.

This place is crowded with company, and indeed may be considered as London in miniature, being in many circumstances an epitome of that vast metropolis. The busy bustling faces which throng this lively town in pursuit of health or pleasure exceeds description, and the Libraries, the Theatre, the Assembly Rooms each in their turn contribute to give a pleasing variety to the changing scene.

Another bumper season benefited both Margate and Ramsgate in 1814.

(o)   [*The Morning Post*, 12 September 1814]

Margate, September 9.

This place is full to an overflow: you may walk from one end to the other, without seeing half a dozen bills; and, it is an absolute fact, that a Gentleman devoted three hours yesterday in search of two beds and one sitting room, and failed in his object.

Ramsgate, [also] September 9.

This town is now so full that a lodging cannot be procured in any leading situation.

The same problem repeated itself in Margate during August 1822.

(p)   [*Ibid.*, 24 August 1822]

Margate, August 22.

To say that this salubrious summer retreat is full, would not half express the state in which the visitors and inhabitants find themselves at this moment, [for] to search for a bed is like looking for the Philosopher's stone, and happy is the individual who can command half a matress as his own. [Moreover] even this accommodation is not to be procured under a half sovereign. [As] the steamboats continue to bring their accustomed importations, [so] the neighbouring towns and villages are filled to excess by the overflowing of our population. It would be an endless task to enumerate the arrivals – suffice it to say that they are more respectable than have been remembered for many years past.

> August and September had produced very long lists of 'Fashionable Arrivals' as published in *The Thanet Magazine* during 1817 (see Doc. 45ff). Pressures on accommodation were fuelled by the fact that supply seemed unable to keep pace with an expanding demand, despite an almost continuous building boom in Margate, beginning in the 1760s, and extending through to the 1830s, which prompted observations such as the following.

(q)   [*The Margate and Ramsgate Guide in Letters to a Friend*, 1797, 17]

Streets, squares, and rows of houses, in different directions, are now to be seen, where, a few years since, the farmer sowed his corn.

(r)   [E.W. Brayley, *The Beauties of England and Wales; or Delineations Topographical, Historical and Descriptive*, VIII: *Kent*, 1808, 956, 960]

MARGATE, though now one of the most fashionable, and best frequented, watering-places in the kingdom, has obtained its principal celebrity within the last . . . fifty years, [during which time] various new streets and ranges of houses have been since raised, and scarcely a year passes without some additions being made.

> During the twenty years 1781 to 1801 the number of houses in Margate had increased more than two and a half fold, from 440 to 1,004, compared to 639 for Ramsgate and 1,282 for Brighton. Between 1801 and 1841 there was a further doubling in Margate from 1,004 to 2,141, but even this sort of increase proved to be insufficient.

(s)   [G.A. Cooke, *A Topographical and Statistical Description of the County of Kent*, New Ed., 1830, xxvii, 297]

Almost a new town has been erected within these few years, of which [Illus. 15a]
    Fort Crescent,
    Fort-place,
    Prospect-place,
    Albany-place,
    Belmont,
    Cliff-terrace,
    Zion-place,
    Brunswick-place,
    Clifton-street,

form a conspicuous part . . . Lodging and boarding houses are numerous, and in many instances extremely convenient. But so great is the increasing notoriety of this place (caused principally . . . by the facility and excellence of the water-conveyence to and from the metropolis) that apartments are still wanting, in most seasons, for the due accommodation of many visitants.

(t) [*Pigot & Co's National, London, and Provincial Commercial Directory for 1833–4*, 5th Ed., 849]

Until about the middle of the last century, Margate ranked but as a small fishing village; but since that period it has been progressing towards its present importance, which is that of a populous town and a bathing place of the first celebrity . . . In the season 2,000 persons frequently land [from the steam packets] in one day. The present buildings are still found insufficient for this vast influx of persons and new ones are constantly erecting.

(u) [*Pigot & Co's Royal National and Commercial Directory and Topography, November 1839*, 339]

The number of passengers visiting Margate . . . in recent years . . . has more than quadrupled that of 1815 . . . For this vast influx of visitors the accommodations of the town have annually been found insufficient, and new buildings are consequently in continual progress of erection.

> The number of visitors attracted to Margate by this time in a season ranged from 60,000 upwards to 100,000, with up to 20,000 crowding the resort at its peak [G.W. Bonner, *The Picturesque Pocket Companion to Margate, Ramsgate, Broadstairs and the Parts Adjacent*, 2nd Ed., 1831, 42; 'Amusements at Margate', *Chambers's Edinburgh Journal*, 1833, 155; Edward Cresy, *Report to the General Board of Health on a Preliminary Inquiry into the Sewerage, Drainage, and Supply of Water, and the Sanitary Condition of the Inhabitants of the Parish of St. John the Baptist, Margate, in the Isle of Thanet, in the County of Kent*, H.M.S.O., 1850, 3]. It is no small wonder then that some considerable 'Difficulty in obtaining Lodgings' was encountered by a visitor to Margate in 1829.

(v) [*Journal of a Tour made by Senor Juan de Vega through Great Britain and Ireland*, I, 1830, 95–8]

Known as 'The Spanish Minstrel', he was, in reality, a young English gentleman named Charles Cochrane.

I ARRIVED at Margate on the 6th of September, and . . . proceeded to look for apartments; after visiting several, for which I was asked twelve shillings per week, and were not in fact so comfortable as the room I had had in Canterbury for five shillings; I then began to despair of getting any that would suit the purse of an *itinerant minstrel*. In every part of the town, I found people in search of the same thing as myself; for two or three steam vessels had just come in from London, with an importation of about a thousand city folk, who had come to pass away the holyday from Saturday afternoon till Monday morning. On these particular days, apartments, nay beds were rare, and difficult to be had; and as about a thousand more were expected [a reference to weekend visitations by 'The Hats boat' or 'The Husbands' boat',] the lodging-house keepers were flattering themselves with a good price, and everybody asked a very high one for their accommodation. 'Have you apartments to let?' and 'Oh! that's too dear' were continually heard in whatever direction I might move. I was amused to see the number of people strolling about the streets for the very same object . . . I went into a cobbler's to ask for apartments, [and] the man's wife took a great deal of trouble to look out for me, [but] she first forewarned me of the great difficulty there would be, in consequence of the numbers of city folks coming in . . . She sent her son out to several of her neighbours to inquire. One of her neighbours coming in . . . was appealed to, and very pleasantly said she had one, and it would be disengaged the following day. Having succeeded thus far, I had to proceed about getting one for the night . . . I positively tried everywhere to get a bed . . . At a common inn . . . the landlord agreed to let me have [one] for two shillings the night, but I must agree, if he could get another customer, to let him have half the bed. Not much admiring having a male fellow, I declined his kind offer, and returned to the cobbler, to tell him of my ill success. My landlady, in consequence, offered to make me up a bed on the floor in her parlour, if I would be content with it . . . I thanked her, and very readily accepted it. I walked down the town, dressed with a small cap, and the collar of my cloak up, in order to escape observation. I went on the pier, where were assembled apparently the whole of the fresh arrivals, listening to the enlivening music of a band that was playing . . . On my returning up the town, I perceived the Raffle Rooms were crowded to excess, . . . and so went on to the little bazaar, called the *Boulevard de Paris*. All the articles for sale appeared to be French [compare Docs. 44 c,d,i,j], attracting a number of buyers, and a greater number of lookers on. The amusement seemed to be the same as at Tuppin's raffling, in which the animated visitors seemed to be risking their superfluity of money.

References made above to the possibility of sleeping two or more to a bed had their counterpart in Gravesend and Milton where despite the number of houses doubling between 1821 and 1841, from 1,108 to 2,293, with the Town and Terrace Piers handling in excess of one million passengers annually by the early 1840s, accommodation was sometimes at such a premium that it was no uncommon occurrence to pay 10s. for the privilege of sleeping, more or less comfortably, in an armchair for the night. In Ramsgate 'a full and lengthened season' was 'confidently expected', according to *The Dover Telegraph and Cinque Ports General Advertiser* of 27 June 1835, where 'with upwards of 1,000 passengers [having] arrived at this fashionable watering place during the week, . . . the number of "*Houses to let*" [is] consequently . . . much diminished.' Contemporary references to visitors having a 'superfluity of money', or to visitors being quickly eased of their money, may be compared with the recollections of a Margate visitor of 1796, drawn from the ranks of the Northamptonshire gentry.

(w) [Henry Homelove, 'On Watering Places', *The Annual Register*, 1796, 481, 482]

As to the settled inhabitants of the place, all who do not get by us view us with dislike, because we raise the price of provisions . . . The lower class have lost every trace of rural simplicity, and are versed in all the arts of low cunning and chicane . . . In the country . . . ¼ hour in the week settled the bills, and few tradesmen wished, and none dared, to practice any imposition where all were known, [but] here the continual fluctuation of company takes away all regard to character; the most respectable and ancient families have no influence any farther than as they scatter their ready cash, and neither gratitude nor respect are felt where there is no bond of mutual attachment, besides the necessities of the present day . . . I am paying for tasteless, unripe fruit, while my own choice wall-fruit is rotting by bushels (also see Doc. 20h).

On a visit to Aberystwyth during July and August 1787 Catherine Hutton, with a woman's eye for such detail, observed how

(x) [Ed: Mrs Catherine Hutton Beale, *Reminiscences of a Gentlewoman of the Last Century: Letters of Catherine Hutton*, Birmingham, 1891, 43, 50–1]

The common people complain that the sea bathers have raised the provisions to an enormous price.

Prices in seaside towns were pushed up during the summer months, because of extra demands which were exerted by visiting holidaymakers, who were out to enjoy themselves, with money in their pockets, seeking during the duration of their holidays higher standards of living than those to which they, and most of the people living in the places which they visited, were normally accustomed. It is a well-known phenomenon of the twentieth century for seaside town residents to complain about higher price levels prevailing during the summer months, compared to the rest of the year. *The Times*, of 27 September 1800, reported that Ramsgate's inhabitants had suffered from rising prices during the season, but equally inland spa towns had been no less astute, the cost difference between the gaiety of Tunbridge Wells in the summer and its dullness out of season being well known.

(y)　[William Durrant Cooper, 'Tunbridge Wells at the Commencement of the Eighteenth Century', *Notes and Queries*, 2nd Series, Volume VI, No. 131, 3 July 1858, 8]

Where are you going to?

To Tunbridge Wells, where do you think?

Change me a guinea, [contrasting with the reply]
To Tunbridge Wells, . . . Give me change for a shilling.
　　Looking back on seaside developments there were said to be

(z)　[George Roberts, *The Social History of the People of the Southern Counties of England in Past Centuries*, 1856, 552]

two prices for articles, one for inhabitants, another for visitors.

In reality prices were affected by all sorts of variables, but even so visitors, as noted elsewhere (see Docs. 19s–v; 20c,h), complained of extortion and of being fleeced at the seaside. When Hardwicke Lewis undertook an excursion to Margate, in June 1786, he felt obliged to raise the subject of extortion, in as discreet a manner as possible.

(aa)　[Hardwicke Lewis, *An Excursion to Margate in the Month of June 1786*, 2nd Ed., 1787, 22–3]

It was not difficult for a quiet man to fix upon an house; in about an hour I was as much at home as if my residence had been here for a century. Rent may be high, but the seasons are short . . . He must be unconscionable indeed who grudges to pay dearly for turning an Englishman out of his castle. Provisions in general are not unreasonable, [and] I should have been quite contented but for two circumstances, that loudly spoke the genius of the place to be Extortion. The milk being tolerable, when compared with the chalk and water of the metropolis, induced me to enquire into the price; and on exclaiming at 3d. per quart, was informed, that not having the luck to be born on the spot 1d. was levied upon me as a foreigner. And Oh! tell it not on Tower-Hill, proclaim it not through the streets at Whitehall, the shoe-black made an additional charge of 100% . . . [Also] it is a custom here to impose a discount of ½% on bank notes by the deputy [Francis Cobb, 1726–1802], who, in this respect, keeps a sort of usurious banking-house.

> Francis Cobb, having established a successful brewery in Margate in 1760, branched out into banking during the 1780s, in partnership with his son, the second Francis Cobb (1759–1831). They established the Margate bank of Cobb & Co. which for more than a century enjoyed an independent existence, until it was absorbed in 1891 by Lloyds Bank. A famous national newspaper reported a fascinating instance of extortion in Ramsgate during August 1799.

(bb) [*The Observer*, 18 August 1799]

A Gentleman just returned from Ramsgate relates that during his stay at that place he hired a boat for a week, at the rate, as he conceived, of 10s. 6d. a day. On the settlement of his account with the watermen, they charged him *four times* that sum, alledging, that they had never taken less in their lives. 'Then you should have told me so before we set out', said the Gentleman, – 'Why so we would, please your Honour, only we thought it might *scare* you.'

Ramsgate again received bad publicity late in the season of 1800.

(cc) [*The Times*, 27 September 1800]

The Inhabitants of Ramsgate held a Meeting on Thursday and resolved to open a subscription for the purpose of convicting and punishing forestalling . . . in their market and town, and [also] unanimously agreed not to pay more than 1s. 2d. per pound for fresh butter sold at the market, an exhorbitant price having been asked for that article . . . [They] recommend to the visitors at Ramsgate to join them in the same resolution, and to request of them not to suffer their servants to pay more than 1s. 2d. per pound for the said article. At the same time, in order to prevent any disturbance, in the market, a number of the inhabitants offered themselves, and were accepted, as extra-constables.

> That great royal patron of Brighton, the Prince of Wales, also felt at that time a compelling need to protect himself against being fleeced on his visits to the seaside.

(dd) [*The Observer*, 17 August 1800]

The Prince of Wales continues at Brighton, and probably to escape the shameful extortion too generally practiced there, receives [even] the most trivial article of consumption throughout his establishment from London. Were the practice more general, the prices of many necessaries would find their level. – Butter is 2s. 6d. per lb.; Eggs, 4s. a dozen; Bacon, 14d. and 15d. per lb.; and many other articles equally exorbitant.

> Many were the trades, services and occupations which profited from a rising curve of holiday expenditure, ranging from the fact that a Tuesday evening masquerade at Margate's Tivoli Gardens (see Docs. 39 b–e), attracted late in July 1835 'more than 2,000 persons, including the élite of the island and its adjacents' [*The Dover Telegraph and Cinque Ports General Advertiser*, 1 August 1835], down to the humble profession of shoe cleaning.

(ee) [*The General Evening Post*, 9–11 July 1795]

There is, we are told, a man at Margate exercising the profession of a *shoe-black* who contrives every season to lay up somewhat more than £100!!!

> This interesting revelation obviously caught the paper's fancy, for a few days later, *ibid.*, 14–16 July 1795, it remarked that

this may literally be said *to be picking money out of the dirt.*

48. '*A Day at Margate*' as featured in *The Times* on 2 October 1795.

> A long and varied day could be spent in Margate and its

immediate vicinity by the mid-1790s. This personal account shows that a considerable range of amusements was on offer, one of the most revealing points being the choice of evening entertainments at the several circulating libraries and bathing rooms, besides the theatre and the assembly rooms.

Rose at seven; went to SAYER's Bathing House, set my name down on the slate: took a walk on the Pier. Came back and waited a quarter of an hour, then bathed ... Returned to my lodgings to dress for breakfast. Finding nobody in the Coffee-room, went back to the Pier, arrived at the happy moment, just as a hoy was vomiting out its sick ... Went to breakfast at BENSON's [The Royal Hotel, in Cecil Square, in conjunction with the Margate Assembly Rooms, was a fashionable hotel and place of resort], having first called at the Post Office [in Charlotte Place near the parish church of St. John the Baptist], and found *not sorted* on the door; ate my shilling's worth, one buttered roll, one dry toasted, and one cold ditto; heard who had won, or lost, at whist, and billiards, the night before; read the newspapers, and wrote a letter. Went over the way to SILVER's Library [also in Cecil Square as a well-established business by this time], who at my request gave me the choice of three rides, observing that I might take a little of each by going round by Kingsgate, the North Foreland, and Broadstairs to Ramsgate. . .

Got back to Margate on my pony, for which I [paid] 18d ... I thought as I rode along on the sands, where I should dine. The boarding houses were all open to me, on paying for a week, or one guinea. This was a great temptation . . . I rode to my lodgings to dress, and went immediately to dinner. After dinner proceeded to the libraries, where the raffling lists were filling fast: was induced to throw in my shillings at SILVER's and WARE's; from thence passed on to WOOD's, SURFLEN's, and GARNER's. At SURFLEN's heard music, and several favourite glees: from thence to the playhouse . . . It was now time to go to supper: I accordingly returned to the Coffee House, and from thence to the Billiard Room. . . I retired at one o'clock in the morning.

49. *Two views of Sandgate in September 1809* (Illus. 12b).

(a) [*MS. The Kentish Portion of an Anonymous Tour of 1809*, KAO, U2402 F1]

Monday, 11 September.

Sandgate . . . is situated on the Beach close to the Sea. Its shore is covered with Pebbles commonly called Shingles and seems well calculated for Bathing in fine weather. A Woman I met at Romney, who was not forty years of Age, told me She remembers when there was not more than two houses there. The whole of the Town therefore is quite new and has an Air of neatness which cannot be exceeded. There is a Circulating Library and Billiard Room and I think to those who are desirous of a Seaside Lounge scarcely any Place that I have seen I should so soon recommend.

(b) [*The Kentish Gazette*, 12 September 1809]

This place (notwithstanding the hitherto unfavourable state of the weather) has been more fashionably and numerously attended this season than at any period since it became a watering place. The lodgings are all full, and in all probability will for some length of time continue so. Purday's Library, recently fitted up with an elegant Reading-Room, has become a very fashionable *lounge*. The balls at Strood's Rooms (which are every fortnight) have been fully attended, and have greatly contributed to the amusements of the place. That of Tuesday evening [5 September 1809] . . . boast [ed] a very large portion both of beauty and fashion. Besides the resident and neighbouring families, the rooms were honoured with the company of the Earl and Countess of Temple, Lords Cobham, Brook and Kinnoul, Sir George and Lady Nugent, Misses Oliver and Campbell, Major Ferris, etc . . . Upwards of ninety partook of an elegant cold collation. . .

The Sea Bathing here is in the greatest perfection, as the waters are *pure* . . . With varied and pleasant walks and rides, cliffs of easy ascent (by the grand military roads), commanding a beautiful view of the British Channel, bounded at a distance by the undulating line of the French coast, the whole of the luxuriant level of Romney Marsh, and a large portion of the neighbouring county of *Sussex*, with a diversity of interesting and romantic scenery in the background, . . . Sandgate can claim . . . at least at *equal* degree of admiration to any watering place in *England*.

50. *An 1828 holiday in Ramsgate with visits to Broadstairs and Margate.*

[*MS Journal of a Holiday in Ramsgate in 1828 including Visits to Broadstairs and Margate*, KAO, U2446 F1]

Specific extracts from this journal relating to the loo table and raffling, and describing an outing to Pegwell Bay, on 18 August 1828, are reproduced elsewhere (see Docs. 38o, 44h). It formed part of

THE FAMILY ALBUM
for the use of
Hawkins Francis James Esq.
open
to the contributions of all
Charitably-disposed persons
among his Family and Friends.
Vol. 1st
Croydon
July 28th 1828

The contributors to the album initialled their respective entries thus:
M.S.
T.J.
E.J.
M.J.
Making up the party were Sutherland, Mrs S. and possibly from the Hawkins family Mary, Emily and Tom. There are references also to 'little Miss Trot', and to 'your pretty little niece M.R.M. Sutherland.' The party or some members of it had obviously travelled from Croydon ahead of the book arriving in Ramsgate on 2 August 1828.

1828, Ramsgate,
2 August.

This book arrived at this place today in a parcel from Croydon containing all sorts of *goodies*, [including] almond sugar plumbs, etc. for the great babies, and some sponge cakes for little Trot, one of which she devoured most voraciously on the beach this morning, and the great babies enjoyed their treat at the same time. I took a dip this morning, the sea was most delicious. M.S.

5 August.

This afternoon our Glasgow friend and relative took us by surprise, for we did not expect him until tomorrow, knowing that there was not a Ramsgate packet before and I did not imagine that he would have set his foot on board a Margate one, but he really did and reached [us] in perfect safety from Margate in a coach. M.S.

6 August.

Mary has told you of my safe arrival. I shall therefore now only acquaint you with the particulars of my visit to Woolwich from whence I started yesterday for Margate. I went to the Stace's last Thursday. There was no one at home but Mr and Mrs Stace and Mary; however, as I had never been to Woolwich before, I amused myself with surveying (?) the Repository and the Arsenal, with both of which I was very much delighted. They have just landed a large brass cannon which was taken in the Burmese war. It is of immense size and weighs 15 tons. The workmanship is very extraordinary for so rude a people, though perhaps it may not be their own casting. There is Arabic and Persian writing on it . . . It is destined for the court-yard of Windsor Castle. Another that was taken [is] of still larger dimension but was lost in the Ganges. What think you of a *Joint Stock Company* to recover it? My plan is to drain off the Ganges and then haul it out of the mud. *You* shall be chief engineer. Wm. Stace, the eldest son, is at Chatham and is getting on very well. Henry, the second, was to pass yesterday at the Military College Woolwich, and he had some chance of the Engineers. I have been strolling out this morning with Sutherland to the library and Billiard room; but there was no news at the one, and 2 stupid people playing at the other. We have all just made an excellent luncheon, which we finished with *Anchovies*; I was *pressed* very much to take some and of course thought it rude to refuse. Emily has been playing a '*la la*' tune, & Baby has been listening.

This is a wretched day, and we have not been able to stir out, little 'trot trot' is now in a dreadful passion and no one knows what is the matter with the young woman. The Duke of Clarence has just passed this place in a steam boat, and a Royal Salute was fired from the harbour. M.S.

7 August.

This morning Sutherland & I took a dip in the sea. It was most delightful indeed. We bathed near Emily and had an opportunity of seeing her duck her locks in the *'azure brine'*. Little Miss Trot shook her hand at us out of the bathing-machine-window. She wants very much to bathe but Mary is afraid it would take *away her breath*. Last Evening we took a stroll to the south in the direction of Pegwell Bay which Emily for the sake of *euphony will* call *'Pigwill Bay'*. We [had] some idea of going there in a boat to-day to call on *'Mr. Pigwell'*, the name that Emily gives to a pole with a tub at the top in the middle of the Bay, but as it is a *'Buoy'* I think she ought to call it *'Master* Pigwell'. There are very nice bathing machines here, very commodious & clean, and have awnings at the back so that those ladies who like may bathe in private, but there are also *'Skeleton Machines'* for which you only pay 'a penny' (at least this is Mary's & Emily's account of the matter) where you are not quite so *private* as some people would wish to be. I will give you sketches of both sorts.

Owing to the roughness of the waves and the rain of St. Swithin, who this year has indeed been as good as his word, we were unable to row to 'Pigwell', so we contented ourselves with a run on the beach, where we collected a very good parcel of shells, and were considerably aided in our research by Miss Mary, who sat on the ground and filled her mouth full of sand.

T.J.

8 August.

Emily has promised to write in your Journal, but as yet has not had time, what with bathing and lying down and playing and one thing and another. We watch the ships passing here every day. From our window we have an excellent view of Deal and the Downs and all the ships lying there. We saw the 'Sir Wm. Paget' sail by yesterday. We have two excellent glasses and can see distinctly the two floating lights off the Goodwin sands. We think some day of taking a row over there and having a promenade on the sands. We have a beautiful pier and harbour [Illus. 11b], the latter of which extends over 48 acres, but which Mary guessed to be 5 or 6! The beach here is not near as good as at Brighton, and we are obliged to walk a long way to get to it.   T.J.

9 August.

This day has been a regular blower, and the poor ladies are terribly blown about. I am just about to put a ribbon to my hat and sally out on the pier; you shall hear when I return if I met with any adventure, unless indeed I am blown into the sea, in which case you hardly expect to hear more from me.   T.J.
I think it is time that I should make a little addition to this book as I see there are several of the pages filled already. Tom is a famous scribbler, and he declares that he has written within the last few months more to you than any one of us. He has made us laugh today by pretending to be so very courageous . . . against the roughness of the sea; he, who used to be ill before he had been on the water half an hour, now declares that he should enjoy to be in some of the little boats we see tossing about, and is sure he should not be ill, but we very much doubt it, after having heard Mary's account of his voyage [to] Scotland. We have had a letter from Anne this morning. Papa and Capt. Walters (?) had some idea of coming down to us today, but from Anne's letter we fear there is little chance of their making their appearance and since the day has proved so very boisterous we are happy to think they are not likely to be on board the packet. Anne was also in hopes she might have made a third as Mrs. Hawkins and Mrs. Godfrey do not pay their visit as soon as she expected. She is very busy at home now, as the dining room is under-going the operation of being stuccoed and we expect to find it quite smart by the time we return. I only regret that the other parts of the house are not to be made to correspond, but as the parlour

cannot be painted until next year, I suppose it will all be done together
if we remain in the house. E.J.

I must beg to correct an error my friend Tom has committed, in saying
I thought the harbour extended over only 5 or 6 acres. You must know
there are two, and I thought he alluded to the small one which perhaps
may cover 8 or 9 so my guess is not so bad as he wishes to make it out.
Tom has just sallied forth in the midst of the wind. He had not
proceeded many steps before he was in danger of losing his hat and his
head. He returned for a bit of black ribbon to secure both, and I am in
momentary expectation of hearing that he is blown over into the deep.

M.S

11 August.

Yesterday was a terrible day, and I do not think there is any prospect of
today being finer. We have several days planned to go on the sea but
have never been able to accomplish our wishes. I do not think you are
aware that Mrs. and the Misses Kings keep this place quite alive. Miss
K. sports a smart hat which she told me the other day was very often
turned inside out and its beauty nearly spoiled. I fancied the other day
I saw the notorious Hatty. M.S.

I met yesterday our old friend Miss Sampson, who as she tells me, has
got small lodgings in Sion place. She says that she often hears from
'Thomas Parry', but that one letter that he promised is not forthcom-
ing. She is looking very well and is in high request at Mrs. King's *coterie*.
Emily King who is not very well goes out for 4 or 5 hours every day to
toss about in the sea. There is an old man with a red jacket who always
goes out with her. Yesterday being Sunday, Sutherland and I went to
the new Church here, which is a most beautiful structure of the florid
Gothic order. It has been built with considerable expense and is but
just finished . . . We walked last evening to 'Pigwell bay' and as I was
amusing myself on the sands I sank in ankle-deep, much to the
mortification of my shoes, my pride and my *silk* stockings. T.J.

12 August.

Today is Sutherland's natal day, and our good Croydon friends did not
forget it, for on our arrival from bathing a welcome basket met us. It
contained everything that is good to eat and entre nous a brace of
partridges which we contemplate eating today. It is one of Sutherland's
favourite dishes and it was very thoughtful and kind of our friends to

think of us. Miss Sampson called on me yesterday. She is anxiously expecting a letter from Thomas Parry Woodcock, who she finds a very good correspondent. Last evening I felt a cold coming on, and I thought in order to stop it a little whey would not be amiss . . .   M.S.
This day is the King's Birthday but we have not heard any rejoicings on that account here yet. It is also Sutherland's. We took a short walk this evening and then came home and played at Écarté. I won sixpence from Mary and lost 2s.6d. to Sutherland.   T.J.

13 August.

There is a sale of Books at Broadstairs to-day and as it is not more than a mile or two, we are going to walk over. Sutherland bought two or three when they were exposed to sale at Ramsgate – 40 plates of horses copied from Carle Vernet would delight you, I think. Yesterday Mary dispatched a letter to you which I daresay you will have read before you receive this. In it I put a little postscript informing you that we were all going to give Papa a handsome seal with his arms upon it and were to subscribe a guinea each . . .   T.J.
We are all returned from Broadstairs. We had a very pleasant walk over and came home in one of the little *Shandrydan* carriages which abound here; it has proved a miserably wet afternoon and we have just witnessed the arrival of the steam packet. I do not envy the situation of the poor folk on board – they must be most miserably cold and wet. We did not fail to pay a visit to the pastry cooks at Broadstairs . . .   E.J.

14 August.

Another wretched rainy day, nothing to be done but read the newspapers, and no news in them except that Corder was executed for the murder of Maria Marten and Mr Connell & Co. kick up their heels for the amusement of John Bull and family. I wrote a letter to-day to Mr. Urquhart who has got the curacy of High Halden near Tenterden in Kent. I have some thoughts of paying them a visit soon. . . Two Steam Boats were obliged to put in this afternoon . . . The light on the end of the pier is lit to-night & it is so misty that we cannot see the lights off Goodwin Sands. I won 1s. 6d. last evening at Écarté and have made 1s. to-night, which I hope I may keep – (Don't you?)   T.J.

15 August.

We discovered this morning that one of the Steam Boats that put into the harbour last evening was conveying the Duke of Cumberland and his son Prince George to the continent on their way to Berlin. They landed yesterday and slept at the Albion Hotel and as the weather was fine this morning they proceeded on their route about 11 o'clock. Mary, Emily & I bustled down to the pier & were just in time not to be too late for a view of them. The guns in the Harbour gave them a Royal salute as they departed. The young Prince is about 9 years old & *after* the Princess Victoria (about the same age), the daughter of the late Duke of Kent, is next heir to the crown of England. His father & he have been in England seeing all the sights for the last 3 or 4 months. [It is] supposed that the Prince had come over to England to be educated, as Parliament a year or two ago voted £6000 a year for him to be brought up in this country, but it seems they have allowed him to continue abroad. The sea is quite calm to-day and we wished very much for a row, but the rain threatens to prevent it.   T.J.

I must not omit to mention that Tom & Sutherland eat sugar plumbs . . . faster than any body I ever saw . . . They both beat me hollow. I went to the pastry cook this afternoon about 5 and bought a shillings-sworth of each, it is now *eight* & I do not think there are more than a couple of each left. They are playing Écarté and eating away. Last evening we were so cold that we enjoyed a fire very much. We intend leaving this for London on Monday week by the steamer. I am quite angry with Mr. Hiden, Sutherland's carriage builder, for he has put such bad locks on our boxes that there are three that already want new ones. Tom is so fond of dear Trot Trot that I am afraid he will quite spoil her. He indulges her in all her various whims, and is constantly feeding her with sweeties. He makes an excellent nurse, and Miss never seems so happy as when she is with her *Munkie*.   M.S.

It is now ½ past 10 o'Clock, and Sutherland & I have just finished a game at Écarté. I have won half a crown this evening which is very good for me. You will find this page rather dirty but the fact is that Mary has been cleaning her watch & Jewels with some Goldsmiths' rouge, & chose to consider this book as a proper place whereon to exercise her employment. This explanation will therefore account for the *pinky hue*. We have been very much amused to-day by an account in the papers of all the letters received by Corder (the murderer) when he advertized for a wife. They are upwards of 50 in number . . .   T.J.

16 August.

This morning we went over to Margate for the first time since my arrival. We were shamefully cruel on a poor horse for we loaded a *shandrydan* carriage with six folks, some of whom were tolerably full-grown, viz. Sutherland, Mary, Mrs. S., Emily, myself & the driver. I thought it a great shame & walked up one hill, but the rest of the party were perfectly callous to [the] poor animal's sufferings . . . It was the first *shandry* we had patronized, but really I prefer my own legs in general. At Margate we saw plenty of 'hoy' people dressed in *buff slippers or shoes, nankeen unspeakables & duffy coats* or *dressing gowns*. They afforded us much amusement & they seemed equally delighted with seeing six in a *shandry*. Mary & Mrs. S. bought up a *host of* scent bottles, at the French Boulevards, which the Margaters call the Bull yards. T.J.

Sunday, 17 August.

Yesterday was the finest day we have had since we have been here, and we made good use of it for we were out the whole day. Directly after breakfast we sallied down to the beach which was crowded with males & females to see one another bathe. Emily exhibited before a great concourse of folk. We afterwards went to Margate which trip Tom has already described. We returned to Ramsgate in time to witness the landing of the passengers from the steam boat and went to the pier in hopes of seeing dear Papa, but alas he was not there. In the evening we were going into the Library but found it was closed. We have been to church today and heard a man who preached as if he had been accustomed to address an audience in the open air, a complete ranter.

M.S.

Sutherland and I took a dip in the sea this morn.g. A ship which we think must be an E. Indiaman has just appeared in sight towed by a steamer. It puts us in mind of you.

T.J.

18 August.

[The day when they succeeded in having an outing by boat to Pegwell Bay, as described in document 38o].

19 August.

This evening we expect some friends to tea, we met quite by chance, Mrs. & the Miss Stewarts, whose brother you know in Calcutta. They

are here for a few days and this evening they drink tea with us. They
are very nice young women.   M.S.

20 August.

Today is very fine. We sent to the pier to see the steam packet come in.
There were a great many passengers on board. There is a Camera
Obscura at the end of the pier. Sutherland, Tom, Emily & myself took
six pennyworth of it to-day, and were highly pleased. Miss Foote is
performing here for two nights and last night we went to see her in 'The
Belles stratagem'. The house is very small but it was very full, and we
were much amused [compare Doc. 43bb].   M.S.

21 August.

. . . This place is filling fast [and] appears to me [to be] already full
[but] certainly not of genteel company . . . Since the Steamers have
frequented it the company has very much fallen off. You have *heard me
speak* of the Dolbys our opposite neighbours and Anne's friends. I hear
they are coming down next Month. They always pay this place an
annual visit. We have been shell hunting this Morning and have made
a tolerable collection. I am sure *my trot* would quite delight you, she is
so fond of horses, dogs, etc. I frequently give her a ride on a donkey on
the sands, and it is worth something to see how she enjoys it. I am sorry
to add that when she is taken off she sometimes cries, but I hope to
correct this when she gets a little older. She is not yet 11 months and for
her age is a wonderful child!! it is very pretty to see her clap her hands
and hold out her face to kiss when she is asked.   M.J.

22 August.

Last afternoon it was wet and disagreeable and after dinner the two
gentlemen got out the cards and began to play at Écarté in daylight. In
the evening Emily and I played them at Whist and they won seven
shillings of each of us, although we only played silver threepences. M.S.
A day or two ago we went to the pier-head where there is a small
lighthouse, the inhabitants of which sell shells, corals, etc. Mary
purchased a beautiful bit of white coral, & a quantity of small foreign
shells. I, dealing in [a] small way, bought some remnants of coral & a
petrifaction. I hope you will not forget to collect some curiosities for me
as I am trying to amass enough to form a little Cabinet. I should think

that you sometimes had good opportunities of collecting these sorts of things. I was in hopes that this book would have been finished before we left Ramsgate but we start next Monday in the Steamer, if Mrs. Sutherland is well enough to bear the journey, for at present she is very poorly. The air here was so cold & the weather so rainy that she caught a stiff neck. Yesterday I heard from my old friend Mr. Urquhart [and] he enquired particularly after you. He is expecting daily Mrs. Urquhart to present him with their first-born. I daresay you fancy he would make a queer husband but they seem very happy in the solitudes of Kent, although their means are rather limited. I have an invitation to go to the Christening, & as they are both such favourites of mine, I shall go, if I possibly can.

I am quite solitary this evening, Mary, Sutherland & Tom being gone to dine at Mr Snowdon's (the medical man here) and Mrs. S. not being able to leave her room, I have just finished practising an hour according to Tom's *strict* injunctions before he left. He is constantly assuring me that the *sole* objects of my coming down here were 'to bathe, to lie down & to practise', & they certainly do occupy the greatest part of my time. I think the bathing is the most *pleasant* of the three, for that I really do enjoy and only wish I could persuade Mary to take a dip with me for I think it would do her so much good. I invited a young visitor to tea with me this evening, & it was no less a personage than little Miss Trot, she behaved herself uncommonly well, and it afforded me great amusement to see the little dear take her bread & butter in her hand, & say ta for every piece, then put it to her mouth. Her nurse as I suppose you know was sent by Martha from Bishopscastle, & she frequently puts us in mind of our own kind Patty. She is devoted to Baby . . . I hear it strike ten, so I must wish you good night.

E.J. alias East India Company.

Although 23 August was written in there are no more entries relating to Ramsgate, Monday, 25 August, being the day when they intended to take the steamboat to London. The next entry shows that these plans were accomplished and that among the party there were some inveterate travellers.

Leamington, Sept. 10th.

You will be surprised to find us all at once transported here. We returned from Ramsgate by the Steamer as we intended, remained in

London a few days and then set off for this place where we have been
nearly a week. Sutherland and I proceed tomorrow morning to
Birmingham on our way to Scotland . . . Tom who accompanied us
here returns to London tomorrow.

The very domestic experiences portrayed in this 1828 visit to
Ramsgate may be compared alongside another diary account of a
holiday spent in that resort during 1829, viz: J. Whyman, 'A
Three-Week Holiday in Ramsgate during July and August 1829',
Archaeologia Cantiana, XCVI, 1980, pages 185–225, being the *MS
Journal of an Excursion to Ramsgate in July and August 1829*, Tyler
Collection (Ramsgate Scrapbook), Cathedral Library and Arc-
hives, Canterbury, to which there are numerous references in this
volume (see Docs. 12, 20m, 25k, 34a, 35g, 37j, 38r, 42cc, 46j, 51b).

51. *A holiday visit to Walmer Castle, the official residence of the Lord Warden
of the Cinque Ports in 1829.*

The following account shows what it was like to spend time with
the Duke of Wellington (1769–1852) who at that time was not
only Lord Warden but also Prime Minister from 1828 to 1830. He
died at Walmer on 14 September 1852.

(a) [Ed: F. Bamford and the Duke of Wellington, *The Journal of Mrs.
Arbuthnot 1820–1832*, II, 1950, 294–301]
Mrs. Harriet Arbuthnot, daughter of the Hon. Henry Fane, M.P.
second son of the 8th Earl of Westmorland, became in 1815 the
second wife of the Rt. Hon. Charles Arbuthnot, M.P. She died from
cholera at the age of 40 on 2 August 1834.

July 1829.

21. – We left London on the 17th of this month and came to Walmer
Castle, where we mean to stay till the end of next week. The Duke got
this house when he succeeded Lord Liverpool as Lord Warden [died 4
December 1828], and he is very much delighted with it. [It became his
favourite residence, and it was there that he died]. It certainly is the
most charming marine château that ever was, close upon the sea, the
Downs constantly full of shipping coming in and going out, and a very

comfortable house with a beautiful pleasure ground, and quite sheltered by plantations. I dare say he will generally spend the summer
here. We are quite alone with him, but the Esterhazys are coming the
end of the week ... I was quite tired of London, was not very strong,
and was charmed to get down here for tranquility and some sea
bathing, which I like better than anything.

29th. – The Esterhazys and Ld Clanwilliam have been staying two
days here and are gone to Hastings. We had not much politics. We
went one day to Dover and another to Ramsgate to amuse the Princess.
[During 1829 the Duchess of Kent and the Princess Victoria spent
some weeks residing at Pierremont House in Broadstairs]. We have
been passing our time here very agreeably. I have bathed almost every
day which has done me great good, and the fresh air, tranquility and
comfort have wrought a miracle upon the Duke; he has grown fat and
looks better than I have seen him for years. . .

Aug. 12th. – We left Walmer on the 31st of July and had a most
dreadful passage in the steam boat from Margate to London. It blew a
hurricane, we were all dreadfully sick and, I think, are completely
disgusted with steam boat expeditions. We were so singularly unfortunate in the weather . . . London was . . . quite empty.

> Holidaying in Ramsgate at this time was Mr. Benham and his
> family. The Duke's visit to Ramsgate took place on Wednesday, 29
> July and attracted the watchful eye of Mr. Benham.

(b)   [*MS Journal of an Excursion to Ramsgate in July and August 1829*,
Tyler Collection (Ramsgate Scrapbook), Cathedral Library and
Archives, Canterbury]

At ½ past 4 walked on the pier [Illus. 11b] to see the steamboat from
London arrive and the duke of Wellington happening to be also on the
pier we had the opportunity for the first time of seeing his grace.

> Following her departure Mrs. Arbuthnot noted that Walmer
> Castle had other visitors.

The Chan^r and L^y L. are at Walmer with *Mrs.* Fox and L^d
Chesterfield. I think the Duke w^d have been more prudent not to have
allowed the latter to make a convenience of his house.

52. *A holidaymakers's impressions of Herne Bay, Ramsgate, Margate, Deal and Dover in 1844.*

[*MS Journal compiled by S. Daniele in 1844*, KAO, U2666 F1, 8–9, 33–4, 36, 38–9, 41–3]

Friday, August 30.

The town of Herne Bay is quite small, and built very irregularly; there is a nice Church, and a Dissenting Chapel; also a Tower on the beach which serves the purposes of a sea-mark, and a town clock, as the church has neither clock or steeple. The neighbourhood is very pretty, and the bathing most delightful; there are two bazaars, and the principal Hotel is a fine building opposite the pier.

Friday, September 6.

We went out directly after breakfast to examine the town [Ramsgate] which is of considerable size, and extends a good away along the Cliffs on either side of the Harbour, and lies on an ascent. There are two churches, one a fine structure, the other a modern building. A very good market [has been] built in the same manner as that at Canterbury and several bazaars and an auction room which is quite a resort for loungers. The Harbour is very fine, of great extent and capable of holding at high tide 700 vessels in case of bad weather. The cliffs are chalky and very high. There are two noble flights of stairs one on each cliff by which you can descend to the beach, without returning to the town. Those on the east cliff are called the Augusta stairs and have 120 steps, those on the west cliff Jacob's Ladder, 104 steps.

Saturday, September 7.

We went to Margate to spend the day . . . [Walked] along the Cliff and returned by the beach, which is superior to that of Ramsgate as the sand is not so loose but closely bound. We picked up some pretty pieces of seaweed and a few starfish. Returned to dinner and as soon as that needful repast was finished started afresh to explore the town. Margate is of considerable extent but does not equal Ramsgate in the beauty of its terraces and houses . . . After leaving here [The Grotto, see Doc. 36] we went to the Pier to watch a London steamer disembark its passengers. . . Returned to Ramsgate, having enjoyed ourselves very much and seen most of the things of interest at Margate.

Tuesday, September 10.

About 3 o'clock we started by coach for Dover and on our way passed
through Deal, which is a long straggling place and does not appear very
pretty to a passer through. The Castle is a singular looking structure
. . . We had a glimpse of Walmer, but it lies enclosed in some woods
and is not a very prominent object from the Dover road. The beauty of
the situation of that ancient sea port I cannot attempt to describe . . .
The town lies between two cliffs.

NOTES ON ILLUSTRATIONS

1. Russell's treatise on sea water was first published in Latin at Oxford in 1750, and the first English translation appeared in 1752. [Reproduced from E.W. Gilbert, *Brighton: Old Ocean's Bauble*, London 1954, facing p. 57].

2a. An illustration of the Old Margate Hoy published by R. Lambe in 1820. [Original in Margate Library].

2b. Broadstairs was still in its infancy as a resort in the 1780s, despite references to bathing machines there from 1754 onwards. [Reproduced from 'Topographical collections for the History of the Isle of Thanet', an unpublished ms. by the Revd. John Pridden, in Margate Library].

3. Two views of the bathing place at Ramsgate, one drawn by R. Green and engraved by V. Green and F. Jukes in 1781, the other from a drawing by Mr. Samuel published by R. Wilkinson and W. Dickinson of London in 1784. [Original prints in KAO, U1287 Z7, 11].

4a. A view of Margate, showing the bathing rooms and machines, drawn by T. Smith and published by R. Pollard in 1786. [Original print in KAO, U1287 Z11].

4b. Illustration by B.T. Pouncey showing Dandelion, a popular tea garden and venue for public breakfasting for visitors staying in all three Thanet resorts before 1815. [Original in Margate Library].

5. Distinguished visitors to Thanet included to Margate in 1787 (a) George Herbert, later Earl of Pembroke (1759–1827) and (b) his wife Elizabeth (1767–93); to Margate in 1798 (c) Henrietta, Countess of Bessborough (1761–1821) and to Broadstairs in 1804 (d) the famous topographical artist and diarist, Joseph Farington, R.A. (1747–1821).

6a.   This cartoon shows exhausted visitors landing at Margate after a journey by hoy in 1790. [Original in Margate Library].

6b.   View of Folkestone from the sea in 1790 showing a small, undeveloped, fishing port. [Original in Margate Library].

7a.   A view of Broadstairs, showing the beginnings of resort development, published by T. Jones and J. Hassell in 1796 [Original print in KAO, U1287 Z10].

7b.   This print of Deal, published by I.T. Hinton, shows more evidence of its traditional maritime activities than there is of sea bathing, despite the introduction of bathing machines there in 1753. [Original in Margate Library].

8.   Original prints of the exterior and interior of the Margate assembly rooms, which opened in 1769, the latter produced for Samuel Silver's circulating library, which operated from at least 1771 until 1808. The former should be compared with the original water colour of the assembly rooms [KAO, U2668] painted by J. Baskerfield in 1792, which is reproduced on the front cover of this volume. It is one of a total of 73 such water colours painted by Baskerfield during a visit to Kent, Sussex and Surrey, and contained in a notebook deliberately designed to form a pictorial record of that visit.

9.   A handout advertising the facilities of the Royal Charlotte, which conveyed passengers between London and Margate, in 1803. [Original in Margate Library].

10a.   An illustration of the great storm of 14–15 January 1808 which severely damaged Margate, drawn and published by J. Hassell. Damage from rough seas has been a recurring problem for seaside resorts and some, such as Margate, have suffered such damage on several occasions. [Original in Margate Library].

10b.   The master of ceremonies of the Margate assembly rooms, Charles Le Bas, as engraved in the frontispiece, together with the accompanying title page, of a Thanet guidebook published in 1809. [Original in Margate Library].

11a.   A view of Broadstairs, showing the further development of this select resort, published by P. Burgess of Ramsgate in 1809. [Original in Margate Library].

11b.   A view of Ramsgate town and harbour from the East Pier Head, showing some of the new developments on the East Cliff, published by P. Burgess in 1809. [Original in Margate Library].

12a.   An illustration of Sandgate, showing the bathing machines near the castle, published by W. Tiffen of Hythe in 1815. [Original in Margate Library].

12b.   This illustration shows two steam vessels, the Victory and the Favorite, both built in 1818, with Margate pier, harbour, town and bathing machines in the background. Facing the harbour were two of Margate's principal hotels, Wright's York Hotel and Creed's White Hart Hotel. [Original in Margate Library].

13a.   The lower end of Margate High Street leading down to the harbour, showing the bathing rooms and Marine Library, in an illustration by T.H. Shepherd and T. Sutherland. [Original in Margate Library].

13b.   Margate was the first seaside resort to popularise donkey rides. This illustration by R. Howell shows an obstinate donkey on Margate beach. [Original in Margate Library].

14a.   An illustration of Samuel Bettison's Hawley Square Library in Margate, published in W.C. Oulton, *Picture of Margate and its Vicinity*, London 1820, p. 51.

14b.   This illustration of Folkestone, published by Rodwell and Martin in 1822, shows the town as seen from the Warren with a Martello Tower in the foreground. [Original in Margate Library].

15.   Plans of Margate and Ramsgate, showing the development of both towns, in 1821 and 1822 respectively. Both maps indicate the principal hotels and other resort buildings such as the assembly and bathing rooms, Theatre Royal, Hawley Square

and Marine libraries at Margate, and the Marine Library, Dyason's and Royal Kent Baths at Ramsgate. [KAO, CCRc/ P37, 39].

16a.   A view of Folkestone from what is now the Leas, drawn by J.M.W. Turner, engraved by Robert Wallis, and published by J. and A. Arch, in 1825–6. [Original in Margate Library].

16b.   An illustration of the third Pegwell Bay regatta held on 23 September 1828, published by George Virtue in 1829, showing the fashionably dressed spectators on the cliffs above.

17a.   An illustration of Margate's Marine Terrace published by Mr. Bettison of the Hawley Square and Marine Library in 1828. The illustration shows the bathing machines on Margate beach and the terraces of fine lodging houses, built on the western side of the town from c. 1800 onwards. [Original in Margate Library].

17b.   An illustration of the barracks and town of Hythe, published by George Virtue in 1829. [Original in Margate Library].

18.   Comparable illustrations of the baths at Gravesend and Margate, published by George Virtue in 1829. The Clifton Baths at Margate were constructed into the chalk cliffs in the 1820s at considerable capital cost, involving substantial coastal excavation and sea defences.

19.   An illustration of Wright's York Hotel at Margate published in *Margate Delineated*, 1829, facing p. 18. It was one of Margate's leading hotels, located on the Marine Parade, facing the harbour and pier, and thus well-placed to attract the custom of passengers arriving by hoy or steamboat.

20a.   Dover from the beach, drawn by W. Westall in 1830, showing it as a fashionable seaside resort, with some fine buildings and with bathing machines at the water's edge. [Original in Margate Library].

20b.   A view of Herne Bay showing the proposed pier as designed by Thomas Telford, and announcing the formation of a company 'for the erection of the above pier . . . to be incorporated by Act of Parliament . . . for the landing of passengers, carriages, etc., at all times of the tide'. [KAO, Office Library].

21a.   An illustration of the Royal Sea Bathing Infirmary at Margate, published in G.W. Bonner, *The Picturesque Pocket Companion to Margate, Ramsgate, Broadstairs and the Parts Adjacent*, London 1831, p. 103.

21b.   A view of Folkestone, etched by E.W. Cooke in 1831, at a time when it was described by the Commissioners on the Municipal Corporations of England and Wales as 'far from being in a flourishing state'. [Original in Margate Library].

22a.   A view of the old and new town of Herne Bay printed for Capper's *Guide* by J. Merrifield, showing the newly constructed pier. [Original in Margate Library].

22b.   An illustration of the King's Arms Library in Snargate Street, Dover, published in W. Batcheller, *The New Dover Guide*, 1838, p. 119.

23a.   An illustration of the West Cliff at Ramsgate, showing the ascent to Nelson Crescent and the Paragon, in 1839. [Original in Margate Library].

23b.   An illustration of Sheerness in the 1840's, showing the dockyard, which contributed most to the town's economy, and the pier, used for the servicing of steamboats between London and the Kent Coast. Sheerness was a late developer as a seaside resort, but the *Maidstone Journal* of 13 June 1848 was able to report that 'the "Season" at this improving and increasingly popular watering place is now commencing, and already many visitors are attracted there, by the . . . facility of access at a very small expense'. [Original in Margate Library].

24.   Two views of Herne Bay published by J. and F. Harwood in 1842–4, showing the Clock Tower erected in 1837 and the concentration of the town on the landward side of the pier [Originals in Margate Library].

INDEX OF PERSONS

INDEX OF PLACES